Affective Betrayal

SUNY series in Chinese Philosophy and Culture
―――――――
Roger T. Ames, editor

Affective Betrayal

Mind, Music, and Embodied Action
in Late Qing China

JEAN TSUI

SUNY PRESS

Published by State University of New York Press, Albany

© 2024 State University of New York

All rights reserved

Printed in the United States of America

No part of this book may be used or reproduced in any manner whatsoever without written permission. No part of this book may be stored in a retrieval system or transmitted in any form or by any means including electronic, electrostatic, magnetic tape, mechanical, photocopying, recording, or otherwise without the prior permission in writing of the publisher.

Links to third-party websites are provided as a convenience and for informational purposes only. They do not constitute an endorsement or an approval of any of the products, services, or opinions of the organization, companies, or individuals. SUNY Press bears no responsibility for the accuracy, legality, or content of a URL, the external website, or for that of subsequent websites.

For information, contact State University of New York Press, Albany, NY
www.sunypress.edu

Library of Congress Cataloging-in-Publication Data

Name: Tsui, Jean, 1983– author.
Title: Affective betrayal : mind, music, and embodied action in late Qing China / Jean Tsui.
Description: Albany : State University of New York Press, [2024]. | Series: SUNY series in Chinese philosophy and culture | Includes bibliographical references and index.
Identifiers: LCCN 2023056366 | ISBN 9781438498782 (hardcover : alk. paper) | ISBN 9781438498805 (ebook)
Subjects: LCSH: Liang, Qichao, 1873–1929—Criticism and interpretation. | Liang, Qichao, 1873–1929—Political and social views. | Affect (Psychology) in literature. | Chinese language—Political aspects. | China—Politics and government. | China—Intellectual life.
Classification: LCC PL2781.A5 Z848 2024 | DDC 320.092—dc23/eng/20240510
LC record available at https://lccn.loc.gov/2023056366

To Hu Ying and Michael Fuller

Even if by some particular disfavor of fate, or by the scanty endowment of a stepmotherly nature, this will should entirely lack the capacity to carry through its purpose; if despite its greatest striving it should still accomplish nothing, and only the good will were to remain (not of course, as a mere wish, but as the summoning of all means that are within our control); then, like a jewel, it would still shine by itself, as something that has full worth in itself.

就令天命不佑，使我抱一善意而不能實行，或竭力實行而無效，但使當保持此志而勿喪失。則自能篤實光輝，坦坦蕩蕩。何以故，有效無效於善意之分量無所增減，故價值全存於自由中故。

—Immanuel Kant, *Groundwork of the Metaphysics of Morals*;
Liang Qichao, "Jinshi diyi dazhe Kangde zhi xueshuo"
〈近世第一大哲康德之學說〉

Contents

Acknowledgments ix

Introduction: An Affective Turn in the Study of
Chinese Political Modernity 1

1. Repairing the Human, Restoring Their Heartmind 35

2. Reclaiming Qing Philology to Recover the
   Innate Moral Order 79

3. To Know *Is* to Act: The Realization of Cosmic-Moral-Political
   Oneness in Action 109

4. Dissolution of Modern Political Languages in the
   Cinematic Spectacle 147

5. Musicality—Representing the Rhythm of Political Revolution
   and the Tenor of Its Moral Discontent 179

Postscript: Let Us Be Taken by Affect, and to Be *Taken* Away
and Afar 219

Notes 233

Bibliography 299

Index 325

Acknowledgments

I cannot remember from where I learned this story: a young monk entered a Buddhist monastery, where everything was in meticulous order. The master priest occasionally wandered around. The young monk wondered: what exactly does the master do? Soon after that, the master went on a journey. Everything in the monastery fell into disarray. The monks fought, and combats ended in bloodshed. Eventually the master returned home, and acted as usual. Tranquillity and order were restored in his presence. To me the years spent studying with Hu Ying was such a religious experience. She rarely gives excessive instruction, but every piece of her seemingly casual remark allows me to be the best of myself. Hu Ying gave me the chance to begin a new life abroad and to live this new life with self-love and self-respect. Over those many years of laborious trying, she never says she tries, nor how hard she has tried *with me*.

I took an independent study class with Michael Fuller in 2010. This class, along with Professor Fuller's scholarly writing, have given me the languages to articulate visions I had struggled to find words for. Professor Fuller continued to comment critically and extensively on earlier drafts of this manuscript. I remember one summer night I was hit by a bike. That summer Professor Fuller continued to identify more shortcomings of this book and proposed more radical ways to revise them. I might not have incorporated all the changes he suggested, but in the process of correcting these errors, I have been given the courage to persevere and to go on trying.

Philip Ivanhoe read nearly all chapter drafts multiple times. In the most difficult days, he remained committed to the project and persisted to encourage me with confidence and good faith. Without his unwavering support, I might not have been able to bring the book to completion.

At UC Irvine, Martin Huang taught me how to read and the importance of reading carefully again. Theoretical texts Rei Terada introduced never failed to be rebelliously illuminating. Constantly I regret not having tried to learn more from her (and this is an apology I owe every one of my teachers).

In various stages of writing, Peter Zarrow, Peter Hershock, Tsuyoshi Ishii, Joshua Fogel, Timothy Guttman, and Lam Ling Hon read portions of the chapters and offered me the most astute suggestions. Peter Hershock asked me to strive to become a liquid crystal. I googled "liquid crystal" but to no avail. Later it took me years to comprehend his words. I thank Peter for his sage words and for introducing me to Buddhist teachings. At a conference Harvey Lederman organized at Princeton in 2021, I met Professor Lin Yueh-hui. Feeling confused by many things, I asked her: Does *liangzhi* 良知 *truly* exist? After a brief moment of silence, Professor Lin looked into my eyes and said, "Are you capable of loving someone?" My chance encounter with Professor Lin and the work by late Araki Kengo illuminated my understanding of *liangzhi*.

Many friends and teachers shared their knowledge and very honest views with me. This book is inspired by them and written *for them*. Beyond the individuals above, in particular I thank Theodore Huters, Man Sing Chan, Erin Huang, Yu Wen, Jennifer Eichman, Lydia Liu, Yiju Huang, Harvey Lederman, Hyun Seon Park, Keren He, Tze-ki Hon, Kai-wing Chow, Chu Hung Lam, Qian Nanxiu, Ren Ke, and Margaret Tillman. Erin Huang and Huili Zheng endeavored to answer my questions in whatever difficult situations they found themselves. Their selflessness demonstrates what it means to be a sincere and upright person.

I thank Roger Ames for gratuitously including this book in SUNY's Chinese Philosophy and Culture series. I am grateful to James Peltz and Diane Ganeles for the sustained efforts they made to bring this book to publication. Three anonymous readers provided very thoughtful suggestions. Their vigorous engagement with this book has allowed me to present a more balanced and comprehensive portrayal of Liang Qichao and his political career.

In New York I have had the good fortune to learn from scholars of Chinese philosophy at the neo-Confucianism seminar sponsored by Columbia University. As Jiang Tao said in one of our late-night drinking days: "This seminar is our home." We all thank On-cho Ng for being our steadfast spiritual leader, and Ari Borrell for being the most reliable family member to return to. Beyond New York, I have a home in Irvine.

In emails we exchanged, Edward Fowler and Yukari Nobumoto constantly ask me to come back to stay with them. As Ying Peterson said, Rouhmei Hsieh, Jessica Liu, Hu Ying, and her are my "four moms." "With *four moms*, what is there to be fearful of?"

At CUNY my former chairperson, Lucas Marchante-Aragón, supported my research and strove to help me overcome many challenges I encountered. Lucas is the most devoted friend one could ask for. Cindy Wong, Janet Dudley, and Maryanne Feola have guided me through my career with patience and unfailing support.

Circle Lo, Sunny Chan, April Tam, Eric Mok, and Eunah Cho remain the most reliable friends. Regardless of where she is, Phyllis Yuen remains close and dear. I am grateful for the friendship of Nicola (Luddie) Sher, Bang-Geul Han, and Martin Siu, and I am fortunate to have been able to spend my Irvine years with Hyonhui Choe, James Goebel, Philip Anselmo, and Vicky Hsieh.

Over the years of trying, I have also encountered many healers. In particular I thank Dr. Yaoshen Cai and Charles Myzwinski. Beyond sparing me from many physical pains, in our acupuncture sessions, Dr. Cai has relentlessly tried to dispel me from "evil influences" of Buddhist teachings and convert me to Christianity. But perhaps Dr. Cai does not know: he listens and listens with deep compassion. His sharing of *dukkha* is itself the finest Buddhist practice. I thank, in addition, the presence of Matthew McAllister in the final stage of book revision. His tender care has made all struggling moments in the past look irrelevant and remote.

My family is always there for me. My uncle Xu Pei guides my learning and growth with fatherly care. My aunt Rosa Suen (Terry Po Po) treats every member of the family with selfless dedication. And, as always, I thank my parents, Jessica and Joshua. Their presence makes being in this world purposeful and worthy.

Introduction

An Affective Turn in the Study of Chinese Political Modernity

In the Qing dynasty (1644–1911), China's imperial examination had become progressively difficult to pass.[1] To stand out in a massive candidate pool and become a state official, students could only direct all their energy to memorizing the textual knowledge prescribed in the Confucian classics and the annotations on these classics sanctioned by the state. This situation continued after China was defeated in the First Sino-Japanese war (1894–95). In order to create a modern nation, including a viable national defense force, both the state and the public activists began to circulate modern political knowledge through schools and reformist publications. Within a few years, scholars competent in the philological investigation of texts were intimately familiar with terms such as "nationalism" (*guojia zhuyi* 國家主義), "liberty" (*ziyou* 自由), and "equality" (*pingdeng* 平等), as well as the series of national independence movements these ideas inspired in the United States and Europe.

Chinese intellectuals had certainly mastered the "discourse" of modern political life. If national history, as postmodern historiography suggests, is a narrative construct fabricated through complex processes of power negotiation and that linguistic changes reflect historical transformations, the country ought to have completed its political modernization in the early 1900s. Although he had done much to help publicize modern political knowledge in China, Liang Qichao 梁啟超 (1873–1929) dismissed the representative power of language as force that could advance the process of modernization. Rather than acknowledging and seeking to make use of his contemporaries' scholarly competence, Liang was distressed by their

1

obsession with textual knowledge, seeing in it a disabling continuation of a discredited traditional approach to understanding that had come to characterize preparation for the imperial examinations. Liang pressed his contemporaries to revisit what they considered to be familiar "textual knowledge," or perhaps the limitation of knowledge as a whole. In the inaugural issue of *New Citizen Journal* (*Xinmin Congbao* 新民叢報), he says, "The *word* nationalism is a fully developed concept in China. Nationalism, as we know (*zhi* 知) on a conceptual level, denotes mutual *feelings* of affinity shared by people with identical ethnic, linguistic, religious, and cultural backgrounds. With determination and resolve, they strive for independence, political sovereignty, and autonomous administrative establishment."[2]

The *linguistic* definition of "nationalism" is unquestionably clear. Liang, however, insisted on challenging the intellectuals of his time: if "nationalism" denotes strong, and often irrational, patriotic feelings one experiences within, does the term mean anything to China if those who talk about it are not *passionately nationalistic*? If people are not *emotionally responsive to* and *affectively engaged* with the word, is it meaningful to go on talking the talk about nationalism and in turn egalitarian democracy, a system of government that thrives on the enlightenment and empowerment of the individual?

Through such rhetorical questions, Liang disclosed an "affective distance" that had estranged and disengaged the Chinese public from the modern political discourse being prescribed and circulated in contemporary reformist publications. The skepticism he expressed regarding language challenges the social constructionist framework, as well as the normative rational presumptions, recent scholarship has relied on to make sense of Chinese modernity. In the past two decades, historians informed by postcolonial studies and postmodern historiography often perceive and approach the formation of Chinese political modernity as a "discursive construct." But having spent years importing modern political knowledge to China, Liang held that language constitutes political reality only as it becomes *personally meaningful*. Sensitive to the intricate difference between "textual knowledge" and "personal intent," the success of China's modern political enlightenment, he believed, was predicated on the way people personally relate to the new words and new ideas. Rather than studying modern political concepts as textual knowledge, Chinese intellectuals needed to undergo a vigorous epistemic reform to modify their habits of "learning." Only by making language an expression of people's affectively lived experience could modern Chinese nationalism, and ultimately the implementation of democratic governance, be truly possible.

An Affective Turn in Chinese Political Modernity

In the hope of making discursive concepts *subjectively*, *affectively*, and *ontologically* meaningful to his contemporaries, in 1902 Liang launched a series of "new" reformist publications. In *New Citizen Journal* and *New Fiction* (*Xin xiaoshuo* 新小說), he experimented with a series of affective representational formats that were calculated to engage and stimulate the bodily senses. His "new prose style" (*xin wenti* 新文體), for instance, mimics the rhyming pattern of Chinese classical parallelism so that the rhapsodic rhythm can resonate with people's heartbeat. To help readers visualize China's modern political development, Liang described various futuristic scenes in dramatic visual and acoustic details that transformed his "new fiction" into a cinematic landscape. Coming to his "historical biographies," Liang portrayed European revolutionaries as superior moral beings who brought their countries national independence through tears, sweat, blood, death, and excruciating pain. The pictorial descriptions of these individuals' intense bodily suffering were designed to elicit empathetic gut reactions.

Liang's formal inventions, innocent as they may seem, radically transformed the scope and the nature of China's modern political reform. By making people's affective engagement the premise of modern political enlightenment, the reformer reinstated some enduring philosophical concerns at the heart of China's modern political transition. To learned individuals of his times (or perhaps postcolonial and postmodern thinkers of ours), Liang urged them to reconsider the following questions: What is man's relationship to language? How is one's affective interiority related to the objective language? If language fails to be *personally meaningful*, can we persist in perceiving it as "generally representative" and "socially relevant"? What, after all, does being "personally meaningful" mean and encompass? Through what kinds of *operating mechanisms* can a person internalize and embody textual knowledge as a subjective experience? What does this new knowledge transmission method look like? China's political order, whether in the Qing dynasty or in ancient times, was sanctioned to a large degree by the state-sponsored intellectual order. If the "text-based" approach to knowledge proved ineffective, how would the rise of an alternative learning method revamp the country's existing intellectual, moral, and philosophical conventions? What, most importantly, have these contending moral and philosophical positions converted modern political concepts into? And what is Chinese political modernity *truly* about?

What Liang Qichao perceived to be a disconnection between "textual meaning" and "personal intent," as it turns out, is so much more than a general interpretative concern. It presents a fundamental epistemic challenge, and ultimately an all-inclusive intellectual, moral, and philosophical transition, that Chinese intellectuals encountered during the political modernization process. In his "new" reformist journals Liang focused as much on the "representational format" as on the "modern political content." By rendering conceptual ideas in musical, visual, and fictional terms, the reformer expanded the reception of textual knowledge from "reading" to "listening and visualizing" experiences. Besides emphasizing the centrality of affect, or people's *lived* ontological experiences, in the process of democratic enlightenment, Liang subtly generated an epistemic shift alongside modern political reform. His attempt to replace the "text-based" approach to knowledge with a "heart-based" approach presents an alarming implication for historians seeking to comprehend Chinese political modernity through the study of the discourse: in late Qing China, the transmission of modern political knowledge took an affective turn. Since the methods for the transmission of knowledge have moved in a new direction, our critical approach to Chinese modernity needs to change accordingly.

What Did "Affect" Mean in Late Qing China?

In recent years, the study of affect has received unprecedented critical attention in the humanities and social sciences. Political scientists, most notably, have frequently emphasized the necessity of reexamining the relation between affect and democratic politics. Those who endorse this approach seem to share a general dissatisfaction: considering passion an integral component of ancient Greek politics, Plato, Socrates, and Aristotle had continued to defend the centrality of human affect in public life.[3] Coming to the seventeenth century, however, the advance of natural science, and subsequently the conception of Cartesian dualism, prompted Enlightenment thinkers to separate "passion" from "reason," and the "body" from the "mind." Since then, the development of philosophy and social theory in Europe has been grounded upon privileging a conception of human subjectivity as rational, autonomous, and disembodied from the nonconscious corporeal drives.

The kind of absolute human subjectivity Enlightenment thinkers upheld seems problematic to modern theorists of our time. First, by repudiating passion in the development of modern liberalism, these early European thinkers had willfully ignored the decisive impact people's affective forces exerted on our political and social decisions. They, moreover, had contemptuously and prematurely denied the prospect of nurturing human affect as a positive ethical and political force that could prove conducive to progressive social transformation. Perceiving affect as an "emancipatory ontological solution,"[4] recent political theorists such as Michael Walzer, Rebecca Kingston, and Leonard Ferry assert that only by "bringing passion back to the public life" can we reorient ourselves with a new view of liberal democracy that incorporates and appreciates all aspects of our emotional life.[5] While modern political theorists protest the dominance of human rationality, Brian Massumi considers the Enlightenment conception of reason a blatant deception. Retrieving an intellectual trajectory that has sporadically but concertedly evolved from Baruch de Spinoza (1632–1677) to Henri Bergson (1859–1941) to Gilles Deleuze (1925–1995), Massumi seeks to challenge the omnipotence of reason that dominates some regions of the academy by turning to the speculative regions of neuroscience.[6] Based on results from biologically based research, he repositions the mind as an embodied property, situated and dependent upon presubjective forces that are experientially and biologically determined. Massumi perceives people as affective beings who find no certainty in their contact with the world. But by acknowledging the kinetic presence of affect, they may at least be able to attend to the "problematique" of our encounter in those accounts of experiences.

At the turn of the early twentieth century, Liang Qichao seemed equally if not more sharply aware of the limitation of analyzing political concepts as normative rational ideals as we standardly approach them nowadays in the Anglo-American tradition. Through the invention of his musical, visual, and fictional representations, Liang's attempt to complement "learning" with people's embodied sensual responses, at first glance, seems to resonate with recent Western theorists' call for an implementation of an "affective turn" in the study of political science. But in the years spent completing this book, I have become keenly aware of the challenges faced by "affect studies." Instead of transporting "affect" as a convenient but unreflexive analytical category to the study of China's modern political reform, we need to step back and rise to a set of unresolved challenges.

First, what exactly makes the study of "affect" applicable to a non-Western cultural tradition? If we are to apply affect as an analytical category in late Qing China, what does the concept suggest and encompass in the local context? Liang called on Chinese intellectuals to look beyond the semantic content of language. Assuming that the invention of his affective presentations began as a protest against the "text-based" approach to knowledge, how did late Qing China's evolving philosophical assumptions, competing academic practices, and existing moral traditions inform those stylistic inventions, and sequentially transform "one-dimensional" rational normative ideals into "three-dimensional" *lived expressions* that embody people's ontological affective intensity? Moving on to more theoretical concerns: affect, in Brian Massumi's and Gilles Deleuze's understanding, refers to the unpredictable corporeal "intensity" that exists prior to, and interruptive of, social logic.[7] With at times a devastating ability to go its own way, this asocial bodily force influences our rational judgment but remains distinct and, on some accounts, disconnected from it. If corporeal intensity and rationality, as affect theorists claim, are categorically and exclusively different from each other, how can Liang expect the Chinese public to be "passionate" about "reason"? Through what kinds of mechanisms can one transform people's "passionate gut reaction" into "emotional expression," and presumably "social and political action"? And how may Liang utilize local philosophical resources to address these unsettled Western theoretical concerns from an East Asian perspective? Lastly, speaking from a more pragmatic point of view: Assuming that affect can be an unpremeditated state of being, and as such difficult to get hold of, how can we capture the presence of affect in available written late Qing documents? In what ways can we discern its transformative impacts on various physical and ideological changes?

Situating the Affective Turn within China's Internal Intellectual Debates

For scholars interested in implementing an "affective turn" in historical and literary analysis after the vastly influential "cultural turn," the questions above are still waiting to be addressed. While I am familiar with recent developments in the "history of emotions" and "affect studies" that center on the United States and Europe, my emphases and methods differ from those used in studies of Western cultures.[8] In the first two chapters of the book, I begin by situating the affective turn Liang Qichao called for in late Qing China's ongoing moral, philosophical, and intellectual debates. Unlike conventional historical studies that focus on his political reform, *Affective Betrayal* examines scholarly essays the reformer published on China's academic practices, philosophical movements, and Confucian ethics. Drawing upon and analyzing the implications of these documents, I argue that the invention of Liang's visual, musical, and fictional presentations is informed by a series of repressed academic practices, marginalized philosophical positions, and underrepresented moral traditions that he sought to restore and incorporate in China's incipient democratic governance. These practices include the Mencian school of Confucianism, the Ming dynasty (1368–1644) philosopher Wang Yangming's 王陽明 (1472–1529) moral theory, traditionally inspired critical reactions to a barren style of learning involving memorization and recitation, and an intellectual movement known as New Text studies (*jinwen jingxue* 今文經學). To elucidate Liang's determination in expanding political reform into an all-inclusive intellectual, philosophical, and moral transition, the book relates the following story.

Since the mid-eighteenth century, learned individuals in China followed a fundamentally "text-based" approach known as the "Learning of Principle" (*lixue* 理學) school of neo-Confucianism. In contrast to Wang Yangming's "Learning of the Heart-Mind" (*xinxue* 心學) school of neo-Confucianism, which insists on recovering people's moral intuition, the "Learning of Principle" school is conventionally, though somewhat unjustly, associated with Zhu Xi 朱熹 (1130–1200), a Southern Song (1127–1279) philosopher who emphasized the importance of obtaining moral knowledge through the careful study of texts combined with investigation of external events and states of affairs.[9] But as intellectuals fell into the habit of mechanically reciting, memorizing, and repeating the lessons of the classics, whether to pass the imperial examinations or to simply to display their erudition, this method and the doctrines it was based upon became so worn out that they ceased to be existentially meaningful.[10] To help people develop and sharpen their critical reflectivity, a group of early Qing scholars established a new academic practice called "evidential scholarship" (*kaozheng xue* 考證學).[11] Sequentially they developed systematic, objective, and sophisticated philological methods to clarify interpretative obscurities that prevailed in the study of Confucian classics. Evidential scholarship later became the leading intellectual practice in the Qing dynasty.

Toward the end of the late nineteenth century, modern political knowledge was introduced to China through state-sponsored campaigns and reformist publications founded by public activists. Having spent years of their careers pursuing a "text-based" approach to knowledge, Chinese scholars were ready to scrutinize the "new" knowledge with investigative research methods developed by evidential scholarship. Liang welcomed the incorporation of scientific objectivism in the study of modern political knowledge and yet he complained that terms such as "nationalism," "liberty," and "people's sovereignty" needed to be understood affectively as well as cognitively.[12] Political modernity, in the end, is not a conceptual property; it is a matter of *being* modern. These new terms and new ideas should manifest a person's awakened consciousness and validate him as a self-sufficient modern political agent. Simply grasping those abstract ideas does not make them *personally* relevant.

Liang believed China had enough Western concepts. What continued to hinder people from becoming truly modern was not the lack of modern knowledge but the intellectual inertia and submissive conformity that prevented them from making the modern political discourse ontologically meaningful.[13] Liang was eager to generate new energies in the stagnant academic scene. To call for an epistemic shift on a national level, he became affiliated with New Text studies,[14] a marginalized exegetic tradition that had persisted for centuries to challenge the orthodox position of "Old Text studies" (*guwen jingxue* 古文經學), a competing interpretative movement with which the "text-based" approach is conventionally associated.[15] Assuming the role of a spokesperson for this oppositional intellectual trend, Liang emphasized the importance of recovering the "affective resonance" between the self and the textual knowledge embodied in the classics, and applying one's "personal meanings" in state affairs.[16] Hoping to utilize New Text studies' exegetic principles in the process of acquiring modern knowledge, Liang saw the possibility of turning his reformist journal into an "affective medium."[17] By rendering new ideas in musical, visual, and fictional terms, Liang soon expanded the reception of modern political concepts from learning to a series of embodied sensory experiences. Beyond finding a substantial way to connect people's ontological interiority with textual knowledge, these affective representations offered him concrete means to introduce a "heart-based" approach to knowledge, and strive for a fine, and much awaited, balance between subjective engagement, critical reflectivity, and empirical verification in China's academic practice.

Liang's creative "formal" protest against the "text-based" learning approach indicated that the establishment of a modern "political" order is contingent on the reformation of the internal "intellectual" order. For many years, historians seemed chiefly interested in China's social and political transformations. But once we situate Liang's "new" reformist publications in the country's unresolved intellectual competitions, it appears that the rise of his affective representations began life as a critical response to an intellectual crisis, if not predicament, that surfaced in the early Qing period but that has escaped recent historians' attention. The "political" reform Liang is conventionally associated with transcends the political domain. It is intricately implicated in a long-awaited internal intellectual transition that seeks to transform Chinese intellectuals' learning habits, the factional divide that separated contentious schools of learning, and ultimately the founding principles of the Qing dynasty's state intellectual practice.[18] In this book, I argue that only by perceiving China's internal intellectual development and the modern political movement as "mutually constitutive" processes can we begin to understand what Chinese political modernity is about and how it has come into being. A simple but compelling reason is that throughout the Qing dynasty, the representative power of language had been repeatedly contested and questioned.[19] It was no longer as illustrative and emblematic as scholars focusing on the study of discourse construction might have assumed. The heavy and at times exclusive emphasis recent studies place on "the study of language" reveals our negligence of China's intensifying intellectual debates, as well as the influence they exerted on the formation of modern political knowledge.

Affective Origins of Chinese Political Modernity

In an academic climate that prioritized the study of language over perceptual intuition, Liang Qichao aspired to stimulate people's sensual responses and channel those premeditated intensities into a constituting component of modern Chinese politics, making "affect" indispensable to the ontological commitments of China's burgeoning democratic liberalism. Coming to the third chapter, the book seeks to address two sets of theoretical challenges associated with his goal. First, what exactly does "affect" mean to Liang? And how could he establish a meaningful connection between people's affective interiority and democratic liberalism? The reformer, in addition, wanted people to be *affectively responsive* to modern political concepts. How could Liang expect people to be "passionate" about "reason"? And through what means did he hope to bridge the discrepancy between "corporeal intensity" and "rational subjectivity"?

To answer these questions, I turn to Liang's essays on a range of apparently unconnected but in fact related topics, which include Cartesian dualism, Western medical physiology, and Indian and Chinese Buddhist metaphysics, that informed the development of the "Learning of the Heart-Mind" school of neo-Confucianism. By comparing Liang's philosophical position with the theoretical premises of "affect studies," I show that the kind of "affective resonance" Liang hoped to recover from the people encompasses but transcends unpremeditated corporeal intensity. It is, as the reformer extensively and comprehensively elaborated in *Mirror for Moral Cultivation* (*Deyu jian* 德育鑑), a moral anthology he distributed in 1903, what the Ming philosopher Wang Yangming called *liangzhi* 良知, a person's a priori moral judgment.[20]

During the Song (960–1276) and the Ming dynasties, Wang Yangming and most neo-Confucian thinkers perceived the universe as a vast, interpenetrating system ordered by a set of transcendental cosmic patterns or principles known as (*li* 理). The cosmic pattern manifests its organizational structure—both moral and physical—in people as well as in myriad forms of beings. While *li* is impeccably structured, it is a set of metaphysical abstractions. As Wang's intellectual contender, Zhu Xi, argued, for abstract principles to manifest their cosmic perfection in physical presence, they needed to "take form" in material substances being known as *qi* 氣. Zhu Xi believed that man shares the unspoiled cosmic moral nature (*xing* 性). But since the *qi* substances that constitute one's physical makeup are contaminated by an evil force that pervades the cosmos, people are perfect in nature but corrupted in person.[21]

Under the influence of Buddhist metaphysics, Wang Yangming rejected Zhu Xi's hypothesis.[22] The universe, as it was believed in early Buddhist teaching, consists of two levels of truth. One is the "ultimate truth" (*paramārtha-satya*; Chin: 勝義諦) pertaining to dharma (Chin: 法), the unchanging cosmic law, while the other is the "conventional or provisional truth" (*saṃvṛti satya*; Chin: 世俗諦), which discloses the living presence of people, stars, flowers, and chariots in everyday lives. This binary division prompts practitioners of Theravāda Buddhism, or the "Lesser Vehicle," to envision a stark, hierarchical contrast between the heavenly realm of metaphysical transcendence and the phenomenal realm of human existence. Nāgārjuna (Chin: 龍樹) (150–250 AD), arguably the most influential thinker in the history of Indian philosophy, repudiated such a view. In *The Middle Way* (*Mūlamadhyamakakārikā*; Chin: 中論), the seminal text establishing the foundational premise of the Madhyamaka (Eng: Middle Way; Chin: 中觀) school of Mahāyāna Buddhism, Nāgārjuna contends that everything in the universe is what it is *in virtue of* its relation to other things. Instead of having any intrinsic self-nature (Sanskrit: *svabhāva*; Chin: 自性), everything and everyone in the universe exist in an "interdependent" fashion. As Nāgārjuna's teaching made its way to China, its metaphysical proposition was further advanced by the homegrown Huayan 華嚴 Buddhism. Wang Yangming, as I discuss in chapter three, incorporated both the Chinese and the Indian Buddhist metaphysics into the teachings of neo-Confucianism. Li the cosmic principle, according to Wang, is *what it is* by relating to the affairs of men. Instead of a transcendental order detached from human existence, *li* the cosmic principle reveals itself in the formative structure of myriad forms of beings. The cosmic principle, in other words, is not "the Way" up high but *the way* we are made, *the way* we breathe, and *the way* we think and act.

Assuming that men's physical and moral compositions are structured in perfect agreement with *li* the cosmic principle, Wang Yangming asserted that people begin life as cosmic moral beings. Whatever individuals do, their "spontaneous response" (*xing* 行), be it perceptual or physical, is the "physical" *disclosure* and *revelation* of the abstract cosmic pattern that they epitomize. Men, in other words, are not a product of heaven but the *living presences of* heaven. In this universe, every man is formed with the identical cosmic pattern. People may share "visible" differences in appearance, ability, and social origins in the realm of human affairs. But beyond these quantifiable attributes, they are essentially *the same as* each other. With all individuals containing within themselves the *shared* cosmic structure, they are homogenous "cosmic members" belonging to the "metaphysical republic" of cosmic oneness.[23] Existing as parts and parcels of an organic entity, people are equal to each other and are inextricably intertwined with each other.[24]

Between Metaphysical Republic and Democratic Governance

Perceiving men as equal cosmic members endowed with unblemished moral goodness, Wang Yangming's moral theory subtly challenged the credibility of autocratic monarchy.[25] Toward the end of the nineteenth century, the arrival of Athenian democratic concepts eventually provided Liang Qichao with concrete means to release the subversive potential of Wang Yangming's moral metaphysics in China's transition to political modernity.[26] While terms such as "national citizen," "rights," "equality," and "civil obligation" (*yiwu* 義務) might seem foreign to most Chinese intellectuals, Liang was quick to discern the affinity between the organizing principle of democratic liberalism and Wang's conception of a metaphysical republic. In a democratic state, each individual is an autonomous agent being promised equal civil and political rights. But to be able to exercise one's rights, people have to fulfill their corresponding civil duties and obligations. Whereas Wang Yangming's "metaphysical republic" emphasizes that people are equal to each other and inextricably intertwined with each other, democratic governance is a unified system that thrives on the cooperation and codependence of each law-abiding citizen. The cosmic structure Wang Yangming envisioned, as it appeared to Liang, offered the finest cosmic moral foundation for an egalitarian government. Having identified the structural affinity between an indigenous "cosmic moral community" and the "democratic political community," the modern reformer, as I believe, saw the apparent attraction of integrating these two systems into a world of "cosmic moral-political oneness."

In Liang's early adult years, he shared the moral faith Wang Yangming placed in the people. Men, as the young reformer once believed, are naturally *predisposed* to discern the a priori totality underlying the organizing structure of their cosmic nature and the democratic political order. If the term "national citizen" speaks to the people, it is because it expresses who we are and the way we are *programmed* to relate to others. Modern political concepts are not foreign conceptual imports; they are modern *political expressions of* men's cosmic nature. For Liang, to be politically modern is about letting the homogeneous "cosmic moral beings" *be* who they *already* are, thereby restoring "the immanence of the metaphysical in the experiential" through China's transition to political modernity.[27]

From "Text" to the "Organization *of* Text"

Liang intended to turn the "learning" of modern political knowledge into a state of "instinctive moral being." How, technically speaking, could he help readers *recognize* modern political concepts as *recollections* of their cosmic nature, and in turn bridge the discrepancy that divides "knowing" the epistemic cognition from "being" the embodied experiential sensation? To make the Chinese public a member of the international community of nation states, Liang had to fulfill the pragmatic need of disseminating modern political concepts as new knowledge, and, at the same time, making new knowledge *personally meaningful* to the people.[28] To satisfy the dual purposes, the young reformer identified a genius solution, which was to shift the reader's attention from "text" to the formal "organization *of* text." Inspired by some of the most cherished practices in the Chinese poetic tradition, Liang began to create a special musical effect in his "new prose style." Music accelerates one's heartbeats and generates excitement. To understand how the syntactic and rhythmical arrangement of words help people restore the "coherence" between their cosmic nature and the modern political structure, I find it useful to consult Michael Fuller's study on Song poetry, a body of scholarship that conducts cross-cultural comparison with great philosophical sophistication.[29]

To explicate how formal poetic structure may resonate with man's moral intuition, Fuller begins by discerning the difference between *wen* 文 (literary or aesthetic pattern) and *yan* 言 (words), two literary expressions that can be easily mistaken for each other.[30] Fuller presents a simple example: in the mid-sixth century, China's capital city, Chang An 長安, was shattered by warfare. The poet Du Fu 杜甫 (712–770) laments in his poem "A Spring Vista" (*chun wang* 春望): "The capital is broken: mountains and rivers remain."[31] The phrases "the capital is broken" (*guopo* 國破) and "mountains and rivers remain" (*shanhezai* 山河在) designate particular facts, objects, and affairs. They are "words," or *yan*, that fully exhaust one's intent (言能盡其意). As soon as Du Fu arranged and juxtaposed these phrases as "國破山河在 *guopo shanghezai*," this particular poetic sequence becomes *wen*, an aesthetic pattern conveying intent without end (文不能盡其意). If organized properly, only a handful of words can unpack boundless meanings. So how can this be?

To elucidate the relationship between "meaning" and the "organization of words," Fuller looks to the ancient Confucian philosopher Xun

Kuang 荀況 (c. 310 BC–c. 220 BC). The human world, according to Xun Kuang, is structured around a larger, and ultimately unfathomable, kind of coherence, which he called "the order of heaven."[32] First, heaven creates people. With their heavenly endowed senses, men are naturally inclined to organize complex human experiences into patterns that epitomize the heavenly order. As a person arranges words into meaningful patterns, the ultimate status of the objects referred to through these words do not matter so long as the intention behind the pointing out of objects is fulfilled.[33] *Wen*, in other words, is man's *embodiment* of intent rather than the *statement* of intent. For ancient Chinese philosophers who attempted to interpret the words of the sages, their concern was less about "the sage's ability to adequately understand the world than in the adequacy of the texts to embody that understanding."[34]

While Xun Kuang believed that men are naturally capable of constructing meaningful patterns that transcend one's rational comprehension, Michael Fuller is careful to identify apparent similarities between Xun Kuang and the German philosopher Immanuel Kant (1724–1804). Kant, like his ancient Chinese counterpart, perceived men as creatures who are predisposed to order human experiences around a set of a priori categories such as space, time, causality, and so on.[35] In his discussion on fine art, Kant asserts that good artists are prone to create work that reveals the transcendental order. These meaningful but unintentional creations reveal the "purposiveness of form."[36] The organizing pattern of certain universal law informs man's artistic creation that reveals patterns. Man, at the same time, is endowed with a purposeful mind that is prone to discern the a priori order, and to experience pleasure in discerning a formal order or structured unity within the world. This particular kind of judgment is known as "aesthetic judgment." Unlike "determinative judgment," which classifies the *reality* of human order by subsuming the particular into categories of meanings,[37] aesthetic judgment thrives on the intuitive coherence people identify between the structuring order of the literary composition and the way we are instinctively predisposed to relate to the world. When the purposeful mind and the purposiveness of form converge, splendid sparks strike. But however pleasurable such an unexpected fleeting encounter might be, the sparks pend in a state of perceptual intuition unmediated by conceptual reasoning. A person, in other words, cannot clearly discern what he knows. Kant called the evanescent encounter an "aesthetic experience," which implies the pleasurable experience of discerning a formal order or structured unity within the world. Since it is the intuitive coherence rather than the rational conceptualization that matters, aesthetic judgment always lingers in a state of unnamable certainty. Comparable to the moments when Theodor Adorno (1903–1969) hears the melodic notes of Beethoven—a person is exposed to the *promise* of perfect coherence without reducing the transcendental to the confinement of the concrete.[38]

Liang was familiar with Immanuel Kant's philosophy. Beyond that, he considered what Kant perceived to be man's a priori knowledge to be the cosmic pattern a person epitomizes in his heartmind.[39] While the German philosopher believes that people are naturally built to identify, process, and react to temporal, spatial, and causal patterns, Liang strove to help readers obtain a comparable kind of "aesthetic moral-political" experience in his affective representations. Similar to learned intellectuals of his times, Liang was well versed in classical Chinese poetry and was familiar with philosophical premises that inform the Chinese lyrical tradition. In "On Feelings Expressed in China's rhapsodic Verse," an elaborate essay he published some years later, Liang divides the structure of Chinese poetry into three geometrical patterns. "The usage of a particular pattern," he says, "is intended to communicate a particular feeling" (那一種情感該用那一種方式).[40] The articulation of strong, candid feelings, for instance, relies on "the method of linear direct explosion" (直線式的奔進表情法 *zhixiang shi de benjin biaoqing fa*). The method of "circular reverberation" (曲線式的迴盪 *quxian shi de huidang*) creates feelings of lingering attachment. And to remain meaningfully suggestive, a poet may reprise subtle musical resonance through the "polygonal concealment" (多角式的含蓄韻藉 *duojiao shi de hanxu yunji*).

Liang's familiarity with the rhythmic structure of classical Chinese poems was reflected in his lyrical reformist journalism. Mimicking the intonation, sound, and rhyming pattern of classical Chinese rhapsody, Liang composed lines structured in parallel couplets, arranged words in resonating rhyming patterns, and juxtaposed his parallel prose with short lines and interjections calculated to create the sense of musical repercussion. By attuning the rhythmical tempo of his musical verses to the pulsating cadence of people's heartbeat, Liang tried to *restore* and *recover* modern political concepts as embodied experiential sensations.

Rethinking Cartesian Dualism

To modern Western theorists, Liang's endeavor may look most bizarre. Man's corporeal "intensity," as Brian Massumi argues, exists prior to, and is interruptive of, social logic. It affects our rational judgment but remains distinct and disconnected from it. If the body and the mind represent two distinct properties, how can "knowing" the epistemic cognition be *the same as* "being" the embodied experiential sensation? While Liang never directly addressed these questions, he opens us to the possibility of rethinking Cartesian dualism with an alternate cultural logic.

Early thinkers from the West, as recent poststructuralist theorists have explicated, tend to divide the transcendental from the existential, man from God, and the body from the mind. But in Madhyamaka Buddhism, the philosophical tradition that inspired the metaphysical premises of the Wang Yangming school of neo-Confucianism, the story was completely opposite. In our universe, everything, according to Nāgārjuna, is what it is *in virtue of* its relation to other things. In these interdependent if not mutually interpenetrative relationships, the cosmic principle is predicated on the presence of man, the "body" on the "mind," and "knowing" on "being." A person, as Wang Yangming once said, cannot *know* the word "hungry" if he has not experienced hunger, nor would he know "bitterness" without a taste of the bitter melon. The case is the same when it comes to performing modern "political" good. Instead of having to *learn* to be an independent political agent through the study of external textual doctrines, the perfection (or restoration, to be precise) of one's cosmic nature rests in crossing over the factitious boundary, be it self-constructed or artificially imposed, that divides a person from his true self. With each individual containing the cosmos *within* himself, a person does not have to connect himself with the external world, for at the deepest level there is no "self-other," "subject-object," "internal-external" dichotomy to begin with. Knowledge, for this reason, is *not* external; it is man's *recognizing responses* to his embodied, existential, and perceptual experiences. Wang Yangming's moral metaphysics, in other words, is about "taking away what has been added on," not "putting more on to it." *To know is to be.*

Liang Qichao was arguably the most influential reformer of his times. Beyond circulating modern political concepts as textual knowledge, parts of his reformist efforts, paradoxical as it may seem, rest in crossing or reducing the "linguistic barrier" that hinders people from manifesting the cosmic principles (*li*) in the world of phenomenal affairs (*shi* 事). Through the invention of his affective representations, Liang tried to channel people's a priori moral goodness into modern political knowledge, making the reception of modern political concepts an aesthetic "moral" experience. The term "national citizen," for instance, should convey the ontological experience of *being* a self-empowered political agent. Rather than a passive learner *of* a modern political concept or a subordinate member *of* a nation, a national citizen is personally responsible *for* the country. The emotional intensity one experiences exhibits his political consciousness and validates him as a self-sufficient political agent. Nationalism, following the same logic, manifests a person's patriotic *feeling* for the state. "People's sovereignty" epitomizes the state of empowered self-sufficiency, while "revolution" expresses one's instinctive impulse to defy the artificial hierarchical order being imposed upon an independent moral and political agent.

In his affective representation Liang endeavored to conflate the state of "ontological being" with "epistemic understanding." Contrary to what recent affect theorists might have assumed, the reformer does not render modern political concepts affectively to "connect" people's moral interiority and external knowledge as two discrete properties. The purpose of his affective presentations rests precisely in obscuring the artificial boundary between the external and the internal, the outside and the inside, and the factual and existential. In his reformist journals, Liang, to parody the German hermeneutic philosopher Wilhelm Dilthey's interpretative concepts, *back-translates* "expressions" to "lived experiences" to make "lived expressions" possible.[41] Rather than finding a way to incorporate the "external" into the "internal," the genius of his musical, visual, and sensational invention lies in moving in the opposite direction: helping the Chinese public "learn" modern political concepts through "un-learning," "know" through "un-knowing," and "conceptualize" through "de-conceptualizing."

In the West, as noted earlier, contemporary theorists such as Brian Massumi perceive affect as nonintentional, noncognitive, and noncultural. By assuming such a hypothesis is misguided by an unreliable, even mystical appeal to neuroscience, Ruth Leys systematically discloses how "emotion"-related research was methodologically and problematically conducted in the United States since the 1950s.[42] In her book Leys says that Massumi's hypothesis should not be taken seriously, and that in particular his claims about affect being nonintentional, noncognitive, and noncultural are incorrect. If affect, as Leys argues, is indeed *not* unintentional, the question that remains unsolved is how can "passion" be related to "reason"? Through a critical reading of Jacques Derrida, Rei Terada reaccentuates the difference between prelinguistic "emotional experiences" and subjective "emotional expressions."[43] To bridge the self-discrepancy between them, it takes a middleman. Terada calls the middleman "feeling," an agent who finds exterior reference for the interior state. Terada's book challenges the illusive unity of a human subject and the assumption that emotion is an expression of the mind and is thus subordinated to it. But in Liang's affective presentation, the reformer offers presumably a counterintuitive response to one of the most contested questions in affect studies: a person does not bridge "passion" with "reason." Only by removing the divide between them can knowledge be personally meaningful. In Wang Yangming's moral metaphysics, this binary opposition does not exist in the first place, and the invention of the body-mind dualism is problematic from the start.

From Discourse Construction to Aesthetic Moral Experiences

In his reformist journals, Liang Qichao tried to turn "words" (*yan* 言) into various forms of "aesthetic patterns" (*wen* 文). My conviction that China's translated political modernity is informed by a historical agent's rhetorical intention, charged with lyrical intensity, and *affectively presented* to the reader is a response to some famous questions Lydia Liu raises in *Translingual Practice* and to further research inspired by her pioneering work.[44] In late Qing China, as Liu argues, the formation of modern political meaning was hardly the result of knowledge transfer and even less the reciprocal exchange of meanings.[45] It was determined by "the contending interests of political and ideological struggles,"[46] and, most importantly, the way people *willfully wished* to be "modern."[47] Theodore Huters shares a comparable observation. Assuming that modern knowledge was shaped by the uncertainty arising from intellectuals' unsettling historical experiences, Huters asserts that people's anxiety reflects a historical situation of *perceived* inequality between languages rather than a failing in the language itself.[48]

I do not question that man's psychological condition shaped the formation of China's modern political discourse. But beyond that, is there a way that we could possibly acknowledge the *presence* of affect without reducing it to linguistic *representation*, a move that annihilates its imperceptible but contentious potentials? Knowing that people's affective sensibilities are too complex and subtle for words, David Wang strives to recuperate the "unspeakable" in "lyrical visions" such as painting, musical composition, calligraphy, operatic performance, and cinematic representations.[49] Indistinct and nonsynchronic as these personal murmurings may sound, they are candid *lived expressions* that reject "strong, holistic" narratives that dogmatically divide China's modernization into processes of revolution and enlightenment.[50]

Lydia Liu and David Wang present two distinct ways of approaching affect in the study of Chinese modernity. While Liu elucidates how affect shapes language, Wang looks away from language. Liang Qichao's reformist journals, somewhat interestingly, point us to a peculiar juncture lying between these two positions: modern political concepts are *affectively presented to* the reader. Besides exposing us to the limitation of approaching the study of China's modernization process as a linguistic construct, Liang's affective representations identify a deep problem in assumptions about meaning: a linguistic script presents words, *not* meanings. Work, as Roland Barthes suggests, epitomizes the author's organizing effort; it is an abstraction of his intentional meanings. A text, on the contrary, is unconstrained by shadows of intentionality. As a person reads, he is free to explore whatever patterns of connection he finds interesting in the play of signifiers."[51] If the meaning of language is contingent on its semantic content as well as the reader's affective engagement, what kinds of modern "political" meaning did Liang intend to present to the reader?

Of modern scholars who work on modern Chinese history, Prasenjit Duara is perhaps most sensitive to the "meaning" *of* languages.[52] In his attempt to delineate the multiplicities associated with the word "nationalism" (*guojia zhuyi* 國家主義), Duara argues that the semantic equivalence between the Chinese and the English terms seems to suggest that China had succumbed to what Lydia Liu would later call the orbit of meaning dominated by the Western power.[53] But in this new global system of nation states and capitalist economy, translatability or commensurability can be only established between languages, not between *positions* and *perspectives* from which a person makes sense of the language.[54] Nationalism, for instance, is an imagined identity a person or community acquires by consciously comparing oneself with others within a fluid network of representations. The awareness of competing in the same "imagined communities" is the *only* quality shared by different "nationalisms," and make "nationalisms" Nationalism. The word speaks for "a phenomenon that registers difference even as it claims a variety of unifying identity."

Political Modernity *as* Confucian Morality

Language, as Duara says, spoke with multiple voices in late Qing China. The same words can often be cited to support mutually contradictory positions and experiential sensibilities. While Duara writes from the perspective of a modern historian, his remark easily reminds us of the founding premise of hermeneutic phenomenology: reality consists of objects and events as they are *perceptually* and *corporeally* experienced in human consciousness and bodily sensations, not of anything independent of the basic structures of human experience. Aristotle was perhaps the first to describe how the eye must be affected by changes as an intervening medium rather than by objects themselves.[55] They, as described, are pictures in our heads, or virtual replicas of that world in an internal representation. People's experience and knowledge of the world, for this reason, are subjective experiences *of* objective facts, interior *of* exterior, and mental *of* physical.

Knowing that one's mental representation varies relentlessly from the objective physical object, Edmund Husserl (1859–1938) presumes that there must be *something there* in a person's head. This intrinsic personal content consists of a vast background of assumptions, memories, associations, and anticipations. They constitute the contents of one's consciousness, and in turn his first-person point of view. Husserl calls this interpretative viewpoint *noesis*, the mental imprint being conditionally shaped by a person's changing psychological episodes.[56] *Noesis* is distinct from *noema*, the *mental act* of seeing. If *noema* is a matter of *to be*, *noesis* points to the intentional state of *being*. The difference between *noema* and *noesis* is comparable to the act of thinking and the thought as such, the act of judging and the judgment, and the act of remembering and the memory itself.

Husserl is interested in the contents of a person's consciousness, or his *intentionality*. Unlike his teacher Husserl, Maurice Merleau-Ponty (1908–1961) believed that the formation of one's "mental imprint" is grounded on his "perception," which, strictly speaking, is neither a mental event nor a mode of thought; it derives from one's embodied experiences or bodily perspective.[57] As embodied beings, people do not experience the world as states of mind but as sensory states of our bodies and our bodily behaviors. A child *perceives* before he thinks. He learns how to think about what we already find ourselves seeing, hearing, and grasping. It is the bodily perspective that provides us with an anchorage through which to get hold of the world. In Merleau-Ponty's understanding, this is what Martin Heidegger (1889–1976) means by *être au monde*. "Being in the world" is essentially a matter of *being bodily there*.

Scholars in the humanities and social sciences have elaborately discussed issues of embodiment—the role of the body on the mind and the self.[58] Following recent developments in neuroscience, the new focus on the brain and its neural networks has shifted attention from issues of the social construction of the body to the ways in which the brain processes and structures corporeal experience, the way it receives sensory data, transforms the significant patterns in that data into memory, and then uses its network of memories in turn to shape the processes of perception. As scholars of the West explore the implications of this embodied account of human experience, Wang Yangming the neo-Confucian thinker compared man's perceptual senses to the inherent pattern of the cosmos. In his Buddhist-inspired moral metaphysics, a person's corporeal body *is* a cosmic body. By emphasizing the affinity between people and the cosmos, Wang underscored the supremacy of man's instinctive moral goodness. Instead of having to *learn* "to be" moral through the study of Confucian classics, a self-sufficient agent recognizes textual knowledge to be manifestations of his affective interiority. Morality, in other words, need not to be obtained from afar; it is man's ontological instinct. The kind of human omnipotence Wang Yangming upheld turned the Confucian classics from being sacred scriptures that should be worshipped by man into the outward expression of one's affective interiority. As the Ming philosopher reversed the "top-down" power hierarchy between man and text into an "inside out" organic entity, he projected a new kind of "human-centered" power dynamics that is packed with subversive potentials.

Coming to the early twentieth century, the arrival of liberal democracy provided Liang Qichao with concrete means to release these bursting subversive potential in the political domain. By making "moral being" the premise of "knowing," Liang creatively expanded one's instinctive "moral" agency to "political" agency. The epistemic shift he initiated reverses man's relationship with the text, as well as the state. These formal inventions, in addition, are designed to attain the far more ambitious goal of expanding the modern "political" movement into an internal "moral" renewal. Liang and Wang believed that human nature is as much about "bodily" nature as it is about "moral" nature. Knowing, therefore, is intertwined with one's moral instinct. Through introducing an affective representational paradigm that emphasizes "moral being *as* knowing," Liang transformed Confucian morality from prescriptive doctrines into "relational" experiences premised on one's cosmic endowment:

in an affective realm that foregrounds the supremacy of man's perceptual moral goodness, meanings are contingent on the way one is morally predisposed to relate to others. A person shares instinctive moral feelings for others, be it one's parents, ruler, or the state. His "sociopolitical" affective dispositions anticipate a corresponding spectrum of political "moral emotions." "Nationalism," "people's sovereignty," and "political revolution," for this reason, are comparable to conformist Confucian moral virtues such as filial piety, loyalty, and righteousness. For Liang, modern political concepts are *meant to be* recollections of one's internal moral perceptions. To become politically modern is essentially the contemporary way of being moral, thereby reappropriating and deploying a range of traditional Confucian ideals and concerns.

In modern scholarship, historians have showed how Liang and his mentor Kang Youwei 康有為 (1858–1927) made strategic use of Confucianism to justify their reformist agenda. But this story can also go the other way around: the political reform gave Liang an opportunity to *reinterpret*, *reinvent*, and *redefine* the meaning of Confucianism in the modern world. By incorporating Wang Yangming's moral theory with a neglected if not wholly forgotten Confucian narrative tradition, Liang made Confucianism an experiential state of moral *being* that empowers people to perform political good. The kind of "moral-political goodness" he called for undermines the established relationship between the people, the text, and the state: instead of waiting for an ideal political leadership to turn people into moral beings, an individual's instinctive moral attributes are sufficient to form a civil society. In recent years, the government of the People's Republic of China shares comparable interest in reinstating Confucianism as a state religion. Schoolchildren, or even party members, are encouraged to recite Confucian classics and observe virtues such as filial piety, loyalty, and righteousness. But in Liang's understanding, "true Confucianism" (*zhen kongxue* 真孔學) never was intended to be a didactic discourse. It is an instinctive moral attribute that *effectuates* democratic governance.

"New Fiction" and "New Historical Biography" as Modern Confucian Classics

Liang Qichao made creative uses of Wang Yangming's moral teachings to bring personal political enlightenment to the Chinese public. In this process, he went as far as transforming "liberty," "people's sovereignty," and "political revolution" into a state of people's "instinctive moral being." Liang's affective representations of modern political concepts defied the established intellectual practice endorsed by the state, the legitimacy of the Qing monarchy, and the hierarchical Confucian paradigm in which one's moral-emotive experiences are contingent on one's social roles and status. The political and epistemic transition Liang initiated may seem treasonous to many. But for this brilliant and creative reformer, democratic liberalism is *not* a foreign political import but an ultimate moral-political ideal shared by Confucius 孔子 (551–479 BC) and his most worthy successors. Sanctioned by the Sage, his musical, visual, and fictional inventions are customized to liberate people from the necessity of having to "learn *to be* good" to actually "*being* good."

Liang, as mentioned earlier, was keen to create a musical effect in his "new prose style." This particular form of musical writing appears most often in a series of historical biographies he composed on European revolutionary heroes. While situated in foreign contexts, these biographies shared the determined purposes of projecting the prospect of realizing the ultimate Confucian moral ideal in democratic governance. In early China, Confucius's teaching formed the foundation of much subsequent speculation on the forms of society and government in which an ideal man should participate. Among the many followers of the Sage, Mencius 孟子 (372–289 BC) was sensitive to recognize and explicate Confucius' endorsement of egalitarian humanism. As a resource for the political modernization process, Liang was invested in reviving the Mencian school of Confucianism, a school that at its heart shared the more affective, personal approach to morality championed by Wang Yangming, and which, of course, Wang saw himself as following and defending.[59] Since 1896, Liang had vigorously propagated the affinity between "revolution" as a Western political concept and Mencius's pursuit of the "Great Harmony." These seemingly unrelated schools of thinking, as Liang believed, are mutually interested in "deposing the autocrat" (獨夫), "punishing "traitors" (*minzei* 民賊), and "justly allotting the land to democratize property distribution" (授田制產).[60] Through drawing an equivalence between political revolution and Mencius' Confucian ideals, Liang sought to reinforce his dual purposes: to justify the moral legitimacy of democratic governance and to make Confucian morality applicable to the modern political construct.

As a faithful follower of the Mencian school of Confucianism, the early Han (206 BC—AD 220) historian Sima Qian 司馬遷 (145–86

BC), according to Liang, strove to show support for political revolution through his biographical writing. The modern reformer considered his own composition of "new historical biographies" to be the modern adaptations of *Records of the Grand Historian* (*Shiji* 史記). During the Han dynasty, the state-sponsored chronicle history focused on delineating the way power was transmitted in an aristocratic hereditary system. Instead of showing unreflective support for the state, Sima Qian believed in individuals' right to overthrow a corruptive political rule. In his historical biographies, he tells stories of individuals in a biographical format. Besides acknowledging historical agents' personal efforts, the grand historian expresses affirmation for those who made revolutionary efforts to replace an imperial monarchy with a righteous order. Liang considered Sima Qian the one who truly understood Confucius and Mencius. To revive what he considered to be "true Confucianism" and its narrative tradition, Liang assumed the role of the "new historian" (*xin shishi* 新史氏). In his historical biographies, Liang shows how Madame Roland (1754–1993), Giuseppe Mazzini (1805–1872), and Lajos Kossuth (1802–1894) struggled to bring their countries liberal democracy through extreme bodily sufferings. His "new" historical biography suggests the following: political revolution is a Confucius-sanctioned way of achieving universal peace. In addition to a virtuous action, it is the contemporary way of realizing the ideal moral-political order that generations of Chinese intellectuals have searched for. Democratic governance, in other words, is a construct that provides modern institutional formats for ideal Confucian governance.

Liang aspired to help people develop "affective moral resonance" with political revolution. Beyond speaking as the "new historian," he assumed the role of a spokesperson for New Text studies, an exegetical tradition that held official interpretation for Confucianism during the Western Han dynasty (141–87 BC). The school's understanding of Confucianism is informed chiefly by *Gongyang Commentary* (*Gongyang zhuan* 公羊傳), an interpretative summary of the *Spring and Autumn Annals* (*Chunqiu* 春秋). According to New Text scholars, the *Annals* is a historical record compiled by Confucius. The book succinctly chronicles events that took place in the state of Lu from 722 to 481 BC. Confucius divides this historical period into "Three Ages": the Age of Disorder (Zhiluan shi 治亂世), the Age of Approaching Peace (Shengping shi 昇平世), and the Age of Universal Peace (Datong shi 大同世). The historical timeline the Sage delineates projects a story of linear progression and prosperity. In reality, however, the state of Lu was annihilated by warfare, political chaos, and moral corruption. Rather than reading the *Annals* as a factual historical record, the *Gongyang Commentary* perceives the book as a constitutional blueprint, or reformist proposal, that Confucius sagaciously conceived for future generations. The new institutional decrees ordering the clan system, legal order, and ritual practices are considered corrective measures the Sage prescribed to restore peace and order.

Arranged in the form of a chronicle, the *Spring and Autumn Annals* was written with oracular succinctness. New Text scholars lauded this particular style of writing as *weiyan dayi* 微言大義: profound moral principles concealed in subtle languages. As the modern spokesperson for New Text studies, Liang was ready to restore the forgotten Confucian exegetic tradition in bringing his contemporaries modern "political" enlightenment. In 1902, he published a novella titled *The Future of New China* (*Xin zhongguo weilai ji* 新中國未來記). While in the *Annals* Confucius stipulates institutional decrees to advance China from the "Age of Approaching Peace" to the "Age of Universal Peace," *New China* relates the following story. After undergoing a series of "revolutionary" activities, in 2062 China has eventually evolved from imperial monarchy to liberal democracy. The historical progression Liang described echoes the "Three Ages" projected by Confucius. Mimicking the way the Sage arranged the *Spring and Autumn Annals*, Liang situated the utopian Confucian sociopolitical ideal in a fictional realm that depicts discursive concepts with visual immediacy and prophetic hints. Through reproducing the forgotten classical ideal in visual transparency, Liang provided his readers with a personal exegetic lens to see modern political concepts through one's own eyes, making modern political knowledge a personal "moral vision" that comes from *within*.

New China was published in 1902. In that year, China was just about to progress from the "Age of Approaching Peace" to an "Age of Universal Peace." At this critical historical juncture, the relationship between the "text" and the "people," as it appeared to Liang, should evolve in alignment with this looming political transition. Rather than going on preaching the Sage's esoteric message *to* the people, *New China* was to prepare those self-sufficient agents for the prospect of seeing, experiencing, and partaking in democratic governance as first-person participants. Democratic liberalism, Liang was convinced, thrives on the independence and empowerment of each individual agent. Once the people have realized the profound moral principles in person, the words or teachings of Confucius should cease to matter. Sharing the positive moral faith Wang Yangming placed in the people, Liang perceived *weiyan dayi* as the ultimate wishes the Sage expressed for the people: that the realization of the ultimate moral-political doctrines thrives on the disappearance of prescriptive Confucian doctrines and its authoritative power. Liang called his literary creation "new" fiction. By "new" the reformer was not only referring to the stories' creative content but also to his endeavor to reinvent Confucianism by incorporating Wang Yangming's moral hermeneutics with the narrative principles of New Text studies.

"Bad" Affect in Modern Politics

Inheriting the way of *how* Confucius expected people to see, and *what* the Sage wanted them to see, Liang invited his contemporaries to inspect democratic governance as embodied visual and acoustic experiences. But his invitation was a strange one. The democratic prosperity Liang projected in *The Future of New China* takes place in 2062, which is one hundred and sixty years after the story's publication date. Of the readers who were reading "New China" in 1902, no one would *ever be able* to participate in democratic governance in person.[61] People, as Wang Yangming said, are the living presence of the cosmos. If participating in democratic governance is to realize one's cosmic nature on earth, what has permanently divided the people from political modernity? And what would this deep and unbridgeable chasm open us to?

At the early stage of his career, Liang embraced the ardent hope of staging a political revolution in China. To stimulate readers' affective resonance for the political revolution, he composed a series of historical biographies on Madame Roland, Giuseppe Mazzini, and Lajos Kossuth, a cohort of European revolutionary heroes who struggled to bring their countries liberal democracy through tears, sweat, blood, death, and excruciating pain. But none of the revolutionary accounts Liang related ended well. In his description of the French Revolution, for instance, Liang disclosed how a political movement driven by people's "instinctive impulses" was followed by the most tragic, fatal, and catastrophic consequences. Madame Roland was beheaded by her political opponents. In the streets of Paris, dismembered corpses spread evenly across the field, and blood dripped over the guillotine. The river Seine turned crimson, with ditches blocked by human flesh. Considering the massive destruction political revolution brought to Europe in the nineteenth century, the political reformer cannot help but admit what "actually" happened in human history.

Liang Qichao strove to incorporate Wang Yangming's moral metaphysics in China's transition to political modernity. What neo-Confucian thinkers believed to be "instinctive moral goodness," as it turns out, can prove to be a cruel, destructive force. At times Liang wondered: To what extent is man's moral instinct reliable? How thoroughly can people transmit their affective disposition to the kind of perfect political-moral ideal he aspired to? And to what extent can one trust and rely on the people?

The above questions do not trouble Liang alone; they present perhaps the greatest fears and anxieties experienced by preceding Confucian thinkers as well as democratic politics since its moment of conception.[62] Western theorists who perceive affect as an "emancipatory ontological commitment" often emphasize the importance of reorienting ourselves with a new view of liberal democracy that incorporates and appreciates all aspects of our emotional life. But in the so-called democratic politics that we have witnessed over the years, this affective force has continued to reveal its own limitations. To observe and contemplate on the compatibility between Wang Yangming's moral metaphysics and political modernity, in 1902 Liang began to look up to the democratic development in Europe and eventually the United States.[63] His observations yielded the following results: in a representative republican government, every individual seems to enjoy equal opportunity for participating in democratic politics. But legislative bodies such as the House and the Senate were constituted by only a handful of representatives. In safeguarding a person or a party's political interests, these representatives do not necessarily defend and pursue the needs and wishes of the general public. Uninformed individuals, moreover, are prone to make irrational decisions. Their dissatisfaction can prematurely undermine many fledgling governing possibilities. In his reflections Liang articulates his biggest worries as well as the general predicament faced by liberal democracy: regardless of how progressive a country has become, it appears that the most ideal form of liberal democracy is not easily achievable.

Clashes of Representational Paradigms

In the early 1900s, the invention of affective presentation offered Liang Qichao the hope of channeling people's instinctive feeling into a positive political and moral force, making it an integral constituent of China's democratic liberalism. This affective turn, ideally speaking, presented a creative solution to conjoin political modernity, Confucian morality, and a worthy but suppressed intellectual tradition. But Liang's idealistic conception soon prompted him to reflect on its practical feasibility. Liang never openly admits that he had opened a Pandora's box, but in the series of "new" reformist journals he published, the "subjective wish" he expressed for the Chinese public persisted to contradict his "objective historical awareness." Liang, for instance, wanted people to be affectively responsive to modern political concepts. In his rhapsodic "new prose style," he celebrated these European historical figures' heroic, moral sacrifices in ecstatic musical rhythm and vivid pictorial descriptions. The acoustic and visual excitement was tailored to resonate with man's perfect moral instinct, creating immediate aesthetic "moral" experiences. But as the historical accounts unfold, these intense bodily sacrifices associated with blood, tears, and death offer evidence of human cruelty and the brutality of political revolution. In these biographies, Liang's creation of musical effect contradicts his rhetorical purposes. Besides creating immediate political confusion for the general public, the affective dissociation exposes the ambivalence of democratic liberalism, as well as the fragility and fragmentation of Chinese political modernity.

Man's spontaneous action, as Wang Yangming explicated in his call for the "oneness of knowing and acting" (*zhixing heyi* 知行合一), is a revelation of his cosmic moral endowment on earth. The cosmos, however, does not look quite the same as promised in the French Revolution. In a series of academic essays composed on Chinese philosophy, Liang readily divides Confucianism into two streams.[64] Assuming that men begin life as perfect moral beings, the school represented by Mencius endeavored to channel people's instinctive moral goodness into a positive political force that supports egalitarian humanism. Xun Kuang, on the contrary, was sensitive to human weakness and sought to suppress humans' evil potential through legal punishment. Liang expected democratic liberalism to bring the ultimate moral-political ideal generations of Chinese intellectuals have searched for. But what is believed to be man's instinctive moral goodness continues to testify to its *own failure*. In his historical biographies, as Liang unwillingly admitted, men seem naturally *incapable* of being moral. Beyond negating the moral foundation he identified for political modernity, the cruelty people displayed in the French Revolution radically questioned the moral optimism China had longed cherished in its philosophical tradition.

The year 1903, as most modern historians are aware of, was a turning point in Liang's career. During that year, Liang abandoned the hope of staging a political revolution in China and began to direct his attention to strengthen the people's public morality (*minde* 民德), intellectual courage (*minzhi* 民智), and readiness for actions (*minli* 民力). If political modernity is indeed what Confucius aspired to in 500 BC, what happened after many years of desultory and often stumbling searching? The confusion and dismay associated with these questions slowly penetrated Liang's writing. In *Intellectual Trends of the Qing Period* (清代學術概論), a book of Chinese intellectual history Liang published in 1921, his critical stance on Wang Yangming is no longer quite the same as it had been twenty years earlier.[65] In the last twenty years of his career, Liang began to devote himself almost exclusively to the restoration of the Chinese cultural tradition. He wrote and compiled an extensive number of works on classical Chinese philosophy and literature. While meticulously researched and gracefully written, these anachronistic accounts at times seem detached and distant from the chaos of the early Republican period.

Materials and Methodological Inventions

Perceiving Chinese modernity as affective experiences exposing the limit of representation and disruptive of the conventional system of language, the final chapters of the book focus on uncovering epistemic uncertainties, or affective dissociations, arising from the dialectic tension between "form" and "content." To explicate how these affective effects have disrupted the semantic consistency of the modern political "discourse," I continue to address the set of questions that appear counterintuitive to the conventional "social constructionist" approach: (1) Why does Liang repudiate the study of language and deny its capacity to bring personal political enlightenment? (2) Assuming that his invention of affective presentations began as a protest against the "text-based" approach to knowledge, how do these corrective intellectual, philosophical, and moral positions inform Liang's affective presentations, and sequentially transform "one-dimensional" rational normative ideals into "three-dimensional" *lived expressions* that embody people's ontological affective intensity? (3) If "form" and "content," as G. W. F. Hegel (1770–1831) suggests, are mutually constitutive, in what ways might Liang's "formal presentation" have transformed, contradicted, or possibly destabilized the modern political discourse? (4) And how, after all, might these contradictions have contributed to the continued political impasse, rather than rationality and progress, that China experienced after the 1911 revolution?

To answer these questions, *Affective Betrayal* conducts a number of concrete case studies. The book, straightly speaking, does not unearth new materials; it reads the readily familiar, though largely untranslated, body of literature differently. For many years, I have frequently returned to the biweekly journals Liang distributed between 1897 and 1905, and studied these periodicals volume by volume. This method is meaningfully different from using the standard anthologies. Being arguably the most influential and prolific intellectual of his times, Liang's complete works have been thematically classified in a twenty-one-volume anthology.[66] Students interested in the development of Liang's political thinking tend to focus on particular genres of writing collected in the anthology. But my concern is that Liang was a complicated man caught in a thorny political and intellectual situation. In the late Qing period, Chinese intellectuals were affiliated with competing academic schools as well as antagonistic political parties. Officially associated with the reformist camp but being a secret supporter of political revolution, Liang's endeavours to synthesize contending schools of political and intellectual thinking through his all-inclusive reform placed him in a vulnerable position. Reluctant to renounce his high-minded moral-political ideal, Liang tactfully and fragmentarily revealed his coherent proposal in his personal poetry, philosophical discussions, plays, and even commercial advertisements published alongside his political writing. Considering the practical constraints Liang faced, I study each volume of his journal as an organic entity and trace the metamorphosis of his implicit political, intellectual, and moral agenda as revealed in these publications. The discoveries I have made so far witness the results of reconnecting bits and pieces that appear, at first, disconnected.

In the following chapters, I analyze Liang's historical biographies, fictional creation, and journalist writing, which are strewn with paradoxical contradictions. Instead of examining these texts in a compartmentalized fashion, I juxtapose them with the academic, philosophical, and moral writing that he published concurrently in the "new" reformist journals. By doing so, I show how Liang's intellectual, philosophical, and moral agenda informed his affective presentations, and how his aspirational agenda as conveyed through these affective presentations was contradicted, negated, and suspended by his factual historical reports.

Chapter Overview

In 1902, to begin with, Liang defined people's participation in democratic governance as a matter of doing "what is good" for the general public. By conjoining the "political" and the "moral" as a symbiotic entity, Liang situated China's transition to political modernity in an ultimate philosophical conundrum: Is moral goodness a natural propensity that is *inside of us*? Or is it something that needs to be acquired *from without*? To Zhu Xi, the neo-Confucianism thinker, man begins life with perfect moral nature. But since his natural endowment is deformed by some polluted physical substances, man becomes morally deficient. To implement a system of democratic governance that thrives on the awakening of self-sufficient moral agents, Liang, as I argue in the first chapter, "Repairing the Human, Restoring Their Heartmind," was ready to intervene in an unresolved philosophical dispute that had persisted to divide generations of neo-Confucian thinkers. Having familiarized himself with Immanuel Kant's mature epistemology, Liang was able to repudiate Zhu Xi's moral metaphysics with structured precision: man, as Kant believes, can cognize only objects that he can in principle intuit. Being a rational agent in possession of pure practical reason, man is predisposed to experience and organize physical reality in keeping with the set of a priori categories directing his reasoning. Such reasoning enables one to discover fundamental moral principles and then specific moral duties. Individuals seeking to *learn* to be moral through the study of texts are in reality recovering the a priori moral order *existing inside of them*. Besides identifying a systematic epistemic framework to validate Wang Yangming's investment in man's possession of perfect moral judgment, the discovery of Kant inspired Liang to project a progressive political vision: being endowed with certain a priori intuitions, man is naturally capable of doing *what is right* and implementing by extension a legislative order that is *good* for the general public. As long as he can observe the legislative provisions derived from one's a priori moral order, the person obtains the "authentic freedom" of being a slave to his own master.

My second chapter, "Reclaiming Qing Philology to Recover the Innate Moral Order," presents Liang's reconstruction of Qing intellectual history. Knowing, as Liang believed, is *not* about acquiring conceptual knowledge but recognizing what appears to be "external" knowledge as "instinctive" feelings one shares with all human beings. In an intellectual climate that prioritized the study of language over man's intuitive understanding, Liang presented modern political concepts in ways that were calculated to stimulate readers' affective responses. The emphasis he placed on a "mind-based" approach to knowledge, Liang argued, was not intended to be a protest against the "text-based" approach. On the contrary, it marked an attempt to recover the *true* spirit of "early" Qing evidential research, a scholarly movement seeking to decipher and restore moral principles prescribed in the early Confucian classics with sophisticated philological and scientific research methods. Objects of experience, as Kant argues, are "mind-dependent." What appears to be an interpretative exercise can only be a form of "embodied" moral combat exhibiting a dialectic competition between the prescriptive moral "law" sanctioned by the state and the a priori moral LAW constituting man's natural moral disposition. As early Qing intellectuals questioned, challenged, and potentially rejected prescriptive moral doctrines with their personal a priori moral intuitions, they were to replace Confucian doctrines and become the ultimate source of moral authority. Through the use of scientific research methods introduced to them by Western missionaries, these Qing intellectuals had succeeded in verifying the reliability of one's moral gut instincts rather than the accuracy of the text. By introducing an epistemic shift that promoted man's natural moral agency, Liang was to restructure the past three hundred years of Chinese intellectual history by directing the poorly executed Qing evidential research back onto the right path. This epistemic shift, in addition, envisions perhaps the most radical possible form of power transition—were people to replace the Qing monarchy with democratic governance, they would not replace the authoritarian rule with the power of the people, but with the LAW of this boundless, indestructible, and interminable universe.

The third chapter, "To Know *Is* to Act: The Realization of Cosmic-Moral-Political Oneness in Action," explores the relationship between body and mind. Liang intended to make man's "instinctive moral agency" the foundation upon which "political modernity" is based. But in China's transition to political modernity, how can a person translate his perfect moral judgment into a functional governmental order? To Liang the answer seemed apparent: Action! The organization of this universe, according to Wang Yangming, reveals *li* the cosmic principle. Being the creation of the universe, man's heartmind (*xin* 心), which is the organ of cognition, epitomizes such structural perfection. As long as a person could restore his mental clarity, whatever inspires his spontaneous action is a crystallization of the perfect cosmic structure he epitomizes in his heartmind. Liang agreed with Wang Yangming that the exposition of man's moral reasoning is *predicated on* his spontaneous action. His incorporation of Wang's moral metaphysics in China's transition to political modernity prompts us to confront a familiar body-mind dilemma: how can "knowing" the epistemic cognition be *the same as* "acting" the embodied corporeal movement? To clarify the nonobtrusive interrelation between "knowing" and "acting," the chapter explicates Wang Yangming's moral theory with the aid of *catuṣkoṭi* (Chin: 四句), the classical Indian tetralemma forming the "four-cornered system" of the Buddhist logico-epistemological tradition. In this universe, the Buddhist believes, everyone and everything are "dependently arisen" upon temporal and situational conditions (*pratītyasamutpāda* 緣起). In a network of undifferentiated interdependence, nothing consists of intrinsic self-nature. "Knowing," without exception, is *dependent on* "acting." Liang encouraged the Chinese public to authenticate their moral conviction in action. Once the people can replace the Qing monarchy with a political revolution, the collective display of their shared cosmic instinct should make all homogeneous cosmic moral members who they *already* are, restoring thereby "the immanence of the transcendental" in the realm of democratic governance.

Coming to the fourth chapter, "Dissolution of Modern Political Languages in the Cinematic Spectacle," I show how Liang Qichao's "subjective moral ideal" and "objective historical awareness" persist to manifest themselves and contradict each other in his "formal presentation" and "narrative content." Compared with other forms of linguistic discursion, fiction, Liang declared, is capable of rendering modern political concepts *virtually present*. In the hope of expanding "political revolution" from a "one-dimensional" historical concept into a "three-dimensional" cinematic experience, in his novella *The Future of New China* Liang carefully depicted the term "revolution" in vivid visual and acoustic details. His attempt to render conceptual ideas with visual vivacity is inspired by the urge to render "profound moral principles concealed in subtle languages" (*weiyan dayi*), an exegetic principle that purportedly informed Confucius's compilation of the *Spring and Autumn Annals*. By restoring neglected aspects of the Confucian exegetical tradition, Liang gave his readers a new and powerful lens through which they could clearly observe modern political concepts with their own eyes, transforming modern political knowledge into a personal "moral vision" arising from within. But having considered the catastrophic consequences created by political revolution, Liang hesitated to consider political modernity as the ultimate moral-political ideal. In *The Future of New China*, he had no choice but to rename "revolutionary" activities "restoration" and "reform." Beyond creating immediate political confusion for the general public, Liang seemed to have made a disheartening prediction: the ideal moral-political vision that Confucius envisioned could not be realized in antiquity, and perhaps it would never take place in any foreseeable future.

In the fifth and final chapter, "Musicality—Representing the Rhythm of Political Revolution and the Tenor of Its Moral Discontent," the book proceeds to explicate how the incorporation of Wang Yangming's moral theory in China's modern political transition exposes the hidden anxieties of Confucianism as well as political modernity. The invention of Liang's musical, visual, and fictional presentations was intended to stimulate people's senses. To trace the presence of largely unrecognized affective effects in his "new prose style," this chapter delineates the rhetorical techniques Liang employed in a series of historical biographies published in the early 1900s. The formal details I analyze range from phonetic arrangement, rhythmical patterns, syntactic structure, and uses of stresses and punctuations to the publication's graphic layout. By introducing an affective representational paradigm that emphasizes "knowing" as "affective moral being," Liang was to transform Confucian morality from didactic doctrines to an instinctive moral agency that effectuates egalitarian democratic governance. His affective presentation, however, consistently contradicts, if not destabilizes, his historical narrative. In the "Biography of Madame Roland," for instance, Liang celebrated the French protagonist's heroic sacrifices in rhapsodic musical rhythm. The acoustic excitement was calculated to elicit people's "affective-moral resonance" for the political revolution. But as his historical account unfolds, Madame Roland's tragic death soon exposes the cruelty of her contemporaries and their animalistic human nature. Political revolution promised to bring China its much awaited "cosmic-moral-political" oneness. But considering the extreme brutality people displayed in the French Revolution, Liang brought home an uneasy discovery: what Confucian thinkers believed to be "instinctive moral goodness" can turn out to be a brutal, destructive force. Besides shaking the moral-metaphysical foundation Liang identified for political modernity, this human destructive potential made one question man's instinctive moral goodness, an article of faith that served as the foundation and inspiration for the Mencian school of Confucianism as well as neo-Confucianism.

Chapter 1

Repairing the Human, Restoring Their Heartmind

A Historical Detour to Mao Mountain

In the mid-1700s, Qian Daxin 錢大忻 (1728–1804) was appointed the commissioner of education and examinations in Guangdong Province. In addition to enjoying a distinguished career in office, Qian, being celebrated as the leading master of Confucianism (*yidai ruzong* 一代儒宗) of his times, was known for the substantial contribution he made to the development of Qing evidential research (*kaozheng xue* 考證學), a scholarly movement seeking to decipher and restore moral principles prescribed in the early Confucian classics with sophisticated philological research methods.[1] Qian Daxin shared with a select group of other scholars a particular interest in acquiring rubbings of bronze and stone inscriptions that had survived from antiquity. To properly date some of the inscriptions he collected, Qian embarked on a number of archeological field trips with his junior colleague Sun Xingyan 孫星衍 (1753–1818). On November 5, 1779, Qian Daxin and Sun Xingyan arrived at a Daoist temple on Mao Mountain (Maoshan 茅山) of Jiangsu province.[2] Delighted by the visit of such distinguished guests, the head abbot duly presented them a precious piece of jade seal the temple had cherished for many generations. Appearing in the shape of a square box, this jade seal, the Daoist suspected, could in fact be the legendary piece of jade Bian He 卞和 presented to the throne during the Warring States period (475–221 BC). Qian Daxin and Sun Xingyan were pleased to receive the seal. Upon examining it, Qian Daxin soon mocked with open contempt: "How hilarious" (殊可笑也)![3] Judging from the characters engraved on the surface, the piece of jade had been carved no earlier than the Southern Song 宋 dynasty (1127–1279). There was no way that it could be the antique seal!

Mao Mountain is a Daoist site notorious for circulating exorcist hearsay. In this cradleland of scam, two eagled-eyed scholars saw through a piece of Song jade *pretending to be* an illustrious artifact. To Qian Daxin and Sun Xingyan, this poor piece of jade was not the only one faking it. Its existence spoke for the collective forgery of multiple generations of "fake Confucian scholars" (*maoru* 貌儒) pretending to have obtained the true moral principles of Confucian teaching during the Song and the Ming 明 (1368–644) dynasties. Before Qing evidential research rose in the mid-seventieth century, Chinese scholars, for nearly six hundred years, participated in a philosophical movement that has come to be known as neo-Confucianism. These "fake Confucian scholars," particularly those who followed the teachings of Wang Yangming 王陽明 (1472–1529), shared a firm conviction: the organization of our universe reveals certain structural patterns known as *li* 理, the cosmic principles.[4] Being the creation of the universe, man begins life as the living presence of such structural perfection. Instead of having to *learn about* the moral principles that the sages prescribed in the Confucian classics, a person should stay focally connected with his endowed moral instinct. As long as a person can restore one's mental clarity and dispel inappropriate thoughts, whatever appears in his mind and inspires spontaneous action is a direct revelation of the deep, underlying cosmic structure the person epitomizes in his mind. A person's natural moral propensity, metaphorically speaking, is like system software constituting one's ethical configuration; it is not a program or application that needs to be installed from the outside.

To pessimists like me, this conviction appears too good to be true. But can it *be true*? To Liang Qichao, the progressive young reformer who aspired to replace the Qing monarchy (1644–1911) with a system of democratic governance, the answer was an absolute Yes! Sharing the great optimism that radiates from Wang Yangming's moral theory, Liang was convinced that men were endowed with certain a priori moral intuitions; they were instinctively capable of doing *what is right* and implementing by extension a legislative order that is *good* for the general public. To Liang, democratic governance was not a Western import, let alone an artificial institutional construct being imposed upon the people. Law and order are the *ways* that the individuals are made. In people's participation in democratic governance, the legislative and constitutional provisions they observe are derived from the a priori moral order that constitutes their instinctive ethical and behavioral composition. To be moral is to be political. In China's transition to political modernity, people should strive to make democratic governance the "public" expression of the natural moral order that makes us human. As long as a person can issue and successively obey decrees derived from one's a priori moral scheme, he becomes a slave to his own master. Having attained a state as such, man obtains "authentic freedom" (*zhenzheng de ziyou* 真正的自由) as both a political and a moral agent.

For those with general knowledge of neo-Confucianism and modern Western philosophy, it should seem apparent that the conception of Liang's ideal moral-political vision entails the assimilation of at least two philosophical traditions: being a rational agent in possession of practical reason, man, according to Immanuel Kant (1724–1804), is predisposed to experience and organize physical reality according to a set of a priori categories that condition his introspective reasoning. The act of reasoning enables one to discover fundamental moral principles and by extension specific moral duties. In a thought experiment presented in *Groundwork of the Metaphysic of Morals* (1785), Kant envisions the prospect of having all rational agents forming what he calls the "Kingdom of Ends" (*Reich der Zwecke*), an ideal form of political governance Liang introduced to his contemporaries as "A Democratic Commonwealth" (*zhong mudi zhi minzhu guo* 眾目的之民主國").[5] Aside from being a member of a political community, each individual, Kant adds, is an independent moral agent capable of moral deliberation. When a person feels compelled to fulfill a moral obligation informed by his causal, deductive reasoning, he must consider whether this self-imposed moral obligation can be justifiably translated into a "legislative" law that is universally applicable for each and every one of his fellow citizens. Both Kant and Wang Yangming, as Liang saw it, believed that men were predisposed to be moral. Having identified what he perceived to be an epistemic framework that unfolds and crystalizes Wang Yangming's moral theory with methodological precision, an exposition I shall further explain and elaborate in the following discussion, Liang took the liberty of assimilating Wang Yangming's moral epistemology into Kant's experimental thought model, projecting thereby an indigenous form of democratic governance, or "peripheral liberalism," that thrives on the metaphysical premise of neo-Confucianism.[6]

The synthesis Liang drew between Wang Yangming's moral metaphysics and Kant's mature epistemology (and in due course political philosophy) is interesting in its own right. But such a synthesis is not what makes his reformism truly radical and altruistically unselfish. Neo-Confucianism, similar to any major moral or philosophical movement, hardly represents a coherent system of thought. Perceiving man as the living presence of the cosmos, Wang Yangming, representing the "Learning of the Mind" school (xinxue 心學) of neo-Confucianism, was convinced that a person is instinctively capable of telling the good from the bad. Speaking on the behalf of the opposing camp, Zhu Xi 朱熹 (1130–1200) believed that man begins life with a perfect moral "nature." But assuming that a person's natural endowment is deformed by polluted qi substances, Zhu Xi asserted that man is morally corrupted and deficient in practices. In order to *learn* to be moral, a person must submit to the study of external references stipulated by an authority. In a political system that rewarded slavish conformity and suppressed instinctive human agency, people were often asked to conform to moral norms as externally defined by the state. Instead of doing what *ought* to be done, most individuals practiced what Western thinkers call "virtue ethics," the display of moral behaviors for the purpose of yielding good consequences.[7]

Liang was born seventy years after the death of Qian Daxin, who famously declared the Confucian classics the ultimate source of moral knowledge. Having been exposed to an intellectual climate that distrusted and undermined man's natural moral agency, Liang came to a dawning realization: the performance of a person's civil obligation entails the fulfillment of his natural moral duty. To implement a system of democratic governance that operates as a "public" expression of man's instinctive moral propensity, one must begin by conceiving a new configuration of "humans," as well as their moral disposition and epistemic, cognitive function. The contrivance of a moral human agent to accommodate his humanist political ideal required Liang to repel and revamp a philosophical tradition that had exerted a shaping influence on China's academic practices and political consciousness since the twelfth century, if not the time of antiquity. To me this is where Liang's genius and contribution truly lie. This chapter situates Liang's political vision in a philosophical and intellectual matrix that contradicted his moral-political reformism and explores how he struggled to reinvent and redirect the neo-Confucian debates with philosophical perspectives informed by Kant's mature epistemology and Buddhist metaphysics. In the end Liang's political reformism cannot be implemented in practice. This idealistic reformer, however, had at least opened a window for us to envision (and perhaps go on envisioning) where China could and should have gone.

The Possibilities as Liang Qichao Understood Them

The Cosmic Heartmind

To comprehend the all-inclusive moral, intellectual, and political reform Liang initiated at the turn of the twentieth century, I want to begin by outlining those dominant philosophical positions he attempted to rectify. Around the first century CE, to begin with, Buddhist teachings had made their way from India to China. Buddhists believe that everyone and everything are interdependent on and mutually constitutive of each other. Being parts and parcels of an organic entity, things and people lack intrinsic character. The early Buddhist philosopher Nāgārjuna (Chin: 龍樹) (150–250 AD) called this state of existence "emptiness" (Sanskrit: Śūnyatā; Chin: 空)—the complete absence of "self-nature" (Sanskrit: svabhāva; Chinese: 自性) in a network of undifferentiated interdependence (and knowing that everything is "what it is" in virtue of its relation to other things, even emptiness itself is empty).

Having been educated and shaped by a Confucian tradition that placed great emphasis on the cultivation of people's moral goodness, some Chinese thinkers were immediately repelled, if not intimidated, by this seemingly nihilist Buddhist interpretation of life. To ground the Confucian moral tradition on an affirmative footing, one early neo-Confucian thinker, Cheng Hao 程顥 (1032–1085), ventured to present a counterproposal: instead of a bottomless abyss that is empty and void, our universe is a vast, interpenetrating system structured by li 理.[8] This cosmic pattern or principle gives shape—both physical and moral—to the universe, and finds expression in every aspect of existence.[9] Being the organizing principle structuring the formation of phenomenal beings, li exhibits its perfection in the structure of things, behavioral disposition of men, and, obviously, the moral and cognitive function of their heart-mind (xin 心), an organ that we today call the heart.[10]

The heartmind is a philosophical concept that receives considerable attention in the work of the ancient Chinese philosopher Mencius 孟子 (372–289 BC). Mencius once made two famous remarks that are relevant to our present concerns: first, a man thinks and feels with his heartmind, an organ that is the locus of conation (emotions, inclinations) and cognition (understanding, beliefs).[11] Second, man is born with nascent moral goodness. When a toddler is about to fall into a well, any bystander would want to save him without hesitation. The person's spontaneous response indicates that man is *instinctively* predisposed to be good. In as early as 300 BC, Mencius had developed a clear philosophical position on man's moral nature, and was sensitive to recognize the heartmind's cognitive function. The philosopher, however, did not develop a systematic moral epistemology explicating the relationship between man's ethical disposition and his cognitive function.

Coming to the tenth century, early neo-Confucian thinkers were under growing pressure to defend Confucianism against challenges arising primarily from Buddhist philosophy. They soon identified a solution to connect man's heartmind and his moral nature: in this universe, there is *li* the all-pervading cosmic principle informing the organization of myriad forms of beings. People, objects, animals, and events may all appear as distinct properties sharing discrete physical and physiological features. But being structured in agreement with *li*, all things "contain within themselves the principle of the world" and they are fundamentally the same as each other and are one with each other.[12] Although distinct properties display different features in appearances, the underlying identity and affinity that people share as the common creation of *li* grant them the innate capacity to think and empathize from the position of others, as well as the imperative to care for everyone and everything as we care for ourselves. Neo-Confucian thinkers called the capacity to experience or feel for others on the basis of the cosmic principles they share "benevolence" (*ren* 仁). In Mencius's teaching, "benevolence," a term that he inherited from Confucius,[13] is the moral seed that sprouts into righteousness (*yi* 義), propriety (*li* 禮), and intellect (*zhi* 智), which are known collectively as the "four moral incipiencies" (*siduan* 四端).[14]

Cheng-Zhu Neo-Confucianism

Buddhists assert that things and people are absent of self-nature. But assuming that there is a generic set of cosmic patterns constituting the deep structure of each individual's heartmind and determining his natural moral composition, the "like-mindedness" of people allows one to experience benevolence and to expand it into other forms of moral goodness. Contrary to what the Buddhist suggests, *li* is immanent in man's moral nature (*xing ji li* 性即理).[15] Such a view framed the way neo-Confucian thinkers pursued learning. "If," as Peter Bol aptly puts it, "there were universal principles and if the mind could grasp them, then it was the mind rather than antiquity that needed attention."[16] As long as a person can make correct use of his heartmind, he, by means of introspective reasoning achieved by his cognitive faculties, should be able to jump directly to the fountainhead of the Way and form a "direct connection" with the heavenly principle.

The conviction that man epitomizes the cosmos in his heartmind forced neo-Confucian thinkers to confront an inevitable question: if man's moral nature is indeed the living presence of *li*, why do people possess dark thoughts and commit evil deeds? Zhang Zai 張載 (1020–1077) answered: *li certainly* informs the compositional structure of the heartmind. But for *li* the metaphysical abstraction to manifest itself in physical presence, it has to take form in *qi* 氣, an all-pervading, kinetic form of matter, which is the vital source of all lives. The relational dependence between *li* and *qi* resembles the relationship between water and gravity. While water flows downward, *qi* moves in accordance with the internal logic of *li*.

Man's original heartmind is perfect in nature. But like a delicate flower or a piece of fresh butter, it faces the inevitable fate of withering away and turning rancid. Zhu Xi shared Zhang Zai's worries but persisted in upholding *li* as the absolute higher cosmic order. At the time Zhu Xi conceived his moral theory, the political partisanship that had divided the Song court continued to tear both the government and the human realm apart. In the hope of preserving *li* the perfect cosmic order when the political reality crumbled, Zhu Xi looked to *qi* and accused it of being the source of pollution that tainted and tarnished the perfection of *li*. The philosopher said: man's heavenly heartmind epitomizes the cosmic principles. The cosmos, unfortunately, has been invaded and disrupted by an errant force. Being a degenerative pollutant immanent in the very flow of existence, this errant force spoils certain *qi* substances, rendering them "muddy," "uneven," and "inherently deficient."[17] While Neo-Confucian thinkers wishfully believed that the corrupted *qi* substances were prone to dissipate, their recurring presence reveals an unwelcome truth: that deviance from the ideal is inexorable and immense.

Having identified the ontological differences between *li* the perfect cosmic principle and *qi* the polluted substances, Zhu Xi severed the realm of metaphysical transcendence from the realm of physical existence, a man's heavenly heart (*daoxin* 道心) from his humanly heart (*renxin* 人心), and sequentially the heartmind's endowed cosmic nature from its functional expressions.[18] Being a manifestation of heaven, man's moral nature, Zhu Xi said, is identical to the cosmic principles (*xing ji li*). It constitutes one's "primordial endowment" (*benti* 本體). Regardless of how the affairs of men fluctuate, the heartmind's moral nature (*xing* 性) remains stable and still (*xing shi wei dong* 性是未動).[19] In contrast to his "heavenly heartmind," man's "humanly heartmind" is a corporeal organ adulterated by polluted *qi*. Once it responds to external stimuli in animated motions (*dong* 動), the humanly heartmind discharges polluted *qi* of which it is made. These *qi* substances, known as human feelings (*qing* 情), are substantially and qualitatively inferior to a person's cosmic moral nature.

In Zhu Xi's moral theory, the anatomy of man's heartmind, metaphorically speaking, is structured as a perfect car engine built to convert power into motion.[20] Once the "cosmic" engine is "put into use" (*fayong* 發用), a person is programmed to manifest the cosmic principles as he acts. In reality, however, the operation of man's heartmind deviates from its manual. The heartmind is certainly "on" when it responds to the external stimuli. But instead of exhibiting the cosmic perfection it epitomizes, it releases inferior *human* feelings, emotions, and desires. How, as one might ask, can the heartmind induce substances that contradict its cosmic moral nature? And from where could these inferior feelings have derived? To explicate the heavenly heartmind's entanglement with this evil force, Zhu Xi recounted the following story.

Before a person comes into contact with the physical reality, his heartmind resides in a state of complete stillness (*ji* 寂). Without any physical movement, it is poised between existence and nonexistence. Then, following the rise of things and affairs (*shiwu* 事物), the heartmind becomes responsive to (*gang* 感) the external stimuli. Still and unmoving as it may seem (*ji wei budong* 幾微不動), the heartmind is about (*ji* 幾) to go. Soon the heartmind shoots forth (*fa* 發), taking off from the phase of "looming issuance" (*weifa* 未發) to "accomplished issuance" (*jifa* 已發). The *qi* substances that permeate the cosmos, theoretically speaking, are governed by the "internal logic" of *li*. They are programmed to give form to the heartmind that has issued forth. But having been contaminated by intrusive evil forces, the movements of certain *qi* substances defy the cosmic law. They cannot be "attached" (*guada* 掛搭) properly to the cosmic patterns the heartmind epitomizes nor can they be "put down" (*andun* 安頓), creating what neo-Confucian thinkers consider to be a "linkage" or "landing" problem. The heartmind certainly shares a perfect moral nature. But once it takes form in the realm of physical existence, its cosmic structure is obscured and deformed by those muddy *qi*. Having manifested themselves as inferior human feelings and emotions, these polluted *qi* continue to overshadow, and to "get the better of" (*sheng* 勝) man's cosmic moral nature.

Zhu Xi knew that *li* was no match for the relentless evil force. And yet he refused to succumb to it. Perceiving a hierarchical distinction between the heavenly order and physical reality, the good and the bad, and by extension the heartmind's endowed cosmic nature and its functional expressions, Zhu Xi asserted that man's primordial cosmic moral nature is *different from* his corrupted human behaviors.[21] Concomitant with the cosmic patterns, one's "heavenly heartmind" shares the perfect moral nature. It is *structurally* perfect. But following the intrusion of the evil force, the "humanly heartmind," adulterated and deformed by debris and dregs, becomes substantially and functionally deficient. With the cosmic patterns permanently failing to reveal themselves in man's physical makeup, the heavenly heartmind has no choice but to operate physically in this malformed humanly heartmind.

Zhu Xi found man's heartmind inherently fragmented (*zhili* 支離). Unable to bridge the marked discrepancy between the heavenly heartmind and the humanly heartmind, the philosopher could hope only to narrow the gap by developing a distinct approach to learning. Zhu Xi emphasized the importance of devoting oneself to the careful study of Confucian classics combined with investigation of external events.[22] A person, he said, cannot purify the *qi* particulars that give shape to his blood and flesh. But by carefully observing the cosmic patterns revealed in the Confucian classics as well as in myriad forms of natural phenomena, he can at least strive to compensate his embodied deficiency with industrious effort (*gongfu* 功夫). Sad as it may seem, man is permanently and innately separated from his own cosmic moral nature. But with firm commitment and relentless effort, he, every now and then, has at least been promised the hope of glimpsing and engaging his buried cosmic perfection.

Wang Yangming's Learning of the Mind

Zhu Xi urged his contemporaries to *learn* to be moral by studying prescriptive moral doctrines that were *outside* of them. But the heartmind, as neo-Confucian thinkers almost unanimously agreed, is formed on the basis of *li*. If the heartmind is indeed the living presence of the cosmos, how is it possible for a person to learn to acquire a "natural propensity" that he was born with? Can human instinct be taught? And how can one *be* himself by learning *to be* something other than himself? Wang Yangming was familiar with Zhu Xi's moral reasoning but found it logically fallacious.[23] The Ming philosopher lived three centuries after Zhu Xi voiced his basic disagreement: *li* is the structuring principle organizing the formation of myriad forms of beings. Manifesting itself in countless numbers of people, things, and natural phenomena, the physical expressions of *li* are bound to be incessantly different. Rather than distorting, deforming, or suppressing the omnipotence of *li*, these "formal" variations only disclose its boundless multiplicities. The heartmind functions in a comparable fashion. Codified by *li*, man's heartmind is *programmed* to operate the way that it is compositionally structured. Its functional expressions exteriorize and exemplify its cosmic moral endowment. It is ontologically *incapable of* discharging erroneous feelings that are quintessentially and qualitatively different from its cosmic nature.

Zhu Xi, as far as Wang Yangming was concerned, had made the fatal mistake of splitting the heartmind into two, inventing the problematic, if not needless, contrast between man's moral nature and his human feelings. Being a living epitome of the cosmos, man's heartmind *is* the cosmic principle (*xin ji li* 心即理). Contrary to what Zhu Xi had claimed, a person's heartmind is so clear and perfect that it transcends the *artificial* human intelligence one acquires from contrived social practices. For one to realize his endowed cosmic perfection that is finer and larger than *what he thinks* he knows, all the person needs is to follow his cosmic instinct. Uninterrupted by man's premeditated intervention, these instinctive responses are his embodied manifestations of the abstract cosmic pattern on earth.

From Heartmind to Text: Philology in the Qing Dynasty

Most neo-Confucian thinkers, particularly those subscribing to the Learning of the Mind school associated with Wang Yangming, believed that there is no value or moral meaning independent of the cosmic heartmind that a person is born with. Exhilarated by the moral faith Wang Yangming invested in the people, a more radical branch of his followers abandoned their study and indulged themselves to the hearts' content.[24] Toward the end of the Ming dynasty, disruptive behaviors spurred by their capricious whims bred widespread social and moral nuisances. In 1644, the Manchus invaded China and conquered the Ming dynasty with military force. Having experienced the fall of the country, some Chinese scholars became fiercely critical of the unwarranted faith neo-Confucian thinkers placed in the omnipotence of the heartmind. Beyond voicing his public condemnation, Dai Zhen 戴震 (1727–1777), a talented philologist and philosopher who was to exert a shaping influence on the development of Qing evidential research, shrewdly identified some fallacies that appeared in the moral epistemology of neo-Confucianism: When neo-Confucian thinkers spoke of *li*, Dai Zhen argued, they referred to it as the cosmic patterns constituting the formative structure of man's heartmind. "Cheng Yi and Zhu Xi related to the cosmic principle as if it is a palpable thing. Having received one's cosmic endowment from heaven, a person epitomizes heaven in his heartmind" (程朱以理為如有物焉, 得於天而具於心).[25] As the person allows his "cosmic endowment" to display itself, how can we be sure that such disclosure is indeed *li* instead of his "subjective opinion" (*yijian* 意見)? Is there really such a "thing" as *li*? What is the relationship between *li* and man's heartmind? Mencius often referred to *li* and perceived the heartmind as the organ of emotions and cognition. The ancient philosopher, however, never seemed to have drawn a direct connection between the two. In this case, what does *li* really mean, and how can we recover Mencius' true intent?

To address these mounting concerns, Dai Zhen and practitioners of Qing evidential research needed to look for a corresponding set of problem-solving tools. Knowing that the conception of Confucian scholarship during the Song and the Ming dynasties was heavily infiltrated by the influence of Buddhism and Daoism, they, as Liang Qichao explained, decided to recover the pristine message of the Confucian classics compiled during (or shortly before and after) the Han dynasty (202 BC—220 AD).[26] As these Qing scholars proceeded, they faced the daunting task of determining which of the many editions of the classics were the true originals and which were forged additions of later centuries. To verify the reliability of sources as evidence for restoring these archaic texts and meanings, Dai Zhen and his fellow philologists felt they must begin by deciphering the meaning of the characters (*shizi* 識字) appearing in these ancient texts. Their reasoning, as Liang saw it, was fairly simple: the meaning of language changed along with the passage of time. In Dai Zhen's research, he liked to begin by identifying the range of definitions a particular character encompassed in the Han dynasty. After that, he would compare these definitions in an extensive number of classical texts to ensure their meanings were consistent with his conjectures.[27] As Dai Zhen and his contemporaries continued their research in paleography (*wenzi* 文字), phonology (*shengyin* 聲音), and textual glosses (*xungu* 訓詁), they quickly realized that the philological definitions of words were shaped by a broad spectrum of social, physical, and anthropological factors. Sequentially practitioners of Qing evidential research undertook the study of physical geography (*dili* 地理), astrology (*tiansuan* 天算), referents and institutions (*mingwu zhidu* 名物制度), inscriptions on bronzes (*jinshi* 金石), and varying editions of print (*banben* 版本) to better consider and document these shaping factors.

Neo-Confucian thinkers sought to obtain moral enlightenment through meditative speculation, whereas practitioners of Qing evidential research were careful to authenticate the meanings of the words that the sages prescribed in early Confucian classics, commentaries, and annotations. By paying attention to minute philological details, collecting extensive evidence, and comparing conflicting samples, practitioners of Qing evidential research learned to verify their speculations with systematic, objective, and scrupulous research methods. Following the invention and application of sophisticated investigative methods, the development of Qing evidential research reached its full maturity in the reigns of Emperors Qianlong 乾隆 (1735–1796) and Jiaqing 嘉慶 (1796–1820). Research methods they developed were incorporated in the school curriculum and progressively evolved to become standardized learning practices for Qing intellectuals who were born and raised between the eighteenth and nineteenth centuries.

This quiet life of scholarly contemplation, fortunately or unfortunately, was short-lived. In the late nineteenth century, China was defeated by a number of foreign military powers. Shaken and saddened by the country's repeated military defeats, certain progressive Chinese intellectuals expressed support for the nationwide reformist campaign initiated by Liang Qichao and his teacher, Kang Youwei. When Liang was a young man, he used to believe that the evolution of world history was governed by a progressive, linear order.[28] To assist China in participating in the global political community as a "self-conscious unity," Liang aspired to replace the Qing monarchy with a system of democratic governance. From 1902 onward, Liang began to explicate particular modern political "characters," "attributes," and "mentalities" in his reformist publication *New Citizen Journal* (*Xinmin congbao* 新民叢報). The modern "attributes" he placed special emphasis on included rights (*quanli* 權利), obligations (*yiwu* 義務), nationalism (*guojia zhuyi* 國家主義), people's sovereignty (*zizhi* 自治), progress (*jinbu* 進步), cooperation (*hequn* 合群), and so on.

The Late Qing Dynasty Predicament

Modern Political Predicament as Philosophical Predicament

At the turn of the twentieth century, China underwent what modern historians call an "unprecedented" historical transition. By replacing the Qing monarchy with a system of democratic governance that thrived on awakening each independent moral agent, the Chinese people, ideally speaking, would assume their personal responsibility and participate in the form of collaborative governance Jean-Jacques Rousseau (1712–1778) depicted in *The Social Contract* (1762). But instead of trying to "live up" to such modern political ideals, many intellectuals, as Liang was quick to note, inherited the "learning" practice from their teachers. Having been trained to decipher the Confucian classics with philological investigative methods conceived by an earlier generation of Qing evidential researchers, they soon fell into the habit of studying, memorizing, and reciting these modern political "attributes" as they examined the Confucian classics.

The learning habits of these Chinese intellectuals gave rise to an immediate question: how can "attributes," "characters," or "mentalities" be studied, memorized, and recited? To Liang the answer was that in some sense they cannot be. As people diligently pursued their study of Western political concepts, they seemed less interested in attending to the unaffected moral feelings they harbored than in manipulating their mastery of modern political knowledge as a form of cultural capital to advance their own benefit. These manipulative uses, as Liang observed, included such things as displaying their erudition of Western knowledge, declaring their alignment with the progressive reformist force, and expressing patriotic spirit kindled momentarily by China's military defeat.[29] For those who liked to "play around" (*wannong* 玩弄) fashionable ideas as catchphrases (*koutouchan* 口頭禪), which they carried around as "charms" (*hushenfu* 護身符) to satisfy their love of fame (*haoming* 好名) and fortune

48 | Affective Betrayal

(*haoli* 好利), Liang wondered: Does not such willful manipulation of words for worldly profit come at the cost of one's sincere moral intent?[30] As I "play around" with these modern concepts, who exactly is playing around with whom?[31] Am I the one playing with the words, or have I been fooled by my abuse of my moral consciousness and lost myself in the game of self-deception?

In the long course of Chinese history, Liang argued, people had often been reminded that a subject must be loyal to the lord, children be filial to the parents, wives be chaste to their husbands, and friends be righteous to each other.[32] Finally China saw the prospect of proceeding with a new form of political governance. As a prospective national citizen who was to interact with the state and his fellow countrymen in a new form of contractual partnership, the expression of his moral feelings should evolve with this new collaborative format. "Morality," as Liang elaborated, "is not something stagnant and unchanging" (德也者, 非一成而不變者也).[33] If private morality (*side* 私德) is about "the relationship between one private individual and another" (一私人對於一私人之事也), "public morality" (公德) concerns "one private individual and the public community" (一私人對於一團體之事也).[34] A "national citizen" is entitled to enjoy his "rights" upon fulfilling his civil "obligations." Scholars of Liang's times, most apparently, were keen about *learning* Western political concepts. But rather than acquiring a new body of bookish knowledge that was quintessentially foreign to a person, *to be* a national citizen is about doing "what is good for" (*you yi yu* 有益於) the people, the public, and the national government, and doing so in a way that does not compromise one's values and principles. Moral expressions may appear infinitely different in private and public contexts, but "they are originated from one primordial body of being" (道德之本體一而已).[35] If there is such thing as public morality, it is essentially the public expression, or extension, of one's private moral feelings. "Public morality and private morality," for this reason, "do not stand in contrast to each other; they are terms that are interconnected with one another" 私德與公德, 非對待之名詞, 而相屬之名詞也.[36]

The Haunted Return of Neo-Confucianism

To Liang, *to be political is to be moral*. By conjoining the political and the moral as a symbiotic entity and accentuating that man's access to modern political power is predicated on his ability to be moral, Liang prompted us to confront perhaps the ultimate moral and philosophical conundrum that had persisted to divide and trouble Chinese thinkers since the eleventh century: if being politically modern is about doing *what is good* for the general public, what does it mean by "doing good"? Is moral goodness a natural propensity that is *inside of us*, as most neo-Confucian thinkers claimed, or is it something that needs to be acquired *from without*, as practitioners of Qing evidential research insisted? Who can decide what is good or what is bad? And where does morality *truly* lie?

Neo-Confucian thinkers and practitioners of Qing evidential research held contending philosophical positions on man's moral nature, and these contending "moral" positions occasioned two distinct approaches to "learning." Sharing the conviction that *li* is immanent in man's heartmind, neo-Confucian thinkers were convinced that men were instinctively capable of being moral. For practitioners of Qing evidential research, however, the connection neo-Confucian thinkers drew between *li* and man's heartmind was a sheer fictional fabrication. Qian Daxin, as said at the beginning of the chapter, was one of the most celebrated philologists, linguists, and historians of the eighteenth century. On his visit to Mao Mountain, Qian poked fun at a piece of Song jade pretending to be the vanished national treasure *heshibi*. To Qian the acclaimed master, neo-Confucian thinkers of the Song and the Ming dynasties resembled this piece of fake jade. Not having any solid (*shi* 實) knowledge of the Confucian classics, their words, empty (*kong* 空) and hollow (*xu* 虛), were "contentions that chisel the air" (*zuo kong zhi lun* 鑿空之論). Having existed as a massive scam, they were fake, vulgar later Confucians (*suru* 俗儒; *houru* 後儒) pretending to be the true, venerable Confucian (*zhenru* 真儒; *xianru* 先儒).[37] Showing strong antipathy for the "fake Confucians'" indulgence in empty metaphysical speculation, Qian considered "the Confucian classics the words of the sages" (經者, 聖人之言也) as well as the ultimate source of moral knowledge. If a student "was to follow their words to search for moral meanings," one, as Qian said, "must begin with textual glosses; outside of textual glosses there are no meanings and principles" (因其言以求其義, 則必訓詁始; 謂訓詁之外別有義理).[38]

For a person to be moral, Qian and his counterparts asked people to return to the Confucian classics and learn about moral principles through the careful study of texts. Coming to the early twentieth century, the unresolved moral conundrum that had persisted to divide disparate schools of philosophical and intellectual practices did not perish with the passage of time. Having been resurrected in the context of democratic governance, such conundrum had translated itself into modern political terms and taken on a new level of urgency: For Chinese intellectuals to proceed to democratic governance, are we looking to assume the new roles this modern democratic game book has assigned us to play, or are we seeking to turn democratic governance into an institutional expression of the instinctive moral goodness that rests *inside* of us? What does and would democracy mean for China? Can democracy be a modern political expression of man's natural moral instinct, or would it remain an artificial institutional construct that requires the people to make profound personal adjustments and be reshaped in its image? Are we to become political robots programmed by rules inculcated in us or independent moral agents knowing the rules by heart?

Among historians who focus on China's transition to political modernity, some have been sensitive to consider neo-Confucianism and the sequential rise of Qing evidential research as sources of moral and philosophical influences informing the conception of Liang's political reformism.[39] But in late Qing China, those philosophical disputes that had divided competing schools of intellectual practices were much more than a remote source of intellectual influence—they were the philosophical climates that shaped the fundamental approaches to learning adopted by Chinese intellectuals and, in turn, their responses to political modernity.

How Can I Be Myself by Learning to Be You?

For Liang, what makes political modernity *truly* unprecedented was not only the replacement of imperial monarchy with a system of democratic governance, but also making the modern political order the "public" expression of the natural moral order that makes us human. By pointing us to the underexamined and yet deeply entangled relationships between "morality" and "political modernity," Liang's seemingly causal remark exposes a common methodological fallacy: with analytical perspectives derived from postcolonial theory and postmodern historiography, historians tend to approach China's transition to modernity as a knowledge-formation process caught in various levels of national and international power competition. But in late Qing China, a person's mastery of textual knowledge does not reflect China's "actual" modern political progress. It may disclose the direct opposite. As Liang declared in the inaugural issue of *New Citizen Journal,* "The more knowledgeable the people become, the more well-versed and knowledgeable slaves and traitors there will be" (夫使一個增若干之學問, 隨即增若干有學問有知識之漢奸奴隸).⁴⁰

Participating in democratic governance, Liang argued, is to do "what is good for" the community in a public arena. For those who abused modern political concepts for worldly gain, they, knowing what was right but refusing to be good, had betrayed their moral consciousness (之善當為而不為, 即是欺良知).⁴¹ Liang condemned his contemporaries as follows:

> The elites living in this contemporary world, having picked up and put down a few new terms, have abandoned the moral tradition inherited from the past. While they found such tradition insignificant, they have failed to take a peek at what contemporary philosophers call the new morality. They declare that they have fulfilled their civil obligation. But before I was able to witness their display of civil virtues, their private virtues have long been banished. 今世所謂識時俊傑者, 口中摭拾一二新學名詞, 遂吐棄古來相傳一切道德。謂為不足輕重, 而於近哲所謂新道德者, 亦未嘗窺見其一指趾。自謂盡公德, 吾未見其公德之有可表見, 而私德則早已蔑棄矣。

People of his times, Liang said, "were unfaithful to themselves" (非誠自得於己).⁴² Those who sought to *learn about* moral principles through the study of "external" references tended to renounce one's truthful feelings in this "learning" process. As one gave up his true self in this state of self-abandonment (*zibao ziqi* 自暴自棄), he was destined to live an inauthentic life.⁴³

Liang expected his contemporaries to evolve from subjects of the state into self-governing agents who are "personally" capable of implementing and participating in modern politics.⁴⁴ To recover the intuitive moral order that rested *within* a person, he needed to revamp the existing intellectual, philosophical, and moral tradition alongside the modern political reform. Without resolving internal moral disputes that had contributed to competing visions of what it means to be human, contending assumptions about their moral nature, and eventually the oppositional learning approaches, Liang would not be able to locate a moral and philosophical foundation to advance his reformist initiative. Having such awareness, Liang began to intervene in the unresolved philosophical dispute that had persisted to divide the "Learning of Principle" from the "Learning of the Mind" schools of Neo-Confucianism, as well as practitioners pursuing "Qing learning" versus "Han learning." And coming to 1903, the reformer seemed to have identified a solution to his conundrum.

Rethinking through Immanuel Kant

In the years of exile spent in Japan, Liang was introduced to the Japanese political theorist Nakae Chōmin's 中江兆民 (1847–1901) translation of Immanuel Kant.[45] Having familiarized himself with Kant's mature epistemology and moral philosophy, Liang was given a new as well as a highly systematic and progressive set of theoretical tools to question and eventually repudiate the "text-based" approach to moral learning: scholars associated with the orthodox school of evidential research insisted that people could learn about moral principles through the study and verification of "facts." But *how*, Liang asked, does a person know about facts? Qian Daxin and his fellow Qing philologists instructed a young generation of Chinese scholars to learn from facts rather than empty metaphysical speculation. To challenge the intellectual position held by Qian as well as his contemporaries, Liang presented the following account in his introduction to Kant: imagine we see a round object appearing in the middle of the sky. It is red, releasing bright light and mildly scorching radiation.[46] As we stay at a distance, we can see its hue with our eyes and feel its warmth through the tactile sensation. This red object, obviously, is the sun. But how can we be sure that we are looking at the sun instead of a red balloon painted over a canvas? A reader may protest: the sun and a painted balloon are "empirically" different! The former is a gigantic star existing out in space, while the latter is an illustration coated with pigment. The two hardly constitute a comparison! But this was not what Liang was asking about. Before Liang became a student of Kang Youwei, he received his formal education at *Xuehai tang* 學海堂, an academy founded by the prominent Qing philologist Ruan Yuan 阮元 (1764–1849) and devoted to philological research methods developed by practitioners associated with the orthodox school of Qing evidential research.[47] By asking *how* a person learns, Liang was pursuing a more fundamental epistemic enquiry: through what kind of cognitive mechanism can a person *relate to* a disparate set of factual data? And how can he discriminate one measuring unit from another?

By comparing one's observation of the sun to a painted balloon, Liang posed a radical challenge to practitioners of Qing evidential research: a person can be presented with an infinite set of data that are empirically different. The objective facts and data per se do not present any meaningful conclusion; a person's reasoning and his associative power do. Our ability to distinguish the sun from the balloon indicates that there is a pre-endowed sense of time and space within us. If an object "appears" to us as the way it is, it is not only because of the object but also because we are pre-endowed with a set of a priori analytical and perceptual categories in the mind.

To explicate Kant's epistemology in further detail, Liang said a person owns multiple pairs of spectacles, each with a distinct lens color.[48] As the person tries on spectacles with different colored lenses, the object he sees changes along with the color of his lenses. So what exactly has changed? The object or the man's perception of the object? Clearly it is the latter. With Liang's example we can further make explicit Kant's revolutionary thinking: not having a direct exposure to the phenomenal world, a person wears multiple pairs of a priori spectacles in his mind. The mind spectacles consist of two intersecting lenses. One frames his sense of time, which informs one's experience of causal sequence, and the other informs him of space, or the perception of geometric organization. Being "a priori intuitions or categories engrained in our perceptual apparatus" (實吾感覺力中所固有之定理), space and time are forms of *Anschauung* (intuition).[49] Aside from time and space, these a priori perceptual lenses consist of several distinct but intersecting forms of intuition, which include the senses of causality, contingency, part and whole, and so on. When a person comes into contact with the physical world, he is *predisposed* to view everything through the a priori spectacles that frame one's perspectives of seeing and to organize those disconnected pieces of information in keeping with the logical order with which one is endowed.

Linguists and philologists of the Qing dynasty would not have heard of Kant. But as foreign as the German philosopher may appear, all aspects of Kantian epistemology, as Liang argued, should be generally familiar to educated readers in China.[50] For instance, there is a basic consensus Kant shares with the school of Yogācāra (Eng: Practice of Yoga; Chin: 瑜伽行派) Buddhism: people do not have access to mind-independent reality; the "external world" exists for us only as it appears.[51] In Yogācāra Buddhism, a branch of Indian Mahāyāna Buddhism that is also known as Cittamātra (Eng: consciousness-only; Chin: 唯識),[52] it is believed that people possess eight kinds of consciousness. The first five consciousnesses (Chin: 五識) refer to a person's sight (Chin: 眼識; *cakṣurvijñāna*), hearing (Chin: 耳識; *śrotravijñāna*), smell (Chin: 鼻識; *ghrāṇavijñāna*), taste (Chin: 舌識; *jihvāvijñāna*), and touch (Chin: 身識; *kāyavijñāna*). A person's initial contact with the physical reality takes place in the intersection of the horizontal (*heng* 橫) and the vertical (*shu* 豎) planes. The Buddhist calls the horizontal plane "*kongjian*" 空間 (space; Sanskrit: *ākāśa*), and the vertical plane "*shijian*" 時間 (time; Sanskrit: *kāla*).[53] For Liang, the Buddhist conception of time and space can be understood as the structural and the perceptual framework that constitutes a person's a priori intuition. As one encounters a physical object with his five consciousnesses, he needs to rely on his sixth consciousness, which is "introspection" (Chinese: 意識; Sanskrit: *manovijñāna*), to draw a meaningful connection between one's a priori intuition and the object he experiences. Operating under the a priori framework of time and space, the sixth consciousness is instinctively capable of "connecting" (*liangjie* 聯結) and "synthesizing all perceptual elements in rational sequence" (綜合一切序次) "so that the logical order does not suffer from disarray" (使有先後而不相離).[54] The renowned Buddhist monk Xuanzang 玄奘 (602–664 AD) introduced the essential sutras of Yogācāra Buddhism to China in the fifth century. Instead of following Xuanzang's standard translation of the sixth consciousness as *yishi* 意識, Liang took the liberty of relating "introspection" to Kant's definition of "reason." Liang names this joint cognitive function *zhihui* 智慧 (which means "wisdom" in Chinese). Unsatisfied with mere disconnected bits of knowledge, reason is predisposed to unify the disparate sensual information a person collects through the five consciousnesses into a coherent, unified, and systematic whole. Thereafter, a rational agent possessing practical reason (*chunzhi* 純知; *chun xing zhuihui* or 純性智慧) and five senses comes to have perceptual feelings (由我五官及我智慧兩相結構, 而生知覺).[55]

When a person encounters an object, Liang emphasized, he can only see the object as it is presented through an endowed set of imperative categories, which are the intrinsic mental perspectives from which we experience the physical world. The order and regularity we encounter in the natural world, in other words, is made possible by the mind's *own* construction of nature and its order. For Kant, the ability to sense objects in time and space presupposes the a priori representation of them, which suggests that our sense of time and space is merely ideal (which is a postulate, or the mind's conceptual abstraction), hence not a property of things in themselves (則此二者、皆非真有、而實由我之假定者也).⁵⁶ It indicates that time and space are not "outside" of us, "not things that exist independently of our intuition," nor are they properties of, nor relations among, such things (非自外來而呈現於我智慧之前).⁵⁷ Rather, they are an endowed set of imperative categories engrained in our perceptual apparatus (實吾感覺力中所固有之定理). Time and space, in other words, originate in the mind; they are a priori: subjective conditions on the possibility of experience (實我之智慧、能自發此兩種形式).⁵⁸

Li Is Here; It Is Who We Are

Liang first introduced Kant to China in 1903. His liberal and often creative adaptation of Kant's philosophy contains a considerable number of interpretative errors.⁵⁹ The reformer, however, did not bring Kant to China solely for education and knowledge circulation purposes. With Western-imported philosophical propositions deriving from Kantian ethics and epistemology, Liang identified a Western philosophical perspective to defend, explicate, and substantiate neo-Confucian thinkers' conception of *li* that informs man's natural moral judgment with logical precision: the concept of *li* and the idea of a priori categories, according to Liang, occupy a central position in the philosophy of neo-Confucianism and Kant. For Kant and most neo-Confucian thinkers, men are structured, or "programmed," on the basis of a certain a priori deterministic order. Instead of a fictional invention, these deterministic orders are constituted by a substantial set of a priori logical, cognitive, and perceptual orders in Kant's epistemology, governing the way individuals think, behave, and reason.

Learned individuals of Liang's times were accustomed to acquiring moral principles and modern political concepts through the study of texts. But those who were determined to *learn about* "the facts" through methods of empirical investigation were ignorant of the founding premise of Kant's epistemology—man can cognize only objects that he can, in principle, intuit. If a person can have knowledge of the world, it is because the world as he experiences it conforms to the conditions of the possibility of experience. It is technically impossible for Chinese intellectuals to detach themselves from the heartmind and learn about modern political concepts through the study of "solid facts," for raw, unmediated facts do not exist. If one is capable of obtaining moral attributes through the study of texts, this is due to the a priori moral order existing *inside of him*. In his mature epistemology and moral theory, Kant explains the relationship between man's possession of practical reason and his natural moral propensity as follows: objects of experience are in some sense mind-dependent. Not having direct access to any physical matters as empirical entities, whatever a person sees, feels, and experiences in this space is known with respect to the geometry of space, the deterministic order of time, and other causal and logical structures, not of anything independent of these basic structures. As Kant says, "Consequently, we can only cognize objects in space and time, appearances. We cannot cognize things in themselves."[60] Besides imposing a predetermined set of organizational order upon a person's perceptual and cognitive experiences, the reasoning capacity arrived at from these a priori conditions enables one to discover the fundamental moral principle. In Liang's interpretation of Kant, moral knowledge is fundamentally a priori in the sense that through reason one can discover the fundamental moral principle, and then deduce from that principle more specific moral duties:

> In our faculty of reason, there is such thing as the moral obligation. Such obligation is being imposed upon us as a natural imperative. Time and again it speaks to our heart in the voice of cautionary alarm: thou *must* be this; thou must not be that. The sense of obligation we share does not belong to the present, neither does it belong to the past nor the future. Having existed independently as a self-governing entity, it is perpetually and permanently unchanging. . . . It is the so-called imperishable. 吾人良智之中, 有所謂道德之責任者存, 此責任者, 實自然之法令, 常赫然臨命於吾心曰: 汝必當如是, 必當毋如是。此責任者不屬於現在, 不屬於過去, 不屬於未來, 實獨立而不倚, 亙古而無變者也 . . . 所謂不滅者。[61]

In his summary of Kant, Liang suggested that man's moral obligation is a conviction deduced from man's possession and application of practical reason. The reasoning faculty informs moral judgment and gives a rational agent the ethical compulsion to fulfill his moral duty by doing what is right. Just as a person is predisposed to organize scattered pieces of information in a meaningful sequence in keeping with the a priori categories, he is obliged to fulfil the natural moral responsibilities (*daode zhi zeren* 道德之責任) informed by his reasoning faculty. When people think of the word "law" (*falü* 法律), they may refer it to a regulation system governmental institutions created to regulate people's behavior. But in Kantian ethics law is an all-encompassing concept. Any command or provision that commands an action can be considered law (凡帶命令之性質, 皆可謂法律).[62] Kant calls the natural moral obligation the "categorical imperative," an unconditional moral command that is binding in all circumstances and is not dependent on a person's inclination or purpose. Among the deterministic causal order informing the physical structure of the universe, the moral order is one of the "general rules" (*gongli* 公例) and "incontrovertible principles" (不可避之理) that predetermines the course a man should follow in his responses to the world. To Liang, this meant that morality expressed a natural law (實自然之法令) instructing one to distinguish right from wrong. Under the governance of this natural moral law, "people might not necessarily do good, but there is no man who does not know that he should be good. Although at times people might commit bad deeds, there is no way that he does not know that evil must be removed" (人雖或不為善, 而無不知善之必當為。雖或偶為惡, 而無不知惡之必當去).[63]

Neo-Confucian thinkers, generally speaking, assumed that there is a generic set of cosmic patterns constituting the deep structure of each individual and his heartmind. Being formed of the same cosmic principles, people share the innate capacity of seeing, acting, and empathizing from the position of others. The "like-mindedness" of one and other thus allows a person to experience benevolence and to expand his empathetic resonance into other forms of moral goodness. For early neo-Confucian thinkers, man's inclination to be good was predicated on the underlying affinities he shared with myriad forms of being. Kant, on the contrary, viewed moral knowledge as fundamentally a priori in the sense that moral knowledge must be the result of careful reasoning (first transcendental, then deductive). In Kantian ethics and early neo-Confucian philosophy, man's moral propensity was derived from discrete origins.[64] The discrepancies between these two streams of philosophical thinking raise two questions: What makes *li* the cosmic pattern and Kantian a priori intuition comparable? And how can Liang possibly justify his decision to repudiate the "text-based" approach to knowledge with a theoretical apparatus derived from a philosophical tradition that is only indirectly relevant to that of his own, let alone China's philosophical tradition in general?

Li and Man's Introspective Cognitive Function

Assuming that man's heartmind is structured in perfect agreement with *li* the cosmic pattern, Wang Yangming had famously argued that man's heartmind is, or is the same as (*ji* 即), *li* the cosmic principle (*xin ji li*). In Wang Yangming's moral teachings, there is a concept known as *liangzhi* 良知, the "good moral knowing" or "innate knowing of the good." Being a functional extension of the heartmind, "good moral knowing" operates as a built-in, premeditated moral censor or detector. It is, as Wang explicated in his "four-cornered doctrines" (*siju jiao* 四句教), inherently capable of discerning good from evil (知善知惡是良知). When a person responds to external stimuli, immediately and automatically his "good moral knowing" determines the merits of such a response. So what exactly do "immediately" and "automatically" mean in this context? And through what kind of mechanism can "good moral knowing" perform such a function? Wang Yangming replied: to know *is* to act, a proposition modern philosophers translate conventionally as the "unity of knowing and acting," or "the unity of knowledge and action." In Wang Yangming's call for the unity of "knowing and acting" (*zhixing heyi* 知行合一), the use of the word "knowing" (知) refers unmistakably to *liangzhi* 良知, the good moral knowing.[65]

In Anglophone scholarship, a good number of contemporary philosophers have attempted to explicate the relationship between "knowing" and "acting" in Wang Yangming's moral philosophy. Their responses, according to Harvey Lederman's classification, can be divided into the "affective-perceptual model" and the "introspective model." Perceiving perfect moral knowing as an omniscient cosmic perspective, philosophers following the "affective-perceptual model" consider *liangzhi* a form of premeditated moral intuition that latently informs and directs people's embodied actions.[66] Lederman rejects this acclaimed interpretation. *Liangzhi*, he argues, is neither a "form of 'seeing as,' nor perceptual propensity, complemented by affect."[67] Instead of the "mastermind" orchestrating, instructing, and overseeing virtuous actions, *liangzhi* is introspective "cognition" that occurs simultaneously with virtuous actions.[68] For Western theorists who are accustomed to envision the body-mind division in dualistic terms, both Wang Yangming and Lederman's interpretations sound startling. In any event, one immediate question suggests itself about Wang's view: What makes the corporeal body interchangeable with the heartmind? Or more simply put, how can the body *be* the mind?

To answer these questions, I would like to return to the basic Buddhist metaphysical premise that informs Wang Yangming's conception of the "unity of knowing and acting." I hope the introduction of this Buddhist perspective will help to elucidate Liang Qichao's as well as Harvey Lederman's illuminating and much-needed reinterpretation of Wang Yangming's moral theory. The development of neo-Confucianism, as noted earlier, began life as a protest against Buddhist metaphysics. In this universe, the Buddhist believes, everyone and everything are mutually constitutive of and dependent on each other. Being part and parcel of each other, we are "dependently arisen" upon temporal and situational conditions. In Wang Yangming's moral philosophy, man's heartmind is informed and constituted by *li* the cosmic pattern. Being dependent on the heartmind, *li* the metaphysical abstraction is what it is by relating to the heartmind. Man's heartmind, following the same logic, is as fluid and as volatile as *li*. Being the physical manifestation of *li* the cosmic pattern, the heartmind is also devoid of self-nature. Whatever shows up in the heartmind is the crystallization of the cosmic pattern it epitomizes. *Liangzhi* operates as the heartmind's moral censor. Being a functional extension *of* the heartmind, "good moral knowing" is just as empty as the heartmind. Aside from telling good from evil, it is devoid of intrinsic self-content, and hence intrinsically incapable of providing either a perspective of seeing or a regulative framework guiding and coordinating the ways virtuous actions are being performed.

Take my experience as an example. In East Asian culture, serving parents good food is a means to display one's filial piety. I intend to be a filial daughter. Both of my parents suffer from high cholesterol. When we see a table of good food, it appears that imposing a restriction on their consumption (and in turn sacrificing myself by eating their share) can be more filial than providing them with good food. In everyday life, the definition of being moral varies from situation to situation. A person does not know about virtues such as filiality by being "perceptually" informed; she *knows* only by being *cognizant of* her mental states as she responds virtuously to external situations. At the moment a person reacts to external stimuli, *liangzhi*'s detective mechanism is *crystalized* and *illuminated* by her spontaneous responses. Without this well-rounded cognitive and epistemic capacity, *liangzhi* would not have *known* that the act is virtuous. To rephrase Lederman's supposition, one genuinely *knows* filiality *if and only if* she is acting filially.[69] Instead of perceptual or affective intuition, the kind of "good moral knowing," or genuine knowledge (真知), a person displays in the course of action is bound to be an "introspective cognitive capacity" and should thus be considered a "cognitive achievement."[70]

In his introduction to Kant, Liang did not provide a systematic account explicating the relationship between *li* the cosmic pattern, man's heartmind, and the heartmind's cognitive function. There, however, there is something the reformer can say for sure: "Wang Yangming's 'good moral knowing' *is* what Kant calls 'my true-self.' Their hypotheses are fundamentally the same" (陽明之良知，即康德之真我。其學說之基礎全同).[71] In China's transition to political modernity, Liang aspired to turn democratic governance into a "public expression" of man's instinctive moral goodness. Knowing that the establishment of this ideal political order is predicated on the consolidation of a corresponding set of moral and philosophical proposition, in 1903 Liang declared, "The moral teaching of Wang Yangming, I believe, is the one and only remedy to cure China from the corruption that prevails in the scholarly community" (竊以為惟王學為今日學界獨一無而之良藥。)[72]

A New Modernity: Liang's "Kantian" Critique of Inherited Intellectual Tradition

Based on the comparison Liang drew between Wang Yangming and Kant, it appears that Chinese philosophers had developed a highly sophisticated moral epistemology since at least the sixteenth century. But instead of trying to realize the full moral and political potential promised by Wang Yangming's moral teachings, practitioners of Qing evidential research denied the heartmind and insisted on looking for moral principles through the investigation of the text. The rise of Qing evidential research in the seventeenth and early eighteenth centuries can be attributed to a number of social, political, economic, and geographical factors.[73] Besides applying scientific knowledge being recently imported from the West, utilizing the rich scholarly resources provided by some prosperous local scholar-gentry communities, and evading political censorship imposed by the Manchurians, it has been interpreted essentially as an intellectual movement seeking to reject the "false" moral epistemology and subsequent indulgence in empty metaphysical speculation characteristic of neo-Confucian thinkers. But Liang was unconvinced by the conventional narrative.[74] To this modern reformer, his contemporaries' false approach to learning was caused by a seemingly unlikely source, which was a fundamentally mistaken moral assumption conceived by Zhu Xi, the great philosopher representing the "Learning of Principle" school of neo-Confucianism. To uncover what he considered to be the true cause that corrupted the Qing intellectuals' unreflective habits of learning, Liang ventured to present a counterintuitive claim that challenges our conception of late imperial Chinese philosophy and intellectual history.

"Early" Qing intellectuals such as Dai Zhen, according to Liang, were suspicious of the connection neo-Confucian thinkers drew between *li* the cosmic pattern and man's heartmind. In order to "search for the truth" (*qiuzhen* 求真), Dai Zhen, he said, scrutinized the Confucian classics with an inquisitive spirit and exceptional intellectual prowess. Since his empirical investigation was predicated on man's "introspective speculation" *of* the Confucian classics, Dai Zhen's learning approach, even without his own awareness, was in reality a continuation and perfection of the Wang Yangming school of neo-Confucianism. To shed light on the mutual emphasis Dai Zhen and Wang Yangming placed upon the "mind," Liang classified Dai Zhen as a practitioner of Qing learning (*qingxue* 清學) or a member of the Enlightenment school (*qimeng pai* 啟蒙派) of Qing evidential research.

In the middle of the 1750s, Qian Daxin was both a patron and a colleague of Dai Zhen.[75] Unlike Dai Zhen, who persisted in his search for the truth, Qian Daxin was fully occupied with primary sources that survived from the Han Dynasty. Qian shared a basic conviction with the leading philologists of the time: "Moral meanings and principles" (*yili* 義理) are moral guidance and doctrines prescribed by the Confucian Sages. Those pursuing philology should aim to bring back the lost or damaged integrity of the ancient texts, or the "ancient meanings" (*guyi* 古義).[76] Liang considered Qian and his fellow philologists to be practitioners of Han learning (*Hanxue* 漢學), or the "orthodox school of Qing evidential research" (*zhengtong pai* 正統派). These "despicable Confucians" (*jianru* 賤儒), Liang said, "attended to tedious details but disowned the master plan; they inherited the form yet relinquished its spirit" (惜存者其瑣節，而絕者其大綱。存者其形式，而絕者卻精神也。)[77] Qian Daxin called neo-Confucian thinkers the "fake Confucians." For Liang, however, Qian and his friends' collective distrust of the heartmind was informed precisely by a false philosophical postulation conceived by Zhu Xi. Instead of a protest against neo-Confucianism as it is generally believed, the orthodox school of Qing evidential research was in fact a reincarnation of the Cheng Yi and Zhu Xi school of neo-Confucianism in the Qing dynasty.

To accentuate the uncanny interconnection between the Zhu Xi school of neo-Confucianism and Qing evidential research, Liang said: having received their training in the composition of eight-legged essays (因為個個都八股出身),[78] Qian Daxin and a number of renowned Qing scholars had been intoxicated by the teachings of Cheng Yi and Zhu Xi (程朱中毒). "Heedless and sloppy, they were a bunch of muddle-minded souls wandering in the company of the ghostly spirits of Cheng Yi and Zhu Xi but covering themselves in jackets bearing the names of Xu Shen and Zheng Xuan" (two eminent philologists of the Eastern Han 東漢 dynasty [25–220]) (一個個都稀稀薄薄,朦朦朧朧的程朱遊魂披上一件許鄭的外套。) "Having devoted themselves into tedious tasks of verification (考證的零碎工作), they placed moral principles aside" (將義理擱在一邊) and had long ceased to care about the most important questions in philosophy.[79]

Learning Made Us the Beasts: Zhu Xi and Evidential Research

Being a firm believer in Wang Yangming, Liang believed in the existence of *li* as well as in man's introspective cognitive function informed by *li*. To express his support for Wang's moral metaphysics, Liang readily translated Wang's position into his own languages: being a person's natural endowment, morality (*dao* 道) belongs to the "domain of personal ethics" (*deyu fanwei* 德育範圍). Learning (*xue* 學) through the investigation of texts and objects, on the contrary, belongs to the "domain of intellectual education" (*zhiyu fanwei* 智育範圍).[80] Being "two" distinct properties, learning and man's moral instinct cannot be "one" with each other. "Zhu Xi," however, "had committed the fallacy of mistaking the way of being intellectual as the way of being moral. He failed to recognize that these two domains were inversely proportional. There was not the slightest chance that the two could be jumbled" (朱子之大失,則誤以智育之方法為德育之方法。而不知兩者之界說,適成反比例,而絲毫不容混也).[81]

As Liang criticized his contemporaries for adopting a "text-based" approach to knowledge, he began to probe into Zhu Xi's personal learning experiences. Having scrutinized an extensive number of personal letters Zhu Xi composed in his later years, Liang presented his contemporaries with an unwelcomed observation: while Zhu Xi urged people to obtain moral knowledge through the study of Confucian classics, this great neo-Confucian thinker was frequently tormented and distressed by his own study. Of the many illuminating passages Liang selected to underscore Zhu Xi's uncertainties, let us look at a letter the neo-Confucian thinker wrote to his friend Lü Zujian 呂祖儉 (?–1198), a scholar-official who was banished from the Southern Song court for defying the throne:

> These years as I look back, the learning that I have pursued has missed the point. Not only did I fail to be my own master, my spirit has also been taken and consumed by those words. This, I'm afraid, is no minor ailment. Whenever I think of it, I tremble with trepidation and fear. I am also worried about my friends. Everything seems fragmented, absent of systematic structure, contoured and confused. There is no means to find my way out. 年來覺得日前為學，不得要領，自身做主不起，反為文字奪卻精神，不為小病。每一念之，惕然自懼，且為朋友憂之。若只如此支離，漫無統紀，輾轉迷惑，無出頭處。[82]

Having identified substantial discrepancies between man's cosmic moral nature and his problematic human feelings, Zhu Xi asserted that man's heartmind is inherently "fragmented" (*zhili*) and disjoined. But in confessions made to his friends, Zhu Xi, somewhat ironically, used the phrase "fragmented" at least three times to describe his own study.[83] The years he spent studying Confucian classics, as it turned out, did not bridge the chasm that had separated the great neo-Confucian thinker from his heavenly heartmind. It only made Zhu Xi feel "fragmented," "shattered," or "disintegrated."

Since the time of Zhu Xi, it appeared to Liang that Chinese intellectuals had departed from their own selves. Those seeking to *learn about* moral principles through the study of "external" sources rather their "personal understanding *of*" the moral sources were destined to drift further and further away from their hearts, their souls, and ultimately their human natures. To Liang this is precisely what had happened to practitioners of Qing evidential research as well as to other intellectuals of his times. As Liang looked to the previous two hundred years of Chinese academic practice, he summarized their learning practice as follows: Mencius considered man's heartmind the locus of conation and cognition. Instead of looking for moral meanings in their own hearts, practitioners of Qing evidential research turned to "remains and fossils being buried underground for over two thousand years" (而與二千年前地下之僵石為伍。)[84] "Scholars of Han learning were those who were disengaged from human society. While they might have composed over a hundred volumes of writing, these works did not attend to the living concerns of their times. As detailed and elaborate as their arguments may seem, they did not spring from the intent of one's primordial heartmind" (漢學者，則立於人間社會以外，雖著述累百卷，而決無一傷時之語；雖辯論千萬言，而皆非出本心之談).[85] Zhuangzi 莊子 (c. 369 BC–c. 286 BC) once made this disheartening remark: "There is no greater sorrow than experiencing the death of one's heart" (哀莫大於心死).[86] Having severed themselves from their hearts, "scholars of Han learning are those guiding all people under heaven and letting their hearts go dead" (漢學家者率天下而心死者也).[87]

Liang was known to be a person who carried himself with a genteel demeanor. But as he thought about the irreversible damage the "text-based" learning approach had caused his contemporaries, Liang bombarded Qian Daxin and a number of "celebrated Qing evidential researchers" (夫盛名鼎鼎之先輩) with manic, explosive anger, calling them "despicable Confucians" (*jianru*) who ravaged China's modern political future and annihilated the country's time-honored moral and cultural tradition:

> Men of my generation live a few hundred years later than the respected teacher [Wang Yangming]. Being vengeful of the virtuous gentleman, those despicable Confucians practicing fake learning destroyed the vein of the Way with all their strength. The profound moral principles concealed in subtle words were completely annihilated and crushed. They and their lingering charm that remained had now vanished without a trace. 我輩生後先生數百年，中間復經賤儒偽學，盜憎主人。摧鋤道脈，不遺餘力。微言大義，流風餘韻，漸滅以盡。[88]

Speaking from Qian Daxin's perspective, neo-Confucian thinkers were fake and vulgar Confucians who indulged themselves in empty metaphysical speculation. But if neo-Confucian thinkers, Liang rebutted, were indeed "fake Confucians," "those who practiced Qing evidential research over the past two hundred years, as far as I see it, had engaged themselves in the study of ox demons and snake spirits. Their intent is precisely the same as these evil spirits (吾見夫本朝二百年來學者之所學, 皆牛鬼蛇神類耳, 而其用心亦正與彼相等).[89] "The holy, absolute truth that can only be experienced through personal obtainment but not communicated to others was shattered in an instant" (神明千聖之學, 一旦而摧毀之).[90] For a younger generation of Chinese intellectuals who had inherited their teachers' investigative approaches and tried to *learn about* modern political "attributes" through the study of texts, these people, "having lost their sense of shame and the ability to distinguish right from wrong, willfully and collectively descended to the beasts" (是非之心與羞惡之心俱絕, 相率而禽獸矣).[91] In this "great moral decline," learning did not make men better people; it reduced bad people to "ox demons and snake spirits," and from ox demons and snake spirits to "wild beasts." "Today," Liang declared, "is a moment in which the human heart has become rotten and corrupted to the extreme" (今日人心腐敗達於極點之時機).[92] "In a world filled with human desires, beasts are all throughout the country" (人欲橫流, 舉國禽獸).[93] "In today's China, the extremity of the moral darkness has become unthinkable" (今日國中, 其道德上之黑闇, 不可思議).[94]

Repudiating Zhu Xi with Kant

Zhu Xi urged people to obtain moral principles through the careful study of Confucian classics combined with the investigation of external things and events. For Liang Qichao, what he perceived to be the "false" learning approach was based on a fatal "interpretative fallacy" caused by Zhu Xi's misapprehension of Buddhist metaphysics. Being the evil seed from which the development of Qing evidential research had sprouted and proliferated, Zhu Xi's interpretative fallacy, as Liang believed, had directly or indirectly inspired the late Qing intellectuals to study modern political ideas as "conceptual knowledge." Having shaped the development of Chinese learning practice for nearly a millennium, what appears to be an abstract, if not irrelevant, philosophical musing had over time caused China's modern political impasse. As Liang sought to implement a modern political order that thrives on the natural moral order, the appearance of Kant eventually offered him a way to revive the Wang Yangming school of neo-Confucianism, rectify the unresolved neo-Confucian debates, and clarify the "true meaning" of neo-Confucianism.

In this universe, the Buddhist says, everyone and everything are mutually constitutive of and dependent on each other. Being part and parcel of an organic entity, we are "dependently arisen" upon temporal and situational conditions. In this network of undifferentiated interdependence, even the most marked antithetical contrasts are absent of intrinsic self-nature. We may honor goodness for the presence of evil. But goodness and evil, being dependently arisen, are neither good nor bad (*wushan wue* 無善無惡). Having experienced the Song dynasty's mounting social and political unrest, Zhu Xi could not tolerate the moral ambivalence created by this seemingly nihilist Buddhist take on life.[95] To salvage the perfection of the heavenly order as the human realm was falling into disarray, Zhu Xi divided man's cosmic moral nature from his corrupted human nature. The sharp distinction Zhu Xi drew between a person's "moral-metaphysical nature" (*yili zhi xing* 義理之性) and his "*qi*-constituted physical nature" (*qizhi zhi xing* 氣質之性) appears as a protest against Buddhist metaphysics.[96] But the conception of such protest, Liang argued, was inspired precisely by the two seemingly contradictory concepts that exist in Buddhist teachings. One is "suchness" (Chin: 真如; Sanskrit: *tathātā*) and the other is "ignorance" (Chin: 無明; Sanskrit: *avidyā*). To explicate Zhu Xi's careful re-appropriation, or perhaps misappropriation of Buddhist metaphysics, Liang said,

> In Buddhist teachings, it is believed that the seeds of suchness [Sanskrit: *tathata*] and the seeds of ignorance [*avidyā*] have coexisted and continued to fumigate each other in the vastness of man's true nature [*bhūtatathatā*] and his eight consciousnesses [*ālayavijñāna*] since time immemorial. Having fumigated their true suchness with ignorance, those ordinary men [*pṛthagjana*] have mistaken their foolishness as consciousness [*vijñāna*]. For those who look for enlightenment, they fumigate ignorance with suchness and turn consciousness into wisdom [*prajña*]. Neo-Confucian thinkers of the Song Dynasty struggled to organize Chinese philosophy with this set of metaphysical propositions. Zhu Xi, for instance, made the distinction between man's "moral-metaphysical nature" and his "physical nature composed by *qi*." In his annotation of *The Great Learning*, the Neo-Confucian thinker says, "Perfect moral nature is an endowment man receives from heaven. Imperceptible and intangible as it is, such endowment keeps one away from the dark, enabling him to comprehend all events and matters created by the same patterns. (Comment: the term "suchness" in Buddhist teachings

is what Kant called "I-in-myself.") But being detained by the *qi* substance and obscured by human desire, man becomes muddled and deluded." (Comment: What the Buddha calls ignorance is what Kant refers to as "I-as-appearance.") 佛說以為吾人自無始以來,即有真如無明之兩種子,含於性海識藏之中而互相薰。凡夫以無明薰真如,故迷智為識,學道者復以真如薰無明,故轉識成智。 宋儒欲用此義例以組織中國哲學。故朱子分出義理之性與氣質之性。其注大學云: 明德者人之所得乎天,而虛靈不昧,以受眾理而應萬事者也。(案即佛所謂真如也,康德所謂真我也) 但為氣稟所拘,人欲所蔽,則有時而昏 (案即佛所謂無明也,康德所謂現象之我也)。[97]

In the realm of human existence, things, people, and events are so inextricably entangled that they prevail in ways that transcend one's comprehension. The Buddhist call this state of being "suchness"—*things as the way they are*. While the complexities of human affairs resist rational conceptualization, most men insist on adhering to their narrow and biased preconceptions. Being misled and dumfounded by their "ignorance," people often fail to recognize the ultimate inexpressible nature of all things. For readers who are new to Buddhist teachings, the contrast between "suchness" and "ignorance" seems to suggest that human existence is sandwiched between two extremes. This ostensible (though deceptive) disparity, Liang said, had prompted Zhu Xi to divide man's "cosmic heartmind" from his "human heartmind"—having received one's cosmic endowment from heaven, man's moral nature is as pure "as such." But once his cosmic endowment, which is a metaphysical abstraction, takes form in polluted *qi* substances, it becomes tarnished and spoiled. Thereafter, a person loses his cosmic moral nature and become ignorant.

"I-as-Appearance" versus "My True Self"

"Suchness" and "being ignorant of the ways things are" appear to be two oppositional properties. But in the world of Buddhist teachings, everything and everyone, once again, are dependently arisen. Being mutually constitutive of each other, they are absent of "self-nature." Zhu Xi the great neo-Confucian thinker could not be ignorant of this basic Buddhist tenet. But being heavily invested in the existence of *absolute* moral goodness, Zhu Xi insisted on disjoining "suchness" and "ignorance" as symbiotic twins for the purpose of rectifying or eradicating what appeared to him to be nihilistic Buddhist pessimism. Sensible as his decision may seem, it is theoretically untenable. To repudiate Zhu Xi's moral theory from the perspective of Kantian philosophy, Liang ventured to explicate the codependent relationship between "suchness" and "ignorance" from what he perceived to be a parallel pair of concepts Kant delineates in his transcendental idealism. These concepts are the twofold roles a rational agent plays as an "appearance" *and* a "thing-in-itself." Considering Kant the lesser German counterpart of the Buddha, in the two pieces of interlinear commentary (*an* 案) that Liang placed in his summary of Zhu Xi's moral theory, the political reformer says that "what the Buddha calls 'suchness' in his teaching is equivalent to Kant's 'my true-self' (or 'I-in-myself')" (佛所謂真如也, 康德所謂真我也), and that "what the Buddha calls ignorance is what Kant refers to as 'I-as-appearance'" (佛所謂無明也, 康德所謂現象之我也).[98] To show how similarities between Kantian philosophy and the Buddhist teachings can shed light on a fatal interpretative fallacy that pertains in the structure of Zhu Xi's moral theory, Liang presented us the following set of cross-cultural comparisons.

Reality, according to Kant, consists of objects and events as they are perceptually and corporeally experienced. Being a rational agent in possession of practical reason, a person is predisposed to experience and organize the physical reality through the mediation of the a priori contingencies. As a person comes into contact with the world, "appearances" (*Erscheinung*) are the "views" he sees through his built-in mental, perceptual, and analytical spectacles. Emerging *as they appear to* the human perceiver, these appearances are subject to the causal deterministic order of time, space, the sense of causality, contingency, and so on.[99] By emphasizing that a person can experience, organize, and respond to the physical reality *based only upon the way* he is made, Kant seems to have disclosed our inherent limitation as humans: as a rational agent, a person can interact with the world only in agreement with the a priori categories with which he is endowed. Unable to take off the built-in mental spectacles, he himself, in this sense, is the same as objects he sees as "appearances," for they are all unanimously subject to the identical set of a priori conditions. Liang translated "I," my phenomenal self, as "I-as-appearance" (*xianxiang zhi wo* 現象之我).

In Kant's transcendental idealism, "appearance," which is the object *of* senses, stands in contrast with, and in relation to, "thing-in-itself" (*Ding an sich*), a posited object that exists independently of perceptual senses.

Aside from a rational agent, man, as we know, is a corporeal piece of blood and flesh. Similar to a table, an apple, or an ant, he is one of the myriad forms of physical beings that exists on this planet. When a man, or any other empirical entity, is not being considered in terms of his epistemic relation to human perceivers, he is called a "thing-in-itself." Considered as an appearance, a person is subject to the deterministic conditions of time, space, contingency, and so on. But considered as a "thing-in-itself," the person can at least consistently be thought of as free. To emphasize the impartial detachment man enjoys as a physical entity, Liang appropriated "thing-in-itself" as "my true self" (*zhenwo* 真我), which is the noumenal self as opposed to the phenomenal self.

The contrast Kant drew between "my true self" and "I-as-appearance," at first glimpse, seems (but *only* seems) generally comparable to the distinction Zhu Xi drew between man's "moral-metaphysical nature" and his "*qi*-composed physical nature": having received one's cosmic endowment from heaven, my "true self" is unaffected by any external influences or restrictions; it is most pure and perfect. But later, as my "true self" takes form in *qi*, my pure and perfect cosmic moral nature is fettered, inhibited, and completely obscured by those polluted physical substances. Thereafter, my true self loses its cosmic moral nature and becomes this ignorant man (or actually woman in my case).

The above comparison, of course, was blatantly mistaken. As Liang was quick to emphasize, those who are prone to draw such analogies have overlooked perhaps the most decisive postulation in Kant's epistemology: as a "physical object" (*wu zisheng* 物自身) living at the intersection of time and space (而與空間時間相倚者也), man's corporeal life (肉體之生命; 眾生之身) is a physical compound made of particles modulated by the law of physics (為物理定例所束縛), which include gravity, relativity, the principles of quantum mechanics, and so on.[100] All the scientific laws run on unalterable courses; there is nothing that is unpredictable (則其所循一定之軌道, 固無不可測知者).[101] "The movements or motions of man are simply parts of the many manifold physical phenomena; they are subject to the inevitable laws of physics and cannot be exempted from them" (其有所動作, 亦不過一現象與凡百庶物之現象, 同皆有不可避之理而不能自肆).[102] If a person's perceptual, cognitive, and ethical propensity is contingent on the causal, deterministic order of time, space, ethical imperative, and other a priori conditions, these constricting contingencies come as a result of a person being a "physical or molecular compound" following the natural law of physics. The law and order that restrict a person are precisely the law and order determining the way that he is built. Since the person is restricted by the law and order that made him a "physical object" rather than any "external" law and order being imposed upon him from *without*, the law that restricts him is precisely who he is and what he is. Being a slave to his own master, a man can ultimately be considered free.

In Buddhist metaphysics there is a comparable set of assumptions that Zhu Xi had either failed or refused to comprehend. Being fixated on the ostensible contrast between "suchness" and "ignorance," Zhu Xi asserted that man's cosmic heartmind is pure "as such." But later as it is spoiled and tarnished by those polluted *qi* substances, the cosmic heartmind loses its moral nature and becomes ignorant. The heartmind, however, cannot be anything *other than* itself. To explicate how Zhu Xi had misinterpreted the relationship between the "heartmind" (Chinese: 心/心體; Sanskrit: *citta*), which is also the organ of emotion and cognition in Buddhist metaphysics, and "ignorance," personally I find it fruitful to turn to *Dacheng qixin lun* 大乘起信論 (*Treatise on Awakening Mahāyāna Faith*), a Chinese translation of the Buddhist treatise *Mahāyāna śraddhotpada śāstra*. Paramārtha (Chin: 真諦) (499–569 CE), the Indian translator, compares the relationship between the "heartmind and ignorance" to "water and wind":

> It is like the wind, which has the characteristic of movement based on there being water. If water were to cease to be, then the wind's characteristic would be eliminated, having no basis. But since water does not cease to be, the wind's characteristic continues. It is only because the wind ceases that the characteristic of movement accordingly ceases. It is not that water ceases to be. It is the same with ignorance, which is based on the intrinsic reality of the mind to move. If the intrinsic reality of the mind were to cease to be, then sentient beings would be eliminated, having no basis [for sentience]. But since the intrinsic reality of the mind does not cease to be, the arising-and-ceasing mind can continue. It is only because delusion ceases to be that the characteristics of the arising and ceasing mind accordingly cease to be. It is not that the mind's nature of cognition ceases to be.[103] 如風依水而有動相, 若水滅者, 則風相斷絕, 無所依止; 以水不滅, 風相相續; 唯風滅故, 動相隨滅, 非是水滅。無明亦爾, 依心體而動,

若心體滅, 則眾生斷絕無所依止; 以體不滅, 心得相續。唯痴滅故心相隨滅, 非心智滅。[104]

Li the cosmic patterns, to repeat Zhu Xi, is the supreme transcendental order governing the formation of man's heartmind and its perfect moral nature. But as the cosmic heartmind is spoiled by *qi*, it becomes wrecked and dysfunctional. Zhu Xi's assertion violates the philosophical premise of Buddhist metaphysics. As Paramārtha suggests in his translation of *Treatise on Awakening Mahāyāna Faith*, the wind blows and water ripples. When there is no water, what is the wind here for? If man's cosmic heartmind is indeed deformed and damaged, as Zhu Xi suggested, how can there be "ignorance" to speak of when the heartmind is dysfunctional and invalid? The motion of the ripples is "dependent on" (*yi* 依) the sweeping of the wind. Its movement exhibits the moving "gesture" (Chinese: *xiang* 相; Sanskrit: *lakṣana*) *of* the wind. Ignorance, in the same vein, is the ripple *of* the heartmind. It moves along *with* the heartmind (依心體而動). Instead of pronouncing the death of the cosmic heartmind, ignorance witnesses precisely its active dynamism. The activities of the heartmind, like any physical phenomenon, are diverse and multifarious. Of these activities, the opposite of "ignorance" is "awakening" (Chinese: *jue* 覺; Sanskrit: *bodhi*); these two states of being denote the incessantly revolving dissolution and enlightenment *of the same mind*.[105]

Man Is the Way

The codependent relationship the Buddhist describes between man's heartmind and its temporary dissolution as manifested in ignorance, as Liang saw it, bears a striking resemblance to the way "my true self" is connected with "I-as-appearance": as an "appearance," I am subject to the causal deterministic order of time, space, causality, and other a priori conditions. The person who imposes the a priori condition upon me *is myself*. While Kant emphasizes that a rational agent is both an "appearance" and a "thing-in-itself," in the world of Buddhist teachings, everything and everyone are dependently arisen. Having placed Kant's philosophy alongside the Buddhist teachings, Liang said,

> When the Buddhist speaks of suchness the Buddhist perceives all sentient beings as one identical body. Ignorance creates

false distinctions and confusion arises. Confusion leads to bad karma. By "my true self," Kant refers solely to the soul of each sentient being. His theory, of course, cannot be as thorough as that of the Buddhist. 佛氏言真如以為眾生本同一體。由妄生分別故有迷惑，有迷惑故有惡業。 康氏所謂真我，則指眾生各自之靈魂而已，其理論自不能如佛氏之圓滿。[106]

To Liang, the mutually constitutive and reciprocally dependent relationship that Kant and the Buddhist depict finds clear resonances in Wang Yangming's moral theory: being the formative pattern constituting the moral and cognitive formation of man's heartmind, *li* the cosmic principle is *not* an *absolute* and unchanging set of metaphysical doctrines existing *outside* of us. It is, on the contrary, the natural law that continues to unfold itself in *the way* people are made, *the way* we breathe, *the way* we reason, and *the way* we respond to the affairs of men. What "appears" to be the supreme cosmic law and order constituting my moral nature is *who I am* as a person. *Li* is the heartmind and the heartmind is *li*. In this constantly changing human reality, different men encounter different situations. Their responses to these situations are destined to be unpredictably varied. What can be defined as good, in this sense, is also infinitely fluid. But regardless of what these changing situations look like, the cosmic pattern that constitutes a person's heartmind will continue to unfold itself along with the person's altering responses to these altering situations. The cosmic principles *are the people* and they evolve *with* the people. Those seemingly different responses are the multifold physical "manifestations" of *li* the cosmic principles of which people are made. Instead of an absolute metaphysical abstraction informing the composition of one's moral nature up high, *li* the cosmic pattern reveals itself in what a person truly, instantly, and intuitively takes to be right—*to be is to be good*.

Assuming that men are moral in nature but debauched in person, Zhu Xi separated man's "moral-metaphysical nature" from the "*qi*-constituted physical nature," and by extension his "cosmic heartmind" from "humanly heartmind." But in Buddhist metaphysics, man's heartmind can be enlightened or benighted. Knowing that "ignorance" is one of the living gestures *of* the heartmind, there can *never* be "two" discrete heartminds as Zhu Xi had claimed. By removing the artificial boundary that Zhu Xi invented, Wang Yangming succeeded in liberating man from the higher, absolute order being imposed upon him from above. Knowing that man's performance of moral action is the spontaneous unfolding of the cosmic law and order of which he is made, man *is* the living presence of the cosmos. What Zhu Xi perceived to be the realm of metaphysical transcendence, in other words, *is* the world of human existence. Rather than having to acquire moral knowledge from the outside, man, ideally speaking, is instinctively capable of establishing legislative and constitutional order on the basis of the natural moral order. Law and order, in other words, do not exist outside of me. During the early 1900s, Liang Qichao endeavored to replace imperial monarchy with a system of governance that thrives on the awakening of each independent moral agent. People, he believed, are natural moral agents who are personally "capable of implementing and participating in modern politics" (能自布政治).[107] Instead of submitting oneself to what the institutional construct defines as right, these self-governing agents should stay faithful to their moral instinct and do *what is right*.

Liang was determined to replace Zhu Xi's moral theory with the teachings of Wang Yangming in China's transition to political modernity. Having repudiated Zhu Xi from the philosophical position shared by Buddhism, Kant, and Wang Yangming, Liang seemed to have located a moral and metaphysical foundation for his political reformism. But still, how can we be sure that Wang Yangming's moral teachings are reliable and true? To attest that man is indeed the living presence of the cosmos, Liang presented what I consider a definitive piece of argument from Kant: as a rational agent, man is naturally obliged to fulfill his moral duty. As a person performs a good deed, he does not do it *for any further, external reason*. To do what is right is unconditional. It is an end in itself. Unlike "hypothetical imperatives," which are commands that hold only if certain conditions are met, the moral law presents us with categorical imperatives.

To clarify the difference between "categorical imperative" and "hypothetical imperative," let me give an example: on a cold winter day, you want to warm yourself with a cup of hot coffee. Before you enter a convenience store, there is a homeless person shivering outside. Should you get him some coffee too? I believe so. But is this virtuous act an expression of your natural moral propensity, or your intention to be good for the deliberate purpose of being so? A hypothetical imperative, simply put, is about a person who does *x* for reason *y*. He is "goal-directed." Since action *x* is dependent on reason *y*, the behavior is "conditional" (*you suowei* 有所為). Liang summarizes Kant's theory in the following words: "if a person does a moral good to achieve some further ends, what appears to be a moral action is 'a means' of achieving that particular

74 | Affective Betrayal

purpose" (為手段而求達他之目的者也。意曰: 必如此乃足以達而目的, 不然則否也).[108] "This action has nothing to do with being moral" (有所為之命令與道德犛然無涉也).[109] In contrast to "hypothetical imperatives," categorical imperatives denote an absolute, unconditional requirement that must be obeyed in all circumstances and are justified as ends in themselves. Saddened by the sight of a homeless person shivering in the snow, my heart aches. The outpouring of everything good in me is a natural impulse I cannot control. Knowing that I did not do *x for y*, my moral action is "unconditional" (*wu shuowei* 無所為).

As a rational agent, a person, Kant says, is predisposed to experience the world through the mediation of his a priori intuition. Being a physical object, or a "thing-in-itself," that exists in this universe, the conditions of a priori reasoning do not come from the outside; they are the constitutive principles of the universe revealing the way a person is made as a "physical being." Under the instruction of the categorical imperative, a person existing as a living presence of the law of the universe is predisposed to fulfill his natural moral duties. The moral obligations that a person feels compelled to obey are not being imposed upon him from external sources; since the law comes from within rather than without, man, from start to finish, is restricted by *his own law*. To submit oneself to the categorical imperative is not about obeying any social, political, or moral order being imposed upon him from the outside. It is about following a priori intuitions that inform one's moral and logical reasoning. Since the fulfilment of man's obligation is not dependent upon any reason, or directed toward any designated purposes, it is an end in itself. *To be*, once again, *is to be good*.

In his moral theory, Zhu Xi claimed that man's cosmic heartmind is contaminated by tarnished *qi* substances, causing people to lose their moral nature and deviate from *li* the cosmic principles. Having familiarized himself with Kantian ethics, Liang repudiates Zhu Xi's proposition with the following words:

> When Zhu Xi spoke of man's heavenly moral nature, he had failed to note that one's personal nature is in fact one body with everything else in the universe. His theory is no match for that of the Buddha. Zhu Xi, in addition, asserted that one's heavenly moral nature is trapped by *qi* substances and blocked by the human desire. Such a remark exposes his failure to distinguish the difference "I-in-myself" that is free and "I-as-appearance" that is not free. Zhu Xi was also no

match for Kant. For Kant, "I-as-myself" cannot be fettered or inhabited by *other* objects. What can be shackled and suppressed is not free. 若朱子之說明德，既未能指其為一體之相，是所以不逮佛也。又說此明德為氣禀所拘，人欲所蔽，其於自由之真我，與不自由之現象我，界限未能分明。是所以不逮康德也。康德之意，謂真我者，決非他物所能拘能蔽也。能拘蔽則是不自由也。[110]

Man's cosmic moral nature, Zhu Xi said, is obscured, shackled, and eventually buried by errant physical substances that are "*outside*" of him. In reality, however, a person is not good *for* a reason. To be good is to follow the *li* of which I am made. Since there is no deliberate purpose to speak of, *li* is not oriented toward any particular destination. When there has *never* been an end to begin with, there is no way that can be blocked, or a course, standard, or principle be deviated from. Men seek for moral principles that are outside of themselves. But knowing that the law and order that command his moral action is the way that he is made, there is no, nor can there be any, *li* that exists *outside* of us. When there is no fixed course of learning, what is there to be learned? Knowing that what appears to have restricted a person is the law and order of which he is made, the person is not restricted by any law and order that is outside of him. "My true self, for this reason, is and will always be free" (故知真我必常自由).[111] Liang concluded Kant's position with the following passage:

> The one who does evil and good is the "I" as a corporeal being and as an appearance. The one who knows that he ought to do what is right and remove what is wrong, it is the me of my soul, or I as my true-self. Since it is I-in-myself [instead of another] who has assigned me my moral obligation upon my heart, it can be sure that my true self is always free. 為善為惡者，肉體之我也，現象之我也。知善之當為，知惡之當去者，靈魂之我也，真我也。以真我能以道德之責任臨命於吾心故，故知真我必常自由。[112]

Just One Push

Between 1901 and 1903, Liang Qichao's definition of democratic governance underwent drastic transformation. Before we proceed to explore the full complexities of his political reformism in the following chapters, it may be possible to generalize his preliminary understanding of democracy as the contractual relationship the state and the people enjoy as described in Jean-Jacques Rousseau's *The Social Contract*. In "On Nationalistic Thought" (論國家思想), Liang asserts that a democratic government is composed of national citizens (*guomin* 國民) "with nationalistic thinking and are self-capable of implementing governmental order" (有國家思想，能自布政治).[113] In this state of governance, each national citizen enjoys his rights and is entitled to elect the government's legislative body, which proposes and adopts legal provisions that are favorable to the public. But the rights a national citizen retains are not absolute. For the person to execute his rights, he is compelled to fulfill his obligation to the government by observing and obeying the law and order stipulated by the state. While a national citizen governs the constitution of the government, he is at the same time being governed *by* it. The same principle applies to the government, which attains its right to exist and to govern by "the consent of the governed." Modern democratic politics rests precisely on the subtle balance of power between these two parties.

Men, as Kant and Wang Yangming argued, are predisposed to be moral. Liang Qichao intended to bring up a new generation of national citizens who are "self-capable" of implementing the governmental order. By emphasizing that man is naturally capable of establishing law and order, Liang insisted that law and order are the ways a person is made. If one is made to follow the law, be it moral, perceptual, or analytical, he is following only the deep, underlying structure of his own mind.

The conjunction Liang made between human morality and political modernity raises the following questions: What makes man's natural "moral" instinct *political*? How can the natural "moral" order, be it *li* or a priori *categories*, be translated into a modern "political" order? And how can one possibly turn man's "radical moral freedom" and "modern political concepts" into a codependent relationship? Liang offered a simple, elegant answer: the categorical imperative, or a person being driven by the imperative need to fulfill one's natural moral duty, is the highest and best form of "political" order. This is *meant to be* the moral and philosophical foundation upon which democratic governance is based. The moral and the political are two sides of the same coin; they cannot be separated. For man, the natural moral being, to be a self-sufficient modern political agent, what is needed is not indoctrination by factual knowledge outside of him, but removing the artificial boundary that divides man's moral nature from his political duty.

For Liang, morality is "one" with the primordial body of being (道德之一本體). If there is such a thing as morality, "private morality" and "public morality" are not terms that stand in contrast to each other. Rather, they are terms that complement one another" (私德與公德, 非對待之名詞, 而相屬之名詞也).[114] "If a person knows private virtue but not public virtue, he only has to apply his personal goodness in one push" (知私德而不知公德, 所缺者只在一推.)[115] So what does "one push" (*yitui* 一推) stand for? How exactly can one "push" the natural "moral" law to become the constitutional "political" law? In particular, how did the indigenous Chinese philosophical, moral, intellectual tradition (and its continuing development between the mid-seventeen and the early nineteenth century) shape these challenges and offer opportunities to respond to them? To answer these questions, we now turn to the next chapters.

Chapter 2

Reclaiming Qing Philology to Recover the Innate Moral Order

In the Qing dynasty, China's intellectual climate was under the heavy influence of "evidential research" (*kaozheng xue* 考證學), an academic practice seeking to clarify interpretative obscurities that prevailed in Confucian classics with sophisticated philological investigative methods. Toward the mid-nineteenth century, modern political concepts such as "nationalism," "liberty," and "equality" were imported to the country. Having spent years of their careers pursuing a "text-based" approach to knowledge, intellectuals who had grown accustomed to deciphering the Confucian classics began to examine these new concepts as "objects" of scholarly investigation. To Liang Qichao, the political reformer who aspired to direct China's transition from imperial monarchy to democratic governance, what China lacked in the modernization process was not familiarity with Western knowledge but the critical reflexivity to make sense of it. As Liang looked back at the development of Qing intellectual history, later practitioners of Qing evidential research had exhausted themselves debating over trivial details such as differences between the words and expressions of texts, or comparisons between the exact years and months (本朝考據家之疲舌戰於字句之異同, 鉤心角於年月之比較).[1] Absent of moral intent and emotional engagement, these pedantic scholars "toyed around" (*wannong* 玩弄) with modern political concepts either as "catchphrases" (*koutouchan* 口頭禪) or as vehicles to display their erudition.[2] In China, Liang declared, there had never been a shortage of new "knowledge" (*zhishi* 智識).[3] While myriad forms of "foreign scholarly thinking" and "Western material civilization" were imported to the country,[4] the arrival of new knowledge had yet to bring people much-needed "wisdom" (*zhihui* 智慧).[5] Those who have appointed themselves the task of importing Western culture, "they may well convert their blind, slavish respect for the ancient sages to a form of slavishness that worships the foreigners and distains people of our own race" (崇拜古人之奴隸性, 而復生出一種崇拜外人, 蔑視本族之奴隸性).[6]

Commenting further on his contemporaries' learning habits, Liang said, "These days, those who expose themselves to new learning and the study of Western classics, they have picked up mostly the formal substance but renounced the spirit" (今所謂涉獵新學, 研究西書者, 亦大率取其形質遺其精神).[7] In China, "as the more available knowledge becomes, the more well-versed and knowledgeable slaves and traitors will be" (夫使一個增若干之學問, 隨即增若干有學問有知識之漢奸奴隸).[8] Having compared textual knowledge to a material object (*wu* 物), Liang asserted that the Chinese scholars' obsession with the text was a matter of "losing one's intent in finding amusement with things" (*wanwu sangzhi* 玩物喪志).[9]

Disheartened by his contemporaries' intellectual hypocrisy and their obsession with "empty words" (*kongyan* 空言), in 1902 Liang began to serialize his *Discourse on the New Citizen* (*Xinmin shuo* 新民說) in *New Citizen Journal* (*Xinmin congbao* 新民叢報).[10] Liang started with a bold question: "For decades our country speaks about the implementation of reformist measures. And yet the results do not seem apparent. How is it so?" (吾國言新法數十年而效不睹者何也)?[11] In "On Public Morality" (*Lun gongde* 論公德), one of his most extensively studied articles, the reformer inserted a brief interlinear comment trying to discern what has contributed to China's immediate impasse.[12] Printed in a font two-thirds the size of the rest of the text, the passage conveys a view that transcends the political reformism Liang was conventionally associated with:

> For recent scholar officials who express support for reform, they call for everything new but dare not to speak about *new morality*. This is because the *slavishness* of the scholarly community cannot be removed, and that the people's love for the nation, the community, and the *truth* remains insincere. 今世士夫談維新者, 諸事皆言新, 惟不敢言新道德。此由學界奴性未去, 愛國愛群愛真理之心未誠也。[13]

In the comment above, Liang subtly included "new morality" (*xin daode* 新道德) as part of the general newness (*xin* 新). Such inclusion presents his famous question about China's political modernization: How can the country go beyond material, physical newness and become spiritually and ideologically modern?[14] While people in the West, Liang argued, were competent in self-governance, the Chinese were deficient in "morality" (*minde* 民德), "intellectual courage" (*minzhi* 民智), and "physical power" (*minli* 民力).[15] Considering "public morality" (*gongde* 公德) the quality that was most desperately needed, Liang attributed the lack of it to China's academic slavishness.[16] For him, only by returning to one's perceptual consciousness could a person "break away from the intellectual slavishness of China's academic practice" (破學界之奴性是也), and make modern political reform *truly* and *thoroughly* possible.[17]

Liang made the lack of public morality the "result" of a cause instead of a "cause" in itself. For so long, his promotion of people's morality, intellectual courage, and physical power has been taken as a critique of the general deficiencies of the Chinese.[18] Instead of perceiving improvement in these aspects as a means to facilitate China's political transition, I argue that the "political" reform Liang launched at the turn of the twentieth century transcends the political. It is an all-inclusive internal "intellectual-moral-political" movement that seeks to transform Chinese intellectuals' learning habits, the factional divide that separated contentious schools of learning, and ultimately the founding principles of the Qing dynasty's state intellectual practice.

Such a reading, seemingly an overinterpretation, points to larger patterns in Liang's reformist project. In the early 1900s, Liang was keen to complement the "learning" (*xue* 學) of language with "intuitive understanding." To accomplish this goal, he made various stylistic and representational inventions to promote an alternative method of knowledge acquisition. In his "new prose style" (*xin wenti* 新文體), for instance, Liang presented translated modern political concepts in a highly rhapsodic rhythm. Through amplifying the musicality of language, he let the aesthetic pleasure of listening expedite the transmission of modern political concepts at the occasional expense of their semantic consistency. As Liang launched *New Fiction* (*Xin xiaoshuo* 新小說) in 1902, he contextualized a similar set of political key words in a visually and acoustically animated fictional landscape. The remediation of "words" into visual terms invited readers to perceive the political modern in its virtual immediacy rather than through discursive definition.

Through amplifying the musicality, visuality, and affective appeal of language, Liang made the reception of modern political knowledge an experience predicated on rational reflexivity as well as on one's embodied aesthetic ambivalence. While the invention of his "new prose style" and "new fiction" marked an attempt to implement an epistemic shift in late Qing China, Liang indicated that his stylistic endeavors were by no means a quintessentially novel idea for China; it was in fact the collective moral-political aspiration that practitioners of a small number of "early" Qing evidential researchers saw themselves defending between the mid-seventeenth and early eighteenth centuries. By directing man's attention to his introspective speculation of Confucian classics, these "early" Qing scholars, whether consciously or unconsciously, were to question, challenge, and ultimately replace the prescriptive moral order sanctioned by the state with man's a priori moral intuition. In the last twenty years of his life, Liang persisted in making an unconventional claim that prompts us to rethink our conception of Qing intellectual history: Assuming that the organization of man's heartmind (*xin* 心) is in perfect agreement with *li* 理 the cosmic pattern, Wang Yangming representing the "Learning of the Mind" school (*xinxue* 心學) of neo-Confucianism, believed that human beings are endowed with *liangzhi* (良知), the "good moral knowing."[19] Being a functional extension of the heartmind, *liangzhi* operates as a built-in, premeditated moral censor or detector. When a person responds to external stimuli, immediately and automatically his "good moral knowing" *discerns* good from evil (知善知惡是良知).[20] If Wang's moral teachings are about recovering man's natural moral endowment and liberating people from the normative moral and social conventions being imposed upon them from without, his personal defiance, as Liang argued, had resurrected in perhaps the most unlikely venue, which was the "early" development of Qing evidential research.[21] "Early" practitioners of Qing evidential research who lived immediately after Wang Yangming *did not* return to the Confucian classics to learn about moral principles. On the contrary, by confronting and contesting prescriptive moral doctrines claimed to be asserted by these classics with one's a priori intuition, they were to liberate people from the confines of prescriptive moral doctrines and let man's a priori moral order be the foundation upon which a looming modern, democratic political order is based. What we have conventionally perceived as a protest against the blind faith neo-Confucian thinkers invested in the omnipotence of the heartmind was in reality a continuation and ultimately completion and perfection of this train of thought.[22] And this time, not only did practitioners of "early" Qing evidential research exercise the native cognitive and moral proposition informed by *liangzhi,* but they also learned to verify the accurateness of such propositions with a systematic set of "scientific research methods" (科學研究方法).[23]

Introspective Speculation or Factual Accuracy?

Liang perceived his stylistic endeavor as an attempt to restore a revolutionary intellectual, moral, and political breakthrough that had been misinterpreted and misunderstood by later practitioners of Qing evidential researchers. As the reformer shifted readers' attention from "text" to their affective engagement *with* text, he was to recover the true meaning of Qing evidential research and to restructure the previous three hundred years of Chinese intellectual history by directing this pioneering but poorly executed intellectual movement back onto the right path.

For readers with general knowledge of Qing intellectual history, I seem to be making an argument that is blatantly, if not outrageously, wrong. Toward the end of the Ming dynasty, as it is generally known, the unwarranted faith Wang Yangming invested in the omnipotence of the heartmind anticipated widespread social and moral nuisances.[24] Having experienced the fall of the Ming dynasty, many early Qing scholars refused to tolerate their contemporaries' indulgence in empty metaphysical contemplation. To retrieve the teachings of the early Confucian sages before they were infiltrated by the advent of Buddhist metaphysics and neo-Confucianism, these individuals looked to return to the study of Confucian classics and a pertinent body of secondary scholarship conceived around the time of the Han 漢 dynasty (202 BC—220 AD). Knowing that these scholars lived nearly two thousand years away from antiquity, they could no longer determine the semantic definition of the words of the Sage or the moral principles (*yili* 義理) the words conveyed. To "attain the truth of meanings and principles" (*de yizhi zhi zhen* 得義理之真) and "bring order to all under heaven" (*zhi tianxia* 治天下),[25] they soon adopted investigative approaches such as paleography, phonology, and etymology as "instruments" and "weapons" to get to "the big ideas" that rested outside of them.[26] This rise of this nationwide restoration movement is known as "Han learning" (*Hanxue* 漢學), which has often been considered a protest against neo-Confucianism, or "Song learning" (*Songxue* 宋學), a philosophical movement devoted to the discussion of abstract moral principles.

Compared with neo-Confucian thinkers, who prioritized man's moral intuition over the objective investigation of facts, it is generally assumed that practitioners of Qing evidential research sought to recover moral prescriptions the early Sages delineated in the Confucian classics. Liang Qichao, however, was unconvinced by the received narrative. In an attempt to clarify what he perceived to be the "true" spirit of Qing evidential research and pitch the epistemic shift he launched at the turn of the twentieth century as both a revival and a restoration of this misconstrued intellectual movement, Liang returned to the origin of this burgeoning intellectual trend and positioned Gu Yanwu 顧炎武 (1613–1682) as the "founder of Qing learning" (清學之祖).[27]

Wang Yangming, as mentioned earlier, believed that men are endowed with *liangzhi*. As long as a person can stay focally connected with his natural moral instinct, his spontaneous responses will unfold in accordance with the heavenly principles. Gu Yanwu was famous for his denunciation of Wang Yangming's moral teachings. To Gu, Wang's teachings were sheer heresy (*xieshuo* 邪說).[28] "From the past to present," Gu protested, "how could there be such thing as the 'Learning of Principle'? The 'Learning of the Classics' *is* the 'Learning of Principle.'"[29] To acknowledge Gu's renowned critique of the "mind-based" approach to moral knowledge, Liang said,

> In his [Gu Yanwu's] understanding, what we have generally perceived as the philosophy of life (nature) or the principle of the universe (the heavenly way) has manifested itself dispersedly in the structural patterns of literary composition or the affairs of things. For those of us who are engaged in scholarly research, it is of paramount importance to stay objective and be attentive to these patterns and structures. The more exhaustive and thorough, the better. This is what it means by "broadening learning through the study of literary patterns." 其意以為，所謂人生哲學(性)，所謂宇宙原理(天道)，都散寄於事物條理(文章)之中。我們做學問，最要緊是用客觀工夫，講求事物條理，越詳博越好，這便是"博學於文"。[30]

Followers of Wang Yangming looked to the heartmind as the source of moral knowledge. Instead of perceiving *li* as a form of metaphysical abstraction waiting to be discovered in man's meditative contemplation, Gu Yanwu considered *li* the "organizational structure" (*tiaoli* 條理) that *presents itself* in the arrangement of the Confucian classics. Assuming that the heavenly pattern has disclosed itself in the structural organization of the Confucian classics, Gu intended to reclaim *li* from the "cosmic endowment" a person personified in his heartmind to the "organizational structure" of text. Gu stated, "There was no 'Learning of Principles' except the 'Learning of the Classics.' The truth can be recovered only directly from the classics" (舍經學無理學, 真直接反求之於古經).[31] To discern the ideal order being manifested in the Confucian classics, a person must shift his attention from empty metaphysical speculation to the careful, exhaustive inspection of the text. The more scrupulous, unbiased, and extensively learned a person was, the more possible he was able to detect and recognize the moral principles being exhibited in the words of the sages.

Gu Yanwu announced his decision about "searching for the truth" (*qiuzhen* 求真) through the investigation of Confucian classics. While his announcement had often been interpreted as a critique against the uninhibited faith Wang Yangming placed in the primacy of the heart-mind, Liang hesitated to interpret his statement verbatim. To uncover subversive implications that transcend Gu Yanwu's personal awareness, Liang encouraged us to rethink this particular piece of Chinese intellectual history from an epistemic point of view: practitioners of Qing evidential research intended to recover the moral knowledge prescribed in the Confucian classics. But Liang proceeded to question: Does man have "direct" access to moral knowledge? If a person is to obtain a philosophical principle, where exactly does it lie? Can moral meanings be located in the "text" per se, or in a person's subjective and introspective reflection *of* the text?

Man, as Liang explicated in his introduction to Immanuel Kant's transcendental idealism, can cognize only objects that he can, in principle, intuit.[32] Being a rational agent in possession of practical reason, a person is endowed with multiple pairs of a priori lenses affixed in his mind. These a priori lenses consist of several distinct but intersecting forms of sensible intuition. As a person comes into contact with physical reality, he is predisposed to perceive the world through the a priori spectacles that frame his perspectives of seeing and organize those disconnected pieces of information in keeping with the analytical categories such as the sense of time, space, causality, contingency, parts and whole, and so on that constitute his cognitive reasoning. Not having any direct access to physical objects as entities in themselves, whatever the person sees, feels, and experiences exhibits the characteristics that deal with the geometry of space, the deterministic order of time, and other causal and logical structures.

Kant's epistemology applies to all forms of cognition. Knowing that a person can have determinate cognition of the world only as it is being perceptually experienced from the a priori conditions that frame his perspectives of seeing, not of anything independent of the basic structures, it appears to Liang that man's reception of the Confucian classics was no exception.[33] Such conviction prompted him to conceive a subtle but radical reinterpretation of early Qing evidential research: man can have knowledge of an object only if it is possible for that object to be given an experience. Just as a person is inherently incapable of knowing an empirical object as a "thing-in-itself," he does not have any direct access to a Confucian classic as a "text-in-itself." When a person is presented with the words of the sages, he can decipher those words only from the mental apparatus that are programmed to organize the subject matter from the perspective of a preconfigured cognitive and perceptual structure. Gu Yanwu fiercely protested against Wang Yangming's moral teachings. For Liang, however, what Gu was *truly* concerned with was not the uninhibited moral faith Wang Yangming invested in the heartmind but the general public's unquestioned, unreflective, and often blind acceptance of his teachings. Being the founder of Qing evidential research, Gu, in other words, blamed people not for their indulgence in the heartmind but for their failure to engage *fully with it*. To uncover the nonconformist spirit that constituted the ethos of this burgeoning Qing intellectual movement, Liang readily aligned Gu's protest with his personal history, missives to friends, and scholarly writings on Confucian philosophy, government, economics, history, and phonology.

Toward the last half century of the Ming dynasty, as Liang recounted, the Wang Yangming school of neo-Confucianism began to gain increasing popularity and influence.[34] Very soon, the school replaced the study of the six classics to become the intellectual warlord (*xuefa* 學閥) of the times.[35] Enticed by the school's growing prestige, scholars who were apprehensive of the authority, according to Liang's interpretation, readily and compliantly accepted Wang's dominant intellectual position.[36] Having grown "indolently dependent" (*yibang* 依傍) on what had conventionally been accepted as the truth, those who looked for personal reputation (*haoming* 好名) were occupied by the need to "borrow the names and titles of the others" (*chengming jiehao* 稱名借號) and "mimic" (*mofang* 摹倣) these authoritative voices.[37] Gu, to quote from one of Liang's citations, asserted that "For men of the Ming period, the books that they had completed were nothing but plagiarism" (有明一代之人, 其所著書,

無非盜竊而已).³⁸ "The trouble with recent writings," Gu continued, "lies entirely in their imitativeness; even they bear uncanny resemblances to that of the ancients, they do not make a great contribution" (近代文章之病, 全在摹倣, 即使逼肖古人, 已非極詣).³⁹ In a letter to his friend, Gu accused the friend as follows: "The trouble with your poem is that it contains Du Fu, and the trouble with your essay is that it contains Han Yu and Ouyang Xiu. With these mental limitation in your heart, all through your life you can never be free from slavish dependence" (君詩之病, 在於有杜; 君文之病, 在於有韓歐; 有此蹊徑於胸中, 便終身不脫依傍).⁴⁰

In Liang's interpretation, Gu Yanwu's fierce endorsement of one's critical engagement *with* the text was reflected in the critique of his contemporaries as well as his personal scholarship. At a time when learned individuals looked up to the authority, Gu tried to deaden all noises to discover his individual voice. To accentuate the emphasis Gu placed on the display of one's "personal creativity" (*guichuang* 貴創), Liang turned to Gu's compilation of the *Record of Daily Knowledge* (*Rizhi lu* 日知錄).⁴¹ Similar to other learned scholars in Chinese history, Gu was well versed in the Confucian classics. Rather than trying to comprehend early ethical percepts under the guidance of the established scholarly interpretations, he was keen to obtain his enlightened understanding (*youde* 有得; *you suo de* 有所得).⁴² To ensure that his contributions were factually grounded, plausibly valid, and surpassed the views of the ancients, Gu often checked his interpretation against the extensive amount of secondary scholarship completed in previous historical eras.⁴³ Upon discovering that the ancients had articulated comparable views, he would not hesitate to omit this piece of thought. In praises of Gu's defense of man's creative spirit, Liang said, "Gu would discard his discoveries upon learning that they resonated with that of the early scholars, and not to speak of plagiarizing the others. . . . With his fierce endorsement, personally creativity had since become a tenant of scholars of the Qing dynasty" (然則雖自己所發明而與前人暗合者, 尚且不屑一顧, 何況剽竊. . . . 自亭林極力提倡此義, 遂成為清代學者重要之信條).⁴⁴ "The writings of Gu Yanwu," Liang continued, "did not contain a single point repeated or borrowed from the ancients."⁴⁵ In the hope of uncovering "the truth" that rested beneath the text, Gu "strived to imbue his scholarship with one's novel, sharp spirit" (*xinrui zhi jingshen* 新銳之精神).⁴⁶

Liang endorsed and celebrated Gu Yanwu's scholarship for its display of "novel, sharp spirit." But what exactly does "novel, sharp" spirit refer to, and how does a person "imbue" his research with it? How, in addition, can we draw a meaningful connection between man's "spirit" and his quest for the "truth"? Having situated Liang's usage of "reason" (*zhihui* 智慧) and "introspection" (*yishi* 意識) in his introduction to Bacon, Kant, and Buddhist metaphysics, it seems evident that by "spirit" (精神), Liang was referring specifically to the application of one's a priori intuition.[47]

In "The Theories of Two Great Precursors of Modern Civilization," an essay Liang devoted to the comparison between Francis Bacon (1561–1626) and René Descartes (1596–1650), he began by identifying some fine but profound differences between two concepts: *zhishi* 智識 (knowledge, or inductive reasoning) and *zhihui* 智慧 (reason). Knowledge, according to Liang's summary of Bacon, is based on "verifications derived from the empirical examination of the material given" (驗諸實物而有所徵).[48] It is "the expressions of matters and things" (*jian shuli zhe* 見事理者).[49] Descartes, on the contrary, disapproved of the emphasis Bacon placed on empirical observation. In his critique of Bacon, Descartes compares knowledge to a mirror that "clearly reflects the matter's manifested surface" (*ming xian yu qian zhe* 明現於其前者) but fails to reveal "what has yet been manifested" (*wei xiang lai zhe* 未現來者) and "what is manifested but unclear" (*xian er bushen ming zhe* 現而不甚明者). Since the mirror displays only what appears on the surface, Descartes, as Liang put it, considers "knowledge a confined zone that is limited and narrowed" (智識之區域本甚狹而有所限制).[50] Being the cause of every misapprehension, it is hence "unreliable" (*buke chi* 不可持) and leads one "astray from the truth" (失真 *shi zhen*).

In contrast to "knowledge," which easily leads to delusion (易生迷妄), Liang argues that Descartes perceives introspection (*yishi*) as "a wide and free-ranged terrain enjoying unlimited possibilities" (區域甚博且自由而無限者也).[51] Knowing that knowledge presents only the superficial surface (*xiang* 相), what is "true" transcends the material given (外物之真相).[52] To uncover such truth, a person must activate his introspection, or the "subjective freedom that distinguishes itself in one's spirit" (精神中則別有自由者存). Through self-reflecting on and speculating about (*zi shen zi yi* 自審自疑) the factual given with such critical "spirit" (*jingshen*), a person can then discern what is obscured and concealed.[53] To Liang, the best way to preserve and exercise such introspective prowess was to be consistently suspicious (*yi* 疑) about conventional wisdom.[54] Aside from discerning the truth, the exercise of critical introspection promises a person the preservation of one's individual freedom (是以之故, 我得保其自由).[55]

Given the background of Liang's discussions of Bacon, Descartes, and Kant, the "truth" was a form of certitude that transcended the superficial surface.[56] To conduct evidential research, in this sense, was to prioritize reason over knowledge, and to critically reflect on and interrogate conceptual bookish knowledge with man's critical introspection. As Gu Yanwu embarked on his "quest for truth," he had awakened a form of subjective awareness that transcended if not contradicted the verification of factual truth.

Scholarship Powered by Blood and Guts

Between the reigns of Emperor Shunzhi 順治 (1644–1661) and Emperor Kangxi 康熙 (1662–1722), the Qing empire suppressed high-minded scholars with pressure and conciliatory policies. As many Ming loyalists faced criminal prosecution, they had no choice but to retreat to the world of quiet scholarly pursuit. It was true that Gu Yanwu directed his attention to the critical introspection of Confucian classics. But being a Ming loyalist striving to resist the tyrannical suppression at a precarious historical juncture, what does it mean to inspect canonical Confucian doctrines with "reason"? Liang answered that sharing the ardent wish to prepare for the construction of new politics, Gu Yanwu and early practitioners of Qing evidential research did not conduct scholarly research for scholarship's sake; they undertook scholarly work *for* the sake of politics (他們不是為學問而學問, 是為政治而學問).[57] Under the instruction of Emperor Wu of Han 漢武帝 (156–87 BC), the six classics had always been considered a symbol of state power (*shili* 勢力) and authority (*quanwei* 權威).[58] Being the time-honored doctrines that shaped China's political atmosphere, these texts constituted the religious conviction of the times (一時之信仰), and had consistently been seen and worshipped as holy texts that could not be infringed.[59] For more than a thousand years, scholars and students living throughout China studied these texts.[60] Although individuals were free to make reference to the six Confucian classics, they were not encouraged to engage with these sacred writings in a critical fashion. The trend, however, reversed following the presence of Gu Yanwu. Being determined to examine, scrutinize, and analyze the Confucian classics with scrupulous care, Gu treated the holy book as "objects" of investigation. His decision was itself a transgressive act anticipating civil disobedience and a radically novel form of power dynamics.

Being endowed with a priori intuition, a rational agent, as said earlier, is predisposed to organize scattered pieces of information in a meaningful or logical sequence. The reasoning faculty informs moral judgment and gives one the ethical compulsion to fulfill his moral obligation. The conception of a priori intuition in Kant's epistemology, as Liang argued, is fundamentally the same as *liangzhi* the good moral knowing.[61] Upon seeing the prescriptive moral doctrines, a person, spurred by this irresistible moral impulse residing inside of him, is enabled by his cognitive and perceptual faculty to confront the Confucian classics and relevant scholarship. That is, by scrutinizing, interrogating, challenging, and potentially repudiating the authoritative moral order with a person's a priori instinct, the undertaking of Qing evidential research signaled the engagement of an introspective mind in a dialectic conversation with the classics, and by extension a man's "active" search for moral meaning. As scholars of early Qing evidential research looked to antiquity, what had conventionally been perceived as an intellectual practice was not an empirical investigation of Confucian literature but a dialectic competition between, if not collision of, two sets of law: one being the prescriptive moral doctrines stipulated by the Confucian Sages, expounded by state interpreters, and sanctioned by authority, and the other is one's a priori intuition, the natural moral order endowed in a person's heartmind and informed by *li* the all-pervasive cosmic patterns.

As Gu Yanwu scrutinized early Confucian scholarship, the active engagement *of* his speculative spirit revised and reversed man's relationship with the text. Rather than looking at the "text-in-itself," his undertaking of early Qing evidential research exemplified man's "introspective speculation" *of* Confucian literature. Being an "object" of investigation, a Confucian text descended from a holy book to become the "target of speculation" enabling the exercise of man's critical *self*-reflexivity. In reality, the Ming loyalists were unable to defy the state in political protests. To free oneself from the shackles and obtain one's ultimate liberation, a person was left with the viable option of battling with the holy books that symbolized state authority. The introspective speculation of Confucian classics then presented perhaps the best arena for showcasing an embodied moral combat between the natural moral law endowed by heaven and the authoritative political order sponsored by the state. *Kaozheng* is an intellectual movement seeking to investigate, verify, and potentially find flaws with the classics. Those who participated in "early" Qing evidential research did not return to the Confucian classics to evade political censorship; they, in contrast, were *there* to interrogate, challenge, and repudiate the state sanctioned authoritative moral order with man's natural ethical order. It was only through the active engagement of the mind can a person replace the state orthodox to become the ultimate source of moral authority that was to guide and direct a new conception of governmental and legislative order.

To unearth Gu Yanwu's rebellious spirit and his fellow practitioners' display of collective resistance, Liang was keen to identify the affective moral force that had subtly transformed into a form of introspective prowess that propelled the development of early Qing evidential research. In a collective historical biography devoted to Gu Yanwu, Huang Zongxi 黃宗羲 (1610–1695), Wang Fuzhi 王夫之 (1619–1692), Liu Jizhuang 劉繼莊 (1648–1695), and Yan Yuan 顏元 (1635–1704), Liang called these early practitioners of Qing evidential research the "five gentlemen" (*wu xiansheng* 五先生) who facilitated China's transition from its old to the new learning practices.[62] The collapse of the Ming dynasty brought them "a level of the pain that was unprecedentedly intense and deep."[63] Stoutly refusing to submit to the Manchurian rule, Gu Yanwu assisted the former Ming prince in staging an insurrection which eventually failed in 1668. Knowing that he could not nurture the moral sprout into full bloom, Gu Yanwu began his nomadic wandering in distress. The rest of the four gentlemen displayed comparable forms of defiance.

Gu and the rest of the gentlemen felt personally obliged to do what was good for the prosperity of their homeland. Charged with ferocious vigor, these "gentlemen of blood and guts" (*xuexing zhi junzi* 血性之君子) were faithful to their natural impulse rather than to the prescriptive moral doctrines. Instead of returning to antiquity to learn from the Confucian sages, their engagement with evidential research symbolized a civil protest that strove to defend one's moral, and ultimately political, autonomy at a time of extreme hegemonic oppression. Of these five gentlemen, some were famous for their fierce opposition to Wang Yangming's moral teachings. To Liang, however, their bitter hostility against Wang Yangming marked precisely a living embodiment of Wang's antagonistic spirit.[64] "The gentlemen might have denied it in person" (也許他們自己不認), but their commitment to the development of "early" Qing evidential research was "reared and bred from the motherly chest of Wang Yangming's teaching" (從陽明學派這位母親的懷裡哺養出來).[65] It was evident that the five gentlemen constituted an oppositional force objecting to Wang Yangming's "mind-based" approach to moral learning (故謂五先生為王學之反動力可也). But at the same time, it is also fair to consider "Wang's teaching the driving force that propelled these five gentlemen [and in turn the development of Qing evidential research] forward" (故謂五先生以王學為原動力可也).[66]

Qing Evidential Research: "Learning" or "Repudiation *of* Learning"

In *Chinese Intellectual History in the Last Three Hundred Years*, Liang declared, "Even if early Qing scholars detested the Wang Yangming school of neo-Confucianism, we must be able to acknowledge the spirit and influence that they inherited from his school of teaching" (那時候的學者，雖厭惡陽明學派，我們卻應該從這裡頭認取陽明派的價值).[67] Qing evidential research had never been a standardized school of practice, and Liang's drastic reinterpretation of this scholarly movement opens us up to its contested and involuted nature. To probe further into the disagreements that divided antithetical schools of Qing evidential research, let us return to the debate between Dai Zhen 戴震 (1727–1777) and Qian Daxin 錢大忻 (1728–1804). Knowledgeable about history, etymology, mathematics, astrology, geography, and linguistics, Dai Zhen and Qian Daxin were deemed two of the most broadly learned scholars of their times. Although the two examined a comparable group of early Confucian scholarship and deciphered these texts with a highly comparable set of investigative methods, their concerns and approaches to learning were directly opposite. I will begin with Dai Zhen's method and concern.

The organization of this universe, as neo-Confucian thinkers claimed, reveals a certain structural perfection known as *li*. Having received one's cosmic endowment from heaven, a person epitomizes the cosmic patterns in his heartmind. In the teachings of Cheng Hao 程顥 (1032–1085) and Zhu Xi 朱熹 (1130–1200), the two, to quote the words of Dai Zhen, spoke of *li* as if it were a "thing," or a predetermined set of dogmatic patterns affixed in a person's heartmind.[68] As people displayed wayward desires or performed evil deeds, thinkers associated with the Zhu Xi school of neo-Confucianism often accused them of deviating from the cosmic patterns of which they were made. Dai Zhen fiercely disagreed with these moral accusations. The connection that neo-Confucian thinkers drew between *li* and man's heartmind, Dai argued, was most problematic. Instead of a positive incentive that promoted moral goodness, such connection had grown into an oppressive force that denied and distorted man's pristine human nature. "Just as ruthless officials commit murders with legal commandment," Dai said, "neo-Confucian thinkers killed people with *li* the cosmic patterns."

Dai Zhen was interested in exploring the meaning of *li* and the dubious connection neo-Confucian thinkers drew between *li* and man's heartmind. To intervene in an unfinished philosophical debate, Dai employed philology, phonology, and textual glosses as investigative tools to pursue his "philosophical" enquires.[69] In the fifteen pieces of annotations published in *An Evidential Study of the Meaning of Terms of the Mengzi* (*Mengzi ziyi shuzheng* 孟子字義疏證), Dai delivered a solid rebuttal of the neo-Confucian thinkers with credible evidence: in the work of Mencius, the Sage explicitly argued that *li* refers to commonalities, traits, tendencies, habits, norms, and patterns that people share *in common*. Rather than heavenly metaphysical perfection that transcends man's comprehension, *li* was a term that described rather than generating the unvarying norm (*buyi zhi ze* 不易之則) each and every of us display. The human "feelings and desires" (*qingyu* 情欲) were part and parcel *of* such norm. They could not be denied or suppressed, as certain neo-Confucian thinkers suggested.

Around the mid-eighteenth century, Dai Zhen and Qian Daxin worked as collaborators in the capital.[70] After reading Dai Zhen's recent study of Mencius, Qian Daxin disapproved of Dai's approach to knowledge for obvious reasons. Moral norms and principles (*yili*), Qian declared, were principles and guidance prescribed by the Confucian Sages, not the meditative mind waiting to be enlightened via empty metaphysical speculation. Those pursuing philology should seek to retrieve the lost or damaged integrity of the ancient texts, or its "primordial meanings" (*guyi* 古義).[71] Knowing that moral meanings and principles were manifested in solid facts (*shi* 實), only by getting hold of concrete evidence could one obtain the truth. Being the ultimate source of knowledge and moral authority, the moral principles the Confucian Sages prescribed were the higher, sacred principles that lay *outside* of us and transcended people's comprehension. People's indulgence in empty metaphysical contemplation triggered the fall of the Ming dynasty. To redirect people's attention from the "heartmind" to the "text," early Qing intellectuals had spent decades conceiving a meticulous set of philological investigative methods. Dai Zhen, however, betrayed the spirit of Qing evidential research. Rather than utilizing his expertise to decipher salient facts showed on the text, he abused this path of liberation to return to the aimless and empty speculation on heartmind.

In Qian Daxin's view, Dai Zhen defied the state practice to retreat to the imprisonment of the heartmind. Liang Qichao was disappointed by Qian's dismissal of Dai Zhen. To Liang, Qian's and the Qing intellectual community's collective denial of Dai Zhen's intellectual endeavor marked the watershed that had since divided the "mind-based" from the "text-based" approaches to knowledge. It was a move that had distracted and deviated Qing evidential research from its original purpose.

As Liang revisited the development of Qing intellectual history, he began by drawing a categorical distinction between these oppositional schools of Qing evidential research. Compared with early Qing "enlightenment thinkers" who "searched for the truth" (*qiuzhen* 求真), Qian Daxin, as Liang remarked, was solely interested in verifying the factual accuracy (*qiushi* 求實) prescribed in the classics.[72] Having exhausted himself with tedious research work that was absent of purpose, Qian and his counterparts were less concerned with "the truth" than with ensuring that the materials they examined were the "true" artifacts that had survived from the Han Dynasty. Having adopted a "text-based" approach to knowledge, these "cheap Confucian scholars" (*jianru* 賤儒) "conducted evidential research for the sake of conducting so and studied the Classics for the sake of studying so" (為考證而考證, 為經學而治經學).[73] Those who were obsessed with the verification of solid facts practiced Han learning and fell into the orthodox school (*zhengtong pai* 正統派) of Qing evidential research. Dai Zhen, however, was different. Instead of upholding the Confucian classics as the ultimate source of moral knowledge, Dai treated the writing of Mencius as an "object" of investigation, and inspected it with relentless curiosity, inquisitive spirit, and intellectual prowess. Having adopted a "mind-based" approach to knowledge, Dai Zhen, along with early Qing intellectuals such as Gu Yanwu and Hu Wei 胡渭 (1633–1714), epitomized the true spirit of Qing evidential research and represented the Enlightenment school (*qimeng pai* 啟蒙派) of Qing evidential research. These early intellectuals practiced Qing learning (*qingxue* 清學) rather than Han learning.[74]

Liangzhi's Introspective Speculation of the Text

Liang was known for his denunciation of Han learning. In *China's Philological Turn*, a monograph seeking to acknowledge the methodological

Reclaiming Qing Philology to Recover the Innate Moral Order | 95

and philosophical contributions Qian Daxin made to the development of Qing evidential research, Ori Sela voices his disagreement with Liang: "Confucian classics," to borrow Sela's citation of Qian Daxin, are "the words of sages" (經者, 聖人之言).[75] The meanings of each word were not restricted to particular stand-alone characters but were also extended from the character to a larger idea. For learning to be meaningful, "new valid knowledge had to be authorized or sanctioned by the past and by antiquity, with the 'mind' playing one part in a learning effort, not dictating or overriding it."[76] Qing evidential research, as Sela argues, was not a "purposeless" activity as Liang claimed. Perceiving the "quantum leap in philology" as an "intellectual campaign" seeking to recover the Way of being a Confucian (*Ru* 儒), Sela asserts that there was no genuine philosophy outside of philology, and true philology was always philosophical in nature.[77]

I agree with Ori Sela that Qing evidential research is a "philosophical" movement seeking to recover "moral" principles through the use of "philological" tools. But having examined the close connection Liang established between Kant's epistemology, the teachings of neo-Confucianism, and Qing intellectual history, I would like to probe into some seemingly trivial interpretative nuances: Qian Daxin perceived philology as the very method of philosophy. If philosophy is an approximation of *yili* (義理), the moral meanings or principles, what exactly does "philosophy" mean and from where can it be found? Does *yili* mean the teachings of the sages as prescribed in the Confucian classics, the "study" of a particular system of theoretical propositions, or a person's enlightened moral understanding of such propositions? Having spent years of his early adulthood pursing Qing evidential research, Liang was sharply aware that his contemporaries conducted philological investigation for the search of moral principles. But in his critique of Qian Daxin and his fellow practitioners of Han learning, perhaps Liang did not find philological investigation problematic for the same reason as that which Ori Sela might have assumed. The ostensibly similar but in fact distinct thematic concerns Sela and Liang share can be displayed in fig. 2.1.

Both Liang Qichao and Ori Sela consider Qing evidential research a "philosophical" movement seeking to recover "moral" principles through the use of "philological" tools. While Ori Sela believes that a person "learns" about moral principles through the study of the Confucian classics, Liang argues that to participate in Qing evidential research was to confront the early Confucian scholarship with one's introspective reasoning capacity embedded in his heartmind.

Figure 2.1. From where did moral knowledge derive? The mind or the text? *Source*: Created by the Author.

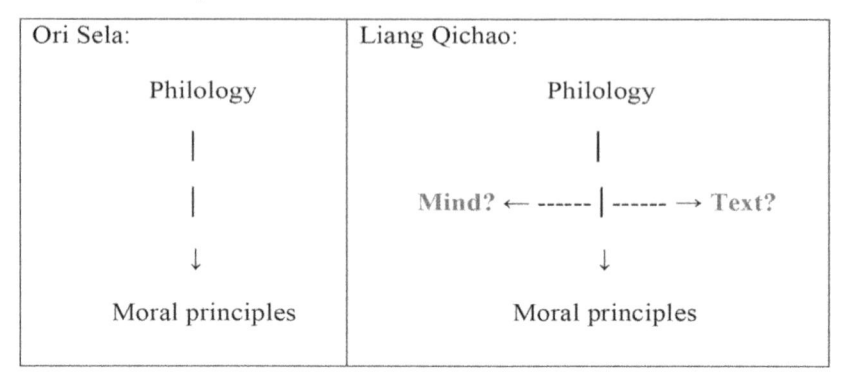

Ori Sela:	Liang Qichao:
Philology │ │ ↓ Moral principles	Philology │ Mind? ← ------ │ ------ → Text? ↓ Moral principles

Confucian classics have always been considered the source of moral knowledge. In his pioneering study on Tang-Song intellectual transition study, Peter Bol presents a compelling case illustrating how Chinese scholars of the Tang dynasty had succeeded in establishing their cultural identity and consolidating their power position through the mastery of Confucian discourse.[78] Coming to the Qing dynasty, the rekindled interested in the investigation of Confucian classics inspired Ori Sela to situate the "knowledge-identity-power" nexus Peter Bol identified in the development and maturation of Qing evidential research.[79] But having examined the elaborate case studies Liang presented in *Intellectual Trends of the Qing Period*, I am reminded of the words of the Greek philosopher Heraclitus (fl. c. 500 BCE): "No man ever steps in the same river twice, for it is not the same river and he is not the same man." The development of neo-Confucianism during the Song and the Ming dynasties inspired the creation of a systematic set of moral epistemology explicating the relationship between man's natural moral disposition and his cognitive function. But having experienced a philosophical sea change that accentuated the centrality of man, his moral agency, and cognitive capacity, it might be fair to question whether or not we can persist in treating the development of Qing evidential research as a continuation or repetition of Tang intellectual history.

To Ori Sela and Peter Bol, power was a source of authority obtained from learned familiarity with the Confucian classics. But having explicated Dai Zhen's and Gu Yanwu's "critical engagement" *with* the Confucian classics, it appears to Liang that the significance of early Qing evidential research rests in the opposite direction. Instead of seeking to recover moral principles from the Confucian classics, to participate in Qing evidential research was to confront the early Confucian scholarship with one's introspective reasoning. The "early" development of this intellectual movement manifested man's endeavor to liberate himself from the authoritative confines of the Confucian classics, and ultimately his attempt to replace the classics to be a subjective source of moral authority. A person, as Liang argued, did not obtain his cultural and moral identity through the mastery of the classics, but by questioning (*yi*) the credibility of the Confucian interpreters and rejecting and repudiating (*bu* 不; *fei* 非) the received Confucian scholarship through his critical interrogation.

A Copernican Revolution in Qing Evidential Research

With the speculative spirit they displayed, Gu Yanwu and Dai Zhen, as Liang argued, evolved from "passive" learners of the Confucian classics to "active" investigators of an "object" of research. In their scholarly practices, the reversal of position between man and text can perhaps be compared to what Immanuel Kant calls a "Copernican revolution of philosophy," a concept the German philosopher employed to emphasize the novelty of his epistemology. In his introduction to Kant, Liang recounted the German's philosopher's revolutionary spirit as follows: since the times of ancient Greece, philosophers in the West had perceived time and space as external properties that are outside of us.[80] For many centuries, they had persisted in questioning: What is the origin of space? When did time begin, and when would it disappear and cease? These questions laid the foundation upon which Western philosophy was based. The conception of Kant's mature epistemology reversed the course of the existing trajectory. Rather than tracing and demarcating the origins of time and space in empirical terms, Kant was interested in exploring from where people's "sense" of time and space arrive from. Man, as Kant suggests, can cognize only objects that he can, in principle, intuit. If an object "appears" to us as the way it is, its appearance is not determined solely by the object's physical properties per se but also by the a priori perceptual order that frames his perceptual point of view. Following the conception of Kant's transcendental idealism, no discussion of reality or knowledge could take place without the awareness of the role the human mind plays in the construction of knowledge and reality.

In Liang's revisit of the previous three hundred years of Qing intellectual history, it might appear to him that Gu Yanwu's and Dai Zhen's critical and introspective engagement *with* the Confucian classics resembled the Copernican revolution Kant heralded in the evolution of Western philosophy. To capture a form of investigative spirit comparable to that displayed by Dai Zhen in his scholarly investigation, Liang pointed us to a piece of his childhood anecdote. When Dai Zhen was a boy, he asked his tutor the following questions:

> "How do we know that those are the words of Confucius recorded by [his student] Zengzi? And how can we be sure that Zengzi's disciples had faithfully documented his words?" The tutor answered, "We learned it from the departed Confucian thinker Zhu Xi's annotation." Dai Zhen wondered, "When did Zhu Xi live?" "The Southern Song dynasty." Dai Zhen questioned further, "When did Confucius and Zengzi live?" The teacher responded, "The Eastern Zhou dynasty." Dai Zhen continued, "How many years are the Zhou and the Song dynasties away from each other?" "Nearly two thousand years." Dai went on to ask, "How, then, can Zhu Xi be certain about his claim?" Finally the tutor stood speechless. 此何以知為孔子之言而曾子述之? 又何以知為曾子之意而門人記之? 師應之曰: 此先儒朱子所注云爾。又問: 朱子何時人? 曰: 南宋。又問: 孔子、曾子何時人? 曰: 東周。又問: 周去宋幾何時? 曰: 幾二千年。又問: 然則朱子何以知其然? 師無以應。[81]

Dai Zhen was skeptical about the association that neo-Confucian thinkers drew between *li* the cosmic patterns and the heartmind. To clarify what *li* truly meant to Mencius, Dai turned to the Confucian classics. While Dai "claimed" to be fiercely critical of the unwarranted faith that neo-Confucian thinkers placed in the omnipotence of the heartmind, what distinguishes his academic practices, somewhat paradoxically, rests precisely in his display of relentless curiosity that promised to liberate his contemporaries from slavish conformity.[82] In Dai Zhen's conversation with his tutor, the tutor took the conventional wisdom as the unquestionable truth. Dai Zhen, on the contrary, was determined to liberate himself from all forms of dependence.[83] Liang argued that as trivial as the above anecdote may seem, it fully and faithfully captures the zeitgeist of Qing learning. In defense of his independent spirit, Dai Zhen declared:

> A scholar should be deluded neither by others nor by himself. . . . The idea of fame has two disadvantages: [it drives] one either to attack past men in order to exhibit himself, or to depend on ancient sages as props, in order to ride their coattails . . . what first enters his mind comes to dominate it and leads him astray for the rest of his life. Perhaps not all of his dependence on other is motivated solely by a desire of riding their coattails. Nevertheless, [in either case] although the mean motive may be absent, the evil consequence is just the same. 學者當不以人蔽己，不以己自蔽 . . . 有名之見，其弊二：非掊擊前人以自表襮，即依傍昔儒以附驥尾。先入為主而惑以終身；或非盡依傍以附驥尾，無鄙陋之心而失與之等.[84]

Dai Zhen and Qian Daxin expressed mutual dissatisfaction with neo-Confucian thinkers' fabrication and distortion of Confucian thinking. To bridge the vast historical, linguistic, and sociological sea change that had divided them from antiquity, the two looked to philology as an instrument to probe into the words, and possibly the intent, of the Confucian Sages. Dai and Qian, however, employed these instruments for nearly the opposite purposes. Perceiving the Confucian classics as the ultimate source of knowledge, Qian was chiefly interested in deciphering etymological and philological definitions of the words of the Sages. To him the "truth" *is* the "concrete fact." Dai Zhen, on the contrary, refused to accept anyone's conclusion without finding the evidence for it. In his praises of Dai Zhen, Liang said, "Dai often found flaws in places that others had neglected and, having found them, would press forward step by step until the point of exhaustion. If in the end he still could not find anything to warrant his confidence, then although they were the words of sages, philosophers, fathers, or teachers, he would not credit them."[85] To Liang, Dai Zhen was critically engaged *with* the Confucian classics. "Those who conduct scholarly investigation," as Dai Zhen announced, "face three kinds of challenges, which are the challenge of being broadly learned, the challenge of being critical, and the challenge of making incisive judgment. Among previous men of extensive learning and powerful memory, some overflowed their houses with their writing. But broadly learned as they were, hardly can they make any incisive judgment."[86]

Moral Intuition Verified by Science

Having identified affinities between the epistemologies of Wang Yangming and Kant, Liang Qichao perceived Qing learning as an intellectual exercise predicated on the application of man's a priori intuition. But having witnessed the widespread social and moral nuisances engendered by Ming intellectuals' indulgence in metaphysical contemplation, how can one be sure that man's a priori intuition is reliable? The heartmind that Wang Yangming deemed flawlessly perfect, after all, had gone wrong in reality. For Qing intellectuals who shared great enthusiasm for questioning the validity of Confucian classics, how can we be certain that the accusations they made were not false and unjust? Having observed the development of Qing intellectual evidential research between the mid-seventeenth and the mid-nineteenth centuries, Liang identified a possible solution: Beyond adopting a "mind-based" approach to knowledge, what makes this scholarly activity *truly* groundbreaking rests in its practitioners' invention of the "scientific research methods," a highly systematic and sophisticated set of verification procedures that served to attest to the validity of one's propositional conjecture.[87] Through the collaboration of Gu Yanwu, Huang Zongxi, Dai Zhen, Duan Yucai 段玉裁 (1735–1815), Wang Niansun 王念孫 (1744–1832), and Ruan Yuan 阮元 (1764–1849), scholars who lived across three generations collectively contributed to a set of research conventions to verify their putative insight and skepticism. Liang summarized the research conventions in six steps.

A good scholar, to begin with, is "vigilant" (*zhuyi* 注意) to details.[88] With a view to discovering subjects worthy of study, he pays special attention to seemingly minute details that most individuals overlook. This attentiveness to details is known as "finding gaps in reading." Upon discovering questionable niceties that cause suspicion and doubt, a person may be prone to make a snap judgment. To ensure one is not dumbfounded by his prejudice, he must "empty his mind" (*kongming qixin* 空明其心) and discard his preconception (*xuji* 虛己). This way, not a shred of personal bias can sneak in and dictate his awareness. To keep one's research oriented, one proceeds to "form a hypothesis" (*lishuo* 立說). A scholar's engagement with evidential research is comparable to a biologist or botanist collecting specimens, or a chemist or physicist conducting experiments in a laboratory. Before a person reaches a conclusion, he must collect an extensive amount of evidence (*shouzheng* 搜證) to determine whether his hypothesis is universally applicable in a broad range of samples.

Dai Zhen's scholarly practice presents one of the finest examples. Dai examined Confucian classics conceived in antiquity. To avoid misinterpreting these historical sources, he first determined the range of definition for a particular character before and during the Han dynasty. Following that, he traced the usages of this character in an extensive number of classical texts to determine whether its definitions agreed with his conjecture. "When there was a single character which was not based on the six scripts, or the meaning of a single word which could not be unvaryingly applied to a relevant body of classics," as Yu Tingcan 余廷燦 (1729–1798), one of Dai's fellow evidential researchers, recalled, "he would not believe it without evidence. As Dai Zhen felt uncertain, he had no peace with himself until he had repeatedly checked the references and the evidence."[89] Dai Zhen proceeded to repeat the investigative process until he arrived at a "conclusive statement."[90]

Dai Zhen's fellow practitioners worked in a comparable fashion. After comparing a large pool of samples and counterevidence, these scholars could finally "deliver a verdict" (duanan 斷案) and explore the possibility of "inferring one's deduction" (tuilun 推論) to comparable cases. Through the application of scientific research methods, Qing evidential researchers succeeded in exposing forgeries of some respected scholarships. Yan Ruoju 閻若璩 (1636–1704), for instance, discovered that the appendix chapters to *Shangshu guwen shuzhen* (尚書古文疏證) published during the Eastern Jin (晉) dynasty (317–420) was forged by scholars of later times. This is also the case for the conception of *Shangshu zhuan* (尚書傳) of Kong Anguo 孔安國 (156–74 BC), a learned scholar of the Han dynasty.[91] And as Hu Wei 胡渭 (1633–1714) studied *Yugong zhuizhi* 禹貢錐指, a chorography conceived purportedly during the Western Zhou 西周 (1045–771 BC) period that documents the geography, territorial boundaries, ethnic makeup, agricultural products, and customs of early China's nine continents, he recognized that the book had been amended and modified consecutively by Kong Anguo and Kong Yingda 孔穎達 (574–648).

Qing learning, as Liang argued, was an intellectual movement that distinguished itself for its practitioners' display of speculative spirit and sequentially their attempt to liberate themselves from dependence on the canonical classics.[92] Having examined the attention Liang devoted to these subversive forces, I venture to extend Liang's analysis to propose a counterintuitive claim that contradicts our conventional understanding of Qing intellectual history: being fiercely antagonistic to the Wang Yangming school of neo-Confucianism, both Gu Yanwu and

Dai Zhen urged their contemporaries to shift their attention from empty metaphysical contemplation to the investigation of text. As these Qing researchers invented and applied systematic "scientific research methods" to verify propositions informed by their introspective reasoning, these research methods were not intended to verify the accuracy of facts but to ensure the efficacy and proper functioning of one's a priori intuition. By certifying and authenticating the cogency of one's personal proposition, a person can confidently determine what is "*truly* true and what is *truly* false" (*zhen shi zhen fei* 真是真非) without repeating the mistake of indulging oneself in his unwarranted, subjective opinion.[93]

The invention of scientific research methods began life as a protest against the Wang Yangming's school of moral teachings. But as practitioners of Qing evidential research directed these scientific verification methods toward authenticating their personal speculations, the rise of Qing evidential research signified that the development of the Wang Yangming school of neo-Confucianism had finally reached its full maturity. Thereafter, man's self-directed meditative efforts could be attested by standardized, institutionalized verification procedures. Practitioners of Qing evidential research may not have been unconsciously aware of this: instead of repudiating Wang Yangming's "heart-based" approach to knowledge, their invention of the scientific research methods had served the paradoxical purposes of advancing, facilitating, and rectifying the application of Wang Yangming's moral theory in practice. What we have conventionally perceived as a protest against Song learning could indeed be the continuation and ultimate completion and perfection of neo-Confucian teaching, rather than a reaction against it.

From A Priori Moral Order to Modern Political Order

In his comparison of Bacon and Descartes, Liang asserted that Descartes' promotion of critical self-reflection abolished people's slavish respect for the conformative religious and philosophical doctrines that had prevailed in Europe.[94] Liang prioritized "heart," "spirit," and "reason" above the material "object," "knowledge," and "scholarly investigation." His endorsement of man's perceptual consciousness, at first glance, remotely echoed Martin Heidegger's (1889–1976) and later Hans-Georg Gadamer's (1900–2002) attempt to introduce a hermeneutic turn in the critique of the dominant scientific culture based on objective rationality. Assuming that a man's *Being* (*Dasein*) comprehends the factual given in terms of his projected relations to the world, understanding, Heidegger argues, is informed by the ontological condition of being in the world, and is therefore both hermeneutic and existential.[95]

Liang's summary of Bacon and Descartes certainly introduced a kind of Western hermeneutics to China. But once we tried to contextualize his comparison of the enlightenment thinkers in the contoured development of Qing intellectual history, it seems apparent that the epistemic shift Liang launched at the turn of the twentieth century was intended to achieve a radical political goal. By pointing the Chinese public to what he considered the most reliable method of understanding, Liang accentuated the supremacy of one's subjective engagement. Assuming that the "truth" was the hidden reality that can be discerned only through man's speculative introspection of the Confucian classics, Liang expected the rise of one's critical reflexivity to liberate a person from the state authority and restore by extension the a priori moral order upon which an alternative political order is based. For sensitive individuals in late Qing China, to accept Liang's modern political proposal alongside the exegetic principles he proposed, to put it in extreme terms, is to envision the prospect of bringing a particular political format that had struggled to surface for three hundred years to its ultimate realization.

Two Kinds of Freedom

Between 1901 and 1903, Liang's exposure to the philosophy of Kant and Rousseau inspired an overly idealistic conviction: man begins life as a rational agent and is instinctively capable of moral deliberation. In a community convened to form democratic governance, each member, Liang believed, must seek to transform the personal moral duties with which he was obliged to comply into legislative provisions with law-binding effects for the general public. Given that moral duty was subjectively assigned, democratic governance was therefore not a socially constructed institutional establishment; it was meant, ideally speaking, to operate as the "political" expression or exposition of man's natural cognitive, perceptual, and moral disposition. To participate in democratic politics was to be one's "true" moral self in the public domain.

Liang expected the absolute monarchy to be replaced by a state governed by "national sovereignty" (*guojia zhuquan* 國家主權), a mutation designating a transfer of power from the ruler to a national government. Alluding to *The Six Books of the Commonwealth* (*Les Six livres de la République*), a seminal work by the early French political theorist Jean Bodin (1530–1596) published in 1575, Liang defined "sovereignty" as "the absolute and perpetual power" of a Republic (主權者，絕對者也，無上者也).[96] A national government enjoys supreme and unsurpassed power over its people. "Marked by the ability to make law without the consent of any other," it is an "issuer of legislative commands rather than a recipient of them" (命令的而非受命的者也).[97] The conventional definition of "sovereignty" raises an immediate question: From whence does power derive? Who or what give the national government the right to dictate the people? Liang conceived a revivifying answer that transcends the confines of political theory.

In his introduction to Kant's political ethics, Liang said that when people think of the term "law" (*falü* 法律), they may associate it with legislative commandments being stipulated, adopted, and enacted by a governmental institution to regulate the behaviors of people.[98] The realm of human existence, however, consists of different spheres of life. Being an all-encompassing concept, and speaking from a broad philosophical sense, "any provisions or commands with law-binding effects can be considered law" (凡帶命令之性質，皆可謂法律).[99] Kant offers perhaps the most notable example in his mature epistemology: the formative organization of man's moral, cognitive, and perceptual disposition is structured in accordance with an assembly of a priori categories, which include time, space, the sense of causality, contingency, and so on. Being a rational agent in possession of practical reason, man's reasoning faculty informs moral judgment and by extension determines his ethical commitment. Irrespective of a person's subjective inclination, the moral duty he is obliged to fulfill is an absolute, unconditional command that is binding in all circumstances and must be obeyed under all conditions. Kant calls the absolute moral command the "categorical imperative." As an imperceptible ethical order being erected *within* a person, it is the absolute, pivotal power dictating the ethical sphere of life. The absolute authority that the categorical imperative exerts on a person, Liang believed, is the same as the authority demonstrated by national sovereignty. Liang presented his analogy as follows:

> The origin of freedom is rooted completely in a person's good will (which is the true self [Sanskrit: *ātman*]). Kant's definition

of a "good will," generally speaking, bears a strikingly similarity to the sovereignty of a republic. National sovereignty is the absolute and the unrivaled. It is an imperative rather than a subject of it. People are entitled to enjoy the latitude of freedom bestowed to them by sovereignty of the state. They have no choice but to obey it. A man's good will is comparable to sovereignty of the state; it is the absolute, unrivaled, and imperative. It is because of the good will (or the true self) that that we are given the right to enjoy our liberty. Therefore, we cannot but obey the good will and our true self. A person obeys sovereignty of the state by fulfilling one's responsibilities to it. When it comes to obeying one's good will, it is about *me* my bodily self carrying out my responsibilities to my true self. To obey one's good will is therefore a moral responsibility. To obey the law and to obtain liberty from one's obedience of it, in other words, are two sides of the same coin. 自由之發源, 全歸於良心 (即真我)是也。大抵康氏良心說, 與國家論者之主權說, 絕相類。主權者, 絕對者也, 無上者也。命令的而非受命的者也。凡人民之自由, 皆以是為原泉。人民皆自由於國家主權所賦與之自由範圍內, 而不可不服從主權。良心亦然, 為絕對的, 無上的, 為命令的。吾人自由之權理所以能成立者, 恃良心故, 恃真我故, 故不可不服從良心、服從真我。服從主權, 則箇人對於國家之責任所從出也。服從良心, 則軀殼之我對於真我之責任所從出也, 故字之曰道德之責任。由是言之, 則自由比與服從為緣。[100]

In this analogy, Liang made explicit that while the categorical imperative and national sovereignty hold absolute and indivisible power, man's observance of these two kinds of legal commandment led to dissimilar results. As a law-abiding subject of the state, one is obliged to comply with the law of the state. By virtue of his compliance with such law, a person is authorized to enjoy the share of "relative" freedom the state bestows on him. But the compliance of the categorical imperative is different. Unlike a political subject who is coerced to observe the legislative commandment stipulated by institutional forces that are *outside* of him (制之於外者), the moral law is the ethical commandant informed by the a priori order that constitutes one's cognitive reasoning.[101] It is the law prescribed by and within the person (制之於中者).[102] Since it is his own law that a person obeys, the person is exempted from all forms of outer restrictions and becomes *truly* and *completely* free. To follow the categorical imperative, in other words, is to obtain absolute and "authentic freedom" (*zhenzheng de ziyou* 真正的自由), rather than the "finite freedom" being conferred to one.[103]

Bringing LAW to law

Kant holds that every rational being has both an innate right to freedom and a duty to enter into a civil condition governed by a social contract in order to realize and preserve that freedom. Upon the development of his epistemology, Kant proceeds to give a social, political dimension to his philosophical thinking. In a thought experiment presented in *Groundwork of the Metaphysic of Morals*, Kant envisions the prospective of people constituting a "Kingdom of Ends," a democratic republic adjoined with the mutual will.[104] The possession and application of practical reason, Kant says, inform moral judgment and place a person under the obligation to do what is right. A Kingdom of Ends witnesses a systematic union of rational agents who are capable of moral deliberation. Sharing analogous forms of a priori cognitive and perceptual disposition, each member is given the equal right "to convert the categorical imperative that binds him into the constitutional provisions of the state" (自以自為目的, 自以自為法令).[105] As a person fulfills his individual moral obligation in a political community, "whatever thought comes across his mind and whatever move he makes, he must consider whether the categorical imperative that binds him can be executed as a legislative order that is universally applicable to all members of this democratic republic" (吾每一動念, 一舉事, 必自審度曰此念此事果可以為此種民主國之法律否).[106]

Liang intended to transform China into a Kingdom of Ends. To the political reformer, participation in democratic governance was less about adopting a foreign set of constitutional orders than replacing the constructed social institutional order with one induced and deduced from the a priori moral order. In the series of writings he continued to publish between 1902 and 1903, Liang began to attach the prefix "authentic" (*zhen* 真 or *zhenzheng de* 真正的), an adjective designating the engagement of one's a priori moral and cognitive properties, to a broad spectrum of modern political key words he had introduced to China since 1895.[107] Rather than emphasizing the importance of becoming national citizens (國民 *guomin*) with political freedom (自由 *ziyou*), Liang wanted the Chinese public to be the "authentic" national citizen (*zhen guomin* 真國

Reclaiming Qing Philology to Recover the Innate Moral Order | 107

民), enjoying "authentic" freedom (*zhen ziyou*) and "authentic" people's sovereignty (*zhen quanli* 真民權). Liang's coinage of these neologisms allowed him to deliver a clear message: democracy is a system of political governance that operates in keeping with man's a priori moral order. In the Kingdom of Ends, each state member, to borrow the words of Kant, is both the legislator and the law-abiding citizen (人人皆立法者皆守法者).[108] Not being restricted by any socially constructed law being imposed upon him from *without*, a person, being a retainer to his personal lord (人人皆君主皆臣從也), obtains "true, ultimate freedom" by submitting himself to his own law.[109] To capture the shining spirit of Kant, Liang presented a luminous translation so poetic that it sheds new light on the German philosopher's turgid prose:

> A good will is good not because of what it effects, or accomplishes, not because of its fitness to attain some intended end, but good just by its willing, i.e., in itself; and, considered by itself, it is to be esteemed beyond compare much higher than anything that could ever be brought about by it in favor of some inclinations, and indeed, if you will, the sum of all inclinations. Even if by some particular disfavor of fate, or by the scanty endowment of a stepmotherly nature, this will should entirely lack the capacity to carry through its purpose; if despite its greatest striving it should still accomplish nothing, and only the good will were to remain (not of course, as a mere wish, but as the summoning of all means that are within our control); then, like a jewel, it would still shine by itself, as something that has full worth in itself.[110] 責任云者, 皆非有所為而為者也。不得以之 (指道德之責任), 為手段而求達他之目的者也。何以故, 手段即目的故。與他種利益絕比較, 非如彼行手段以求利益者, 或趨或舍, 聽吾之自擇也。康德又曰: 就令天命不佑, 使我抱一善意而不能實行, 或竭力實行而無效, 但使當保持此志而勿喪失。則自能篤實光輝, 坦坦蕩蕩。何以故, 有效無效於善意之分量無所增減, 故價值全存於自由中故。[111]

The emphasis Liang placed on "authenticity" allowed him to draw a clear distinction between "factual knowledge," "subjective perception of factual knowledge," and "knowledge as ontologically *lived* experience." By urging his contemporaries to submit to the political law derived from the a priori moral order, Liang pointed the Chinese public to what he considered to be the true meaning of democracy: providing that one can act in accordance with the social-institutional provisions informed by one's a priori disposition, a person is liberated from all forms of oppressive restriction and becomes a ruler of his own. In China's transition to political modernity, to encourage the general public to erect the constitutional commandment instructed by the categorical imperative was to envision perhaps the most radical form of power transition possible—being a physical object, or a "thing-in-itself," that exists in this world, the creation of man epitomizes the causal deterministic order informing the physical structure of our universe. In a civil society in which people are governed by their collective will, not only would the absolute monarchy be replaced by the power of the people, but the LAW of this boundless, indestructible, and interminable universe.

Chapter 3

To Know *Is* to Act

The Realization of Cosmic-Moral-Political Oneness in Action

For many years, some lingering thoughts and memories persisted in Liang Qichao's writing, refusing to let go despite the passage of time. In 1903, Liang wrote that if a political revolution is merely about toppling one political regime with military actions, that was the path China was heading toward.[1] But this, as he protested in nostalgic anguish, was *not* what he and his comrades expected a political revolution to mean, nor what a political revolution *could* or *should* mean. In Buddhist teachings, there is a concept called *saṃsāra* (Chin: 輪迴), an existence filled with unending cycles of suffering and bitter sorrow. The opposite of *saṃsāra* is *nirvāṇa* (Chin: 涅磐), the cessation of beginnings, or the Path to Liberation. China, unfortunately, had missed her chance to escape from its unending cycle of sorrow. Similar to hundreds of other political revolutions that had taken place in Chinese history, the one Liang saw approaching was marshalled by adventurists (*yexin jia* 野心家) intoxicated by power and greed.[2] The military course they took was destined to embark on a narrow means leading to a narrow end. And this, as Liang looked back to the ill-starred Hundred Days' Reform, was not the kind of *revolutionary* changes his dear friend Tan Sitong 譚嗣同 (1865–1898) had died for in 1898.[3]

Since China had been defeated in the First Sino-Japanese War (1894–95), Liang had envisioned the prospect of replacing the Qing monarchy with democratic governance.[4] Having spent a year circulating revolutionary ideas at the Hunan Academy of Current Affairs (*Hunan shiwu xuetang* 湖南時務學堂), Liang and Tan were called to the capitol to participate in a nationwide reformist campaign looking to modernize China through the implementation of constitutional monarchy and a Western schooling system. The young emperor who sponsored the reform was most liberal and progressive. But the matriarch Empress Dowager Cixi 慈禧 (1835–1908) was no fool. Sensitive to the subversive potential the political "reform" posed to the Qing monarchy (1644–1911), she soon plotted a crackdown on the movement.[5] Liang and Tan were advised to run. Liang fled to Japan. Tan chose to stay. Six days later Tan was decapitated in public.

Four years after Tan's execution, Liang embarked on extensive fundraising trips in the United States and Europe to collect donations for their unfinished revolutionary project. Having met Sun Yat-sen's 孫中山 (1866–1925) patrons abroad, Liang knew that his contender had seized most available resources to overthrow the Qing monarchy. His chance was gone, permanently gone. Upon returning home from his travels, Liang's newspaper editorials were filled with his memories of Tan.[6] In one of these editorials, Liang wrote that compared with the "narrow-ended definition of political revolution" (*xiayi zhi geming* 狹義之革命) China was heading toward, the "board, all-embracing form of political revolution" (*guangyi zhi geming* 廣義之革命) that he and Tan had once aspired for was intended to bring about "a profound transformation in every perceptible and imperceptible matter in this society" (社會上一切無形有形之事物所生之大變動).[7] "Having shared the noble wish of shedding his blood to save all sentient beings for long" (烈士發為眾生流血之大願久矣), Tan the martyr, according to Liang, had "his body killed to restore one's undivided oneness" (*shashen chengren* 殺身成仁) with the people, the state, and his cosmic moral nature.[8] In the *Analects*, Confucius (551–479 BC) first mentions the saying *shashen chengren* to celebrate the nobility of sacrificing one's life for benevolence (*ren* 仁) or higher moral principles.[9] But the word *ren* had come to mean something radically different to Liang and Tan.

Before Tan Sitong was executed in public, the young martyr completed a monograph titled *An Exposition of Benevolence* (*renxue* 仁學).[10] In this book, Tan Sitong prescribes a total of twenty-seven definitions for *ren*. If the young martyr were to summarize his elaborate definitions in one word, being *ren* is about being "interconnected" (*tong* 通) with everyone and everything in the cosmos. As Tan shed his blood (*liuxue* 流血) in the 1898 reform, the shattering of his corporeal body (*shashen* 殺身), as Liang believed, *was not* a political incident; it was the *Way* opening China to its much-awaited political and spiritual transcendence.[11] Apparently Tan died a political death. Beyond being consumed by the urge to vindicate his friend's tragic death, why did Liang insist on lionizing Tan's political execution as a form of spiritual, religious, and cosmic transcendence? In China's transition to political modernity, why should a person exemplify one's cosmic nature and strive to be an undivided oneness with the cosmos? And how could the person fulfill such wish through the destruction of his corporeal body? To answer these questions, the chapter visits a few underexamined philosophical assumptions that informed the conception of Tan's progressive political reformism, a vision that eventually led to the divide of the reformist camp. To situate Tan's death in a complex and evolving philosophical matrix that inspired him to become "one" with the cosmos, let us return to his final words, in which the young martyr explained his looming suicide and political reformism from the perspective of Buddhist metaphysics.

Defining Political Transcendence

As Tan Sitong defined it in the opening section of *An Exposition of Benevolence*, to be *ren* is to be "interconnected" with everyone and everything. His usage of the term being "interconnected" may seem puzzling to some. I am, for instance, "connected" with my dear friend Sunny. But how do I "interconnect" with her, and successively with inanimate objects such as a table, a tree, and the cat living next door? How tightly can I hold the cat to grow her tail and fur? And if being an interconnected entity is about showing selfless care for Sunny or the table, what can I do for the table to lose myself in it? In Tan's understanding, being "interconnected" rests in our realization that things and people are "interdependent" with each other. The young martyr presented his explication in the equations shown in figure 3.1.

In everyday life, people may see a clear contrast between binary dualisms such as "you and I," "people and the state," "man and object," and "life and death." Once these seemingly antithetical properties are measured in algebraic calculations, the results look otherwise. Take "life and death" as an example. In the arithmetic equations below, Tan established the following algebraic properties: if "being born" (*sheng* 生) is symbolized as 甲 (or "*x*" in modern alphabetic terms), "unborn" (*busheng* 不生) can be rendered as 不 (non) × 甲 (¬× *x*). "Coming to cease" (*mie* 滅) can be represented as 乙 ("*y*"), and "unceasing" (*bumie* 不滅) as 不×乙" (¬× *y*). Having established these properties, Tan showed how these items are all *equal to* each other. His steps can be translated as shown in figure 3.2.

For Qing intellectuals who were new to algebra, Tan summarized the above steps with the following words: "If 'unborn' (¬× *x*), arithmetically speaking, is equal to 'unceasing' (¬× *y*), 'being born' (*x*) is equivalent to 'coming to cease' (*y*). 'To be born and to cease' (*x*/ *y*) is ultimately *the same as* 'unborn and unceasing'" (¬× *x* / ¬× *y*) (不生與不滅平等, 則生與滅平等, 生滅與不生不滅亦平等).[12] By straightening out the algebraic computation, Tan attested methodically that all contradictions (and by extension the contradictions *of* contradictions) are *equal to* each other. The "unvarying equivalence" (*pingdeng* 平等) between discernible distinctions (*fenbie* 分別), to use his words, is the "ultimate substance of undivided oneness" (*ren zhi ti* 仁之體).[13]

Figure 3.1. The sameness between life and death. *Source*: Tan Sitong, *Renxue* (Taipei: Xuesheng shuju, 1998), 7.

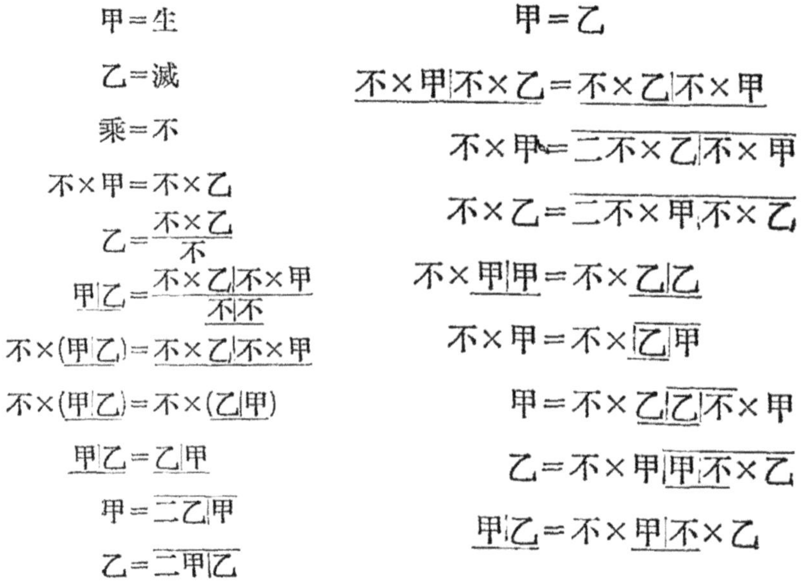

Figure 3.2. Tan Sitong's arithmetic equation. *Source*: Created by the author.

$\neg \times x = \neg \times y$	$x = y$
$y/0 = \dfrac{\neg \times y}{\neg}$	$\neg \times x / \neg \times y = \neg \times y / \neg \times x$
$\dfrac{x}{y} = \dfrac{\neg \times y / \neg \times x}{\neg \quad \neg}$	$\neg \times x = 2 \neg \times y / \neg \times x$
	$\neg \times y = 2 \neg \times x / \neg \times y$
$\neg \times (x/y) = \neg \times y / \neg \times x$	$\neg \times x/x = \neg \times y/y$
$\neg \times (x/y) = \neg \times (x/y)$	$\neg \times x = \neg \times y/y/x$
$(x/y) = (y/x)$	$x = \neg \times y/y / \neg \times x$
$x = 2y/x \quad y = 2x/y$	$y = \neg \times x/x / \neg \times y$
$y = 2x/y$	$x/y = \neg \times x / \neg \times y$

Tan's algebraic computation is accurate in arithmetic terms. But when it comes to matters such as "life and death," how can one positively suggest that "being born" and "passing away" are essentially *the same as* "unceasing and unborn"? To explicate Tan's contention from a more expansive philosophical viewpoint, let us to return to the emphasis the young martyr placed on "unborn [Sanskrit: *anutpanna*] and unceasing [Sanskrit: *aniruddha*]," a phrase that had traveled to China through the Kuchean missionary Kumārajīva's (Chin: 鳩摩羅什) (344–413 CE) translation of *The Middle Way* (*Mūlamadhyamakakārikā*; Chin: 中論). Completed by the Buddhist philosopher Nāgārjuna (Chin: 龍樹) (150–250) in the second century, *The Middle Way* is the seminal text establishing the foundational premise of the Madhyamaka (Eng: Middle Way; Chin: 中觀) school of Mahāyāna Buddhism. At the beginning of the book, Kumārajīva translates the prefatory verse that Nāgārjuna dedicated to the Buddha:

> Unceasing, unborn,
> Unannihilated, not permanent,
> Not coming, not going,

Without distinction, without identity,
And free from conceptual construction.
I prostrate to the Perfect Buddha,
The best of teachers, who taught
Whatever dependently arisen is.[14]

不生亦不滅 不常亦不斷
不一亦不異 不來亦不出
能說是因緣 善滅諸戲論
我稽首禮佛 諸說中第一[15]

In early Buddhist teachings, it was believed that the universe consists of two levels of truth. One is the "ultimate truth" (*paramārtha-satya*; Chin: 勝義諦) pertaining to dharma (Chin: 法), the unchanging cosmic law, while the other is the "conventional or provisional truth" (*saṃvṛti satya*; Chin: 世俗諦), which discloses the existence of all forms of material presences in everyday life. Practitioners of Theravada Buddhism, or the "Lesser Vehicle," envision a stark, hierarchal contrast between the realm of metaphysical transcendence and the world of human existence. Nāgārjuna repudiated such a view. In *The Middle Way*, Nāgārjuna says: in this universe, everything is what it is *in virtue of* its relation to other things. Instead of having any intrinsic identity or self-nature (Sanskrit: *svabhāva*; Chin: 自性), things are dependently arisen upon temporal and situational conditions (*pratītyasamutpāda*; Chin: 緣起). To return to my earlier example: some fifteen years ago I met Sunny on our college campus in Hong Kong. Since then, I have been defined in part by my friendship *with* her. In 2015, I moved into my tree-surrounded apartment, and have been occasionally frustrated by my futile attempts to protest against a wicked cat living next door. To be Jean Tsui, in a sense, is to be a particular locus in a complex network of ever-evolving relationships. What appears to be *her* is a momentary collection dominated by egotistic cravings and false notions about what is real.

In Madhyamaka Buddhism, man's relational dependence with his surrounding environment resembles the ridge beams and rafters.[16] A ridge beam establishes the high point of a roof. Without the support of the rafter, the ridge beam cannot hold the roof aloft. Having studied with Yang Wenhui 楊文會 (1837–1911), one of the leading Buddhist scholars of the Qing dynasty, Tan Sitong pondered: if everything in this universe exists *in relation to* other things, why should the imperial monarchy exercise oppressive dominance over the people? To justify the political changes they called for, Tan was ready to interpret China's existing social, political, and cosmic imagination from a Buddhist perspective: in a realm of relational dependence, the emperor cannot be the ruler *of* the people; he exists interdependently *with* the people. The father, by extension, is interdependent *with* the son, men *with* women, self *with* other, the East *with* the West, the body (*tipo* 體魄) *with* the soul (*linghun* 靈魂), and people *with* myriad forms of beings in heaven and earth (*tiandi wanwu* 天地萬物). Nāgārjuna calls this state of universal dependence "emptiness" (Sanskrit: *Śūnyatā*; Chin: 空)—the complete disappearance of self-nature in a network of undifferentiated interdependence. And if you and I, the "*self*" (*wo* 我) and "other" (*ren* 人) are devoid of conventional self-identities that we possess in ourselves, then, as Tan reiterates Nāgārjuna's words, there is no longer "being born" nor "coming to cease" to speak of. Once the distinction between "being born" and "coming to cease" disappears, even distinction itself ceases to exist. In this state of ultimate homogeneous lucidity, the universe finds itself "unceasing and unborn" (*busheng bumie* 不生不滅). This, in Madhyamaka Buddhism, is where *nirvāṇa* lies.

Kang Youwei on Human Nature

Toward the end of the nineteenth century, Tan Sitong inspired Liang Qichao to envision the prospect of removing the institutional boundary that divided the ruler from the people, thereby reconnecting the Chinese public as an equalitarian democratic community. After the First Sino-Japanese War, the country's national defeat prompted Liang and Tan to harbor a greater ambition: through replacing the imperial monarchy with democratic governance, they were to realize the opaque political ideal that Confucius purportedly projected in his compilation of the *Spring and Autumn Annals* (*Chunqiu* 春秋). To transform China into the world of the "Great Unity" (*datong* 大同), a place where all men live harmoniously as equal social members, Liang began to circulate his revolutionary thinking at the Hunan Academy of Current Affairs, where he told the students: in Confucius' compilation of the *Spring and Autumn Annals*, the Sage's usage of the word "King" (*wang* 王) defies "the throne of the times" (*dangshi zhi jun* 當時之君); it stands "at best as a synonym of the universal, common law" (不過公法二字之代數而已)

that complies with "the Way of the benevolent government" (*wangdao* 王道).[17] Liang's teacher, Kang Youwei, was supposedly the person who inspired his search for democracy and people's sovereignty.

In *An Investigation of Confucius as a Reformer* (*Kongzi gaizhi kao* 孔子改制考), a wildly imaginative yet controversial monograph completed in the 1880s, Kang Youwei perceived parliamentary democracy as a form of governance espoused by Confucius and the former Sage Kings of antiquity.[18] Unlike Liang the young idealist, Kang was a highly complex if not "impenetrable," man.[19] Kang did not trust the people, nor their ability to participate in democratic governance.[20] Sharing an overly pessimistic view on the disposition of human nature, Kang believed that the current national and international unrest was caused by one obvious reason—some men were born inferior, or perhaps considerably inferior, to others. Kang's demoralizing proposition can partly be attributed to a conceptual shift that had appeared in the recent development of neo-Confucianism.

Neo-Confucian thinkers of the Song and the Ming dynasties, as discussed in the first chapter, perceived *li* (理) as the underlying cosmic pattern that unfolds itself in the formative structure and behavioral deposition of men and things. *Li*, according to Zhang Zai 張載 (1020–1077), was the supreme metaphysical order governing the movement of *qi* (氣), the all-pervading material substance that forms the physical composition of men and things. Beginning in the early Qing dynasty, however, the relationship between *li* and *qi* reversed.[21] Being the formative substance that lays the foundation of human civilization, *qi*, as it appeared to Wang Fuzhi 王夫之 (1619–1692), Gu Yanwu 顧炎武 (1613–1682), and Huang Zongxi 黃宗羲 (1610–1695), is the primal origin of *li* the cosmic principle. It is the vital energy that informs and governs the organization of *li*. Kang Youwei was in agreement with these thinkers. In *The Esoteric and Exoteric Essays of Master Kang* (*Kangzi neiwai pian* 康子內外篇) (1886–87), Kang explicates how *qi* takes precedence over *li*: "Men," Kang said, "take form in physical substances before they begin to develop their intellect. With intelligence there are principles. Principles are the creation of men" 夫有人形而後有智, 有智而後有理。理者, 人之所立.[22] Since most *qi* are muddy and impure, the intellect of men made with deficient *qi* can never reach a level of sophistication that enables them to develop the conception of principles.[23] This is why Sages appear so rarely in human history.

Kang found most men inherently inferior and evil (*e* 惡). Having contemplated on what he considered to be excessive savagery men displayed in the French Revolution and on the Indian's inability to resist colonialization by Britain, Kang expected democratic governance to be a state-sponsored constitutional reform supervised by a handful of highly talented individuals.[24] To enable these gifted men's participation in democratic governance, he encouraged Emperor Guangxu 光緒 (1875–1908) "to establish a national congress that incorporated views of the general public" (設議院以通下情).[25] In a memorial Kang wrote, "The national congress is the place where the throne and the people assemble to discuss state affairs and formulate corresponding public policies in collaboration" (國會者，君與國民共議一國之政法).[26] To ensure that their collective governance was transparent and efficient, China must observe the practice of *trias politica* (*sanquan fenli* 三權分立), a philosophy the French enlightenment philosopher Charles de Montesquieu (1689–1755) conceived to accentuate the separation of powers between legislation, administration, and jurisdiction. In the Qing dynasty, the throne was in direct charge of the Six Ministries (*Liubu* 六部), which include the Board of Civil Appointments (*Libu* 吏部), the Board of Revenue (*Hubu* 戶部), the Board of Rites (*Libu* 禮部), the Board of War (*Bingbu* 兵部), the Board of Punishments (*Xingbu* 刑部), and the Board of Works (*Gongbu* 工部). Instead of holding himself accountable for all state policies, the throne should confer his law-making power to the congress. And "the congress should stipulate the rule of law, the department of justice should enforce the law, and the state government should implement these legislative stipulations as an administrative unit" (以國會立法，以法官司法，以政府行政).[27]

To assist the throne in "supervising the constitutional reform and reorganizing the existing bureaucratic structure" (統籌全局，改定官制),[28] Kang persuaded Emperor Guangxu to establish the New Planning Board (*Xinzhen ju* 新政局), a temporary governing agency that "bypasses the existing administrative structure."[29] Operating as a provisional congress being answerable solely to the throne, the New Planning Board should consist of twenty reform-minded individuals being recruited across the nation. "Inaugurated in the court the Board should meet to reconceive all state policies" (開制度局於宮中，將一切政事重新商定) in three steps.[30] First, the committee should study and compare federal constitutions codified by modern nations such as Japan, the United States, and other modern

European nations.³¹ Upon identifying the constitutional model that was most applicable to China, the committee should draft a modern constitution that clarified the definition of a responsible government, determined the rights of the state government, certified the independence of its jurisdiction, and stipulated election law to regulate the electoral system, voting rights, and election management bodies. Upon the completion of the provisional constitution, the board should eventually "decide on the date to commence the national congress" (預定國會之期).³²

The New Planning Board, as Liang explained in retrospect, was intended to operate as the preparatory Senate (*guizu yuan* 貴族院), or the Upper House of the Congress, whereas the establishment of the Southern Learning Society (*Nanxue hui* 南學會) prepared for the creation of the House of Representatives. In concert these two organizations should establish China's modern central government.³³ Once the preparatory Congress came into being, the New Planning Board would disband the Six Ministries and form twelve new administrative bureaus (*shier ju* 十二局). Following the principle of *trias politica*, these twelve bureaus were administrative units sharing the sole responsibility of implementing and executing legislative policies.³⁴ The strict separation of power between legislation, administration, and jurisdiction should also be closely observed on the provincial level.³⁵

Tan Sitong's Protest against Kang Youwei

Kang Youwei, Liang Qichao, and Tan Sitong expressed equal enthusiasm in realizing the "Great Unity" Confucius projected in the *Spring and Autumn Annals*. This new generation of New Text scholars, however, faced an immediate challenge: what was the best means to realize the Great Unity in practice? Kang Youwei and his students, most apparently, did not fully agree with each other. Having spent years learning Buddhist teachings and Western sciences, Tan Sitong argued that regardless of our universe is governed by *li* or *qi*, everyone and everything will "always" *be the same as* each other and *equal to* (*pingdeng* 平等) each other. Being born as identical creatures, people are naturally entitled to enjoy equal political rights. What makes democratic governance truly remarkable is not the invention of the institutional construct but that it presents a "formal" political structure to express and accommodate people's heavenly nature.

Speaking from the perspective of Western chemistry and physics, in *An Explication of Benevolence* Tan Sitong remarked that things and people are made of sixty-four elements (*yuanzhi* 元質).[36] These sixty-four elements can be conjoined with each other through an adhesive substance called the ether (*yitai* 以太).[37] In the human body, the cranial nerves residing in one's brain monitor the five sense organs. Being the most complex and powerful organ, man's brain consists of the largest amount of particles. The density of these particles makes the brain ether most responsive. When a person thinks, ether conjoins the large amount of elements residing in the cerebrum with the rest of the elements that constitute the myriad forms of beings. People's connection with things and people, in this sense, is not a "personal" matter but rather epitomizes the amalgamation of the sixty-four elements of which *everything* and *everyone* is made. The cohesion of these universal elements makes all individuals a body of undifferentiated uniformity.

Kang Youwei, as said earlier, asserted that men made of polluted *qi* are inherently inferior and evil. But assuming that everything and everyone are constituted by the identical elements, Tan believed that the "consolidation of these elements through the ether made a person one body with myriad forms of beings in heaven and earth" (以太通天地萬物人我為一身).[38] No one, for this reason, is superior nor inferior to another. Early neo-Confucian thinkers assuming that the universe was governed by *li* rather than *qi* arrived at a similar conclusion.

In the eleventh century, Cheng Hao 程顥 (1032–1085) famously declared that "the sages, or the benevolent ones, are 'one' with myriad forms of beings in heaven and earth" (仁者天地萬物為一體). The Confucian sages, Cheng said, shared a lucent, spotless heartmind (*xin* 心) that reveals the structure of the cosmos. While ordinary men were distracted by the appearance of things, the sages were free from these prejudices. Whatever the sages saw was not the thing or person per se, but a direct reflection of the all-pervading cosmic principles informing the compositional structure of his heartmind. Having a cosmic heartmind as such is to not have one (*shengren wuxin* 聖人無心).[39] Cheng Hao asserted that the benevolent ones were "one body" (*yiti* 一體) with myriad forms of beings. So what does Cheng mean by "one body"? And how can the sages practically be "one body" with the trees and, say, a random cat living next door? In a recent symposium, the contemporary Buddhist philosopher Graham Priest posed nearly an identical question to Philip Ivanhoe, the modern neo-Confucian scholar: "What does it mean for two things to be one?"[40] To contribute a Buddhism-inspired, or obviously Tan Sitong–inspired, solution to the discussion, I venture to construe Cheng Hao's remark with three logic diagrams in figure 3.3.

Neo-Confucian thinkers, as said, perceived *li* as the organizing principles exhibited in the formative structure and behavioral deposition of men and things. In diagram 1, *l* symbolizes *li*, the cosmic patterns governing the formative structure of *all* forms of beings in the universe. The sages (*s*), the trees (*t*), and the cat (*c*) certainly look *very* different. But assuming that "everything in the world," to borrow Philip Ivanhoe's apt summary, "contained within itself all the principles or patterns in the universe," the compositional structure of the sages (*s*), the tree (*t*), and the cat (*c*) reveals the identical cosmic patterns.[41] Sharing a cosmic heartmind of absolute transparency, the sages' metaphysical construct is *the same as* the cosmic patterns (*l*). In the tree diagram, their structural equivalence can be represented as $s = l$. Knowing that the myriad forms of beings in the universe exhibit the identical cosmic patterns, the compositional structure of the tree and the cat are also an equivalence of *li* ($t = l$; $c = l$). Since the formative structure of the sage, the tree, and the cat discloses the unvarying patterns, *l*, *s*, *t*, and *c*, as it is shown in diagram 2, are all identical to each other ($l = s = t = c$). If the structures of these properties are completely identical, they are also mutually commensurate and interchangeable with each other. In a web of undifferentiated affinity, these seemingly distinct properties become

Figure 3.3. Explicating "oneness" in three logic diagrams. *Source*: Created by the author.

Diagram 1	Diagram 2	Diagram 3
l ↙ ↓ ↘ *s* *t* *c* ↙ ↙ ↓ ↘ ↘ ⋮ *l* ⋮ ↙ ↓ ↘ *s* *t* *c* ↙ ↙ ↓ ↘ ↘ ⋮ ⋮ ⋮	⋮ ↕ ⋯ *c* ↔ *l* ↔ *s* ⋯ ↕ ⋯ ↔ *t* ↔ ⋯ ↕ ⋯ *c* ↔ *l* ↔ *s* ⋯ ↕ ⋮	⋮ ↕ ⋯ *o* ↔ *o* ↔ *o* ⋯ ↕ ⋯ ↔ *o* ↔ ⋯ ↕ ⋯ *o* ↔ *o* ↔ *o* ⋯ ↕ ⋮

indistinguishable from each other. As ostensible differences between *l*, *s*, *t*, and *c* vanish, what is left in the diagram is *pure structure*, or a state of undifferentiated uniformity.

By "one body," perhaps what Cheng Hao meant was the *disappearance of ostensible differences* in a cosmos of things and people manifesting the exact *selfsame* patterns. In a cosmos without boundaries, the sages, the tree, the cat, the human, the objects, heaven and earth, the transcendental, the existential, and so on are completely *the same as* each other. Not only are the sages "one body" with the cosmos, the sages are *the* cosmos. Such a law should hold true for all men. For neo-Confucian thinkers, people may "appear" as distinct individuals sharing discrete physiological features and temperament. But being formed of the same cosmic principles, the affinity we share discloses the *pure structure* of the cosmos. Being part and parcel of an all-encompassing whole, people share the innate capacity of seeing, acting, and emphasizing from the position of others.[42]

Tan Sitong, similar to his reassuring neo-Confucian predecessors, was convinced that men coexist as an undifferentiated entity. He called the organizing structure revealing the underlying coherence *tiaoli* 條理, which is his modern rendition of *li* the cosmic principle.[43] To Tan, to be coextensive with the cosmic principles is to be good (*shan* 善). For the sake of the advancing one's personal interest, some wicked men, as he was sad to report, invented "names" (*ming* 名) as artificial constructs to create hierarchal differences and antagonistic contrasts. People ignorant of the organizing principles of the universe tend to perceive these fabricated contrasts as "substantial" differences. Tan believed in the existence of evil. But instead of a wicked cosmic force pervading *qi*, as some neo-Confucian thinkers suggested, evil arose from misnaming and disrupting this underlying organizing structure.[44]

In *On Confucius as a Reformer*, Kang fashioned Confucius as a messianic prophet. Considering himself the modern reincarnation of this messianic prophet, Kang was to guide the global community toward the Great Unity by assimilating the world population into one race, one family, and one nation.[45] To Tan, however, Kang seemed to have misunderstood and misinterpreted Confucius. As creatures of the cosmos, people's actions, thoughts, and corporeal makeup, Tan argued, were physically *programmed* to connect as an undivided oneness. As Confucius composed the *Spring and Autumn Annals*, the Sage purposefully tried to dismantle the fabricated distinction the ruler had maliciously imposed to divide oneself from the people who were created equal to him. In a letter addressed to his teacher Ouyang Zhonggu (歐陽中鵠) (1849–1911), Tan wrote,

> Assuming that heaven belongs exclusively to Christianity, the Westerner finds our holy religion inadequate. They do not know that heaven was something that we have always had. During the Xia [c. 2070–1600 BCE], the Shang [c. 1600–1046 BCE], and the Zhou [1046–256 BCE] dynasties, men were close and friendly with heaven. But as the throne rose to power, people lost their rights as well as their interconnection with heaven and earth. The throne enjoyed the exclusive right to offer a sacrifice to heaven, and the people looked up to the throne as if he were heaven. Since then the throne has manipulated his use of heaven to reign over the world. When all people felt inferior, he himself rose. Confucius was concerned and therefore composed the *Spring and Autumn Annals*. Being a book seeking to govern in compliance with the law of heaven, the *Annals* took the liberty of expressing praises as well as denunciations toward the throne and the feudal lords. This was why Confucius appointed himself the uncrowned king. (西人) 因秘天為彼教所獨有, 轉疑我聖教之有缺, 不知是皆吾所舊有也。三代以上, 人與天親, 自君權日盛, 民權日衰, 遂乃絕地天通, 惟天子始得祀天, 天下人望天子儼然一天。而天子以遂挾一天以制天下。天下俱卑, 天子孤立。孔子憂之, 於是乎作春秋。春秋稱天而治者也, 故自天子、諸侯, 皆得其褒貶, 而自立為素王。[46]

Being a student of Buddhist teachings, Tan Sitong drew an illuminating synthesis between the Great Unity and his Buddhist-inspired definition of "benevolence." Confucius, according to Tan's interpretation, was a noble man seeking to restore all men as "heavenly creatures" (*tianren* 天人). Instead of the "Chosen One" being appointed by the higher divine force, a "heavenly man" denotes an objective fact evincing the metaphysical structure of the cosmos and the ways all men are made. As Confucius strived to endorse people's civil rights (*xing minquan* 興民權), what made his projection of the Great Unity *truly* precious was not the implementation of a constitutional construct but the humanitarian conviction that people are born and created equal. To Tan, Confucius sought to remove the hierarchal distinctions that had divided the emperor from the people. But since Confucius "violated the interests of those who were in support of imperial monarchy, his teaching remained unpopular" (然其學不昌者, 亦為與君主之學相悖而已矣).[47] "For those who wish to become religious leaders," Tan continued, "they cannot declare themselves people of a particular nation. They must consider themselves the 'heavenly men'" (凡欲為教主者, 不可自說我是某國人, 當自命為天人).[48] As Kang Youwei announced his racial modification and international unification projects, not only did he fail to advance the Great Unity, he had reimposed and reenforced the artificial distinctions Confucius had attempted to eradicate in the first place.

Heaven as Democratic Governance

Toward the end of the nineteenth century, the import of modern political ideas such as "national citizen," "rights," "civil obligation," and "equality" to China challenged the legitimacy of the Qing monarchy. As foreign as these democratic concepts may have seemed, Tan discerned the affinity between the organizing principle of democratic governance and the "cosmic metaphysical republic" envisioned by early neo-Confucian thinkers.[49] Assuming that humans' formative structure is in perfect agreement with the cosmic pattern, Tan asserted that man and the world belong to an organic oneness. They are identical *to* each other and *are* each other.[50] People may share visible differences in appearance, ability, and social origins in the realm of human affairs. But beyond these quantifiable differences, people endowed with unblemished moral perfection are homogenous "cosmic members" belonging to the "metaphysical republic" of equalitarian uniformity.[51] The cosmic structure as envisioned by neo-Confucian thinkers, in this sense, resonates with the founding premise of democratic liberalism: in a democratic state, each individual is promised equal civil and political rights. But to be able to exercise the rights one is entitled to enjoy, a person is obliged to fulfill his corresponding share of civil duties. Whereas the neo-Confucian "metaphysical republic" emphasizes that people are equal to each other and inextricably intertwined with each other, democratic governance is a unified system that thrives on the collaboration and interdependence of each law-abiding citizen.

The affinity underlying political modernity and the moral metaphysics of neo-Confucianism transcends a person's creative endeavours; it reflects perhaps a utopian political vision that scholars pursuing the study of New Text Confucianism aspired to revive and implement in China's transition to political modernity. But in the course of restoring what Liang and Tan might perceive to be the *true* meaning of Confucianism, the two needed to amend their teacher's self-possessed distortion of Confucius, help people realize their cosmic nature, and have every individual participating in democratic governance as an undivided organic unity. Their solution rests readily in Tan's own words. In *An Exposition of Benevolence*, the young martyr makes what I consider to be an apocalyptic remark foreshadowing the all-inclusive intellectual, moral, and philosophical reform that Liang had persisted in introducing in the early 1900s:

> Critics may say, "The ideas you advance are really high-sounding, but what is the point of babbling on about these empty things since they cannot be practiced?" My answer is: I value knowledge, but I do not value acting. Knowledge is something of the soul, whereas acting is something of the body. . . . Hence there is a limit for acting, but there is no limit for knowledge; for acting has an end, whereas knowledge has not. In addition, it is inevitable that acting will always lag behind knowledge. What is reached by the hands and feet surely cannot be as far as what is reached by the ears and eyes. What is kept in the memory surely cannot be as great as the power of understanding. What is measured by weights and rulers surely cannot be as precise as the skill of surveying. What is put down in facts cannot be as subtle as the principle of *sunyata*. For how can all these facts be changed by force? Mean scholars lament the fact that they are able to know but unable to act. This is not *genuine knowing*, for with *genuine knowing* there can be no inability to act. 難者曰: "子陳義高矣, 既已不能行, 而滔滔然爲空言, 復奚益乎?" 曰吾貴知, 不貴行也。知者, 靈魂之事也; 行者, 體魄之事也。 . . . 是行有限而知無限, 行有窮而知無窮也。且行之不能及知, 又無可如何之勢也。手足之所接, 必不及耳目之遠; 記性之所至, 必不及悟性之廣; 權尺之所量, 必不及測量之確; 實事之所肇, 必不及空理之精; 夫孰能強易之哉? 僻儒所患能知而不能行者, 非<u>真知</u>也, <u>真知</u>則無不能行矣。[52]

Tan's statement looks straightforward at first glance: compared with the experience of acquiring encyclopedic knowledge, there is only a limited range of actions a person can perform. "Acting" (*xing* 行), most naturally, is limited, while "knowing" (*zhi* 知) is limitless. While Tan prioritized "knowledge" over "action," he went on to suggest that there is *one and only one* exception to what appears to be a thoroughgoing dualism: "genuine knowing" (*zhenzhi* 真知).[53] Coined by Wang Yangming, the Ming neo-Confucian thinker, the term "genuine knowing" refers to "knowing" in its purest form, untouched and uncontaminated by any form of conceptual or perceptual inference.[54] For Tan Sitong, the Buddhist practitioner, to *know* in the absence of perceptual boundaries is to be *empty*—upon the ultimate realization that everything is dependently arisen, one's momentary collections of all distinctions are dissolved into a universe that is unceasing and unborn. "Once a person *genuinely knows*, there is no action that he cannot perform" (真知則無不能行); because thereafter the boundary that divides "knowing" from "acting" has disappeared, along with the dissolution of all perceptions.

Tan Sitong saw the world as a place of undivided oneness. The ultimate equivalence of this kind could have arrived only with the disappearance of all conceptual notions, and ultimately the very existence of concepts themselves. Tan's understanding of *ren*, or undivided modern political-cosmic oneness, resonates with the Buddhist search for transcendence. In Western culture, transcendence has often been perceived as an internal state of affairs. It is the attainment of particular, subjectively experienced altered states and supernatural powers, or the realization of intellectual or rhetorical brilliance. But in Buddhist teachings, to transcend, to quote Peter Hershock's brilliant elucidation, is to be connected with things and people in the way we are meant to be connected.[55] Once a person erases "the boundaries imposed on the meaning of things by our customary relationship with them," he expands along with the world.[56] The relinquishment of self-imposed perception, thereafter, renders one infinite and boundless.

Obviously, Tan's solution was inspired by Buddhist metaphysics as well as the emphasis Wang Yangming placed on the "oneness of knowing and acting." Wang, as noted in the first chapter, shared a firm conviction: the organization of our universe reveals certain organizational patterns being known as *li* the cosmic principle. Being the creation of the universe, man begins life as the living presence of such structural perfection. Instead of having to *learn about* the moral principles that the sages prescribed in the Confucian classics, a person should stay focally connected with his endowed moral instinct. As long as he can restore his mental clarity and dispel inappropriate thoughts, whatever appears in his mind and inspires his spontaneous action (*xing*) is a direct revelation of the deep, underlying cosmic structure he epitomizes in his mind. Wang describes the integration of man's cosmic instinct and the embodied expressions of such instinct as *zhixing heyi* (知行合一), which modern philosophers translate standardly as the "unity of knowledge and action."

For Western theorists who are more accustomed to envision the body-mind division in dualistic terms, Wang's remark sounds most bizarre. Gilles Deleuze and Brian Massumi, for instance, perceive man's corporeal intensity as an asocial corporeal force that influences our rational judgment but remains disconnected from it. The body, in other words, is inherently and biologically predisposed to go its own way. Wang Yangming should agree that a person knows *through* the body. But in the emphasis he placed on the "oneness of knowledge and action," man's bodily acting, which constitutes his being, is not just the "ground" on which knowing takes place. Acting *is* knowing. So how can "knowing" the epistemic cognition be *the same as* "acting" the corporeal movement and sensation? Or how can the body *be* the mind? Knowing that Liang Qichao had later urged his contemporaries to "authenticate" their modern political knowledge with embodied practices, a topic I will explicate in further detail, these questions, aside from their immediate historical relevance, promise a key to scrutinizing the subtle philosophical complexities involved in China's transition to political modernity, as well as some illuminating but hitherto unexamined dialogues between Buddhism and the Wang Yangming school of neo-Confucianism. They cannot be treated lightly, nor be deposed causally as a rhetorical gimmick. To clarify the nonobtrusive interrelation between "knowing" and "acting" and sequentially fine idiosyncrasies that distinguish this Chinese notion from general views held by recent poststructuralist and affect theorists, in the following discussion I try to elucidate the premise of Wang Yangming's moral position from the perspectives of Buddhist metaphysics.

The Oneness of Knowledge and Action

Neo-Confucianism, as explicated in the first chapter, can be divided generally into two schools. Assuming that the structure of man's heart-mind is in perfect agreement with the cosmic pattern, Wang Yangming believed that moral principles are immanent in man's moral nature. For a person to be moral takes only staying true to his heartmind. Zhu Xi also believed that man shares perfect moral nature. But assuming that the physical composition of his heartmind is adulterated by polluted physical substances, Zhu Xi asserted that once a person's heavenly heartmind (*dioxin* 道心) takes "form" in his humanly heartmind (*renxin* 人心) as a corporeal organ, it discharges inferior substances known as "human feelings" (*qing* 情). For this reason, man was disconnected from his heavenly moral nature.[57] In order to learn to be good again, he must devote himself to the study of Confucian classics combined with investigation of external events.

Wang Yangming considered Zhu's position logically fallacious. Wang voiced a basic disagreement: being the structuring principle informing the organizational formation of myriad forms of beings, the physical displays of *li* are bound to be incessantly different. Those formal, physical variations do not distort, deform, or suppress the omnipotence of *li*; on the contrary, they manifest its boundless multiplicities. Codified by *li* the cosmic patterns, man's heartmind is programmed to operate the way it is compositionally structured. Its functional expressions exteriorize and exemplify its cosmic moral endowment. It is ontologically incapable of discharging erroneous feelings that are quintessentially and qualitatively different from its cosmic nature. One cannot possibly divide the heartmind's cosmic moral endowment from its functional expressions.

Disapproving of the binary dichotomy Zhu Xi envisioned, Wang criticized the Song philosopher for splitting the heartmind into two, inventing the problematic, if not needless, contrast between man's moral nature and his human feelings. To reveal that the heartmind's "cosmic moral endowment" is in perfect agreement with its "functional expression," Wang excluded erroneous desires and feelings that should have *not* existed at the first place. "Man's heartmind," as stated in his "four-cornered doctrine" (*siju jiao* 四句教), "is absent from the distinction between good and evil" (*wu shan wu e xin zhi ti* 無善無惡心之體). It is untainted by any form of polluted material substances. Wang's complete doctrine goes as follows:

> The absence of good and evil characterizes the substance of heartmind.
> The presence of good and evil characterizes the movement of its intentions.
> The knowledge of good and evil characterizes its *liangzhi*.

The doing of good and ridding of evil characterizes the investigation of things.[58]

無善無惡心之體 有善有惡意之動
知善知惡是良知 為善去惡是格物

Wang believed that the heartmind is neither good nor evil. Residing in a state of amorphous absence, it is virtually free from any form of antithesis. By repeating the adjective "absent" (*wu* 無), the Ming philosopher appeared to have evacuated the heavenly endowed heartmind and turned it into a space of empty void. Enraged by Wang's seemingly nihilist remark, followers of Zhu Xi accused him of infusing Confucian orthodoxy with the practice of heretical Chan Buddhism (*xie chan* 邪禪). In addition to absolving people of their ethical responsibilities and rendering learning irrelevant, they held Wang responsible for instigating social corruption and for causing the moral deterioration that had run rampant toward the end of the Ming dynasty.[59] Wang's contenders were angry for a reason. Zhu Xi, as mentioned earlier, affirmed that men were moral in nature. If the heartmind's compositional structure epitomizes the cosmic pattern and coordinates in synchronicity with its functional expressions as Wang argued, how can it be a place of complete "absence" or "nonexistence"? Being the living expression of the perfect cosmic patterns, how can the heartmind, and by extension the cosmos, *not* be intrinsically moral and good?

The Emptiness of the Heart

Wang's bold remark looks puzzling for certain. But those who accused him of spreading nihilistic doctrines seemed to have missed an important piece of cultural background. The Ming philosopher's formulation of the "four-cornered doctrine," as most of Wang's contemporaries and our modern philosophers have overlooked, has little if anything to do with general "dicta" or "axioms," as the Chinese characters and their English translations suggest.[60] Originated from Sanskrit, the term *siju* (四句) derives from the Kuchean missionary Kumārajīva's Chinese translation of *catuṣkoṭi*, the classical Indian tetralemma forming the "four-cornered system" of the Buddhist logico-epistemological tradition.[61] By reiterating the key word *wu* (無) (absent of; empty of) in his "four-cornered doctrine," what

Wang aspired to achieve is quite the opposite of amoral nihilism; it is a state of undivided oneness in which everyone and everything have surrendered their self-nature in a network of undifferentiated interdependence.

To understand (1) how Wang Yangming incorporated the premise of Madhyamaka Buddhism into the moral metaphysics of neo-Confucianism, (2) some immediate challenges the Buddhist conception of the universe posed to the "Learning of Principle" school of neo-Confucianism, and (3) the means by which Liang Qichao had assimilated Wang Yangming's call for the "oneness of knowledge and action" into his modern political reform, let us visit a major debate that *catuṣkoṭi* sparked in early India, and the ways in which that debate facilitated the philosophical developments of Indian and Chinese Buddhism.

Catuṣkoṭi, to begin with, involves the systematic examination of each of four tenable logical propositions, *P*:[62]

1. *P* is true (affirmative).

2. *P* is false (negative).

3. *P* is both true *and* false (both affirmative and negative).

4. *P* is neither true *nor* false (neither affirmative nor negative).

These positions, similar to the legs of a table, are interrelated to and interdependent on each other. They are known as the four *koṭi* (corners; *sanskrit*: कोटि). Being widely employed as both a pedagogical and a dialectic device in elucidating the Buddhist cosmic law and order, *catuṣ koṭi* allows the Buddha to describe the *dharma*, the unchanging cosmic law, in four tenable clauses:

1. The dharma is real (affirmative).

2. The dharma is unreal (negative).

3. The dharma is real and unreal (both affirmative and negative).

4. The dharma is neither real nor unreal (neither affirmative nor negative).

Having stipulated these four clauses, the Buddha never tries to clarify the exact meaning of each clause, nor the correlation between them. The *catuṣkoṭi* riddle remains one of those *avyākṛta* (Chin: 無記)—inexplicable questions—that the Buddha left answered, for any answer to them, whether in the negative or the affirmation, would mislead the enquirer. Of the competing interpretations available, the oldest, and presumably most contentious, appears in *Abhidharma* (Chin: 論), the early Buddhist doctrines associated with Theravada Buddhism.

Early Buddhist teachings, as mentioned earlier, maintain that the universe consists of two levels of truth. One is the "ultimate truth" and the other the "phenomenal or provisional truth." An early commentator of the *Abhidharma* explicates these two levels of truth as follows: in our everyday life, the physical beings, thoughts, emotions, and cognitions that we experience with our five senses are all "effable." These effable experiences belong to the "phenomenal or provisional truth." In the phenomenal reality, while we can feel a person or an object, everything we feel, see, and hear is impermanent. As distinct and concrete as these things and people might appear to be, they exist conditionally as atomic units flowing in this fleeting temporal space. For instance, there is a pitcher of water. When the pitcher is broken into shards, the infinitesimal particles of which these shards are made transform into other forms of beings. The pitcher that we have touched and treasured disappears. Our cognition of the pitcher, on the contrary, is "ineffable." Being a metaphysical abstraction, the conceptual notion of the pitcher is independent from the pitcher as a physical object. The persisting notion is imperishable. Such is the ultimate truth that transcends empirical phenomena and verbal expression.

Having envisioned a clear, hierarchical contrast between the "higher ineffable truth" and the "fleeting phenomenal truth," followers of Theravada Buddhism perceive the dharma as the all-pervading "ultimate truth" that exists *out here* but remains inaccessible to the layman. The early Buddhists' imagination of the dharma, the unchanging cosmic law, prompted them to interpret the four-cornered *catuṣkoṭi* riddle as follows: in the first clause, the Buddha speaks of dharma as if it is real, so that he can lead beings to venerate his omniscience. In the second clause, the Buddha says that the dharma is unreal, because those who are dumbfounded by their perceptual experiences have confused the impermanent phenomena as real and the dharma as unreal. Coming to the third clause, the Buddha teaches some hearers that phenomena are both real and unreal. The difference is contingent on one's point of view. The worldly beings who have not obtained enlightenment perceive worldly phenomena as real. But for enlightened individuals, what the worldly beings perceive to be real is unreal. The fourth clause is the refutation of the third and captures, as best one can in words, the perspective of emptiness. Speaking to those who are practically free from passion and wrong views, the Buddha affirms that everything is neither real nor unreal.[63]

For practitioners of Theravada Buddhism, anything a person sees and feels is impermanent. Subject to undergoing modifications, there is nothing real about it. The dharma is different. It is the only thing that is "real." Being the unchanging cosmic law, it is the ultimate unchanging truth that shares its intrinsic self-nature (*svabhāva*).[64] The Theravada and the Mahāyāna schools of Buddhism hold opposing views on the ways the "ultimate truth" is related to the "phenomenal truth." To erase the traditional boundary that divided worldly beings from dharma, Nāgārjuna repudiated the supposition held by the Theravada school. Nothing in the universe, according to Nāgārjuna, not even the dharma, has *svabhāva*. Empty of self-nature, everything is what it is *in virtue of* its relation to other things. Nāgārjuna's protest against the *Abhidharma* metaphysics heralded the establishment of a new form of Buddhism, the Madhyamaka school of Mahāyāna Buddhism. The "Greater Vehicle" movement that was to exert dominant influence on the development of Buddhist cultures in Central and East Asia.

Nāgārjuna rejected *Abhidharma*'s exposition of *catuṣkoṭi* in completion, and considered its interpretation of the third *koṭi* problematic in particular.[65] The third *koṭi* says that the dharma is both real and unreal. *Abhidharma* explains the clause as follows: those who are enlightened know that the dharma is real. People who have failed to look beyond phenomenal truth have mistaken phenomenal truth as real and the dharma as unreal. Nāgārjuna rejects his interpretation, for it violates the principle of noncontradiction—what is *true* cannot be *false*. If the dharma is *real*, it cannot be *unreal*. As a universal rule, true and false, and real and unreal, could not exist at the same time. Just as a person cannot be both dead and alive, and fire does not burn some parts of the fuel but not others.

In Nāgārjuna's protest against *Abhidharma*'s interpretation of *catuṣ koṭi*, the Buddhist philosopher dismantled the stark contrast Theravada Buddhism drew between the ultimate truth and phenomenal truth. In our universe, Nāgārjuna argues, everything and everyone are dependently originated, necessarily coexistent, and positionally inseparable. Instead of sharing any intrinsic self-identity, people and things are constituted essentially by the place they happen to occupy in that web of relations. Something's being the thing that it is, is its bearing a bunch of relations to other things. Everything in the world, as Jay Garfield succinctly explicates in his annotation of the *Heart Sutra*, the canonical Buddhist sutra informing Nāgārjuna's conception of "emptiness" and the founding premise of the Madhyamaka school of Buddhism, is mutually and communally dependent in three important senses: "First, dependent upon causes and conditions for its existence; second, dependent on its parts and on the wholes in which it figures for its existence and identity; and third, dependent on conceptual imputation for its identity."[66] Since everything is dependently arisen, there is no ultimate ground to reality.

Nāgārjuna asserted that all material phenomena are dependently arisen. If there is no exception to this rule, we may wonder: What about dharma? If dharma is empty, is our existence suspended in a state of nihilist abstraction? Emptiness, once again, should not be confused with "nonexistence." Everything exists, but exists without "self-nature." If this is the case, what does dharma, the unchanging cosmic law, depend on? The answer is simple: the ultimate truth depends on phenomenal truth. Being mutually dependent upon each other, both the ultimate reality (conceptual notion) and the phenomenal reality (physical object) are as empty as the other. As duality ceases to exists, there is no longer "being empty" and "not being empty" to speak of. Even emptiness itself is empty.

Following Nāgārjuna's founding of the Madhyamaka school, his conception of emptiness had been reinterpreted by various schools of Mahāyāna Buddhism. Of the philosophical developments that continued to evolve in India and East Asia, the rise of Huayan 華嚴 ("Flower Garland") Buddhism in China is most relevant to our concern. Having made its way to China, Mahāyāna Buddhism grew into distinctive forms of local Buddhist practices.[67] The Huayan school was the most philosophically complex among these homegrown branches. Dushun 杜順 (557–640) and Fazang 法藏 (643–712) were the first and third patriarchs of this local school. Under the influence of the indigenous Chinese philosophical traditions, the two took the concept of "relational dependence" to a new level.

In the Chinese Daoist tradition, it is assumed that there exists a supreme principle behind the flow of events. The worldly phenomena that surround us do not constitute things *in themselves*; they are manifestations of *dao* (道) or *li* (理) the supreme way. Having assimilated the Indian notion of emptiness into the local Daoist belief, Dushun and Fazang suggest the following: being the presence or expression of *li*, the worldly phenomena or affairs (*shi* 事) are absent of intrinsic self-nature. It is precisely the same for *li*. Being a metaphysical abstraction, the presence or expression of *li* depends on them in order to be what it is. Absent of self-nature, *li* can be observed only through *shi*, the worldly affairs that manifest themselves in the physical reality. The ontological structure of *li*, in other words, contains the ontological structure of *shi*, and vice versa. Being an interpenetrative identity, *li* and *shi* are essentially *the same as* (*ji* 即) each other. Besides affirming that things are *interdependent on* each other, Dushun and Fazang parlayed the Indian notion of emptiness into a picture of the world in which the "ultimate reality" and the "phenomenal reality" *interpenetrate* each other. Their way of perceiving "ultimate reality" and "phenomenal reality" as a mutually constitutive identity, as far as I believe, exerted a profound influence on Wang Yangming's reinvention of the heartmind.

Wang devoted substantial years of his early adulthood to the study of Buddhist teachings. While he hesitated to honor this piece of personal history, the Buddhist metaphysics that had evolved from both the Indian and the Chinese philosophical traditions had penetrated his moral philosophy in a way that is seamless and deep. Neo-Confucian philosophers, as discussed in various sections of this book, perceive *li* as the all-pervading cosmic principle informing the compositional structure of myriad forms of creatures. Being the chief architect of the "Learning of the Principle" school of neo-Confucianism, Zhu Xi upheld that *li* the higher absolute order is seamlessly perfect. The Song philosopher lived at a time of social and political turmoil. Reluctant to accuse *li* of causing human corruption, he turned to the muddy *qi* substances and accused them of failing to materialize *li*'s structural perfection in the corresponding physical presence.

Familiar with the Buddhist metaphysics that evolved from the Madhyamaka school, the Yogācāra school, and eventually China's homegrown Huayan school, Wang Yangming agreed that *li* is the metaphysical abstraction *informing* the compositional structure of the heartmind.[68] But being a metaphysical abstraction, *li* is fluid and volatile. Unable to manifest itself in perceptible forms, the appearance of *li* is predicated on the myriad forms of worldly phenomena that disclose its formative structure. If the compositional structure of man's heartmind epitomizes *li* the cosmic pattern, *li* is *what it is* by relating to the heartmind. In this interpenetrative relationship, the ontological structure of the heartmind contains and encodes the ontological structure of *li* the cosmic patterns. To explicate their nonobstructive dependence, Wang declares that "the heartmind is *the same as* the cosmic pattern" (*xin ji li* 心即理).[69] Wang Yangming was certainly not the first to claim identity between the heartmind and the cosmic pattern in the development of neo-Confucianism. The brothers Cheng Hao and Cheng Yi made comparable remarks. In addition to that, even Zhu Xi himself mentioned that "the heartmind is the cosmic pattern; the cosmic pattern is the heartmind" (*xin ji li* 心即理; *li ji xin* 理即心).[70]

In Huayan Buddhism, Wang's use of the notion *ji* (即) ("is the same as") can be considered a Buddhist equivalence to the equals sign (=) indicating equality in Western mathematics. Derived from the Latin word *æqualis* and converted into a mathematical symbol by Robert Recorde (1512–1558), the equals sign is placed between two expressions sharing *the same value*, or for which one studies the conditions under which they share the same value. Having established an equivalence between the heartmind and the cosmic pattern, Wang's call for *xin ji li* can be represented as follows:

$$x \text{ (xin: heartmind)} = l \text{ (li: cosmic patterns)}$$

$$x = l$$

The equals sign, once again, is placed between two expressions sharing *the same value*. If the heartmind is *the same as* the *li* the cosmic patterns ($x = l$), it would be equally true to say that the cosmic pattern *is* the heartmind ($l = x$). Quantifying the heartmind and the cosmic pattern as identical and mutually convertible properties, Wang Yangming demolishes the boundary that divides the realm of metaphysical transcendence from the realm of human existence. Man's heartmind, unlike what Zhu Xi had claimed, is not a defective duplicate *of* heaven. *The heartmind is heaven*. What has been perceived to be two distinct realms of existence is indeed an organic oneness. Heaven is not *way up* there. It is here, and it is *us*.

Wang Yangming's repudiation of Zhu Xi's moral metaphysics remotely resonates with Nāgārjuna's rejection of the early Buddhist *Abhidharma*. Perceiving the dharma as the unchanging cosmic law, practitioners of Theravada Buddhism envisioned a rigid dichotomy between the "ineffable" ultimate truth and "effable" phenomenal truth. For Nāgārjuna, however, everything in the universe is dependently risen. Knowing that the "ineffable" ultimate truth is what it is *in virtue of* its relation to the "effable" phenomenal truth, Nāgārjuna replaces the hierarchical contrast that separates these two realms of truth into a relationship of "mutual dependence." In this relational existence, neither the "ineffable" ultimate truth nor "effable" phenomenal truth shares any intrinsic self-nature. These two realms of beings are as empty as each other. Such is the adapted instruction of the Buddha.

Having been exposed to the metaphysical premise of Madhyamaka and, successively, Huayan Buddhism, Wang Yangming asserted that man's heartmind *is the same as* the cosmic pattern. In this interpenetrative and interconnected relationship, *li* the abstract cosmic pattern is *what it is* by relating to man's heartmind. It is absent of self-nature. Being the physical manifestation *of* the cosmic pattern, the heartmind is just as empty as *li*. Not having any self-identity, whatever shows up in the heartmind is the crystallization of the cosmic pattern it epitomizes. Being "a form of substance that is *absent of* the evil as well as the good" (無善無惡心之體), the heartmind is free from intrinsic content, not to mention what Zhu Xi perceives to be *qing*, inferior human feelings.

Parliamentary Democracy: A Modern Experiment in Hunan

In Wang's teaching, *liangzhi* 良知 operates as the heartmind's moral censor. Being a functional extension of the heartmind, *liangzhi* the "good moral knowing" is just as empty as the heartmind. Aside from distinguishing good from evil, it is devoid of intrinsic self-content, and hence intrinsically incapable of providing either a perspective of seeing or a regulative framework guiding and coordinating the ways virtuous actions are being performed. Knowing that *liangzhi* is devoid of intrinsic self-content, its value is externally determined. So, what does *liangzhi* depend on? Acting, most obviously.

Sharing divergent conceptions of the heartmind, Zhu Xi and Wang Yangming developed distinctive approaches to learning. While Zhu Xi urged people to investigate the cosmic pattern disclosed in the Confucian classics, Wang Yangming reduced a person's deliberative consideration (*silü* 思慮) and wilful arrangement (*anpai sisuo* 安排思索) to matters of biased cleverness (*yongzhi zisi* 用智自私).[71] Being a living epitome of the cosmos, the heartmind is so clear and perfect that it transcends the *artificial* human intelligence one acquires from contrived social practices. For one to realize his endowed cosmic perfection that is finer than *what he thinks* he knows, a person needs to follow his cosmic instinct. Man's "*spontaneous* response" (*xing* 行), be it perceptual or physical, is the *revelation* of the heavenly principles.[72] Uninterrupted by man's premeditated intervention, this instinctive response is a person's embodied exteriorization of the abstract cosmic pattern on earth.

What I considered to be Wang Yangming's Buddhist-inspired interpretation of the oneness of knowledge and action brims with philosophical brilliance. Coming to the late nineteenth century, the precedent of democratic governance offered Tan Sitong an unprecedented opportunity to identify the affinity between China's prevailing "cosmic moral community" and the "modern political community," and, by extension, the attraction of integrating these two systems into a world of "cosmic moral-political oneness." To be politically modern, as it appeared to the young martyr, is about letting the homogeneous "cosmic moral members" *be* who they *already* are, thereby restoring "the immanence of the transcendental in the experiential" through China's transition to political modernity.[73]

Liang Qichao and Tan Sitong intended to put their philosophical vision into actual political practice. But later as their teacher Kang Youwei drafted multiple petitions to Emperor Guangxu seeking his endorsement to implement wholesale institutional reform to refurbish China's legislative and jurisdiction constructs, Liang and Tan grew impatient. On the eve of what he perceived to be the crumbling of China, Liang ventured to present a "contingency plan" to Chen Baozhen 陳寶箴 (1831–1900), the liberal-minded governor of Hunan (湖南) province.[74] In his missives Liang wrote: "Were we to thrust the reform to the gentlemen of the state, the Southern Mountain will be displaced and the Eastern Sea will be drained, but still the reform would not be put in place" (欲以變法之事, 望政府諸賢, 南山可移, 東海可涸, 而法終不可得變).[75] If the colonial powers were to subjugate China as they conquered Africa, India, and Vietnam as Kang Youwei predicted,[76] "let us assume the personal responsibility of transforming Hunan province into a self-determining political sovereignty."[77] Self-governed by cabinet members constituted exclusively by the local gentry, Hunan the "New China" would become an autonomous modern nation-state independent from China the multiethnic empire reigned by the Manchurian. In this "newly founded autonomous nation" (新造自

立之國), a national congress operated by parliamentary democracy and modern jurisdiction systems would be established.[78]

Liang was sharply aware that his "contingency plan was rebelliously unethical and widely deviant" (大逆不道, 狂悖之論).[79] It was so risky yet so propitious that it made his heart "throb uncontrollably and his hot blood boil, as if it were a flame that was to gush out from his throat" (心突突不能自制, 熱血騰騰焉, 將焰出於腔).[80] But, as Liang assured Chen Baozhen, so long as "one shares the determination to be independent" (存自立之心), to be willing to "burn all bridges and risk ten thousand deaths" (破斧沉舟, 萬死一生之策), and to set his mind on "having one or two hinterland provinces ready to declare its independence" (必有腹地一二省可以自立), "China would be able hold on to this last thread of hope" (然後中國有一綫之生路).[81]

A modern nation-state consists of members who cherish their national identity and seek to achieve self-determination. In Hunan, as Liang was aware, nearly all gentry members were foreign to modern governance. For the local gentry to comprehend the operating principles of democratic governance and fulfil their civil obligations, Chen Baozhen must "empower the local gentry" (*xing xiangquan* 興鄉權) by granting them the opportunity to learn to *become* modern legislators by partaking in a "trial" parliamentary congress.[82] This "trial" congress, Liang proposed, should take place in the Southern Learning Society (*Nan xuehui* 南學會), an organization that excluded the participation of individuals from other provinces. Aside from highly confidential topics, thereafter all the provisional policies to be implemented in Hunan should be passed directly to members of the Southern Learning Society for discussion and deliberation.[83] To restrict law makers' authority (定權限) and ensure "the separation of power in legislation and administration" (議事與行事分而為二), members of the Southern Learning Society were allowed to appoint only administrative personnel to implement the new policies.[84] After members had convened to discuss the feasibility of these provisional legislations for a year or so, over half of them would be qualified to assume the duty of modern congressmen.[85] These qualified congressmen could either renew their appointment or be dispatched to legislative councils to be established in counties and prefectures nearby.

Xuehui (學會) is often associated with a "learning group" or a "professional association" dedicated to the study of a particular subject of interest. But the Southern Learning Society that Liang proposed to Chen Baozhen was expected to operate as the prototype Lower Chamber (*Zhong yiyuan*

眾議院) of the national congress.[86] In the Southern Learning Society, as Tan disclosed to his teacher Ouyang Zhonggu, each member was expected to participate fully in the legislative process. When a magisterial officer needed to implement a new policy, he must first present the proposal to the Southern Learning Society for approval.[87] "The Southern Learning Society does not share the 'name' of the congress, but it operates in 'reality' *as* the congress" (無議院之名而有議院之實).[88] In the process of performing its legislative functions, this prototype congress should "assume 'actual' political power and eventuate in practice the bureaucratic reform that has not been introduced in public" (於是無變官制之名而又變官制之實).[89] Once the Southern Learning Society was ready to replace the magisterial office to be the venue in which institutional proceedings were processed, "it would actualize a legal reform that has yet been officially brought about" (於是無變法律制度之名, 而有變法律制度之實).[90]

As radical as their plan may seem, Liang's and Tan's preparation for Hunan's transition to a parliamentary democracy was publicly acknowledged by reform-minded intellectuals of their times. "When Tan Sitong first asked to create the Learning Society, Huang Zunxian 黃遵憲 [1848–1905] at once took his proposal as the establishment of the parliamentary congress" (譚復生等稟請開學會, 黃公度即以爲議院).[91] A reader, Chen Guangfu 陳光孚, wrote to *Hunan Newspaper* (*Xiang Bao* 湘報) in 1897. His letter displayed the general public's familiarity with Liang's undeclared purpose: "In terms of state governance, people from the West attach the greatest weight to the congress. . . . At present, the creation of the Southern Learning Society was meant to remold the state officials as modern legislators" (西人治國之道, 最重議院 . . . 今學會之設, 意在化官為士).[92] Wang Kangnian 汪康年 (1860–1911), the cofounder of Liang's early reformist journal *Chinese Progress* (*Shiwu bao* 時務報), was ready to envision the election and appointment processes of the congress.[93] Later, as Liang's proposal was outlawed by conversative officials, Huang Junlong 黃均隆 (?–1911), the imperial censor, said, "Liang and his associates published the *Chinese Progress* in Shanghai. They expressed enthusiastic support for democracy and the commencement of the congress. . . . Later the circle turned to the founding of the Southern Learning Society, an organization that substantiated the inception of the congress" (梁啓超者曾在上海刊刻時務報, 力倡民主議院之說者也。 . . . 又改建南學會, 以爲議院之權輿).[94]

The gravity of Liang's objectives should seem apparent to Chen Baozhen. On November 21, 1897, Liang wrote to Chen seeking the "independence" (*zili* 自立) of Hunan.⁹⁵ A month later, Tan submitted a follow-up petition. Calling Chen "my respected honor," Tan considered Chen "the only person in the country who is capable of granting sovereignty to the people" (方今海內能興民權者, 惟一我公).⁹⁶ Beyond establishing the Southern Learning Society as the preparational foundation of the national congress, Tan urged Chen Baozhen to ensure the prototype congress's administrative efficacy by conferring upon it "actual" political power. Chen was advised to establish a centralized "State Police Department" (*jingbu* 警部) under the command of the Southern Learning Society (在南學會下成立警部).⁹⁷ "The gentry's governmental authority," according to Tan, "should surpass that of the local magistrates" (其治地方之權, 反重於州縣官).⁹⁸ What he called defense (*baowei* 保衛) should be understood as an equivalence and revival of *baojia* (保甲), a community-based law enforcement and civil control system that Wang Anshi 王安石 (1021–1086), the Northern Song (960–1127) chancellor, invented and incorporated into his controversial socioeconomic reform.⁹⁹

In the spring of 1898, Tsarist Russia wrested from China a long-term lease for Port Arthur. Distressed by China's approaching calamity, Chen approved the request of Liang and Tan. The Southern Learning Society was founded officially in Hunan.¹⁰⁰ In the same year, Chen established the Bureau of Safety Defense (*Baowei ju* 保衛局) and placed the department under the command of the Southern Learning Society. Having reserved a budget from the Bureau of Taxation, Chen set up a modern military academy to prepare two thousand young men for military combat. Tan was appointed the supervisor to oversee the development of the new academy.¹⁰¹

Liang Qichao and Tan Sitong outlined what they perceived to be a viable institutional model in which Chinese "political modernity" could begin to take form. Following the establishment of the Southern Learning Society, Liang looked to introduce the local gentry to the origins, historical development, and legislative functions of parliamentary governance.¹⁰² In "A Study of Ancient Parliaments" (*Gu yiyuan kao* 古議院考), Liang wrote, "The parliament serves as the foundation to strengthen a nation, whereas the schools are that upon which the parliament is based" (故強國家以議院為本, 議院以學校爲本).¹⁰³ To persuade Chen Baozhen, Liang said, "To promote the sovereignty of the people, it would be wise to begin by empowering the gentry. To empower the gentry, it would be wise to start by founding a learning society" (欲興民權, 宜先興紳權。欲興紳權, 宜以學會為之起點).¹⁰⁴ "The degree of political right a person enjoys," Liang continued, "is proportional to his intellect" (是故權之與智相倚者也).[105] "To promote people's sovereignty, one must prioritize the need of enlightening the general public" (今日欲伸民權，必以廣民智為第一義).[106] In 1897, Liang was appointed the instructor in chief at the Hunan Academy of Current Affairs, a modern school where he began to "passionately publicize the political revolution" (盛倡革命).[107] In the hope of awakening a young generation of Hunan natives, Liang further encouraged Chen to convert local academies (*shuyuan* 書院) devoted to classic learning into modern schools (*xueyuan/ xuetang* 學院/學堂).[108]

Liang's support for public education and the establishment of professional societies appeared to project distinct but closely connected aspects of the "reform" he aspired to implement in the Qing monarchy to strengthen its rule. But as soon as a reader turns to historical documents chronicling Liang's revolutionary schemes, it becomes clear that Hunan's modern educational reform was intended to facilitate the local population's participation in burgeoning parliamentary governance. In a letter to his fellow comrade, Di Baoxiang 狄葆賢 (1873–1941), Liang envisioned China's national independence movement to unfold as such: following the precedent of Hunan, all provinces in China would establish their local "trial" congresses and practice self-governance. Once a local congress could operate autonomously as an independent legislative unit, "any province could become independent" (隨舉一省皆可自立).[109] For this day to arrive, each individual province must invest in its local military force. As insurgents revolted to overthrow the Qing monarchy, the Independence Society (Zili hui 自立會), the headquarters that oversaw and orchestrated the national liberation movement, "would certify all southeastern provinces as independent and newly established nations" (指定東南各行省為新造自立之國).[110] Subsequently the eighteen provincial "sovereignties" could be unified as one nation to resist the invasion of foreign powers (合十八省為一國，以拒外人).[111] In this new, modern nation an official congress would be established. Tan Sitong, the one who is most intelligent and knowledgeable, "should make a perfect candidate for president" (伯里璽之選也).[112]

Politicizing Wang Yangming's Moral Metaphysics

The progressive political vision Liang Qichao and Tan Sitong shared, as readers familiar with this piece of modern Chinese history know, had never been realized. In his attempt to *enact* the Great Unity in a way that was radically different from that of Kang Youwei, Tan Sitong the young martyr ultimately exhibited his enlightened understanding through his own death. Having obtained his Buddhist enlightenment, perhaps Tan would not have thought that he would "die."[113] His death, however, mattered to Liang Qichao. Having invited his dear friend to participate in the 1898 reform, Liang had since been tormented both by Tan's passing and by his own chances of survival.[114] To display the finest form of knowing from a friend, Liang struggled to contextualize Tan's death in the most expansive political, intellectual, and philosophical framework possible. In his preface to *An Exposition of Benevolence*, Liang writes,

> Why did Tan Sitong compose *An Exposition of Benevolence*? He wrote it to glorify the teachings of Nanhai [Kang Youwei] and to integrate the essential ideas of the world's great philosophers in an effort to save sentient beings all over the world. Nanhai used to teach his students: "make the pursuit of benevolence one's primary goal, the search for the Great Unity one's guiding principle, the salvation of China one's primary goal, and the annihilation of oneself and one's family one's ultimate commitment." *An Exposition of Benevolence* is a book that elucidates these objectives, and Tan the martyr is the man who enacted these goals in action. 《仁學》何為而作也？將以光大南海之宗旨，會通世界聖哲學之心法，以救全世界之眾生也。南海之教學者曰：以求仁為宗旨，以大同為條理，以救中國為下手，以殺身破家為究竟。《仁學》者，即發揮此語之書也，而烈士者即實行此語之人也。[115]

To justify Tan's volitional political execution, Liang asserted that his friend had composed *An Exposition of Benevolence* to glorify their teacher Kang Youwei's determination to realize the Great Unity and had sequentially "enacted" (*shixing*) this progressive political ideal in action. While the Great Unity projects the prospect of all men living harmoniously in a community of undivided oneness, Tan decided that he must be "interconnected" with everything and everyone in this universe. By creating a subtle yet illuminating synthesis between the Great Unity and Tan's Buddhist-inspired definition of "benevolence," Liang tactfully incorporated Buddhist metaphysics into the evolving development of New Text Confucianism. And in the years that followed, he continued to emphasize the importance of enacting Tan's conviction in collective political actions.

Similar to Wang Yangming, Liang perceived man's innate moral goodness as a dispositional propensity that is latent, abstract, and imperceptible. For the imperceptible propensity to take shape in true, concrete knowledge, it *has to be* experienced and obtained through external, formal outlets (真知識非實地經驗之後是無從得着的), which include physical actions, embodied sensual responses, and myriad forms of other empirical experiences.[116] "*Li* the cosmic principle," as Liang recounted in retrospect, "does not exist in separation from the heartmind and physical objects for certain" (理當然不能離心物而存在).[117] "Once the subjective inclination is detached from objective matter, it loses its purpose and amounts to nonexistence" (因為主觀的意不涉着到客觀的物時，便失其作用，等於不存在).[118] Being an imperceptible abstraction, one's latent moral propensity is *contingent* on the concrete empirical experience. Its expression is externally defined and proceeds to reinvent, reconstitute, and re-present itself in the changing circumstances.[119] Regardless of how these external expressions have changed, they remain the most truthful expressions of one's endowed moral goodness.

In a series of writings published in the early 1900s, Liang seemed to have conveyed and accentuated a singular message: for modern political concepts to be *true*, they must manifest a person's sincere moral intent. Instead of "learning" through the investigation of texts, such moral propensity can only be *lived*, *enacted*, and *experienced* through embodied actions. To emphasize the importance of enactment, and communicate Wang Yangming's moral theory to his contemporaries, in 1903 Liang compiled an anthology of moral precepts titled *Mirror for Moral Cultivation* (*Deyu jian* 德育鑑).[120] Having collected a substantial number of moral dicta prescribed by thinkers that range from Confucius to Qing philosophers, Liang summed up six steps to help his contemporaries obtain "authentic" (*zhen* 真; *zhenzheng de* 真正的) modern political knowledge. Of these steps, the first requires one to "discern and recover one's natural moral intuition" (*bianshu* 辨術). Following that, one should make the effort of "becoming resolute" (*lizhi* 立志). Upon "recognizing the primal importance" (*zhiben* 知本), a person must persist in "preserving it through nurturing cultivation" (*cunyang* 存養) as well as "self-reflection and restraint" (*xingke* 省克). Once the person has succeeded in recognizing, securing, and preserving the instinctive moral goodness drawing upon Wang's teachings, Liang championed the idea that the person must *enact* (*yingyong* 應用) this instinct in *embodied* actions. It is only by materializing one's moral goodness *in practice* that a person can transform a conceptual notion into a moral attitude, and from an attitude to a moral behavior producing positive social, political changes.

To retrieve what he perceived to be a philosophical foundation for Wang Yangming's moral optimism, in *Mirror for Moral Cultivation* Liang returns to a number of remarks Confucius made about humans' nature. Then by skillfully juxtaposing the words of Confucius and Mencius with those of Wang, Liang the political activist argued that in the Mencian school of Confucian teaching, it is generally believed that human beings begin life as self-sufficient moral beings. Wang Yangming inherited and substantially advanced the Mencian school of Confucianism in the Ming dynasty. Being faithful followers of Wang's teaching, later philosophers such as Nie Shuangjian 聶雙江 (1487–1563), Wang Longxi 王龍溪 (1498–1583), Luo Nianan 羅念菴 (1504–1564), and Liu Zongzhou 劉宗周 (1587–1645) proceeded to defend and develop the moral metaphysical intricacies of his philosophy to their full potential. Liang shared the moral faith Wang Yangming placed in the people. By showcasing how the belief in man's instinctive moral goodness had systematically evolved from Mencius, Wang Yangming, and more recent neo-Confucian thinkers, Liang's anthology subtly presents and reconstructs a moral-intellectual genealogy fortifying the legitimacy of the Learning of the Mind school of neo-Confucianism. His support for the "heart-based" over the "text-based" approach to learning is perhaps most clearly reflected in the title of his anthology: to be moral is to look into oneself in the mirror.[121]

To bridge the gap that had hindered men from internalizing the imported political concepts as ontologically *lived* experiences, in the same year Liang compiled a second anthology titled *China's Bushido* (中國之武士道). In Chinese history, Liang said, people had long cherished the tradition of realizing their moral conviction through self-mutilation. The most celebrated episodes appear in the grand historian Sima Qian's 司馬遷 (c. 145–85 BC) *The Records of the Grand Historian*. To execute what Liang perceived to be prototypical forms of "political revolution" in China, those early "revolutionary" heroes had willingly smashed their heads against pillars, slashed their throats with swords, and performed other suicidal acts. Liang's compilation of these self-destruction accounts was warmly endorsed by his contemporaries. Yang Du 楊度 (1875–1931), an influential revolutionary thinker of his time, favorably commented on these early political suicides: "'Life and death,' as the Japanese Zen

Buddhist monk Hakuin Ekaku 白隱慧鶴 (1686–1769) once said, are actual facts" (死生者事實也).[122] "It is not the kind of empty talk and empty discussion that one does for the sake of fooling oneself or others" (非可以空言空論自慰以慰人者).[123]

Man's moral propensity, as Liang emphasized, "loses its purpose and amounts to nonexistent once it is detached from empirical experiences" (便失其作用，等於不存在).[124] To illustrate how corporeal bodily experiences can give abstract conceptual ideas blood and bone in both a literal and a metaphoric sense, Liang was equally careful to accentuate the intensity of physical suffering in his recounting of modern European history. In his composition of the *Biography of the Three Heroes Who Founded Italy* (*Yidali jianguo sanjie zhuan* 意大利建國三傑傳), Liang calls Giuseppe Garibaldi (1807–1882) an "authentic" nationalist (*zhen aiguo zhe* 真愛國者).[125] In contrast to the hypocritical Qing intellectuals, the Italian hero shared a moral calling that outweighed his love for life. To realize his moral and political vision through Italy's unification project, Garibaldi was ready to endure a series of extreme bodily tortures. When the heroic man was first punished for organizing political protests, he declared "his wish to smash his brain and liver on the land of Italy" (欲塗肝腦於本國之土地).[126] Garibaldi proceeded to demonstrate in the Italian Congress with his naked body covered by dripping blood (鮮血淋漓, 軀幹全赤) and blood-splattered eyes (濺血之眼).[127] Garibaldi's wife, who was eight months pregnant at the time, endured with him on the battlefield. Before the heroic woman died giving birth to a dead infant, she bid farewell to her husband with "blood-shot teary eyes" (猩紅之淚眼) and "a waxy yellowish smiling face" (蠟黃之笑臉).[128] Having experienced extreme physical and emotional torment, Garibaldi obtained the ultimate conviction that Italy's unification could be achieved only by squeezing his brain marrow (絞腦髓) and slashing the blood of his neck (擲頸血).[129]

Man's Instinctive Moral Goodness: Broken or Intact?

A person, Liang argued, does not "learn" about moral goodness from learning; he realizes and enacts it with his corporeal body. In Liang's historical biography, Garibaldi the Italian hero expressed clear determination in breaking up his flesh into flaking pieces. In reality, Tan Sitong literally lost his head. Practically speaking, to what extent can Liang's ideal cosmic, moral vision be virtually feasible? In the world of neo-Confucianism, man's moral perfection is a reflection of cosmic coherence. From the twelfth century onward, the conception of such cosmic imagination had given Chinese intellectuals much-needed hope to hold on to during a time of historical turmoil.[130] But at the same time, the anxiety and distrust they expressed for the oneness model, alongside their attempts to suppress or deny one's deep suspicion of the model, seems to have played an equally if not more decisive role in shaping the development of the Chinese history. Zhu Xi believed that men share a perfect cosmic nature. But since such nature has been substantially polluted by the deficient substances of which he is made, man can "learn" to be good only through the study of texts combined with the investigation of external events and states of affairs. Wang Yangming recognized the human deficiencies Zhu Xi identified.[131] But to rekindle the moral hope, Wang redirected his attention from the harsh reality and asked people to focus on restoring their perfect cosmic nature. For Wang Yangming, what Zhu Xi considered to be perfect moral potential *could be* actual. As long as a person is willing to put in effort, there is a good possibility that he can materialize his imperceptible moral instinct in perceptible physical actions. Once the cosmic abstraction becomes *real*, one relinquishes the boundary dividing metaphysical transcendence from human existence. To *live* is to be in heaven.

The emphasis Wang Yangming placed on the "Oneness of Knowledge and Action" expects more than man's spontaneous moral behavior; it struggles to bring together the metaphysical and the existential, positively putting an end to the irony of oneness that had persisted in the philosophical tradition of neo-Confucianism. Liang Qichao endorsed the moral faith Wang Yangming shared for people. Seized by the urge to justify his friend's tragic death, the modern reformer repeatedly emphasized that a modern political concept can be *true* only if it becomes an embodied enactment of one's spontaneous moral intent. Perceiving his contemporaries as equal cosmic members of the metaphysical republic, Liang envisioned the hope of having people live as one organic cosmic, moral, and political body in a republican government.[132] Of the many things a person can do to be one, there, as he saw it, was *a way* that promised to remove all existing barriers dividing the human from heaven, knowing from acting, and the people from the state. *The way* rests in people's collective participation in a political revolution.

Proceeding to the next two chapters, it is time to return to the questions I raised earlier. Liang wanted people to make the earth heaven.

Later as he tried to explicate and assess such a possibility in his depiction of the French Revolution, what did "heaven" turn out to look like? If being a "cosmic" creature enacting his cosmic potentials is about drowning oneself in a river packed with blood and dismembered human flesh, what kind of a cosmos had Liang disclosed in the early twentieth century? As noble as Liang Qichao's vision may be, it was destined to fail in a tragic fashion. If man's moral nature proves to be questionable, what kind of property would the lack of morality turn political modernity into? What would it mean for China to proceed to political modernity without moral intent? And once the cosmic vision was to be shattered along with Liang's modern reformist project, what could China hold on to in the years that were to follow? However reluctant I am to enter the heart of darkness, we should now turn to Liang's celebration, and, at the time, painful denial of the French Revolution. Without unearthing unresolved anxieties, incongruities, and contradictions pertaining to a philosophical trajectory that seems remotely relevant to the late Qing political reform, we cannot understand how Liang's reformist project was supposed to work and, more importantly, how it failed to work.

Chapter 4

Dissolution of Modern Political Languages in the Cinematic Spectacle

In 1902, Liang Qichao began to serialize his novella *The Future of New China*, a story taking place in 2062, 160 years after the year in which the story was published. The novella unfolds with China celebrating its "fiftieth restoration anniversary" (*wushinian weixin zhudian* 五十年維新祝典). By inserting an intertextual comment, "Attention" (*zhuyi* 注意), with a uniquely personal voice, Liang, the narrator, draws readers' attention to the World Exposition held in Shanghai, where tens of thousands of international visitors have arrived to attend the exposition. As most of the celebrations are staged in Shanghai, the world leaders attending the International Peace Congress (Wangguo taiping huiyi 萬國太平會議) in Nanjing 南京, a city five hundred miles away, send naval vessels to pay China their tribute.[1] With vessels lined up along the coast of Shanghai, Liang presents a panoramic view of a crowd that spreads from Shanghai to Jiangbei 江北, Wusongkou 吳淞口, and Chongming County 崇明縣. Marveling at the breadth and scale of these celebration events, with wonder and awe Liang exclaims: "How magnificent! How magnificent!" (*kuozhai, kuozhai* 闊哉、闊哉).[2]

Having unveiled the panoramic topographical viewpoint, the novella zooms in on the interior decor of the largest exhibition hall in Shanghai. A clock on the wall indicates it is nearly twelve thirty. An audience of twenty thousand has arrived from the countries of Great Britain, the United States, Germany, France, Russia, Japan, the Philippines, and India to attend a keynote speech that is about to be given.[3] Mimicking the tone of a vernacular storyteller, to the *kanguan* 看官, viewers who are physically presented in the marketplace,[4] Liang presents a graphic vision: the clock hanging over the wall strikes twelve thirty.[5] The chairperson of the historical association walks onto the stage. With a deep bow he welcomes the audience. As the chairperson finishes his welcoming speech, Dr. Kong appears on the second rank of the stairs on the left. Robed in his formal gown, the old gentleman wears a medal of honor upon his chest. With a bright and gentle smile, this honorable man makes his way slowly to the stage. Dr. Kong makes a graceful gesture, at which clapping reverberates around the hall like the sound of landslides and roaring waves.[6]

The Future of New China was published in the inaugural issue of *New Fiction*. In "On the Relationship between Fiction and Public Governance" (論小說與群治之關係), an essay issued alongside the first installment of the novella, Liang wrote that fiction is capable of creating "a life beyond one's life, and a world beyond that of one's own" (身外之身, 世界外之世界).[7] In this realm novel of experiences, readers embrace imaginings that exceed the ordinary. Among the different genres of writing, no other form of literary expressions is as evocatively descriptive as fiction (而諸文之中, 能極其妙而神其技者, 莫小說曰).[8] Through the visual description of a topographic landscape, the furnishing decor of a modern lecture hall, the appearances of refined garments, and the applause of the engaged audience, Liang strived to transform China's political future into a vivid cinematic landscape. Beyond constructing a discursive modern national imagination, as most scholars believe Liang was doing,[9] the pictorial and acoustic immediacy the reformer communicated to the reader indicates that the use of new fiction rests in its *ekphrasical* potential to make abstract "ideas" *look* real by creating pictures with words.[10] First discussed in Plato's *The Republic*, *ekphrasis* is "the name of a literary genre, or at least a *topos*, that seeks to imitate in words an object of the plastic arts."[11] Motivated by man's desire for the natural sign, the creation of *ekphrasis* is understood generally as "a sign that is to be taken as a visual substitute for its referent."[12] Often a poet is captured by his naïve wish to see the immediacy of the picture. To realize such a wish, the poet describes the physical qualities of a scene or object in visual terms. Sometimes his verbal descriptions may appear so transparent and *real* that the mimetic account animates the object with its representational transparency and mistakes the words as the "real" referent, thereafter rendering the mediating linguistic codes irrelevant.

As discussed in the previous chapters, Liang was distressed by his contemporaries' obsession with textual knowledge, seeing in it a disabling continuation of a discredited traditional approach to understanding that had come to characterize preparation for the imperial examinations. Assuming that words as signifiers are inadequate in representing the modern political reality being signified, in 1902 Liang declared that "the reformation of people's government *must* begin with a revolution in fiction, and the renovation of the people *must* begin with the renovation of fiction."[13] In *The Future of New China*, Liang attempted to make conceptual ideas "look" animated and real. By remediating the conceptual into lively pictorial and acoustic presences, his invention of "new" fiction as a new means of representation, to borrow Anne Friedberg's contemporary terms, "constitutes the frame of a window"[14] and unfolds "an intermedial space through which new ways of seeing can emerge."[15] As Liang presents spectators with different perspectives from which to view familiar pieces of conceptual knowledge, the limits and multiplicities of the frame of vision redefine the boundaries and multiplicities of the physical reality.[16]

Liang's fictional animation of the conceptual reminds one of the rise of the "visual turn" in today's print journalism.[17] In this multimedia age, television, film, and digital technologies such as virtual reality and computer graphics present the audience our world as seen before the screen. To compete with these visual and digital media, the prose writing in print media, as Jay David Bolter discusses in his study of popular media culture, strives to "emulate computer graphics."[18] Rather than relying on semantic signs to convey information as discursive knowledge, newspaper and tabloid writing exploit the expressive potential of words, imageries, and other literary devices to conjure up various visual imaginations. With the written text projecting vivid visual imaginations, popular prose invites the reader to "pass through the sign to the thing represented by it."[19]

In his attempt to transform "one-dimensional" conceptual ideas into the "three-dimensional" fictional representation, Liang asserted that fiction was capable of performing a task that could not be easily accomplished by linguistic discursion. Considering fiction the *most* indispensable tool for renewing the people and enlightening them with modern political knowledge, Liang exemplified how one can subvert the legitimacy of one representational medium and shift it to another. At the turn of the twentieth century, different discourses representing different political forces were competing for meaning and legitimacy. While this was a time for inventing and modifying the new discourse, it was also a time in which one was given the rare opportunity of questioning, repudiating, and potentially disabling the representative power of discourse as a whole. Liang's introduction of fiction as a more faithful means of communication indicates that not only was late Qing China in a state of linguistic fluidity, it was also in a state of "representational fluidity."

In the following discussion, I hope to explore the new representational paradigms Liang employed to reinvent and redefine modern political knowledge, and how the multiplicity of these representational formats was intended to achieve the paradoxical purpose of challenging and obscuring the modern political knowledge he had created in the first place. The chapter begins by addressing two fundamental concerns: Why in 1902 was Liang determined to convert modern political languages into a vernacular system of visuality and physicality? And why is it that one can renew the people only by remediating the readily available modern political key words into three-dimensional fictional presences?

New representational frameworks, as contemporary Western theorists suggest, open up new ways of seeing. In *New China*, Liang strove to transform the conceptual given into a virtual realm of experiential presence. Beyond his prophetic projection of China's political future, his novella is known for its depiction of a debate between two young men sharing conflicting political views. Huang Keqiang 黃克強, on one hand, is in support of moderate reform; his friend Li Qubing 李去病, on the other hand, remains convinced that only a political revolution can save China from its predicament. As the story unfolds, Huang Keqiang eventually succeeds in realizing his "reformist" proposals, which lead to the great prosperity China enjoys in 2062. By utilizing the expressive potential of fiction, which serves as conversion tool to make pictures with words, Liang transforms restoration (*weixin* 維新) and revolution (*geming* 革命), two recently translated political key words, into an animated cinematic narrative. Rather than conceptualizing "restoration" and "revolution" in discursive terms, his fictional transfiguration of modern political lexicons embodies a form of "remediation," the rendition of an identical body of knowledge through a new means of representation.[20] Knowing that Liang shared the firm conviction that fictional representation is capable of representing the truth more faithfully than semantic discursion, the chapter examines whether Liang's decision to communicate modern political concepts as virtual cinematic presences anticipated an epistemic shift, and eventually an unexpected epistemic crisis, in late Qing China. By examining the ways in which the fictional imaginations Liang evokes for these modern political concepts have contradicted their prescribed semantic content, the chapter questions whether these *ekphrasical* fictional descriptions run the risk of destabilizing the signifying power of modern political languages and exposing the vulnerability of the recently translated political discourse as a whole.

Between Learning and Religious Truth

In his essay "On the Relationship between Fiction and Public Governance," Liang Qichao asserts that fiction is capable of transforming the reader and society through the affective means of thurification (*xun* 薰), immersion (*jin* 浸), stimulation (*ci* 刺), and lifting (*ti* 提).[21] Of Buddhist origins, the emotive power of such knowledge transmission mechanisms promises to induce perceptual awareness without relying on linguistic discursion. While many have discussed the cultural origins and functions of "thurification," "immersion," "stimulation," and "lifting,"[22] we have yet to fully consider what makes these *nondiscursive* means of communication instrumental in bringing people modern political enlightenment.[23] Let us begin by examining these nondiscursive communication mechanisms alongside Liang's promotion of Buddhism in the early 1900s.

On the day "Fiction and Public Governance" was issued in *New Fiction*, Liang published a corresponding article titled "The Strengths and Shortcomings of the Religious Thinker and the Philosopher" (宗教與哲學家之長短得失) in *New Citizen Journal*.[24] In the latter article, Liang starts by drawing a distinction between philosophy (*zhexue* 哲學) and religion (*zongjiao* 宗教). The study of philosophy, he says, can be divided into two schools[25]—one is the "school of objects" (*weiwu pai* 唯物派), while the other is "the school of mind" (*weixin pai* 唯心派).[26] Those associated with the "school of mind," as Liang continues, are chiefly interested in "scholarly knowledge" (*xuewen* 學問), "academic study" (*xueshu* 學術), "theoretical thinking" (*xueshuo* 學說), and "the theory of science" (*gezhi xueli* 格致學理).[27] By attaching the common prefix *xue* 學 (the learning of), a term he uses often to refer to the acquisition of knowledge based on the careful investigation of a text or language rather than introspective contemplation, to these classification categories, Liang reduces philosophy (*zhexue*) to one form of bookish learning. Rather than the rational investigation of principles of being, in his writing philosophy refers specifically to investigations based on the study of *words* or a text-based approach to knowledge. Then based on the equivalence he draws between philosophy and the study of words, Liang further trivializes philosophy as the "study of the names" (*mingxue* 名學) and the "study of the mathematics" (*suanxue* 算學).[28]

Liang's definition of philosophy deviates from conventional wisdom. Having reduced philosophy to the study of words or the learning of conceptual knowledge, he astutely includes "new, or Western, learning" (*xinxue* 新學), a subject sharing the suffix *xue* 學, in the philosophy category. Philosophy, Liang declares, is in general inferior to religion. The reformer states,

> In recent times, those so-called outstanding figures are busy showing off the few terminologies they acquired from new learning. They abandon all moral traditions we inherit from the past and claim that these traditions have little significance. And as for the new moral teachings conceived by recent philosophers, they fail to comprehend even the most trivial aspects of them. 今世所謂識時俊傑者，口中撿拾一二新學名詞，遂吐棄古來相傳一切道德，謂為不足輕重。而於近哲所謂新道德者，亦未嘗窺見其一指趾。[29]

In his protest against the "fashionable young people" pursuing the "new learning," Liang accuses them of being ignorant about the Western intellectual traditions that foreground the evolution of most modern concepts. What these people think they have acquired as "Western learning" (*siguo xueshuo* 西國學說) is in fact little more than "new lexicons" (*xinxue mingci* 新學名詞).[30] To criticize those who are oblivious to the "true" meanings these modern concepts represent, Liang gives a few examples illustrating the ways in which the thinking of Adam Smith (1723–1790), Charles Darwin (1809–1882), John Locke (1632–1704), and Immanuel Kant (1724–1804) have been misconstrued by individuals who adopt a text-based approach to learning.[31] The term "original wealth" (*yuanfu* 原富), he says, first appears in Yan Fu's translation of *The Wealth of Nations* (1776).[32] Taking *yuanfu* verbatim, people interpret the term as the accumulation of private riches instead of the creation of public wealth.[33] The same interpretative practice extends to Yan Fu's translation of Darwin's evolutionary theory as *wujing zhi lun* 物競之

論 (the theory on the competition between species). Instead of being aware of the urgency of forming national communities at a time of growing international conflict, these people construe Darwin's theory as competition between members of one's community.[34] Locke's and Kant's conceptions of the notion "freedom of will" (*yiyu ziyou* 意欲自由), more unfortunately, validate certain individuals' excessive self-indulgence as a right bestowed by God.[35]

The translation of Western political, philosophical, and scientific concepts promised the advent of modern knowledge.[36] But in his reductionist account, Liang reduces "Western learning" to linguistic "signifiers" detached and separated from their "signified" meanings.[37] Liang denounces his contemporaries' "learning" (*xue*) of philosophy as a meaningless quest for idle words. Of the various forms of "philosophical" practices, he considers new learning the most inferior of all.

Having voiced his criticism of the study of philosophy, Liang asserts that "thinkers pursuing philosophy and religion share views and approaches that are directly opposite" (宗教家言與哲學家言往往相反對者也), and these schools should thus be classified as antithetical practices. Philosophy, for instance, focuses on the acquisition of knowledge that has form (*youxing* 有形), whereas religion is invested in the formless (*wuxing* 無形) truth that transcends practical knowledge.[38] The reformer says: "It is true that the philosopher exceeds the religious thinker in the realm of metaphysical discursion, but the former cannot be a match for the latter when it comes to the management of practical state affairs" (雖然言窮理則宗教不如哲學家, 言治事則哲學家不如宗教家). To further explicate the contrast in concrete terms, Liang compares formal knowledge prescribed in philosophical teaching to the physical body (*shen* 身) and religious enlightenment to the heart (*xin* 心) and soul (*linghun* 靈魂).[39] Assuming that learned individuals in China have abandoned their souls in pursuit of the body, Liang asserts that were China to become *truly* modernized, people would have to devote themselves to religious practice rather than continuing their "study" of philosophical knowledge.

In his comparison between philosophy and religion, Liang, somewhat interestingly, classifies Buddhism and the Learning of the Mind school of neo-Confucianism as "categories of religious practices" (宗教之類也).[40] By comparing China's present political situation to that of Meiji Japan, Liang asserts that "religious thinking makes the best remedy when it comes to reforming a country" (論革新國是者, 宗教思想為之也).[41] When it comes to *New China*, Liang reasserts that "the adoption of the teachings of

Wang Yangming and Lu Xiangshan 陸象山 (1139–1192) offer the finest solution to save China from its political predicament" (陸王學是今日救時第一法門).[42] The reformer argues,

> The Wang Yangming school of Neo-Confucianism in China can also be classified as the Learning of the Mind. People who can truly understand some of its principles will become strong and determined, and will become more aggressive at whatever they set their minds on. The manner and practices displayed by Ming Confucian scholars offer good examples. In the last two hundred years of this reign, this school of learning has lost its popularity. Certain branches of the school have made their way across the East Sea. The success of the Meiji restoration is attributable to the Learning of the Mind. The Learning of the Mind, fairly speaking, is the most superior form of practice among different religions. 吾國之王學，唯心派也，苟學此而得者，則其人必發強剛毅，而任事必加勇猛，觀明儒者之風節，可見也。本朝二百餘年，斯學銷沉，而其支流超渡東海。遂成日本維新之治，是心學之為用也。心學者實宗教之最上乘也。[43]

Wang Yangming's representation of the Learning of the Mind school of neo-Confucianism, as discussed in earlier chapters, emphasizes the importance of cultivating intuitive knowledge without relying overly on the study of texts. Considering the intellectual and cultural background in which Lu-Wang's moral teachings were conceived, the Learning of the Mind school of neo-Confucianism has been generally considered a philosophical school.[44] Liang, however, insists on classifying the Lu-Wang school of neo-Confucianism as *xinxue* 心學 (the Learning of the Mind), the Learning of Wang Yangming (*wangxue* 王學), and the Learning of Lu-Wang (*luwang xue* 陸王學) as "religion" (*jiao* 教). Such liberal classification presents that following implication: "enlightened" understanding of modern political concepts is anathema to "learned" familiarity with modern political languages. In his writing, what Liang was truly concerned with may not have been the difference between philosophy and religion. By dividing philosophy and religion into two oppositional categories and creating a contrast between "the body and the soul" and, by extension, "the form and the formless," Liang was to accentuate the difference between the "study" of discursive modern political concepts and obtaining an "enlightened understanding" of them. The categorical distinction he drew between "philosophy" and "religion," in this sense, is metaphorical. It cannot be taken verbatim.

Among Buddhism, Intuitive Knowledge, and New Fiction

To break with the slavish conformity that had hindered the Chinese public from becoming truly modern, Liang sought to replace "learning" with the kind of "intuitive understanding" endorsed by Buddhism and the Learning of the Mind school of neo-Confucianism. His aspiration to transmit modern political knowledge without relying excessively on discursive textual explication was manifested repeatedly in 1902. In "The Political Theory of Aristotle" (亞里士多德之政治學說), an essay published two weeks after "The Philosopher and the Religious Thinker," Liang compares man's enlightened understanding of democracy to the attainment of Buddhahood.[45] As for how the intuitive mode of knowledge transmission can be incorporated in the transmission of modern political knowledge, it appears that Liang's solution rests in drawing a connection between Buddhism and fiction.

To Liang, the creation of an animated cinematic narrative can move people without stating the explicit. By comparing the affective power of fiction to Buddhist knowledge transmission mechanisms such as "thurification," "immersion," "stimulation," and "lifting," he accentuates the similarity between fictional communication and the "religious" mode of intuitive knowledge transmission. Having disclosed the ways in which fiction's communication mechanisms are similar to those of Buddhism, Liang further explains why fiction is the most nondiscursive means of communication among other genres of writing:

> The Chan Buddhist method of "hitting and shouting" [at students] also resorts to the power of stimulation to lead men from their folly to sudden enlightenment. This power is more effective in speech than in writing. However, the effect of the spoken word is spatially and temporally limited. Because of the inherent limitations of speech, we must turn to writing. As for writing, the vernacular is a more effective medium than the classical language and the parable is a more effective form than the formal statement. Hence, nothing possesses more

power of stimulation than fiction. 禪宗之一棒一喝, 皆利用此刺激力以度人者, 此力之為用也。文字不如語言, 然語言力所被不能久也。於是不得不乞靈於文字。在文字中, 則文言不如其俗語, 莊論不如其寓言, 故具此力最大者, 非小說末由。[46]

In the above statement, Liang presents a fairly contoured logic to dissociate fictional representation from linguistic discursion. Chan Buddhism, as he elaborates more extensively in "On General Transformational Trends of Chinese Academic Thoughts" (論中國學術思想變遷之大勢), is known for its insistence on transmitting its teaching through nonverbal acts. Liang writes,

> The teaching of Chan is independent of language, whether spoken or written. It points towards discovering one's own [Buddha] nature; so that one might become a Buddha through his realization [of that nature]. 禪宗以不著語言, 不立文字, 直指本心, 見性成佛為教義。[47]

Doctrines of Chan Buddhism are not transmitted through language. Since the practitioner "does not have any words written" (*bu zhu yizi* 不著一字), "nor does he give any formal lectures or have any texts written" (*bu shuofa, bu zhushu* 不說法, 不著書), the knowledge transmission method the Chan Buddhist pursues is analogous to the "formless spiritual truth" as defined and delineated in "The Religious Thinker and the Philosopher."[48] Chan Buddhism, as Liang is fully aware of, looks for the complete discarding of words. To justify the use of language in his fictional creation, Liang presents the following reasoning: compared with "written words" (*wenzi* 文字), "speech" (*yuyan* 語言) is a more effective medium in kindling Buddhist enlightenment. Since "speech" does not travel far, one has no choice but to resort to "written words." Of the various forms of verbal expressions, the classical language is not as expressive as slang; slang is not as expressive as formal statements; and formal statements are not as expressive as parables. Knowing that the parable is created through fictional fabrication, fiction is hence the most effective mean to induce Buddhist enlightenment. Liang praises Buddhism and the Learning of the Mind school of neo-Confucianism for their capacity to transmit the unrepresentable truth through nondiscursive means of communication. To accentuate the affinity between fiction and religious practices, Liang considers "the Learning of the Mind School of neo-Confucianism the most superior form of religion" (心學者實宗教之最上乘者), and "fiction the most superior form of literature" (小說為文學之最上乘也).[49]

In China's transition to democratic governance, Liang attributed the country's political impasse to the "learning" of "formal" Western philosophical theories. Comparing the Chinese public to the "lost and foolish ones" (*mi er yu zhe* 迷而愚者) in Buddhist teachings, Liang asserted that his contemporaries were "not qualified to obtain Buddhahood" (未能有一切成佛之資格),[50] not to mention the prospect of creating a modern new world (無望能做新世界焉矣).[51] Liang looked to the invention of new fiction to bring his contemporaries personal political enlightenment. It is generally assumed that Liang reinvented the Chinese fictional tradition by politicizing its narrative content. But having situated the reformer's promotion of new fiction alongside his critique of the Chinese intellectuals' learning habits, it appears that his adoption of fiction as a "non-discursive" means of communication was intended to break his contemporaries' learning habits through the introduction of an epistemic shift. What concerns the reformer was not *what* kind of novel narrative content fiction can encompass but *how* it can communicate such content more faithfully than discursive reasoning.

An Epistemic Shift: From Name to Nameless Fictional Truth

In 1902, the editorials, short stories, and translated fiction Liang contributed to the inaugural issue of *New Fiction* corresponded closely to his endorsement of nondiscursive modes of intuitive religious communication. On the day "The Philosopher and the Religious Thinker" and "Fiction and Public Governance" were issued, Liang published a translated short story titled "Last Days of the World" (世界末日記) alongside the first chapter of *New China*.[52] His translation was a re-rendition of *Sekai no matsujitsu* (世界の末日), a work of science fiction that the Japanese writer Tokutomi Roka 德冨蘆花 (1868–1927) rendered from French to Japanese.[53]

In "Last Days of the World," readers are told that a massive glacier has frozen the globe. During the demolition of geographical landscapes and the complete annihilation of humans and other animals, one living being after another disappears. As all forms of physical existences are about to be wiped out, a young couple and their dog spend their final moments on a piece of land covered by ice. Assuming that new fiction is intended to bring the late Qing reader enlightened understanding of the political modern, readers may ask: Why would Liang want to publish a story of massive destruction in the inaugural issue of *New Fiction*?[54] And by what means might the portrayal of complete destruction serve his purpose?[55] In his translator's afterword Liang readily answers:

> Under the Bodhi tree my Buddha stood, then summoned on the *Avatamsaka* for the Great *Bodhisattvas*. As if deaf and mute all the *srāvaka* [the hearer; the general disciple] became. The purpose of translating this story is to speak to the *bodhisattvas*, not to the ordinary men or the *srāvaka*. 我佛從菩提樹下起, 為大菩薩說華嚴, 一切聲聞凡夫, 如聾如啞。(謂佛入定, 何以故。緣未熟故。) 吾之譯此文, 以語菩薩, 非以語凡夫, 語聲聞也。[56]

In Buddhist teachings, the Buddha (*fo* 佛) is the enlightened one, while Bodhisattvas (*pusa* 菩薩) are the enlightened beings who decline to enter *nirvaṇa* before all sentient beings have attained salvation. Since everything is "known" between the Buddha and the Bodhisattvas, their inexplicit exchange is unintelligible to the laymen. The communication between these enlightened beings resonates the differences between philosophical learning and intuitive religious communication. Philosophical learning, as discussed in "The Religious Thinker and the Philosopher," is based on the study of discursive language, while religious teaching refers to understanding formless spiritual truth by heart. To Liang fictional creation resembles the teachings of the Buddha. Rather than telling a story through the provision of a fictional narrative, his translation of "The Last Days of the World" was intended to communicate the unrepresentable truth to the enlightened.

In his translation Liang urges his readers to *diting* 諦聽 (listen). Through the use of the Buddhist term, he positions the readers as Buddhist practitioners. To the modern laypersons he says, "Listen, Listen, good men and good women. Everything dies, but only the imperishable being survives" 諦聽, 諦聽, 善男子, 善女人, 一切皆死, 而獨有不死者存.[57] In the Buddhist sutra, "imperishable being" (*busizhe* 不死者) means the spirit or the soul.[58] Compared with man's physical body (*tipo* 體魄;

shenqu 身軀), which is composed of elements and minerals such as iron, metal, wood, carbon, sugar, salt, and water, man's soul survives decay and death, and is therefore superior to the body.[59] To scholars concerned with the preservation of China's cultural identity in its transition to modernity, it may seem as if Liang introduced the soul to accentuate the indispensability of the country's national spirit.[60] In the above examples, however, his discussion of the "soul" or the "imperishable being" refers specifically to the formless truth that resists linguistic representation. The hierarchal contrast Liang drew between "form" and "formlessness," and by extension "the body" and "the spirit," underscores the difference between "the signifier" and "the signified." The kind of transcendence Liang pursued, once again, is emblematically figurative.

Assuming that the formless truth survives and transcends formal material presences, Liang's translation of "The Last Days of the World" is a story that repeats and reaccentuates his conviction in vivid fictional terms. In this story, a massive glacier swiftly freezes the earth. Slowly the radiance of the sun disappears and the earth begins to revolve aimlessly around a gigantic black ball.[61] As the young couple is about to die in each other's arms, the two utter:

> Among all the formal presence in the universe, everything has died. Among all forms of appearances, everything has died. Among all colors, everything has died; among all sounds, everything has died. 太空萬有之形, 一切既死, 萬有之相, 一切既死。萬有之色, 一切既死, 萬有之聲, 一切既死。[62]

In Buddhist teachings, *xing* 形 (material form), *xiang* 相 (physical appearance), *sheng* 聲 (sound), and *se* 色 (visual images and color) refer to various forms of material presence. While Liang announces the complete destruction of all forms of beings, his seemingly gloomy description is free from pessimism. The young couple gracefully accepts that they cannot escape the fate of death (*bude busi* 不得不死). To woman the man says, "The imperishable being of us will live on" (*wo bei you bushizhe cun* 我輩有不死者存).[63] The woman readily agrees: "The imperishable being of us will live on. And as for all other mortals, their imperishable being will also persist" (我輩有不死者存, 一切眾生, 皆有不死者存).[64] These are the last words the young couple say to each other. Liang calls the young couple "the lovers" (*xiangai zhe* 相愛者),[65] announcing that the flower of their "love" that will always be in full bloom (*aizhihua shang kai* 「愛」之花尚開).⁶⁶ In his conclusion Liang rearticulates his familiar remark: "Everything dies; only the imperishable being survives" (一切皆死, 而獨有不死者存).⁶⁷ Liang's concluding statement echoes the emphasis he repeats elsewhere in *New Fiction* and the *New Citizen Journal*: the formless, spiritual truth shall transcend all formal presences.

Competition between Political Discourse and Fictional Representation

The first issues of *The Future of New China* and "The Last Days of the World" were published on the same day in 1902. In *New China*, both Liang Qichao and Dr. Kong assert that the purpose of composing this story is to translate the conceptual political idea into the fictional *presence*, a representational format that promises to depict new ideas more faithfully than discursive modern political knowledge. In Dr. Kong's keynote speech, the old gentleman asserts that he intended to recount the past one hundred years of Chinese history.⁶⁸ But having consulted Liang, the chief editor of *New Fiction* (*Xiaoshuo bao zhuren* 小說報主人), he decides to convert the "formal, official national history" (堂堂正正的國史) into fictional narrative.⁶⁹ "The founder of *New Fiction* of Yokohama," Dr. Kong announces, "instructs me to fill in his column with the lecture I am delivering. Again and again, he asks me to transform the lecture into the genre of fiction" (橫濱小說報主人要將我這講義充他的篇幅, 再三諄囑, 演成小說體裁).⁷⁰ As Dr. Kong describes *New China* as a "fictional" *presence* of the official, national history, Liang reaffirms this remark. In his author's preface to *New China*, Liang says that as he rereads the chapters he has completed so far, the story "appears to be fiction but not quite so; it appears to be unofficial history but not quite so; and it appears to be political discussion but not quite so" (似說部非說部, 似稗史非稗史, 似論著非論著).⁷¹ While Liang was unable to refrain from laughing at the story's categorical ambivalence, his comment positions new fiction as a representational format that serves as a remediation of discursive, formal knowledge.

Dr. Kong, in addition, delivers his lecture in 2062, and Liang published the old gentleman's lecture script in 1902. On the day Dr. Kong makes his appearance, readers are told that "a member from the historical association has taken notes and wired his speech to the headquarters of *New Fiction* in Yokohama for publication."[72] By inserting a playful note complaining of the high cost of telegraphs, Liang eradicates the temporal distance that divides the remote future from the present.[73] This transtemporal exchange further suggests that the futuristic presence projected in the novella emphasizes the figurative discrepancy between formal materiality and the formless, unrepresentable truth.

Liang celebrates fiction for its easy comprehensibility and its power to entertain. Based on this claim, it is generally assumed that in China's transition to political modernity, the importance of fiction rests in its capacity to transmit new words and new ideas to the general public by further explaining these concepts in an easily comprehensible fictional narrative.[74] New fiction, in other words, is an auxiliary tool serving the pragmatic purpose of circulating modern political knowledge to the general public, rather than a producer actively contributing to the formation of modern political knowledge. The political elevated the status of fiction by making fiction its subordinate. Such is the conventional understanding.

So far, however, what I argue is that in the second half of 1902, Liang set up a hierarchical contrast between knowledge of "what has form" and the "formless, intuitive truth." Fiction, he argues, can best capture and communicate the formless truth the way it is. Instead of a representation *of* the concept, the acoustic and visual effects created by fictional representations generate a physical "presence" of the concept in a tangible context. Through situating modern political concepts in a fictional reality, Liang aspires to depict modern political knowledge as a higher level of truth that failed to be represented by language. The "signified" fictional description exposes the "signifier's" failure in bridging the gap between its role as a representative tool and the truth it is meant to represent. The fictional presentation of a modern political concept, for this reason, is *different from* and *more authentic than* the political lexicon. Liang's attempt to re-create the formless, intuitive truth in the realm of virtual fictional presence, in other words, is more of an *antagonist* response to formal political languages than an effort to facilitate its circulation. By comparing religion to philosophy and foregrounding nonverbal Buddhist knowledge transmission as the most effective means of communication, the reformer challenged the representative power of recently translated political languages as a whole. For Liang, fiction is neither a supplementary nor an ancillary instrument enabling the circulation of modern political discourse. His decision to depict modern political concepts in a fictional presence initiated a competition between discursive language and three-dimensional fictional representation. The relationship between new fiction and modern political discourse, for this reason, is *confrontational* rather than *complementary*.

Between New Text Studies and New Fiction

In *The Future of New China*, Liang experimented with the possibility of producing and circulating modern political concepts with an alternative knowledge transmission method. Assuming that the modern political reform he called for was implicated in an all-inclusive internal intellectual, philosophical, and moral transition, I hope to probe further into the following questions: what are some underexamined intellectual and philosophical currents that informed the epistemic shift Liang initiated? How did these competing epistemic frameworks reconfigure conceptual Western democratic ideals into embodied ontological experiences? And in what ways might Liang's assimilation of equalitarian democratic ideal reveal some hitherto uncharted internal intellectual transitions in late Qing China?

The Qing dynasty's intellectual climate, as discussed in the second chapter, was under the heavy influence of the development of evidential research, an academic practice that conceived systematic and objective philological methods to clarify interpretative obscurities that prevailed in the study of the Confucian classics.[75] As learned individuals focused on verifying obscurities pertaining to dating, textual editions, philological content, and factual accuracy, these textual doctrines became so overanalyzed that they had ceased to be existentially meaningful. To combat the ills bred by excessive intellectualism, a small group of Qing intellectuals were determined to rekindle the "moral resonance" people should have shared for the Confucian classics, and to channel by extension their "personal moral meanings" into the handling of practical state affairs (*jingshi* 經世).[76] This intellectual movement was being known as "New Text studies" (*Jinwen jingxue* 今文經學), a peripheral school of Confucianism that had persisted for centuries to challenge the authority of "Old Text studies" (*Guwen jinxue* 古文經學). Of the individuals associated with New Text studies, Zhuang Cunyu 莊存與 (1719–1788) played arguably the most decisive role in redirecting his contemporaries' attention from the scriptures' philological content to the "profound moral principles [that early Confucian sages] concealed in subtle language" (*weiyan dayi* 微言大義).

Zhuang Cunyu's search for *weiyan dayi* was inspired by his reading of the *Spring and Autumn Annals*, a historical record composed purportedly by Confucius in late 400 BC.[77] In brief entries that range from one to forty-seven characters, Confucius was said to have chronicled events that took place from 722 to 481 BC in the state of Lu 魯. Confucius divided 242 years of history into the Three Ages (*Sanshi* 三世), which evolved progressively from the Age of Disorder (*Juluan shi* 據亂世) to the Age of Approaching Peace (*Shengping shi* 昇平世), and ultimately the Age of Universal Peace (*Taiping shi* 太平世). While Confucius' chronological account projects a story of progressive order, peace, and prosperity, the state of Lu was shattered in reality by warfare and political chaos. Scholars and political thinkers of the Han dynasty (202 BC–220 AD) presented two competing explanations for Confucius' unfathomable decision. One group of scholars considered the *Annals* a factual historical record. But having inspected the *Gongyang Commentary* (*Gongyang zhuan* 公羊傳), an annotation an anonymous author conceived for the *Annals* during the Warring States period (475–221 BC), Dong Zhongshu 董仲舒 (179–104 BC) and He Xiu 何休 (129–182 AD), who were associated with New Text Confucianism, called the *Annals* the progressive constitutional blueprint Confucius had sagely conceived for the future generations. According to Dong and He, Confucius lived at a time of social and political unrest. To rectify social practices that he deemed morally unacceptable and to guide people toward wholesale institutional reform, the Sage decided to lay down new conventional decrees pertaining to the clan system and legal order as well as ritual and music that served moralizing purposes. However terse the entries in the *Annals* may seem, its subtle language conveys the subjective judgments Confucius cautiously and judiciously prescribed to express his "approval or denunciation" (*baopian* 褒貶) of each event.

Dong Zhongshu and He Xiu interpreted the *Annals* as a political blueprint outlining Confucius' ideal sociopolitical order. By presenting Confucius' astute comments to Han rulers as the Sage's liberal reformist visions, they strove to implement the progressive social, political order the Sage projected in the *Annals* as the lawful constitutional order.[78] Later power competition intensified in the Han court, and the two's progressive social-political reformism fell out of favor.[79] Having faded into obscurity for nearly two millennia, the progressive interpretation of Dong and He made a surprising return. Toward the late 1800s, Kang Youwei revisited the *Gongyang Commentary* and agreed with Dong and He that Confucius had been a farsighted political theorist. Beyond prescribing social reformist measures to ensure bureaucratic efficiency, the progressive political blueprint the Sage stipulated in the *Annals* projects to a clear path toward facilitating China's transition to the "Great Unity."[80]

In *On Confucius as a Reformer* (孔子改制考), a book he completed in 1892, Kang makes a radical claim: neo-Confucian scholars liked to treat Confucianism as "learning of the sagely moral way" (*shengxue* 聖學). Attention to man's personal moral cultivation caused them to neglect the emphasis Confucius placed on "political governance" (*wangdao* 王道).[81] The cultivation of a person's "inner moral goodness" (*neisheng* 內聖), as Kang believed, should be channeled into and expressed in the management of "outer state affairs" (*waiwang* 外王). The modern political predicament China faced at the turn of the century soon prompted Kang to reinterpret the "Three Age" theory and envision novel interpretative possibilities in conjoining Confucian morality and modern political governance. Perceiving Confucius as a radical political reformer in support of democratic governance, Kang stated that in the past China had been governed by "authoritarian rule" (*junzhu* 君主) and that the country had founded itself in the "Age of Disorder" (*Zhiluan shi* 治亂世). As soon as the country underwent institutional reform and implemented a "constitutional monarchy" (*junmin gongzhu* 君民共主), China would proceed to the "Age of Approaching Peace." As people developed greater political awareness over the passage of time, "constitutional monarchy" would be replaced by "democratic governance" (*minzhu* 民主). China would then officially proceed to the "Age of the Great Unity" that Confucius had envisioned in the *Annals*.

At first, Liang was "madly excited" (*xi ruo kuang* 喜若狂) by his teacher's progressive interpretation.[82] In the hope of communicating this liberal political vision to the general public, Liang propagated the synthesis Kang drew between Confucius and democratic governance as follows. Confucian teaching was divided into two schools after the death of the Sage.[83] One was represented by Mencius and the other by Xunzi 荀子.[84] While followers of the school of Xunzi circulated ideas prescribed in the classics (*chuanjing* 傳經), the Mencian school sought to realize the unfinished social, political ideal that Confucius had projected in the *Annals*. Having committed himself to putting Confucius' teachings into practice (*xingjiao* 行教),[85] Mencius emphasized the necessity of deposing "autocrats" (*dufu* 獨夫), punishing "traitors" (*minzei* 民賊), "having those skilled in making war be given the most severe sentences" (*shanzhan fu shangxing* 善戰服上刑), and "justly allotting the land to democratize property distribution" (*shoutian zhichan* 授田制產).[86] Collectively these ideals outlined a prototypical form of "democratic governance" (*minzhu*) in early China. Of these two schools of Confucianism, Liang asserted that only the Mencian school could be considered "true Confucianism" (*zhen kongxue* 真孔學).[87] Since the incipient democracy Mencius envisioned jeopardized the interests of the ruler, "it had never been implemented since the time of its conception" (至今未嘗一行于天下) and "had remained politically obscure" (不顯于世).[88] To rectify "the great misfortunate" (*da buxing* 大不幸) that had hindered Confucianism from fulfilling its true social and political undertakings, Liang expressed his and "a handful of his comrades' commitment in accomplishing this grand mission" (今二三子既有志于大道).[89]

Liang and his teacher, Kang Youwei, were determined to realize Confucius' great mission. The two, however, envisioned different means to put the ideal into practice. Calling Confucius the uncrowned king (*suwang* 素王) who had received the mandate of heaven, Kang Youwei asserted that he had inherited his reformist measures directly from the Sage. As Kang tactically appropriated if not exploited Confucius' conception of the "Three Ages" to justify the legitimacy of his political reformism, Liang was disheartened by his teacher's attempt to invoke the authority of the Sage. To Liang, the most notable contribution that New Text Confucianism made to China's modern political development rested in accentuating that the meanings of words were *contingent upon* the profound messages the Sage strove to express. But having attempted to impose certain interpretative possibilities as imperative commands, Kang "restricted his visions to words and sentences of the classics he shared an affinity with" (見局見縛於所比附之文句) and "had since given up one's search for the truth" (不復追求其真義之所存).[90] At a time when Kang made manipulative uses of Confucius to justify his reformist objectives, Liang declared that his adoration for the truth exceeded his adoration for Confucius (吾愛孔子, 吾尤愛真理).[91] He, in addition, remained convinced that Confucius shared his persistence in the pursuit of the truth (又知孔子之愛真理).[92] In "The Preservation of Teaching Is Not the Reason to Venerate Confucius" (保教非所以尊孔論) (1902), Liang writes, "Certain individuals justify the lawfulness of their reformist proposals by claiming that 'Confucius had imposed comparable changes through comparable means'" (某某孔子所以知也, 某某孔子所曾言也).[93] Their slavish conformity is self-restricting: "If one failed to identify corresponding equivalences in the Confucian classics, he would not venture to embark on a path that he knew was *truly* true" (萬一遍索諸四書六經而終無可比附者，則將明知為真理而亦不敢從矣).⁹⁴

While Kang Youwei turned Confucius into the "Sage King" who had received the mandate of heaven, Liang considered the Sage a transmitter or interpreter of the way of heaven. In *The Future of New China*, Liang dubs the modern descendant of Confucius, Dr. Kong Juemin, *boshi* (博士), a title conferred to erudite scholars well versed in the Five Classics during the Han dynasty. By making Dr. Kong the spokesperson for the chief editor of *New Fiction* as well as the transmitter of modern Chinese history, Liang posed a subtle claim to challenge his teacher: scholars who supported the *Gongyang Commentary*'s interpretation of the *Annals* should generally agree that the ideal institutional structure, social etiquette, and moral order that Confucius envisioned for later generations were articulated *not* in discursive prescription but in his implied judgments, shrewd comments, and corrective propositions. The communicational strategy Confucius adopted was known as *weiyan dayi*, in which profound moral principles were concealed in subtle languages. New Text studies was not an intellectual movement seeking to implement the "Three Ages" as Confucius' dogmatic instruction in the modern world. Such a move would only reinforce the hierarchy that divided the authority from the subject, intensifying in consequence the slavish conformity that has hindered Chinese intellectuals from becoming self-empowered participants of democratic governance. Following the exegetic tradition of New Text studies, the creation of "new" fiction offered Liang a concrete means to replicate a Confucian moral-political ideal through his formal invention. In the preface to *New China*, Liang calls some of his plots "parables" (*yuyan* 寓言) that he has "conceived with great consideration and care" (頗費覃思，不敢草草).⁹⁵ "Parable," as explicated in "Fiction and Public Governance," is a synonym for "fiction," and is by far the most faithful means of epitomizing the unrepresentable truth. By categorizing plots in *New China* as parables, Liang asserted that the significance of his fictional creation rested in transmitting the formless "truth" through nondiscursive means.

Reinventing New Text Studies with New Fiction

The *Annals*, as followers of the *Gongyang* commentary suggest, is a sacred text providing practical "political" instruction for people of the future. In

Liang's composition of *New China*, a sense of continuity exists between the *Annals* and his fictional creation. Mimicking the way the Sage arranged and presented the *Annals*, Liang situated the utopic Confucian sociopolitical ideal in a fictional realm that depicts the progressive formation of democratic governance with visual immediacy and prophetic hints. In the story, China systematically evolves from "authoritarian rule" to the "joint ruling of monarch and people" to a "republican democracy." Being a modern parable or reincarnation of the *Annals*, *New China* is told from the perspective of Dr. Kong, the contemporary heir of Confucius. While the ancient Sage promulgated the forward-looking reformist scheme at a time of warfare and social unrest, his modern descendant exemplifies how progressive institutional transformations can take place in modern forms of political governance. In the story, as a series of modern political transformations unfold between 1962 and 2062, Dr. Kong is careful to convert the political reform Confucius purportedly projected in 500 BC from the liturgical calendar to the Confucian calendar. The 1962 restoration, for instance, takes place in Confucian year 2453. By the time the political movement replaces the Qing dynasty's authoritarian rule with republican democracy in 2002, China finds itself in the Confucian year 2513.

Fiction, as Liang said, promises to unfold a "physical presence beyond one's physical surrounding and a world beyond his world." Aside from converting the "Three Ages" into a fictional adaptation of the *Annals* that merges the Confucian calendar with the linear modern political progress, Liang made various attempts to let the "visual description" take over "semantic textual discursion." Knowing that meanings are contingent upon individuals' personal moral enlightenment, it is only through the awakening of the people that democratic liberalism is possible. By bringing a reader to see what he sees, hear what he hears, and feel what he feels, Liang's fictional description yields to the people the interpretive, moral, and, ultimately, political power. While Kang Youwei, and presumably followers of New Text studies, focused on unearthing the profound meaning the Sage concealed in the subtle languages, Liang's attempt to make his fictional creation a modern expression of the *Annals* turned the exegetic principles of New Text studies into an intellectual proposition that emphasizes the interpretative power of the individual. By passing to the reader a pair of exegetic lenses with unobstructed exposure to the signified, Liang's employment of storytelling as a medium refreshed the meaning of *weiyan dayi*. Aside from implementing a new intellectual order alongside the modern political order, Liang revived and reinvented this marginalized intellectual practice through his formal invention.[96]

Remediating Political "Revolution" in "Reformist" Terms

New China situates the "reformist" activities in a fictional context and invites the late Qing reader to reimagine the word "reform" from a new epistemic paradigm. Although Liang declared that the purpose of delineating the signified truth is to assist the late Qing reader in obtaining enlightened understanding of, rather than linguistic familiarity with, modern political knowledge, the story is in fact more intriguing than that.

In Dr. Kong's lecture, the old gentleman recounts the great prosperity China enjoys one hundred years after the *"reformist"* (*weixin* 維新) movements. Before the "reform" takes place, Dr. Kong introduces us to two friends who share conflicting political views. Similar to Liang, the two friends, Huang Keqiang and Li Qubing, first emphasize that *The Future of New China* is a novella seeking to depict the formless, unrepresentable truth. Repeating the protest Liang voices in "The of Strengths and Shortcomings of the Religious Thinker and the Philosopher," Huang Keqiang begins by complaining about his contemporaries' unreflective learning habits. Young intellectuals of his time, Huang says, study modern political lexicons as textual knowledge; they do not seek to comprehend what these modern political concepts *truly* mean. Having interpreted "liberty" and "equality" in a literal sense, they manipulate these keywords to justify corruptive behaviors such as drinking, visiting brothels, and skipping schools.[97] Their abuse of modern political lexicons has turned "liberty" and "equality" into "expressions of great evil and sin" (罪大惡極的名詞).[98] The meanings of "reform" and "restoration," as Huang continues, have been more badly misunderstood. These days, he says, those "leading reformers and restoration leaders" (維新改革第一流人物) are "a bunch of thieves and bandits" (一羣民賊).[99] They administer the reformist movement as a profit-making enterprise, and receive foreigners as pimps welcoming brothel visitors.[100] Not having any enlightened understanding of modern politics, the words "reform" and "restoration" articulated by these thieves and bandits are absent of *true* political significance. Huang says:

Dissolution of Modern Political Languages | 169

For those thieves and bandits who are in power, they can mouth such things as reform and restoration. If you were to ask them, do you think they would know what reform and restoration really mean? 那政府當道一羣民賊：他們嘴裡頭，講什麼維新，什麼改革，你問他們知道維新改革這兩個字，是什麼一句話麼?[101]

Huang Keqiang intends to modernize China through "true" political reform. But his friend Li Qubing disagrees with him. Having failed to see the hope of implementing changes to the imperial monarchy, Li Qubing is determined to overthrow the Qing dynasty with a political revolution (*geming*). Li considers Huang the Chinese equivalent of the Italian politician Camillo Cavour (1810–1861)[102] and describes his "reformist" proposals as a preliminary form of "constitutional monarchy" (君主立憲主義).[103] Comparing himself to the Italian revolutionary hero Giuseppe Mazzini (1805–1872), Li, on the contrary, calls himself "a person with true revolutionary thinking" (有真正革命思想的人). Li announces:[104]

> Today, for a person with true revolutionary thinking, his views are surely the same as mine. For one without such vision, even if he intends to talk about revolution, he will not be able to do it irrespective of how capable he is. It would be fine if China does not have any revolution in the days to come. But if China does have one, these thieves' and bandits' sinful associates are destined to enter the nirvana without remainder [*anupadhiśeṣanirvāṇa*], having no hope of being redeemed nor reincarnated. 今日有真正革命思想的人，他見識一定是和我一樣。沒有這種思想的人，他要講革命，任憑他多大本事，一定是做不成的。中國往後沒有革命便罷，若有革命，這些民賊的孽苗，是要人無餘涅槃而滅度之的了。[105]

In the above statement Li makes three points. First, while his friend Huang Keqiang intends to initiate a *true* political "reform," he is the person who knows the *true* meaning of revolution. Second, for those who do not know what revolution *truly* means, the kind of "revolution" they "talk about" (*jian* 講) is bound to be erroneous. Third, if those thieves and bandits insist on staging a "revolution" *as* they understand it, their "revolution" can never be the *true revolution*. To clarify what a *true revolution* is, Li soon lists a number of progressive political movements that support his vision. These movements include assisting all provinces in China in declaring independence from the Qing monarchy, replacing the imperial rule with a republican government, establishing a national congress, and eventually holding the country's first presidential election.

Huang Keqiang and Li Qubing exchanged their divergent political views in 1902. Years later as history unfolds, we learn from Dr. Kong's lecture that Huang the Chinese Camillo Cavour had eventually succeeded in completing his "reformist" career (*weixin shiye* 維新事業).[106] The old gentleman recounts the past hundred years of Chinese history as follows. In the nineteenth century, China was under the rule of the imperial monarchy. Driven by the hope of liberating the people from authoritarian rule, Huang initiated a series of "reformist" movements. Of these movements, the first was the independence of Guangdong (*Guangdong rishi* 廣東自治) that took place after the Alliance's invasion of Beijing (*lianjun po Beijing* 聯軍破北京) in 1900.[107] In that year, Huang formed the Constitutional Party (*xianzheng dang* 憲政黨), which gathered more than four million members in Guangdong province. With the help of nine million supporters scattered across other provinces, the party was determined to fight for Guangdong's independence. Upon learning about the rise of this local military force, "the emperor was moved and crafty officials were scared out of their wits" (天子動容，權奸褫魄).[108] In his description of the ruler's and his subjects' emotional shock, Dr. Kong indicates that the independence movement was not a move sponsored by the throne. Very quickly Guangdong province declared independence from the Qing monarchy and became the first province governed by constitutional law. Following Guangdong's success, other provinces declared independence in succession. Soon the national congress (*guohui* 國會) was formed, and the last Qing emperor, Luo Zaitian 羅在田, became the first president (*datongling* 大統領) of China. The establishment of the national congress was predicated on the collapse of the Qing imperial rule. When the emperor was in his first presidential term, he sagely decided that it was time to concede his presidency to the people, and was praised for his perceptive understanding of the political situation (前王英明能審時勢排羣議，讓權與民).[109] Immediately after the emperor resigned, Huang Keqiang was elected the first president of China. The decade-long "reformist" movement reached its official completion.

Between Liang's Fictional Invention and Political Indeterminacy

Being the person who knew the *true* meaning of "reform," Huang materialized his "reformist goals." Knowing that these "reformist" movements included declaring the independence of Guangdong, liberating all provinces in China from the Qing monarchy, replacing the imperial rule with the national congress, holding the presidential election, and revoking Luo Zaitian's presidency with the people's collective will, the "reformist" activities Dr. Kong recounts in his fictional description, somewhat paradoxically, are precisely what Li Qubing meant by "*true* revolution."[110] Huang Keqiang and Li Qubing seem fully aware of this glaring contradiction.

In *New China*, Huang and Li repeatedly emphasize that the "words" reform and revolution *cannot* reflect the "true/ authentic" (*zhenzheng de* 真正的) meaning of reform and revolution. As Liang expands the meanings of the "word" reform by associating it with revolutionary activities, his attempt to dissociate the word "reform" from its conventional interpretation declares his denouncement of the received meaning of the word to achieve the paradoxical goal of giving "reform" its true revolutionary connotations. Liang's reinvention of "reform" in *New China* can be considered a fictional supplement to "Exegesis on Ge" (釋革), an essay published on the date Huang's and Li's heated debates appeared in *New Fiction*.[111]

In "Exegesis of Ge," Liang extracts the character *ge* 革 appearing in *gaige* 改革 (reform) and *geming* 革命 (revolution), arguing that *gaige* and *geming* mean in fact the same matter. "Revolution" (*geming*), he says, refers to "the implementation of momentous changes through pulling out the root and recreating a new world" (從根底處掀翻之，而別造一新世界).[112] Compared with these sweeping sea changes, the replacement of a particular dynasty is too trivial to be considered "revo," an abbreviation Liang conceives for "revolution" (皆指王朝易姓而言，是不足以當 revo).[113] In his time what people perceived to be the political revolution was only a matter of "*bianqe*" 變革 (change). "What others called *geming* (revolution) in the past," Liang declares, "is what I now call *bianqe* (change). It is the one and only solution to save China" (即日人所謂革命，今我所謂變革，為今日就中國獨一無二法門).[114] By glossing over the resemblance between *bianqe* 變革 and *gaige* 改革, Liang concludes that political revolution is essentially the same as *gaige* 改革 (reform).[115]

In *New China*, Liang has gone as far as associating the visual and fictional imagination of revolution with the word "reform." To label visual imaginations with a lexicon to which they are not conventionally associated with marks Liang's attempt to reorganize modern political knowledge through introducing nondiscursive means of communication. In this sense, not only does the fictional description in *New China* try to transcend language, it provides what is absent in translated political languages, enabling "words" to say more than its semantic meaning. Once we situate the composition of *The Future of New China* in the recent development of Liang's political career, there also seems to be an uncanny parallel between his fictional creation and personal political indeterminacy.

At the turn of the twentieth century, as it is generally known, the reformist and the revolutionary camps began to divide into two competing forces. As their antagonism intensified, the construction of a realm of virtual, fictional imagination seemed to have offered Liang a rare opportunity to help the public reenvisage and reconceive what "reform" (*weixin*) should *truly* mean and encompass. To situate Liang's creation of a fictional realm amid the immediate political predicament he faced in the early 1900s: in September 1898, Dowager Cixi cracked down the Hundred Days Reform. Immediately after that, Liang and his teacher Kang Youwei were driven into exile. Having received Emperor Guangxu's endorsement and support, Kang was determined to restore the power of the throne and implement a state-sponsored constitutional reform from above. To do so, he was to stage a military uprising and assassinate Cixi. Liang did not like his teacher's plans but had eventually agreed to assist him. To build their military troops, Liang approached the chivalrous fighter Wang Wu 王五 (1844–1900) and leaders of the Elder Brothers Society (*Gelaohui* 哥老會), a secret society seeking to rebel against the Manchurian rule.[116] Liang also made plans to employ skirmishers, or light cavalry soldiers, from the Philippines.[117] To facilitate the purchase and transportation of firearms from abroad, he established an ironware company in Hong Kong and envisioned creating a silkworm production company.[118] By offering young workers English lessons after work, Liang looked to turn these workers into an armed troop and to prepare them for military combat.[119]

Liang continued to gather and mobilize resources to rescue the throne. But the more he tried, the more uncertain he became. In his letters to Kang, Liang voiced a few alarming concerns. Many times, he said, he wrote to their party's headquarters in Macau. These messages never received a reply. If the reformist camp were to restore the unfinished constitutional reform, all party members would be ready to form a cabinet and assume the duty of a central government. But so far, their teammates seemed unprepared to assume office.[120] There had been recent rumors suggesting that the emperor was critically ill. If the upcoming military uprising was intended solely to rescue the throne, perhaps this was a goal that could not be achieved.[121] The reformist camp, in addition, planned "to stage the uprising either in Canton or in provinces along the Long River" (長江沿岸各省起兵).[122] The emperor, however, was imprisoned in Beijing. How and why could staging an uprising in Southern China save the throne in the north?[123] Were the reformist camp to transport the uprising to Beijing, it seemed unlikely that their amateur troops could outpower the imperial military force and presumably the intervention of the Russian Army.

Liang questioned the validity and viability of restoring the unfinished constitutional reform. As practical concerns continued to exaggerate disagreements that had estranged Liang from his teacher, his friendship with Sun Yat-sen 孫中山 (1866–1925) deepened.[124] In Japan, Sun encouraged Liang and Kang to join him in overthrowing the Qing monarchy with a political revolution. While Kang, who had been promoted to personal advisor of the throne, firmly rejected the invitation, Liang thought differently.[125] Perceiving democracy as a form of government in which the people enjoy the right and authority to deliberate legislation, Liang expected absolute monarchy to be replaced by a state of "national sovereignty" (*guojia zhuquan* 國家主權), a mutation designating a transfer of power from the ruler to a national government. In April 1902, Liang announced to Kang his wish to stage a political revolution:[126]

> Overthrowing the Shogun is the most appropriate solution to Japan's political predicaments, and overthrowing the Manchurian the most appropriate solution to China. According to your humble student's view, there is nothing more fitting than this. The Manchurian bureaucracy has been hopeless for so long. Day after day, we hope our Majesty can resume his rule and restore his authority. But how can this be possible? Even if there is such a possibility, we have so many enemies in the court. Our initial campaigns have been deserted for so long. Even if we can be reappointed by the throne, hardly

can our aspirations be realized. Sir, you are afraid of destructions. I cannot possibly say that I am not. But if destruction cannot be avoided eventually, the longer we wait the more destructive it becomes. Perhaps it is better early than late. Even if we do not speak of revolution, others will. How can speaking about this [the political revolution] be prohibited? 日本以討幕為最適宜之主義，中國以討滿為最適宜之主義。弟子所見，謂無以易此矣。滿廷之無可望久矣，今日日望歸朝，望復辟，夫何可得？即得矣，滿朝皆仇敵，百事腐敗已久，雖召吾黨歸用之，而亦決不能行其志也。先生懼破壞，弟子亦未始不懼，然以為破壞終不可免，越遲則越慘，毋寧早耳。且我不言，他人亦言之，豈能禁乎？[127]

Having foreseen the difficulties in implementing institutional changes to the Qing bureaucracy, Liang urged his teacher to "overthrow the Manchus" (*taoman* 討滿), a euphemism for the political revolution. But his persuasion was fruitless. Kang called Liang "capricious and fickle" (*liu zhi yi bian* 流質易變). To Liang he said, "Since you have become interested in staging a revolution, your heart changed so radically to the point that these broken pieces can hardly be put together again. Since our principles are different, our ties would have been broken even if we were father and son" 自汝言革命后，人心大變大散，幾不可合。蓋宗旨不同，則父子亦決裂矣。[128]

Despite Kang's fierce condemnation,[129] Liang remained committed to his political vision and formed a secret alliance with Sun Yat-sen.[130] Due to a series of misunderstandings, later Liang was permanently expelled from the revolutionary camp.[131] Knowing that he could no longer collaborate with Sun, Liang began to travel across the globe to collect donations for his own political revolution. Upon realizing that most such resources were already in Sun's possession, Liang had no choice but to return to the reformist camp. As a "reformer" seeking to initiate a political "revolution," the prevailing linguistic distinction between "reform" and "revolution" occasioned by China's corresponding political divide, in his view, did not reflect the *true* meanings of these terms.[132] Rather than elaborating on the bookish definition of "reform" and "restoration" (*weixin*) as linguistic "signifiers," in *New China* Liang begins to recover the "signified" truth that the words had failed to represent. Beyond converting the formal language into the formless truth, Liang's fictional representation completes the "corrective" task

Dissolution of Modern Political Languages | 175

of associating the political key word with *true* meanings that it was *meant* to represent.

Rectifying the Name through Its Own Subversion

Having decided and declared that *gaige* and *bianqe* can represent revolution more accurately than *geming*, Liang further tries to situate *geming* in China's dynastic history and connect the word with violence, immorality, and brutal dynastic upheaval. Huang Keqiang and Li Qubing, for instance, associate *geming* with stories of bloody dynastic replacement in China's imperial past and compare China's current revolutionary leaders to notorious usurpers such as Emperor Qin Shi Huang 秦始皇 (260–210 BC), Emperor Wu of Han 漢武帝 (156–87 BC), and Emperor Zhu Yuanzhang 朱元璋 (1328–1398). The two equate revolution with chaos, and label what they call China's first-generation revolutionaries "robbers (*qiangdao* 強盜), rascals (*wulai* 無賴), and insidious thieves" (*jianzei* 奸賊) who had completely discarded good moral conduct.[133] "Over the last two thousand years," the two claim, "China has undergone enormous revolutions and chaos" (中國這兩千年來, 革了又革, 亂了又亂).[134]

In the early 1900s, Liang's endeavor to initiate movements such as "poetic revolution" and "religious revolution" in China transformed the word "revolution" into a symbol of linear historical progression. While Liang enjoyed the liberty of inventing and circulating new semantic meanings for translated modern political concepts, he was also in a position to restore the word *geming*'s premodern connotations. In "Exegesis on Ge," Liang intends to replace *geming* (revolution) with *gaige* and *bianqe* through his skillful rhetorical arrangement. Regardless of the apparent mismatch, he goes so far as to position *geming* as a mistranslation for "revo" (revolution), an initial he often juxtaposes with another initial "ref" (reform). To argue that *gaige* and *bianqe* are more accurate descriptions for the *true* revolution Liang declares that calling "revo" *geming* is a matter of "misnaming and disrupting the legality of language" (名不正, 言不順). He says,

> Nowadays, the translation of revolution as "revo" has confined learned gentlemen to the literal definitions of words. It makes them assume that mentioning this word declares one's antagonistic relationship with the imperial monarchy. Now

it is too late to correct such assumption. Those who are in power also find the association harmful. They try to suppress and destroy it, making it impossible for a country to make adjustments to keep pace with the international trends. If this is the case, incorrect names and incongruous language are there to be blamed. 今日革命譯 Revo, 遂使天下君子拘墟於字面。以為談及此義, 必與現在王朝一人一姓為敵, 迴之若將晚已, 而彼憑權籍勢力者, 亦恃曰是不利我也。相與室遏之摧鋤之, 使一國不能順應於世界大勢以自存, 若是者, 皆名不正, 言不順為害也。[135]

At the time "Exegesis on Ge" was published, there was a certain public consensus on the difference between reform and revolution. For this reason, it is difficult for Liang's rhetorical persuasion in the "Exegesis of Ge" to go beyond word play. The attempt to make the word "reform" an equivalent of "revolution" is not an easy task. And in Liang's case, a greater obstacle is that the word *geming* is officially affiliated with the revolutionary camp led by Sun Yat-sen. While Liang might have had an opportunity to launch his own revolution, it was difficult for him, a person who had been permanently expelled from the revolutionary camp, to adopt the exact word *geming* in his later political campaigns.[136]

For many years we have tended to understand late Qing political modernity as a constructed discourse resulting from cross-cultural exchanges and consolidated by power relations on both the local and the international level.[137] But in *Discourse on the New Citizen* (*Xinmin shuo* 新民說), Liang's promotion of intellectual courage (*zhi* 智) exposes the fallacy of studying Western concepts as textual knowledge. In a concluding remark he made in "On Public Civility" (*Lun gongde* 論公德), Liang asserts, "I'm afraid that the more sophisticated the country becomes in the domain of knowledge, the weaker in the moral cultivation."[138] To emphasize his concern, Liang goes as far to claim that "as soon as Western material civilization is fully imported to China, the four billion people will turn collectively into beasts" (泰西物質文明盡輸入中國, 而四萬萬人且相率而為禽獸也).[139]

Late Qing intellectuals had struggled to grapple with the new and the foreign. But as new words and new meanings had finally become familiar, Liang negated the recently acquired familiarity by announcing that there was something *truer* than the discursive given. By emphasizing the adjectives "authentic" and "true" (*zhen* 真), Liang drew a hierarchal contrast between "authentic" modern political truth and "textual" political knowledge, reducing the discursive given to the deceptive and the untrue.

In writings published in 1902, Liang reminds the late Qing reader that *true* modern political "meanings" and modern political "languages" are *different*, and that formal language cannot faithfully represent the formless truth. Sharing such assumption, Liang argues that fiction, which is capable of transmitting intuitive understanding as Chan Buddhism does, is capable of transmitting the formless truth more faithfully than language. Liang's introduction of fiction as a "competing means of representation" discloses the pitfalls of examining the formation of late Qing political modernity as a "competition of discourses." In this chapter, I am chiefly interested in exploring how Liang's conjuration of the contrast between the "name" (*ming* 名) and the "substance" (*shi* 實) undermines the validity of the recently translated modern political discourse and makes it an unreliable and deceptive whole. It has been widely acknowledged that from 1902 onward, Liang made renewing the people and transforming them into modern citizens his primary concern. In *New Citizen Journal*, Liang carefully elucidates and consolidates semantic definitions for recently translated modern political concepts. But as he did so he exposed the fallacy of learning these concepts as discursive knowledge. The late Qing intellectual, in other words, performed the paradoxical tasks of creating modern political discourse and subverting the legitimacy of such a creation.

Chapter 5

Musicality—Representing the Rhythm of Political Revolution and the Tenor of Its Moral Discontent

In 1898, the Hundred Days Reform ended abruptly with the exile of its leaders, Liang Qichao and Kang Youwei. Refusing to give up on the political changes he had long hoped for, Liang proceeded to promote modern political concepts and advocate ideological reforms in journals he founded in Japan. In an editorial, "A Respectful Announcement to My Fellow Reformists" (敬告我同業諸君), that he published in *New Citizen Journal* in 1902, Liang compares his new role as a modern journalist to the grand historian Sima Qian 司馬遷 (c. 145–86 BC).[1] As "the person to guide the national citizen toward the path of evolution,"[2] the modern historian, Liang declares, is responsible for transmitting what he considers the most relevant and favorable modern political knowledge to the public with "objectivity" (*keguan* 客觀).[3] To ensure that the modern historian could fully convince the public of the importance of these concepts, Liang, somewhat paradoxically, declares that the historian is entitled to elaborate these concepts in a "subjective" (*zhuguan* 主觀) voice.[4] "Slightly biased and radical" (*shaopian shaoji* 少偏稍激) his "extreme remarks" (*jiduan zhi yilun* 極端之議論) might be, they should not be deemed problematic.[5]

Partiality, radicalness, and political instigation, as Liang was aware, violated a journalist's code of ethics. But by comparing the modern journalist to the historian and asserting that the historian wrote for the people's benefit, Liang exploited an ambiguity to his advantage. At the time that Liang published this editorial, he spoke as the leader of the most influential reformist party in China. The professional conduct Liang tried to engage in and the strategic goal he aimed to achieve bear a striking similarity to the tension between "the philosophical ideal of life" and "the rhetorical ideal of life" in ancient Greece. The former, according to Werner Jaeger, was "based on knowledge of human nature and of what is best for it," while the latter intends to "create pleasure and win approval."[6]

Moral concern and rhetorical intention, be they in Liang's announcement or in ancient Greece, can always be intricately if not hopelessly entangled. In Liang's editorial, perhaps the most crucial implication for understanding the origins of Chinese political modernity is that his translated political concepts began life in a "rhetorical situation" and were *affectively presented* to the reader. By declaring himself a historian who lived "to benefit the national citizen" (*yi li guomin* 以利國民), Liang assumed the role of a political orator in the Athenian agora to which he had transformed *New Citizen Journal*.[7] Besides transmitting modern political knowledge, the historian-orator was determined to move and to persuade. Modern political concepts, as articulated in the reformist journal, were vivid embodiments of logos, pathos, and ethos.

Liang was convinced that "the persuasive power of pathos is far greater than logical reasoning" (*qinggan de yingxiangli yuanzai lizhi zhishang* 情感的影響力遠在理智之上), and that music was by far the most effective instrument in moving people with pathos.[8] Having analyzed political writing Liang published between 1897 and 1903, Xia Xiaohong argues that the "poetic revolution" (*shijie geming* 詩界革命) that Liang sponsored in 1899 reflects the reformer's determination to popularize modern political knowledge by utilizing the formal features of language to make music.[9] To maximize the persuasive power of his writing, Liang purposefully amplified the rhythmical effects of his prose, making it a signature of his "new prose style."[10] Xia's observation resonates with Liang's personal reflection. Some years later, as Liang looked back to his career as a modern journalist, he acknowledged that his new prose style, which finally reached its full maturity in writing he published in *New Citizen Journal*, was invested with "*ganqing*" 感情 (affective power). As Liang wrote, "Since then [1902], I had made circulating modern political ideas my primary occupation. . . . Often emotionally charged, my writings had a certain magical power over the reader" (自是啟超復以宣傳為業 . . . 筆鋒常帶感情, 對於讀者別有一種魔力焉.)[11]

Musicality—Representing the Rhythm of Political Revolution | 181

Both Xia and Liang himself suggest that modern political knowledge was *affectively* presented to the late Qing reader in *New Citizen Journal*. But beyond trying to move the reader, Liang the political reformer confessed in his reflection that the *ganqing* that permeated in his political writing was also the expression of his most truthful and intimate "feelings." Liang wrote,

> At the time I was not happy with what the revolutionaries were doing. But having become excessively careful and conscious, I only modified my political views slightly. My conservativeness and aggressiveness went on to battle within the chest and exploded with my *ganqing*. My words, for this reason, were often self-contradictory. 啟超亦不慊於當時革命家之所為, 懲羹而吹齏, 持論稍變矣。然其保守性與進取性常交戰於胸中, 隨感情而發, 所執往往前後相矛盾。[12]

In this brief confession, Liang exposes us to two faces of *ganqing*: one is the unmediated and often uncontainable affective experience, and the other is his rhetorical persuasion charged with affective power. While the former derives from "the spontaneous overflow of powerful feelings," the latter was cautiously informed by the reformer's strategic calculation. These two faces of affect, according to Liang, found themselves alongside and, at the same time, at odds with each other. Sometimes the presence of the unmediated emotion was too intense that it ran the risk of contradicting if not annihilating the reformer's rhetorical purpose.

Affect and emotion are unmediated and prelinguistic states of being, and as such, they are difficult to get hold of. By analyzing how the modern political concept "national citizen" (*guomin* 國民) is affectively presented in Liang's "Biography of the Hungarian Patriot Kossuth" (*Xiongyali aiguozhe Gesushi zhuan* 匈牙利愛國者噶蘇士傳), the first part of the chapter addresses the following questions: Why did Liang Qichao want to imbue his representation of "national citizen" with *ganqing*? What kinds of emotion and subjective perception have been projected into the concept? Through what means can affect and emotion find their way to Liang's historical narrative, or perhaps the modern political discourse as a whole? And how does the affective dimension communicate to the late Qing reader? The second part of the chapter focuses on the much-contested political concept "revolution" (*geming* 革

命) in Liang's "Biography of Madame Roland, the Greatest Heroine in the Contemporary World" (*Jinshi diyi nüjie Luolan furen zhuan* 近世第一女傑羅蘭夫人傳). Having examined Liang's political activities in 1902 and the growing antagonism between the reformist and the revolutionary campus in the previous chapter, the last chapter proceeds to explore what might have prompted Liang to depict *geming* so passionately in this biography. Since the word *geming*, or political revolution, is affectively charged, is it possible to assume that the *meanings* being communicated to late Qing intellectuals rest *beyond*, and are *different from*, the word's semantic content? If Liang's affective presentation, whether informed by his rhetorical intention or by lyrical intensity, ran the risk of challenging, obscuring, and even destabilizing the word's semantic content, what kinds of "meanings" could Liang have presented to his late Qing readers? By asking these questions, we return to the affective origins of translated political modernity in late Qing China. Only then can we question the extent to which the study of discourse is a reliable way of understanding the nature of Chinese political modernity in general, and reflect on the ways "affect and emotion" as new analytical categories can transform our imagination of the Chinese "modern."

Between Modern Political Concepts and Political Ethics

Democratic governance, as Liang explicated in affinities he identified between the moral theory of Wang Yangming and Immanuel Kant, was intended to operate as the "political" expression or exposition of man's innate cognitive, perceptual, and moral disposition. To bridge the gap that has divided "objective" knowledge from people's "subjective" consciousness, from 1902 onward Liang began to attach the prefix "authentic" (*zhen* 真 or *zhenzheng de* 真正的) to some of the most popular modern political key words. The coinage of the terms "authentic national citizen" (*zhen guomin* 真國民), "authentic liberty" (*zhen ziyou* 真自由), and "authentic people's sovereignty" (*zhen quanli* 真民權) allowed him to accentuate the importance of staying faithful to one's perceptual sensitivities and making the engagement of one's unpremeditated ontological experiences the condition of becoming *truly* politically modern.

To underscore that participation in democratic politics is a matter of being one's "true" moral self in the realm of democratic governance,

Liang accentuated the need of discerning the differences between *learning about* the national citizen as a conceptual idea and embodying the ontological experience of *being* an "authentic" national citizen in a concrete historical context. In each issue of New Citizen Journal, Liang liked to elaborate on one particular modern political concept from various interpretative perspectives. In his scholarly essays, he first explicated the definition of "the national citizen" with factual objectivity. After that, the reformer situated the concept in a series of historical biographies featuring Hungary's transition to political modernity. Speaking lastly from a third-person omniscient perspective, Liang the "new historian" (*xin shi shi* 新史氏) took the liberty of elucidating what the concept meant to the European historical agents he personally admired and to people who found themselves undergoing a comparable form of historical transition.

In the "Biography of the Hungarian Patriot Kossuth," a historical biography serialized in New Citizen Journal in 1902, for instance, Liang introduces the reader to supporters of the Hungarian political leader Lajos Kossuth (1802–1894).[13] In his learned scholarly essays and editorials, Liang asserts that a national citizen is entitled to confront the state or a foreign country if the latter violates one's obligation in the contractual relationship they establish. But the Hungarians were no ordinary national citizens. Austria, as stated at the beginning of the biography, sought to colonize Hungary at the price of violating the Golden Bull edict. The Hungarians were immediately enraged by Austria's aggression. To trace these two countries' unresolved historical entanglement, Liang presents the following account. In the long course of the Seven Year's War (1756–1763), the alliance of France and Prussia invaded Austria with military forces. As "righteous men born with knight-errant spirit," the Hungarians refused to tolerate behaviors that violated benevolence and propriety. "Driven by righteous wrath (*yifen* 義憤), the Hungarians expelled the Alliance in defense of their neighbor."[14] But later, as Austria's foreign minister, Klemens von Metternich (1773–1859), resumed power, he was determined to colonize Hungary by disregarding the Hungarians' benevolence. Liang accused the Austrian of "responding to benevolence with jealousy and distrust" and "returning the favor with revenge."[15] To the new historian, the determination the Hungarians displayed in fighting the Austrian's colonial invasion was not driven by the need for national survival; rather, Austria had violated propriety and the good practice of reciprocity. The Hungarians, in a word, were defending their rights on a moral rather than a legal ground.

Propriety is an integral component of Confucian morality. By characterizing Hungary as the benefactor and Austria the beneficiary, Liang replaces these countries' legal, contractual relationship with a moral one. Later, as the Hungarians stood up to repel Austria's invasion with arms, Liang describes their military combat as "the right they shared to fight against tyranny" (baozheng 暴政), a term implying moral illegitimacy in the Chinese cultural and political tradition. Having situated the Hungarians' fight for national independence within a Chinese moral paradigm, Liang, the new historian, implies that to exercise one's rights is more about reasserting the lawful moral order than striving for the balance between one's civil rights and obligation in modern politics. By rendering the Hungarians as the righteous knights-errants and fashioning their battle to transform the country into a nation-state as an attempt to reinstall the appropriate moral order, Liang imbues nationalist spirit with morality and turns modern national citizens into natural moral agents.

Confucian morality emphasizes the need to be filial (xiao 孝) to one's parents and loyal (zhong 忠) to one's lord.[16] In a modern nation-state, Liang believes that one shares moral obligation (yiwu 義務) as well as civil political obligation. As Liang explicates in his historical biography, Austria's foreign minister attempted to oppress Hungary by closing down its Congress. Upon learning of the decision, Kossuth, the national hero, was determined to fight for Hungary's independence. Being a man "with great determination, mental prowess, and physical power,"[17] Kossuth's insistence on "cultivating his character and bettering his moral behavior" distinguishes him from most politicians.[18] While Kossuth was a great man (weiren 偉人), a hero (yingxiong 英雄), and a knight-errant (haojie 豪傑), the national citizens he gathered, according to Liang, were equally virtuous and heroic. Sharing pure, noble, and burning patriotic love for the country, the Hungarians were determined to follow their great leader Kossuth, a great man they respected, loved, and worshipped. "Upon receiving the newspaper the great man published, the national citizen felt as if they could finally see the rains after the drought, and relieve their thirst with water."[19] These people considered Kossuth their benefactor (enren 恩人).[20] Kossuth was imprisoned for his protest against Austria. After his release, "the Hungarians welcomed their benefactor in Budapest, [and] their joyous sound had suddenly shaken the mountain."[21] Later as Kossuth decided to launch a revolution, "people in the provinces were deeply grateful for his virtuous deeds. Several thousand of them were ready to die for their national leader."[22]

In the "Biography of Kossuth," Hungarian national citizens aspire to turn their country into an independent nation-state. Besides exemplifying the conceptual definition of being a national citizen in a lived historical context, Liang describes the Hungarians' love for Kossuth and the country with highly affective languages. Terms he uses include "love," "respect," "fantasize," "worship," "feeling grateful," and "to die for." As fierce and passionate as they may seem, these affective sentiments, Liang believes, are consonant with Confucian morality. In "On Public Morality" (*Lun gongde* 論公德), an editorial issued on the day the first installment of the "Biography of Kossuth" was published, Liang asserts that "public morality" (*gongde* 公德) is essentially an extension, transfiguration, and external manifestation of "private morality" (*side* 私德) in the modern democratic domain.[23] Instead of two distinct sets of proprieties, they are identical sentiments manifested in different contexts and in turn are characterized with different terms. To Liang, how a country treats its people is analogous to parents' care for their children.[24] Since these kinds of care are comparable, one is obligated to serve one's parents and one's country with same devotion. While the Hungarians' emotional sentiments cannot be categorized in Confucian moral terms, their intense emotional engagement in the modern political transition elevated them from national citizens to "authentic" national citizens. "Authenticity," in other words, is predicated on sharing and realizing one's sincere moral intent, and modern political concepts are meant to be experienced and practiced as "modern political-moral goodness."

An Onto-Hermeneutic Turn in Political Modernization

As Liang urged his contemporaries to uncover "true" meanings beyond the semantic content of language, his integration of a moral component into the acquisition of modern political knowledge entailed the introduction of a new hermeneutic paradigm. Liang's reasoning can perhaps be succinctly theorized with Chung-ying Cheng's 成中英 "onto-hermeneutics" (*yixue quanshi xue* 易學詮釋學), a philosophical supposition seeking to bridge the gap between hermeneutics and ontology.[25] Cheng's conception of onto-hermeneutics, as On-cho Ng elaborates with great intellectual vigor, aims to achieve two purposes: first, to invent a new hermeneutics to accurately describe the Confucian onto-cosmological conception of reality; second, to expand the scope and depth of Martin Heidegger's and Hans-Georg Gadamer's hermeneutic theories by incorporating the Confucian exegetical principle as a comparative perspective.[26]

In the Confucian tradition, Chung-ying Cheng argues, proper understanding of the classics can be achieved only through one's emotional identification with its teachings and in turn the realization of teaching in action. Knowing that understanding begins with the "comprehensive observation" of both the symbolic and textual meaning of the discursive scripture, one's emotional responses to the text alter one's existential makeup and transform one's understanding of the scripture into an embodied, ontological experience. As a person puts moral teachings into practice, he materializes one's ontologically premised understanding of Confucian teaching by realizing his moral potential in action. The existential application of moral wisdom transcends the dichotomies of fact and value, knowledge and reality, and virtue and reason.

Understanding, according to Cheng, is more "the ontological conflation of epistemological exercise and experiential exertion" than a disembodied, narrowly instrumental, and mechanistically technical process.[27] Liang's insistence on transforming the study of modern political knowledge into an ontological moral experience calls for a comparable form of hermeneutic exercise. For the political reformer, the most effective means of assisting the reader in "becoming" an authentic national citizen was to expose them to the virtual experience of *being*. Rather than explicating the term "national citizen" as a piece of conceptual knowledge, in the "Biography of Kossuth," the creation of visual and musical immediacy engages the reader as the audience attending an oration Kossuth delivers in public. In his speech, Kossuth tells his followers *in person* what it takes for a person to become an authentic national citizen:

> What is to happen today is the one and only solution to safeguard the independence of Hungary. It also concerns the life and death of my national citizen. Gentlemen, if you want liberty, please wait patiently until this internal crisis is appeased. Thereafter, we and our children shall always be able to obtain eternal life in the realm of independence. Our success depends on today; our fall depends on today; our survival, Gentlemen, depends on you; our demise, Gen-

tlemen, depends on you. However incapable I am, I have been appointed with this mission. Today, shedding rivulets of tears and quick drops of blood, holding my heart, draining my gallbladder, and creeping on the ground rubbing my belly against it, I present this proposal before my heroic, honorable Hungarian *national citizens'* hearts and chests. Gentlemen, O Gentlemen, if only we could manifest our pure and noble patriotism.[28] 今日之事，實維持匈牙利國家之不二法門，而我國民生死之問題也。諸君若愛自由乎，請忍耐以待此內難之削平。則我輩及我子孫皆永得永生於獨立之天地。其成耶，在今日。其敗耶，在今日。其生耶，在諸君，其死耶，在諸君。某也不才，忝受委托。今日搵縷縷之淚，瀝滴滴之血，捧心瀝膽，匍匐俯伏以提出此案於我有血性、有榮譽的匈加利國民胸臆之前，諸君乎諸君乎，若我輩各出其高尚純潔之愛國心。

Assuming that the Hungarian and the Chinese belong to the same ethnic origin and have suffered from comparable imperial invasions, Liang asserts that the Hungarian national hero is a role model for "those who are yellow, who have been oppressed by autocracy, and who live in an age of frustration."[29] To convince his contemporaries of the urgency of becoming an "authentic" national citizen, in the above passage Liang seeks to reproduce the acoustic immediacy of a speech through various literary strategies.[30] Liang's Hungarian hero, to begin with, addresses himself as "the humble one" (*mou* 某) and addresses his audience as "Gentlemen" (*zhujun* 諸君), "my national citizen" (*wo guomin* 我國民), and "we" (*wo bei* 我輩). These terms of address, as Barbara Mittler observes in her study of Liang's journalistic writing, turn an author into a "subjective presence."[31] Collectively they give the reader the impression that one is being directly engaged and is encouraged to identify oneself with the addressee, which in this case is the national citizen. The audience, or the late Qing reader, is called upon as many as five times in the short speech. By putting the emphatic particle *hu* 乎 between the repetition of "Gentlemen" (*zhujun hu zhujun* 諸君乎諸君), the addresser conveys his emotions affectively to the reader and forms a feeling of intimacy between them.

To emphasize the urgent need of transforming Hungary into a nation-state, and to convince the reader that one can accomplish this goal only through self-sacrifice, Liang includes the following parallel prose in Kossuth's speech:

188 | Affective Betrayal

> Our success depends on today; our fall depends on today; our survival, Gentlemen, depends on you; our demise, Gentlemen, depends on you.
>
> 其成耶，在今日。其敗耶，在今日。
> 其生耶，在諸君，其死耶，在諸君。

The short parallel prose consists of four couplets. They share duplicate grammatical structures, and the parallel prose is a repetition of certain phrases and characters. The first lines of each couplet are organized in the identical pattern of "*qi* 其 *cheng* 成/ *bai* 敗/ *sheng* 生/ *si* 死 *ye* 也," and these couplets conclude either with the phrase "*zai jintian*" 在今天 (depends on today) or "*zai zhujun*" 在諸君 (depends on you, Gentlemen). Although the words "success" (*cheng* 成) and "fall" (*bai* 敗) in the beginning couplets are replaced by "survival" (*sheng* 生) and "demise" (*si* 死) in the concluding couplets, the short prose lines are semantically parallel. These repetitive, if not redundant, couplets can be categorized as "contrived parallelism." Contrived parallelism, according to Ronald Egan, "results from padding a statement so that it comes out in parallel phrases even though the sense does not require the matching."[32] To Egan the purpose of aligning parallel lines with a corresponding intonation and end rhyme is "to keep the rhythm going,"[33] and the creation of contrived parallelism often indicates that the poet "has given priority to rhythm over sense."[34]

Egan's observation seems immediately applicable to Liang's "poetic" endeavor. Having romanized the short parallel prose in Mandarin pinyin, the phonetic duplication appears ostensible:

> Qi cheng ye, zai jinri. Qi bai ye, zai jinri.
>
> Qi shen ye, zai zhujun. Qi zi ye, zai zhujun.

In addition to *cheng*, *bai*, *sheng*, and *si*, Liang's parallel prose is constructed by the repetition of five phonological units (*qi*, *ye*, *zai*, *jintian*, and *zhujun*). With a limited number of monosyllabic sounds repeating themselves in the duplicate grammatical pattern, the passage constitutes a certain rhythm. Although these couplets represent two directly opposed political outcomes, the parallel syntactic structure and semantic units form an organic phonological unity in its own right. By repeating a monotonous group of sounds in a predictable sequence, Liang's musical arrangement attunes the reader to a particular acoustic rhythm. His creation of musical effect distantly resonates with what George Steiner considers a poet's attempt to turn from "the linear, denotative, logically determined bonds of linguistic syntax" to "the simultaneities, immediacies, and free play of musical form."[35] The use of contrived parallelism, which is characteristic of Liang's new prose style, demonstrates how the reformer succeeds in producing an audio text through careful syntactic and phonological organization and in expanding the reading experience into a listening one.

Aside from making the short passage "speak" to the reader, Kossuth's speech creates the simultaneous effect of exposing the reader to the cinematic experience of seeing. In his speech the Hungarian patriot addresses his audience as "knight-errant-like national citizens" (*xiayi zhi guomin* 俠義之國民) who "act upon their *righteous* wrath" (*ji yu yifen* 激於義憤).[36] While Kossuth humbly suggests that he and the Hungarian national citizen stand on an equal footing, the moral binding between them is repeatedly emphasized. Liang, for instance, introduces Kossuth as a "great man" (*weiren*) and a "hero" (*yingxiong*).[37] On the day Kossuth is released from prison for anti-Austrian activities, it is said that "Hungarians welcomed their 'benefactor' [*enren* 恩人] in Budapest, with the joyous sound abruptly quaking the mountains."[38] Feeling "deeply thankful for Kossuth's good deeds . . . thousands of civilians were ready to sacrifice their lives for him."[39] To arouse the national citizen's determination to sacrifice oneself for the country, Kossuth presents himself as a wounded man who has endured excruciating torment in the process of transforming Hungary into a nation-state. Kossuth expects the national citizens to undergo the same trials. By announcing to the people that he is speaking in tears and blood, and that to communicate these words is to present to them his heart in both hands, drain the bile of his gallbladder, and crawl toward them rubbing his belly against the ground, Kossuth skillfully glosses over the remote parallel between fulfilling a person's civil obligation as a national citizen and performing one's righteous duty to a friend in the Chinese moral and fictional traditions.[40]

The Hungarian hero prides himself on the extreme physical suffering he endures. Tears, blood, heart, gallbladder, and crawling on all fours are bodily images that gratify immediate voyeuristic pleasure. The musical rhythm of his speech intensifies the corporeal sensation promised by the virtual exhibition. Following the short parallel prose constituted by the group of three-character phrases, Liang introduces an additional pair of parallel couplets in Kossuth's speech: "With rivulets of tears running down and the blood shedding drop after drop" (*wen liuliu zhi lei, lü didi zhi xue* 搵縷縷之淚, 濾滴滴之血). The extended sentence length and the reduplications *liuliu* and *didi* decelerate the pace of the speech and generate tension. The repetition of sounds prolongs Kossuth's physical suffering and retains the reader's attention in a suspended moment. In the succeeding couplet, "presenting my heart, draining my gallbladder, creeping on the ground, and rubbing my belly against it" (*pěng xīn lì dǎn, pú fú fǔ fú* 捧心瀝胆, 匍匐俯伏), the phonetic resemblance between the last four characters makes the tension and suspension more pronounced. The speech finally resumes its pace as it arrives at the three-character couplet "my heroic and my honorable" (*you xuexing, you rongyu* 有血性、有榮譽). As the melodic tempo of the speech is about to reach its crescendo, Kossuth draws his people's attention in the timeliest manner, calling them "Gentlemen, O Gentlemen" (*zhujun hu zhujun* 諸君乎諸君).

In Kossuth's speech, the rhetorical implication of being a national citizen in this biography differs radically from the objective and learned definition Liang delineates in the editorials he published in the same journal. Aside from "people with nationalistic thinking and capable of implementing and participating in the modern political system" (有國家思想, 能自布政治), a modern national citizen, as Kossuth implies, is expected to sacrifice his life and endure extreme physical suffering for the country, and presumably the political leader.[41] What leads the subjective historian's national citizen further away from the modern journalist's objective definition is that Liang, through the creation of acoustic and visual effects, presents his rhetorical call *affectively* to the late Qing reader. The creation of affective resonance with the reader on acoustic, visual, and sensory dimensions, in this sense, is as important as circulating modern political knowledge through the narrative.

From Linguistic Text to Acoustic Text

In early China, thinkers used to be able to envision an underlying coherence between learning (*xue* 學), the moral way (*dao* 道), and political governance (*zhi* 治).[42] The sense of coherence, however, had gradually fallen apart since the time of Confucius in sixth century BC. Coming to the early eighteenth century, the Qing monarchy performed excessive

Musicality—Representing the Rhythm of Political Revolution | 191

and demeaning rituals to deride the Han literati. Accompanied by this emblematic condemnation was an imposition of rigid state ideology that denied people's thinking and feelings. The court's manipulative distortions of the cultural and literary traditions anticipated the spread of what Judith Whitbeck calls "vulgar cultural manifestation" as expressed in one's ruthless pursuit of *wen* 文, overrefinement of culture and literary inquisition; *ming* 明, the quest for reputation or fame (as opposed to reality and substance); and "specious appearance" (*xiaomao* 笑貌), the high court officials' display of hypocritical demeanors as Gong Zizhen 龔自珍 (1792–1841) criticized in the essay "On Private Interest." Gong Zizhen was familiar with music's parabolic symbolism. To denounce the cultural and moral decline of the Qing empire, he began to flatten the vibrant distinction between the five tones. "To draw out the contrasts between an age of order and that of decline," as Whitbeck observes, "Gong examined forms of cultural expression. Colors were transformed so that in age of decline, black and white blended together and the five colors were discarded." In music, the pentatonic scale was reduced to a single eerie drone as the "highest note of the scale [*gong* 宮] and the lowest note [*yu* 羽] are discarded and the others blend together."[43]

Similar to Gong Zizhen, Liang berated his contemporaries for their mental inertia and indulgence in meaningless philological investigation. In his attempt to replace the Qing monarchy with a state of democratic governance that thrived on the subjective engagement of independent political agents, Liang's search for personal moral autonomy entailed a corresponding form of musical representation. While Gong denounced the Qing autocracy by flattening the five tones, Liang restored the high and low tones, a musical arrangement that anticipated the awakening of strong human feelings and psychological complexities, to publicize his call for progressive political reformism. Speaking from the perspective of a "new historian," in the "Biography of Kossuth" Liang asserts that the purpose of situating the historical narration in a public oration is to "arouse" (*xing* 興) the reader's resolve to become a national citizen in China's transition to democratic governance. *Xing* is a literary device used to stimulate readers' emotional responses.[44] To emphasize his rhetorical call, Liang aligns himself with Mencius. The reformer says, "Didn't Mencius say that 'invigorated by the ancients, a bystander cannot help but being deeply moved [*xing qi* 興起], and not to mention those have shared similar experiences.' . . . Alas, for readers of this biography, they should be inspired and moved."[45]

In the speech Kossuth delivers to his national citizens, what is being emphasized is not only the national citizen's moral binding with the political leader but also the virtual experience of *being* a national citizen on the eve of an unprecedented historical transition. The immediate aesthetic experiences to which Liang's affective presentation can potentially transport a reader might have easily taken precedence over the semantic content of words. Judging from Kossuth's speech, Liang is conscious of the power of music and skillful in making music with formal features of language. While Liang had never systematically presented his reason for creating a musical order alongside a descriptive historical narrative, nor explained what makes the musicality of language a compelling vehicle for political persuasion, one might try to locate some hints from some contemporary Chinese and Western theorists.

In ancient China, according to Kenneth Berthel, sound's intrinsic ability to spread itself across had been understood as "sympathetic resonance." For early Chinese philosophers, "the idea that different kinds of sounds transmitted different information or emotional content intersubjectively was seen as typologically equivalent to the physical phenomenon of sympathetic resonance so readily observable in nature."[46] In studying the connection between language and music, and the complementary role the two play in communicating one's intent, Berthel suggests that "expression is certainly not a simple case of mimetic reproduction of the nonmusical sounds of the external world, but rather a deployment of musical sounds that represent the human affect that arises from external arousal."[47] Focusing on the role music played in transmitting reality and principle in ancient China, Berthel hopes to achieve the more ambitious goal of questioning the "centrality of language in representing our worldview,"[48] an objective that has been more elaborately discussed in Kao Yu-kung's study of classical Chinese poetry.

"Emotion," as said in the "Great Preface to Mao's Odes" (*Maoshi daxu* 毛詩大序), "is stirred in the heart and takes shape in poetry" 在心為志, 發言為詩.[49] Subscribing to the assumption that the creation of poetic form is driven by the poet's desire to manifest one's intent (*shi yan zhi* 詩言志),[50] Kao Yu-kung notes that "the poetic impulse arises from the desire to express the mental states and acts of the poet through artistic language."[51] Since one's interiority cannot be fully expressed in discursive language, the creation of a formal structure often manifests the poet's "manipulation of rules to adapt to his creative imagination, and his effort of attaining his vision through his specific form."[52] Formal structure is thus "an integral part of the poet's intention and is inextricable from the realization of the poet's vision."[53]

The supposition that the "musicality" conveyed by the formal and phonetic structure of language as a means of self-expression is shared by Western theorists such as Theodor Adorno (1903–1969). The human subject, Adorno believes, is constituted by subjective consciousness as well as unmediated experiences that struggle to override his rationalizing power. Classifying the "name" as something "chained to the form of judgment and proposition and thereby to the synthetic form of the concept,"[54] Adorno, being equally suspicious about the signifying power of language, categorizes music as an "aconceptual synthesis" that refuses to reduce the empirical experience into the conceptual.[55] Compared with "signifying languages" that always "say the absolute in a mediated way," music has the potential to reach "the absolute immediately."[56] In his discussion of Friedrich Hölderlin's (1770–1843) late poetry, Adorno argues that to conceive an internal musical rhythm within a poetic composition is to resist the discursive power of linguistic conceptualization. While Adorno is keen to celebrate the realization of man's personal freedom in the musicality of language, in "Parataxis" he strongly emphasizes that the musical quality of Hölderlin's language cannot be considered more authentic or reliable than the semantic narrative. This is simply because when a person expresses his aconceptual self in language, this unconscious self can be found only in the aconceptual musical quality *of* language. The truth content of language lies in the uncertainty and obscurity unwrapped by the musicality of the semantic content. Adorno describes the infinite interpretive possibility conditioned by the tension between the form and the content as a state of "constitutive dissociation."[57] The "path followed by the determinate negation of meaning," he states, "is the path to the truth content."[58]

For Chinese and Western theorists, the musicality of language does not convey the "true meaning"; it opens us to interpretative possibilities that rest beyond the linguistic representation. If the formal structure is indeed "the objectification of an inner state," we might have good reason to suspect that Liang's conception of an affective musical order alongside his discursive historical narrative serves the need of capturing and conveying the unmediated experiences of *being* an authentic national citizen, a state of existential authenticity that transcends rational conceptualization. Democratic governance, as Liang explicated in his comparison between Wang Yangming and Kant, was intended to operate as the "political" expression of man's natural cognitive, perceptual, and moral disposition. In studies of modern Chinese literature and history, historians tend to perceive the rise of subjectivity to be the foundation on which Chinese modernity is based. And yet, the personal authenticity Liang calls for is different from the kind of subjectivity being defined from a Eurocentric philosophical trajectory.[59] Being sharply aware of the limitations of objective rationality, to Liang the inner authenticity that informs the formal expression transcends the perspective mental content; it is what Wang Yangming called *liangzhi*, the good moral knowing.

In Wang Yangming's moral theory, the Ming philosopher compared man's perceptual sense to the inherent pattern of the cosmos. By emphasizing the affinity between the organizational principle of a person's heartmind and that of the cosmos, Wang underscored the supremacy of human moral intuition. As a self-sufficient moral agent, a person recognizes textual knowledge to be a manifestation of one's subjective feelings and makes use of textual knowledge as reference serving self-regulatory purposes. The kind of human omnipotence Wang upheld promised to transform textual knowledge from prescriptive scriptures meant be learned by man to the outward expression of one's affective, moral interiority. As Wang reversed the "top-down" power hierarchy between man and text into an "inside-out" organic entity, he projected a new form of "man-centered" power dynamics that was packed with subversive potential.[60] This subversive potential met a new outlet in China's transition to political modernity. Liang wishfully believed that man was naturally capable of manifesting his moral instinct in action. To ensure that modern political "knowledge" would resonate with the reader's a priori moral disposition, Liang took the liberty of inventing a coextensive musical order that accompanies the rhythmical structure of his historical narrative. To Kao Yu-kung, the contemporary scholar of Chinese poetry, the aesthetic experience anticipated by the interplay between form and content allows the poet and the reader to communicate beyond the textual meaning.[61] This "aesthetics," he says, "is an interpretative code" that derives its expressive potential from presenting itself indirectly.[62] While "it is difficult to articulate this aesthetic as a code," "the very fact that it never becomes fully explicit protects its power to suggest, to change, and to develop."[63]

Political Transcendence in Action: The French Revolution

Perceiving his contemporaries as equal cosmic members of the metaphysical republic, Liang, as discussed in chapter three, celebrated the nobility of enacting one's cosmic nature through embodied political actions. To make his voice heard, Liang composed a series of historical biographies on Madame Roland, Giuseppe Mazzini, and Lajos Kossuth, a cohort of European revolutionary heroes who struggled to bring their countries liberal democracy through tears, sweat, blood, death, and excruciating pain. In the "Biography of Madame Roland," Liang describes the French heroine as a benevolent sage (*renren* 仁人) who is compassionate (*ciai* 慈愛), noble (*gaoshang* 高尚), and pure (*jiebai* 潔白). From Madame Roland's early girlhood days until the day she was executed on the guillotine, her perfect cosmic moral nature remained uncontaminated by any evil influence. According to the biography, Madame Roland called for the French Revolution in 1789. As a physical "enactment" of her perfect heartmind, Madame Roland's participation in the French Revolution promised to disclose and eventuate the heavenly cosmic order that transcends one's rational comprehension. But what happened in the historical reality was anything but compassionate, noble, or pure. However reluctant he is to do so, Liang describes the destructive outcome of the French Revolution in most vivid details:

> The wild billows of the revolution were bombing the sky and shaking the earth. The guillotine had grown tired of man's blood. Making the *sa-sa* sound, the wind roared with the fishy smell of human flesh that blocked the river. With the miserable rain they made this a misty season. 革命之狂瀾轟天撼地，斷頭機厭人之血，布鄂河塞人之肉腥颯颯慘雨濛濛之時節.[64]

In his pictorial description above, Liang points to readers blood dripping down the guillotine and dismembered bodies being spread evenly across the fields. The city of Paris is covered with blood, and ditches are blocked by human flesh. To fully unfold the French Revolution's destructive force, Liang continues,

> Madame Roland's ideal has now been realized. Assuming that the peaceful construction is underway, she is staggered

to learn that new challenges have been posed before the prevailing ones can be overcome. One tries to block the tiger at her front door and yet the wolf is crouching at the back gate. While the biggest enemies on top are dead, the biggest enemies from below are growing in full maturity. At present, Madame Roland has no choice but to toss herself into the revolutionary torrent that she has generated, and to be enfold, consumed, and taken away. 羅蘭夫人之理想，今已現於實際。以為太平建設指日可待，豈意一波未平，一波又起。前門拒虎，后門近狼。在上之大敵已斃，而在下之大敵人，羽翼正成。今也，羅蘭夫人遂不得不投身於己所造出之革命急潮之中，而被裹被挾被捲以去。[65]

Liang calls the French Revolution the "reality" (*shiji* 實際) of Madame Roland's high, lofty ideal (*lixiang* 理想). Instead of actualizing her perfect moral goodness in the physical existence, the French heroine was devoured and destroyed by the collective political action she called for. Liang names the crowd that killed her tigers and wolves, and characterizes their murderous rage as "mad waves, petrifying billows" (*kuangtao xielang* 狂濤駭浪), and ocean currents (*jichao* 急潮). By comparing people's murderous instincts to meteorological phenomena, Liang dehumanizes their destructive impulse as natural forces that go beyond one's control. To underscore the overpowering presence of these natural forces, Liang repeats the passive voice "being" (*bei* 被) as many as three times to indicate that Madame Roland "has no choice but" (*budebu* 不得不) being enfolded, consumed, and taken away (*beiguo beixie beijuan* 被裹被挾被捲). The repetition accentuates how the French heroine's perfect moral goodness has been devoured by the dehumanized revolutionary currents she has summoned at the first place.

Man's heartmind, according to Wang Yangming, crystalizes the organizational principles of the cosmos. Sharing the heartmind of a sage, Madame Roland is uncontaminated by human prejudices or desires. The revolutionary activities for which she dies for are *meant* to be the disclosure of the heavenly order. In the French Revolution, however, the "enactment" of people's cosmic, moral nature contradicts their heavenly endowment. How, after all, did men's transcendental moral instincts become passive animalistic forces? Madame Roland might be more sensible than most people. But the perfect heartmind, as Wang argued, is shared universally by all beings. If a person's instinctive responses indeed reveal heaven, from whence do the evil forces come? And what can these behaviors tell us about the "perfect" cosmic order?

Evil as Hesitation to Be True to Oneself

Speaking from the perspective of Western theorists, the murderous furies people displayed in the French Revolution are "affective" intensities that present themselves *ahead* of our conscious awareness. Having drawn an equivalence between man's heartmind and the cosmic pattern, Wang Yangming asserted that the heartmind is free from the intrusion of savage feelings and desires. His purification of the heartmind presents an immediate question: men exhibit all kinds of wicked cruelty and evil thoughts. If their heartmind is indeed a revelation of the cosmos and therefore absent of self-nature, from whence does evil arrive? This certainly is not the first time that Wang Yangming's moral teachings were put to the test. The Ming philosopher once responded to the challenge in his "four-cornered doctrine": the presence of goodness and evil come along with the movement of our inclinations (*you shan you e yi zhi dong* 有善有惡意之動). To properly understand Wang's explanation, let us begin with his definition of "inclination" (*yi* 意).[66]

"Inclination," Wang Yangming said, substantiates "what is emanated from the heartmind" (心之所發便是意).[67] In our everyday life, "inclination is manifested in the external matters (*wu* 物) upon which it directs toward" (意之所在便是物).[68] These external matters can refer to physical objects as well as the general affairs of men (*shi* 事).[69] A person, for instance, serves his parents with filial piety. The circumstance of serving one's parents is a state of *shi*, and the loving sincerity he expresses toward this state of affairs manifests inclination.[70] Of the broad spectrum of natural propensities a person displays, Wang divided them into two categories: one is emotion (*qing* 情), and the other is moral knowing (*zhi* 知). Having compared man's heartmind to the cosmos, Wang suggested that a person is instinctively capable of knowing brotherly love (*zhi di* 知悌) and being compassionate (*zhi ceyin* 知惻隱). His natural moral inclinations are manifested in the same fashion as his instinctual responses.[71] When a person smells a stinky smell, he is sickened by the smell. When he sees an attractive woman, he is aroused.

Man's heartmind, as Wang emphasized, epitomizes the cosmos; its primordial cosmic endowment cannot be erroneous (蓋心之本體本無不

正).⁷² Being the inclination of the heartmind, *yi* is upright and sincere (*chenyi* 誠意). In reality, however, the inclination originated from one's heartmind often becomes inauthentic when it is directed toward external affairs (自其意念發動, 而後有不正). The corruption of *yi*, as Wang believed, has neither to do with external affairs nor with the cosmic endowment that informs its presence. It is caused by man's "lingering hesitation" (*jinian liuji* 一念留滯) and his "reluctance" to be true to oneself (*bie nian guadai* 別念掛帶). Inclination manifests the natural propensity heartmind directs toward the external objects. However absolute and pure one's inclination is, a person may feel uncertain about his instinctive disposition. As the person hesitates, his inclination becomes stuck (*ji* 滯), fixed (*liu* 留), attached (*zhu* 著), and adulterated (*za* 雜). The indecisiveness then detains inclination in a vulnerable and unstable position (*bu anwen chu* 不安穩處), exposing it to risks and latent dangers (*wei* 危). Man shares aversion for putrid smells and instant liking for a beautiful woman. But once these feelings have been overprocessed, they can be turned into rage (*nuqing* 怒情) and sorrow (*aiqing* 哀情).

A person's hesitation, Wang said, reveals the irreconcilable discrepancies between his pristine cosmic nature and our societies' mundane "practices and conventions" (*xi* 習). Across different social and geographical contexts, people tend to invent norms and practices in accordance with their own will. These received practices foster debauched customs (風俗之頹靡). Following the passage of time, debauched customs become common standards.⁷³ They infiltrate a person as if they were oil staining and covering his face (習俗移人, 如油漬面).⁷⁴ Men are the living presences of the cosmos. Having being exposed to these corrupted social conventions for a period of time, they begin to second-guess their cosmic instinct. Once they hesitate, uncertainty and doubt spoil one's cosmic instinct, turning sincere inclination (*chengyi* 誠意) into selfish intent (*siyi* 私意). Wang did not blame men for succumbing to the corrupting social conventions; he found them largely powerless in resisting them.⁷⁵ To acknowledge men's predicament, Wang presented a vivid metaphor: swamped and submerged by these received social practices, a person lives as if he resides in a pickled fish store. Gradually he loses his sensitivity to the bad smell and begins to stink like fish.⁷⁶

Both Zhu Xi and Wang Yangming believed that the cosmic patterns were flawlessly perfect. But assuming that the cosmic patterns informing the structure of one's moral nature were obscured by *qi* the muddy substances, Zhu Xi considered man's corporeal heartmind filthy and deformed. Wang Yangming tried to purify the filthy heartmind by dispelling the evil from without. Instead of accusing the heartmind of being contaminated by pollutants, Wang blamed established social practices for spoiling its natural purity. For Wang Yangming, man's pristine human nature emits kind thoughts (善念者, 本性也).[77] "The occurrence of evil thought manifests social conventions" (惡念者, 習氣也) coming from *without*.[78]

A Futile Defense of the Heavenly Order

Being an avid defender of Wang Yangming, Wang Ji 王畿 (style name Longxi 龍溪) (1498–1583) made continuous attempts to salvage the perfection of the cosmos as embodied in man's heartmind. To restore his contemporaries' confidence in *liangzhi*, or good moral knowing, Wang Ji sought to justify people's wicked behaviors as follows: Men, as Wang Yangming and Mencius believed, begin life as perfect moral beings. A person's moral intuition can be categorized finely as "ontological moral goodness" (*liangzhi benti* 良知本體).[79] Once the person's ontological moral propensity is activated in thinking, feeling, and embodied actions, his latent moral potential becomes "perceptible" in mental and physical activities. Wang Ji called the outward expression of one's moral propensity "the presence of good moral knowing" (*jianzai liangzhi* 見在良知). "The presence of good moral knowing" is meant to be an unadulterated disclosure of the cosmic pattern as epitomized by a person's heartmind. In reality, however, men are social beings living in a relational context. When a person interacts with his environment, he can be easily distracted by external stimuli. The person might mistake his "sensory responses" (*zhijue* 知覺) to these exterior stimuli as expressions *of* his good moral knowing. Similar to his teacher Wang Yangming, Wang Ji believed that man's heartmind contains the cosmos; it is an absolute good unpolluted by any form of evil influences. When a person responds or behaves in a vicious manner, these depraved behaviors *do not* disclose his moral nature. They, on the contrary, are indications signaling that his good moral knowing has been adulterated (*liangzhi chanhe* 良知摻和) by the intrusion of sensory responses, which include his sight, hearing, smell, taste, and touch of the physical reality.

Applying Wang Ji's reasoning, one might be tempted to perceive the atrocity people displayed in the French Revolution as sensory responses being misconstrued as expressions of their cosmic nature. Wang Ji's defense of man's good moral knowing may seem reasonable in theory. But once we return to Wang Yangming's call for the "oneness of knowledge and action," such defense becomes untenable. The emphasis Wang places on "the *oneness* of knowledge and action," once again, was informed by interpenetrative relationships delineated by Huayan Buddhism.[80] *Liangzhi* operates as the heartmind's detective censor. Being a functional extension of the heartmind, *liangzhi*, similar to the abstract cosmic pattern it epitomizes, does not contain any self-nature or substantial self-content. To *know* a person's imperceptible cosmic moral propensity, we can learn *only* from the tangible outlets through which *liangzhi* finds concrete expression. In this mutually interpenetrative relationship, the ontological structure of good moral *knowing* is contained and encoded in the ontological structure of man's *bodily being*. What lies within the heartmind, in other words, is predicated on (and crystalized in) the external outlets from without. Good moral knowing, as I far as I believe, is not a self-isolated form of epistemic or cognitive function.[81] Knowing *is* action. This is why Wang Yangming emphasized the "oneness" *of* knowledge *and* action.

In his defense of Wang Yangming, Wang Ji took people's malicious behaviors as their "sensory responses" *to* the external stimuli rather than expressions *of* their perfect moral knowing. The distinction Wang Ji delineated between man's perfect moral knowing and their sensory responses is absent in Wang Yangming's moral metaphysics. A person, as Wang believed, can *only be* who he is and *know only* what is *within* him. Feeling hungry, for instance, expresses one's recognition of hunger.[82] And when a person knows that he is in pain, such knowledge acknowledges the "presence" of his prevailing ailment. Liang Qichao was familiar with Wang's logical reasoning. Embodied responses, and by extension one's recognition of such responses, as Liang explicated in his exposition of the "oneness of knowledge and action," epitomize an actual fact (感覺 (知) 的本身, 已是一種事實).[83] Being the disclosure of one's *lived* experiential sensations, one's embodied responses manifest the "presence" of his imperceptible cosmic moral propensity. Instead of sensory responses to external stimuli, people's vicious behaviors disclose their moral nature. *We are what we do*. In Wang Yangming's call for the "oneness of knowledge and action," there is no duality to speak of.

Are People's Spontaneous Responses *Posthuman*?

Sharing divergent conceptions of the heartmind, Zhu Xi and Wang Yangming developed distinctive approaches to learning. While Zhu Xi urged people to investigate the cosmic pattern disclosed in the Confucian classics as well as myriad forms of natural phenomena, Wang reduced a person's deliberate consideration (*silü* 思慮) and willful arrangement (*anpai sisuo* 安排思索) to biased cleverness (*yongzhi zisi* 用智自私).[84] Being a living presence of the cosmos, a person's heartmind is so clear and perfect that it transcends the *artificial* human intelligence one acquires from contrived social practices. For a person to realize his endowed cosmic perfection, which is finer and larger than *what he thinks* he knows, the person must follow his cosmic instinct. Uninterrupted by man's premeditated intervention, these "*spontaneous* responses" (*xing* 行), be they perceptual or physical, epitomize the exteriorization of abstract cosmic patterns on earth.

Wang's metaphysical musing was not restricted to current philosophical discussions; it was widely reflected in the literary culture of his times. During the Ming and the early Qing periods, Chinese literati were keen to celebrate the intensity and authenticity (*zhen* 真) of one's romantic passions (*qing* 情).[85] While recent literary historians perceive the flourishing of romantic passions as a testament of the blossoming of human subjectivity induced by the development of the city and its burgeoning bourgeois culture, Ling Hon Lam presents an alternative view.[86] In contemporary Western culture, Lam says, it is generally assumed that emotion is a feeling *inside* of us. Being the exterior of one's psychological interiority, emotion relates a story of suppression and emancipation, and has hence been taken as a token of a person's self-sovereignty. While modern Western culture affirms "the superiority of the emotive interior," Lam reverses the familiar assumption upside-down and inside-out.[87] In Ming and Qing China's theatrical and fictional creation, as Lam brilliantly argues, the passionate intensity a person experiences testifies precisely the *absence* and transparency of human subjectivity. Strong feelings are *impersonal* and are completely *outside* of us. They *do not* come from within.

Under the influence of neo-Confucianism, Chinese novelists of the seventeenth and eighteenth century were accustomed to perceive men as cosmic beings. Instead of inferior human feelings bred by the muddy *qi* substance, the strong emotions one experiences evince "an all-pervading field of cosmological force" that penetrates and trespasses a person without him being consciously aware of it. To experience emotion, as the Ming novelist Feng Menglong 馮夢龍 (1574–1646) described, is to be *taken*, *penetrated*, and *possessed* by cosmic forces. "Having been delivered outside in the world," one experiences emotions as a process of self-displacement.[88] In this fleeting moment of incomprehension, a person, to borrow what Theodor Adorno calls the "liquidation, or annihilation of I," is temporarily dislocated from his rational cognition.[89] Being superseded by cosmic forces of which he is made, man, in moments as such, feels *without a self*. For a person to return to himself, he can do so only by *recollecting* one's emotions from *without*. Theatrical performance had grown into a new dominant art form toward the beginning of the Ming dynasty. Beyond contributing to the formation of urban culture, this particular art form vividly showcased what was it like *to be* human.[90] People have feelings. But the feelings they believe to have experienced are in fact the mimicry of their outward appearances. Men, in other words, are all actors, if not impersonators, assuming our cosmic roles on the stage known as the world. We *become* ourselves by pretending to be ourselves.

Similar to neo-Confucian thinkers of the past, contemporary Western theorists share comparable enthusiasm in tracing and recognizing the presence of a noncognitive force that goes its own way. In the early wave of affect theory, Silvan Tomkins, Eve Kosofsky Sedgwick, and Brian Massumi associate affective forces with bodily intensities that cannot be contained by intentionality or reduced to narratives of purpose.[91] Being something out there and in play before we are aware of it, affect distinguishes itself in two ways. First, it is a force of intensity that resists rational conceptualization. Second, such intensity presents itself ahead of our knowledge. By the time we realize that it is here, we have already *been* affected by what we do not *know* we own. As an unintentional intensity that denies one's conscious access, the presence of affect undercuts our pretense of autonomy and undermines our sense of selves as coherent subjects.

As affect theorists blame man's corporeal body for his senseless incomprehensibility, certain poststructuralist thinkers seek to locate the "empty, affective space" in one's mind. Rei Terada's work presents a fine example. In her reading of *Of Grammatology* and *Writing and Difference*, Terada notes that Jacques Derrida (1930–2004) tries to capture the ways fear and horror are experienced in man. The human "subject," as Terada elaborates, is constituted by two distinct entities. One is the "self" and the other is "subjectivity." The "self" experiences prelinguistic psychological intensities that cannot be expressed in conceptual terms. Unlike the kind of bodily "affect" René Descartes (1596–1650) describes, this fierce intensity is originated from the "self," rather than physiological sensations felt by the body. To distinguish the difference between the corporeal and the experiential, Terada calls these unnamable intensities "emotions." Emotions one experiences, as said earlier, cannot be described by words. To makes sense of these *lived* empirical intensities, a person has to *translate* his "emotions" into "emotional expressions." While "emotions" belong to the experiential realm, "emotional expressions" belong to the conceptual one. These properties are empirically different, and their differences expose the inherent "self-difference" that divides one's "self" from his rational "subjectivity." To bridge this discrepancy, the two need a middleman to form an artificial connection between them. Terada calls the middleman "feeling," an agent that seeks to identify a frame, reference, or representation appearing in the form of "emotional expression" to make sense of the ineffable "emotion." Instead of the biological twin of "self/ emotion," "subjectivity as manifested in emotional expression" works only as a correspondence that helps to form a "semantic token of unity" between the two.[92] Through a careful reading of Derrida and the work of other modern philosophers, Terada challenges the illusive unity of a human subject and the assumption that emotion is an expression of the mind and is thus subordinated to it.

The poststructuralist and the neo-Confucian thinker relied on their own systems of thought to identify the limitations of human subjectivity. While poststructuralist thinkers pronounce the "death of the subject," Wang Yangming perceived "affective absence" as the revelation of man's cosmic nature. Man's heartmind, as Wang says, is *the same as* the cosmic pattern. In the spontaneous moments of incomprehension, one's cosmic "first nature" erupts within the "unhomelike" space of reified socially adaptive "second nature." Taken by the cosmic coherence that defines us, man becomes the cosmos by losing oneself in this heavenly instant.

Dialectic Tension between the Rhetorical and the Lyrical

In the "Biography of Madame Roland," Liang describes the French Revolution as "violent" and "cruel." On the year the biography was published, Liang spoke as the leader of the reformist party. Considering the party's growing antagonism toward the revolutionary movement led by Sun Yat-sen, it might be fair to speculate that Liang was to warn the general public of the perils of the revolution by amplifying its catastrophic consequences. Intellectual and literary historians have long been interested in delineating the changing definition of "revolution" in the early twentieth century, and how the term has evolved from a cultural taboo into a collective political passion. In his study of Liang Qichao's political reformism, Tang Xiaobing considers the reformer's composition of the "Biography of Madame Roland" the ultimate renunciation of the revolution. At an early stage of Liang's career, Tang argues, a conviction in the universal law of progress convinced the reformer that China could become a nation-state and eventually a member of the modern global community only by undergoing a political revolution.[93] Coming to 1902, however, Liang's growing familiarity with the Hungarian independence movement, the Unification of Italy, and the French Revolution slowly reminded him of the revolution's lethal consequences. The ferocious narrative details presented in the "Biography of Madame Roland" manifest Liang's latest reflection as well as his rejection of the political revolution.

Chen Jianhua shares a comparable view. Liang's early usages of *geming*, according to his etymological study, were informed by the Japanese word *kakumei* 革命, a term that refers to a broad range of social, institutional, and ideological reforms, as opposed to an overt overthrow of the status quo.[94] Later, as Liang's celebration of "poetic revolution" began to generate unexpected enthusiasm for the "political revolution" led by Sun Yat-sen, the reformer was determined to differentiate *geming* as a metaphor for reform from *geming* as a form of actual physical destruction. Informed by translingual mediations as well as the historical agent's "political motivations and social affiliations,"[95] Liang's denunciation of the political revolution in 1902 should thus be interpreted as a public statement announcing the growing antagonism between the reformist and the revolutionary camps.[96] In the "Biography of Madame Roland," Liang's protest against the political revolution, at first glance, seems consistent with the interpretation of Xiaobing Tang and Jianhua Chen. The reformer says,

> She [Madame Roland] was someone affectionate instead of someone cruel; she was someone who loved peace instead someone who enjoyed violence. Alas! For the benevolent and the martyr who live in an age of revolution, who is not noble

Musicality—Representing the Rhythm of Political Revolution | 205

and virtuous? And who does not love the people passionately? If one hasn't found herself in desperation, why would she be happy to shed, to splash, and to squander her blood with the blood of hundreds and thousands of civilians? As one hope after another is dashed, and as one disappointment is followed by another, one has no choice but to sever her benevolence, repress her love, swallow her pain, and shed her tears. Alas! Madame Roland was so tender and innocent a person. But why *exactly* was she left with the unwilling choice of throwing herself to the swirl of the unprecedented tragedy in history and bidding farewell to the world by meeting her death? Who, *exactly*, should be responsible for her plight?[97] 彼慈愛之人, 非殘酷之人也。樂和平之人, 非好暴亂之人也。嗚呼! 自古革命時代之仁人志士, 何一非高尚潔白之性質, 具視民如傷之熱情? 苟非萬不得已, 豈樂以一身之血, 與萬眾之血, 相注相搏相糜爛以為快也? 望之無可望, 待之無可待, 乃不得不割慈忍愛, 茹痛揮淚, 以出于此一途。嗚呼! 以肫肫煦煦之羅蘭夫人, 而其究也, 乃至投身於千古大悲劇之盤渦中, 一死以謝天下。誰實為之, 而令若此?

Similar to Liang's depiction of national citizen (*guomin*), the "political revolution" (*geming*) has been rendered in the reformer's signature new prose style. In the biography, Liang says that the affectionate and peace-loving French heroine is destined "to shed, to splash, and to squander" her blood "with the blood of hundreds and thousands of civilians." Having swallowed her pain and shed her tears, Madame Roland has no choice but to "meet her death" (*yisi* 一死) in the "unprecedented tragedy in history" (*qiangu da beiju* 千古大悲劇). Through detailing the distressing consequences, Liang underscores the French heroine's hesitation in initiating a revolution. In his rhetorical question, "If one hasn't found herself in desperation, why would she be happy to . . . ?" Liang depicts the revolution as an event to avoid at all costs. In the following couplet, "as one hope is dashed after another, and when one disappointment is followed by another" (*wang zi wu ke wang, dai zi wu ke dai* 望之無可望, 待之無可待), the repetition of *wang* (望) and *dai* (待), the negation *wuke* (無可), and the use of the redundant grammatical unit *zi* (之) generates a sense of endless prolongation. Together they exhibit Madame Roland's refusal to participate in the revolution and deepen her burning agony. Immediately after this disavowing statement, the French heroine's reluctance is accentuated by the double negation "have no choice but" (*budebu*), which is a repetition of the negation *bude* in the rhetorical question "If one hasn't found herself in desperation . . ." (*gou fei wan bude yi* 苟非萬不得已) aforementioned. Finally, Madame Roland's frustration is announced by the theatrical exclamation, "Alas!" (*wuhu* 嗚呼). With an additional rhetorical question asking "who, *exactly*, should be responsible for her plight?" Liang accused the political revolution of causing Madame Roland's tragic death.

The long passage above consists of a good number of parallel couplets, empathetic particles, and rhetorical questions. The interplay of long and short lines, the rhyming pattern, and the repetition of sounds constitute a distinct musical pattern, making the passage an acoustic entity in its own right. The description of blood, tears, and death are presented in a highly rhythmical pattern, which magnifies the passage's sensory appeal. Judging from Liang's antagonist relations with the revolutionary party, one might assume that Liang's creation of cinematic effects was intended to satisfy his immediate strategic needs. But the meanings of the modern political concepts that Liang communicated to the reader, as I argued in the earlier discussion, rest in the interplay between the semantic content of the words and their affective presentations. To decide what the political revolution means in the passage and how the acoustic and visual effects can affect the late Qing reader's perception of *geming*, we need to conduct a careful analysis of the tension between Liang's formal arrangement and his textual narrative. To begin with the opening lines announcing Madame Roland's reluctance to die for the political revolution:

> For the benevolent and the martyr who live in an age of revolution, who is not noble and virtuous? And who does not love the people passionately? If one hasn't found herself in desperation, why would she be happy to shed, to splash, and to squander her blood with the blood of hundreds and thousands of civilians? 自古革命時代之仁人志士, 何一非高尚潔白之性質, 具視民如傷之熱情? 苟非萬不得已, 豈樂以一身之血, (與)萬眾之血, 相注相搏相糜爛以為快也?

This short passage is composed of three parallel couplets. The first couplet consists of two seven-word lines (高尚潔白之性質, [具]視民如傷之熱情). The following parallel pair is a four-word couplet (一身之血,

[與]萬眾之血), and the last couplet contains three short phrases (相注相搏相糜爛). The gradual length reduction (which can be represented numerally as 11-(3)7-(1)7-6-(3)4-(1)4-2-2-3-(3)1) accelerates the pace of the passage and increases the tension. As the accumulated tension exhales its ultimate relief at the empty word ye (也), the passage reaches its musical crescendo.

The rhythmical quality of the passage is inconsistent with the semantic narrative. The musical tempo, for instance, accelerates when Liang announces Madame Roland's reluctance to participate in the political revolution. The impatience and fervor conveyed by the accelerating rhythmical pace contradict her hesitation. As the French heroine's physical torment is being emphasized, the passage arrives at its melodic climax. Rather than lamenting Madame Roland's tragic death, the empty word ye rejoices at the much-anticipated orgasmic relief. Certain words, as fig. 5.1 shows, appear recurrently in the passage.

Figure 5.1. A rhymical passage from the "Biography of Madame Roland"

S1.	彼慈愛之人，非殘酷之人也。樂和平之人，非好暴亂之人也。	5 - 5 **(1)** - 5 - 6 **(1)** 2 -11
S2.	嗚呼！自古革命時代之仁人志士，	(3) 7 - (1) 7
S3.	(何一非) 高尚潔白之性質，具視民如傷之熱情？	6 - (3) 4 - (1) 4
S4.	苟非萬不得已，豈樂以一身之血，與萬眾之血，	2 - 2- 3 - (3) 1
S5.	相注相搏相糜爛以為快也？	
S1.	She [Madame Roland] was someone affectionate instead of someone cruel; she was someone who loved peace instead someone who enjoyed violence.	
S2.	Alas! For the benevolent and the martyr who live in an age of revolution,	
S3.	Who is not noble and virtuous? And who does not love the people passionately?	
S4.	If she hasn't found herself in desperation, why would she be happy … with the blood of hundreds and thousands of civilians	
S5.	To shed, to splash, and to squander her blood?	

Sentence one consists of as many as four *zhi ren* (之人, someone; a person of). The possessive case *zhi* (之) appears twice in sentence three, whereas *zhi xue* (之血, the blood of) appears twice in sentence four. In the last sentence, the adverb *xiang* (相 jointly) appears three times. The repetition of these words turns the passage into cyclical acoustic cycles. The sense of repetition and undifferentiated conformity is accentuated by the words' phonological monotony. To parse the first sentence further:

Line 1: 彼慈愛之人

b**ei** ci oi zi j**an**

Line 2: 非殘酷之人也

f**ei** caan huk zi j**an** j**aa**

Line 3: 樂和平之人

lok wo ping zi j**an**

Line 4: 非好暴亂之人也

f**ei** h**ou** b**ou** lyun zi j**an** j**aa**

The characters in this extended parallelism are romanized in modern Cantonese, which was Liang's mother tongue as well as the dialect in which he fine-tuned the sounds of his lyrical composition. The reformer creates alliteration in lines 1, 2, and 4 by repeating the *-ei* vowel (b*ei*, f*ei*, and f*ei*). The lines in the passage all rhyme in the *-a-* vowel (j*an*, j*aa*, j*an*, and j*aa*). Liang, as the romanization indicates, tends to repeat the same vowel in each line. Besides softening the brutality of the political revolution, the phonetic solidarity once again shifts the reader's attention from words to sounds. With syntactic patterns giving rise to rhythmical totality and the repetition of sound creating an acoustic euphony, the *formal* organization of the passage is an organic metrical entity. The anticipation, enthusiasm, and impatience conveyed by the musical development "speak" against Madame Roland's hesitation as declared in the passage. After a careful examination of Liang's syntactic and phonological arrangement, one begins to question whether the exclamation "Alas!" (*wuhu*), double negation *budebu*, and repeated emphases on Madame Roland's unwillingness are intended to deny the legitimacy of the revolution, or if they are placed to create formal cohesion.

Lyrical Suspension of Political Revolution

So what does political revolution *truly* and *actually* mean to Liang Qichao? Having traced the linguistic origins of recently translated political key words and examined how translation has generated new semantic meanings under the reference of Chinese, English, and Japanese linguistic, cultural, and political systems, modern historians tend to comprehend the formation of Chinese political modernity as a constructed discourse resulting from cross-cultural exchanges and consolidated by power relations at both the local and the international levels. In our study of *geming*, however, it appears that the affective power of Liang's quasiparallel prose, together with his torn ambivalence toward political revolution, can be said to have created what the modern theorist Michel Poizat calls the *jouissance*, or phonic ecstasy, formed by the rhythmic and acoustic effects of language.[98]

In his study on the interplay between words and music in operatic performances, Poizat posits that "language accents bring vocal materiality to the foreground."[99] And the "corporeality" of acoustic language, as another theorist Mladen Dolar elaborates, provides "aesthetic pleasure" to the reader and easily becomes "an object of fetish reverence."[100] For Poizat and Dolar, phonic sensations offer a reader the aesthetic pleasure of listening, but, at the same time, such pleasure inevitably distracts one from self-reflexivity. "The *jouissance* associated with vocal materiality," writes Poizat, "tends to corrode or erode the signifying scansion of language."[101] The aesthetic enjoyment derived from the acoustic effects thus "prevents a clear understanding of the text"[102] and can come only "at the expense of meanings."[103] Roland Barthes provides an equally compelling account of how informative language can be "unworked" by senseless sound.[104] While the musicality of language reserves its potential to signify, it cannot convey any substantial content. What has been expressed and denoted by sound and rhythm is the *secret*, "which, concealed in reality, can reach human consciousness only through a code, which serves simultaneously to encipher and to decipher the reality."[105]

In this book, it is the production of *meanings* rather than the formation of semantic definitions in the burgeoning modern political discourse that I am concerned with. As a late Qing reader read an animated speech written on paper, he was presented with a semantic text that delivered intelligible information as well as an audio text transmitting "an unconscious knowledge" encoded in the musicality of language. Since the musical code is often received in oblivion, it might be fair to speculate whether the reader-listener in late Qing China was conscious enough to realize that one might be "listening to the modulations and harmonies of that voice without hearing what it is saying."[106] If the "meanings" of the modern political concepts Liang communicated to his readers were indeed *different* from their semantic definitions, what exactly do these concepts signify? By exploring the affective power of Liang's new prose style, I argue that the meanings of the modern political concepts Liang communicated with his readers rest in the "affective disruption," or "acoustic dissociation," unwrapped and complicated by the formal structure of his new prose style. In *Writing and Difference*, Jacques Derrida argues that language is different and deferred from the truth content. To explicate how language fails to signify the unrepresentable truth, the theorist says, "The conscious text is thus not a transcription, because there is no text present elsewhere as unconscious one to be transposed or transported. For the value of presence can also dangerously affect the concept of the unconscious. There is then no unconscious truth to be rediscovered by virtue of having been written elsewhere."[107]

Derrida points us to the alarming consequences of studying "what it is not" as "what it is." Aside from emphasizing that the true meaning rests elsewhere than language, Derrida opens us to the "intimate distance" that might have potentially divided the late Qing reader from translated political modernity. The acoustic effects of Liang's new prose style expedited the transmission of translated political modernity by speaking directly to the reader and appealing to his senses. While the musicality of language captures a person's attention, the sensory and aesthetic experiences can come only at the expense of obscuring and unsettling the semantic consistency. The late Qing reader's reception of political modernity, in this sense, implies an *estrangement*, if not a *rational discharge*, from what has been prescribed and promised by the readily available modern linguistic apparatus. Knowing that meanings rest in the interplay between the new prose style operating as a semantic text, an audio text, and a pictorial text, when a reader responded to the concepts Liang circulated, one can hardly be certain whether his responses indicated a rational comprehension of these concepts, or what Barthes calls the "commitment to this voice as a site of opacity."[108]

Displacement of Truth from the Discursive Given

In Liang's historical biography, his denunciation of the political revolution is devoid of semantic ambiguity. But once the rhythmical and acoustic effects of the passage we analyze are taken into consideration, "the authority of the meaning engendered by the grammatical structure," to borrow the words of Paul de Man, "is *fully obscured* by the duplicity of a figure that cries out for the differentiation that it conceals."[109] Aside from the "acoustic dissociation" unbridled by the tension between the semantic content and its musical effect, Liang's depictions of extreme physical torment also make one wonder whether the political revolution is an absolute negativity.

Kossuth the Hungarian hero fashions himself as a wounded man suffering from extreme physical pain. In his public oration, Kossuth asserts that a modern nation-state can come only at the expense of blood, tears, and death. Upon listening to Kossuth's call, the Hungarian national citizens echo him, yearning, "Give me Liberty or give me Death" (*buziyou, wuningsi* 不自由，毋寧死).[110] In the historical biographies Liang published in 1902, blood, tears, and death are often evidence of one's moral superiority rather than of destructive physical torture. In the "Biography of the Three Italian Heroes Who Founded Italy" (*Yidali jianguo sanjie zhuan* 意大利建國三傑傳), which was serialized immediately after the "Biography of Kossuth," Liang declares that Giuseppe Mazzini's (1805–1872) and Giuseppe Garibaldi's (1807–1882) determination to unify Italy was motivated purely by their affectionate concern for the public.[111] Having carefully described the various levels of physical torment that Mazzini and Garibaldi endured, Liang announces that the shedding of people's blood and tears authenticates their moral superiority and prepares Italy for its much-anticipated historical evolution. More intriguing descriptions of bodily suffering appear in the "Biography of Madame Roland." The French heroine, according to Liang, had since the age of ten identified herself with many ancient "knight errant" figures.[112] Among the books she read, Madame Roland was particularly fond of biographies detailing Christ's crucifixion. The young woman incessantly regretted not having been born in Sparta, an ancient state that derived its national pride from the citizen's capacity to endure extreme physical torture.[113]

People's tears, blood, and death witness the massive destruction created by the French Revolution. But once Liang's descriptions of extreme physical suffering are contextualized in the historical biographies he published in the same year, it becomes evident that collective sacrifice and extreme physical torture are celebrated with glorification. Liang's endorsement of political revolution persists to appear in his untiring support for Madame Roland:

> Although Heaven refuses to let Madame Roland enjoy domestic bliss toward the rest of her life, the history of France and the history of the world have to rely on the name of Madame Roland to magnify their glories. Slowly the wind was blowing, clouds getting tangled, thunders striking, and the water pouring. Xi-Xi-Chu-Chu! The French Revolution! Jie-jie-qu-qu. France, finally, can no longer avoid a revolution!!! 雖然天不許羅蘭夫人享家庭之幸福以終天年也, 法蘭西歷史, 世界歷史, 必要以羅蘭夫人之名以增其光焰也。於是風漸起, 雲漸亂, 電漸進, 水漸湧, 譆譆出出! 法國革命!! 嗟嗟詛詛! 法國遂不免於大革命!!![114]

Liang suggests that French history and world history have been lionized and brightened by the revolution Madame Roland initiated. Whether or not to participate in a political revolution was no longer Madame Roland's personal decision; it was her historical mission. While the definition of "revolution" in the above passage contradicts the long passage I analyzed earlier, the rhythmical structure and musical effects of the text bear a striking resemblance. And this time, Liang apparently interprets the revolution in a positive light:

> Thinking that the revolution has now been staged, Madame Roland believes that now the republicanism she has always aspired to finally has a chance to be realized. Madame Roland does not love the revolution. But because of her love for France, she has no choice but to love the revolution. She believes that today's France is dead, and the revolution is the only thing that can bring the country back to life. For this reason, the couple has made cultivating revolutionary spirit and circulating revolutionary thinking their vocation. 以為革命既起, 平生所夢想之共和主義, 今已得實現之機會。夫人非

愛革命, 然以愛法國故, 不得不愛革命。彼以為今日之法國已死, 致死而之生之, 舍革命末由。於是夫妻專以孕育革命精神, 弘布革命思想為事。[115]

By making the political revolution a fine medley of one's moral conviction and the political modern, Liang affirms the legitimacy of revolution by transforming it into a superior moral good. And yet, the "authentic" revolution he celebrates remains a paradoxical existence. In the "Biography of Madame Roland," the French heroine is willing to sacrifice her life to realize her moral vision through revolutionary ends. But judging from what happened in the French Revolution, it becomes evident that once "authentic" political conviction was materialized in embodied actions, it could result only in the most cruel and brutal consequences. Authenticity, in a sense, is a form of existence that thrives on its apparent absence. While it is futile to study modern political ideas as conceptual knowledge, "authentic" political modernity remains an opaque conviction that is yet to be defined.

Liang was as sharply aware of this reluctant suspense as I am. In the second half of the "Biography of Madame Roland," Liang accuses the word "liberty" (*ziyou*) of being a false signifier for "authentic" liberty. Toward the end of 1793, Madame Roland, as his narrative suggests, is sent to the guillotine. Before her head is to be removed, the French heroine sees a statue of the god of liberty. The French heroine steps forth and asks the statue a rhetorical question: "Alas, Liberty, Liberty, in this world, how many crimes in the past and present have been committed under your *name*?" (嗚呼, 自由自由, 天下古今幾多之罪惡, 假汝之名以行).[116] Madame Roland repeats the same question Liang raises at the beginning of the biography.[117] Before Liang is to repeat this question after his announcement of the French heroine's tragic death, Madame Roland makes the following declaration:

> Today's world is dirty and chaotic, with people drinking men's blood as wine. I would be more than happy to leave, with nothing to linger on. I only wish my national citizens would be able to obtain the *true liberty*. 今日此等污濁混亂以人血為酒漿之世界, 余甚樂脫離之, 無所留戀。余惟願我國民速得真正之自由。[118]

In her one-way dialogue with the god of liberty, Madame Roland addresses the god she worships in his "name," only to lament how the name has been used as an excuse to commit evil deeds.[119] Her rhetorical question indicates one's keen awareness of the difference between "the god" of liberty she speaks to and "the name" of the god that she is addressing. While Madame Roland questions the representative power of the name as a signifier, she has no choice but to address the god with its name. To ask the rhetorical question is to affirm her belief in the existence of the god as well as to acknowledge her failure to designate the god she believes in. Madame Roland's question begins with the lamentation *wuhu* 嗚呼, which refers to lamentation and astonishment as well as glorification.[120] Standing on the guillotine and speaking for the very last time to the god of liberty she worships, the French heroine articulates that her frustrated attempts to implement liberty in the political reality has turned liberty into an excuse to destroy her. And yet these lamentations and accusations could have come only from the ardent love and passion she has shared for the liberty she aspires to.

Knowing how the present linguistic condition has deprived her of the chance to designate the kind of liberty she has aspired to, Madame Roland wishes only that her "fellow" citizens will soon be able to obtain "authentic" liberty. Through her emphasis of the word "authentic," Madame Roland repudiates the "word" liberty as a contaminated signifier. But the French heroine, somewhat ironically, can try to designate the "truth content" only with the word "authentic." What liberty truly means remains a deferred suspension, leaving the French heroine with anguish, disappointment, and frustrated passion for the falsity of its name.

Fake Reformers versus True Revolutionaries: A Crisis of Meaning

Aside from the above examples, meanings of *geming* in the "Biography of Madame Roland" can be further unsettled by an intertextual reading. These linguistic ambiguities point us to more epistemic certainties in late Qing China. Being the key contributor to the biweekly *New Citizen Journal*, Liang was under pressure to complete a substantive amount of writing within a short period of time. Rather than introducing a broad range of subjects in each issue of the journal, he liked to explicate a singular modern political concept from multiple interpretative perspectives. The "Biography of Madame Roland," for instance, was serialized in volumes seventeen and eighteen of the Journal. In editorials published in the same volumes, Liang, somewhat paradoxically, denies the bitter denunciation of the political revolution he makes in the "Biography of Madam Roland."

In "A Respectful Announcement to my Fellow Reformists," an editorial published in volume seventeen of *New Citizen Journal*, Liang reasserts that a historian is allowed to articulate his subjective views in an extreme and biased fashion. At the time when Western learning was first introduced to China, many learned Chinese scholars, Liang says, were intimidated by its idiosyncrasy.[121] But later, as political reformers began to demand and defend people's civil rights (*minquan* 民權), Western learning ceased to be terrifying by comparison.[122] Liang intends to help people dispel their fear of political reform. In this editorial, he says he can achieve this goal only by threatening and terrifying the general public with a notion that is more daunting than political reform. The notion, apparently, was the political revolution:

> To familiarize the people with the civil rights they are entitled to enjoy, one has no choice but to frighten them with the political revolution. As the talk of revolution becomes commonplace, people will be too terrified to develop fear of discussions of civil rights, not to mention of political reform. 欲導民以民權也, 則不可不駭之以革命。當革命論起, 則並民權亦不暇駭, 而變法無論矣。[123]

Liang asserts that he is deeply frustrated by his contemporaries' lukewarm responses to his calls. To facilitate China's modern political reform, Liang announces that thereafter, he would present *geming* in the most extreme fashion possible. These extreme depictions, as he believes, "are measures a newspaper office has no choice but to adopt for the sake of guiding and directing the national citizens toward a positive political cause" (某以為報館之所以導國民者, 不可不操此術).[124]

The second half of the "Biography of Madame Roland" was serialized in volume eighteen of *New Citizen Journal*. In this issue, Liang presents his editorial in an open letter. In "A Respectful Note to Those in Power" (*Jinggao dangdaozhe* 敬告當道者), Liang writes that having spent years importing the Western political system and liberal ideals to China, he has finally introduced people to the rights they are entitled to enjoy.[125] But instead of rejoicing in his success, he is devastated by his fellow reformists' indolence, stupidity, and selfishness. Liang considers his comrades "fake reformers" (*wei gaigezhe* 偽改革者) who have turned his efforts into a fatal weapon against him.[126] Having directed most of their energies positioning themselves as progressive reformers, these individuals hardly try to implement the reformist measures they promised to impose. Liang warns against the "fake reformers": if people persist in "talking about" fake reform (*wei gaigezhe* 偽改革), China would soon face "the most tragic and radical consequences" (最慘最劇之現象), accompanied by the political revolution.[127] Liang says that he has no intention of condemning the political revolution. The disastrous consequences accompanied by political revolution should soon testify the efforts revolutionaries make to correct the ills of fake reform. To draw a clear contrast between "fake reformers" and "true revolutionaries," Liang readily includes Madame Roland, Giuseppe Mazzini, and the Japanese thinker Yoshida Shoin 吉田松蔭 (1830–1859) as "true revolutionaries" for whom he shares unmatched admiration. By drawing a comparison as such, Liang again implies that only *the political revolution can be the true reform*.

From the late nineteenth century onward, as Liang proceeds to argue, Chinese students who studied abroad had been introduced to reformist teaching. But having been bitterly disappointed by false promises made by those fake reformers, they had come to believe that men could obtain their freedom and rights only through replacing the Qing monarchy with political revolution. Sharing an ardent hope and love for China, these passionate young people were willing to sacrifice their lives for their political ideals. Considering the "true" political revolution a corrective measure to the "fake" reform, Liang reinforces his claim: were a person to talk about reform, he was left either with the "fake reform," or the true reform to be manifested in political revolution.

In 1903, an anonymous author contributed a sequel to Liang's composition of *The Future of New China*.[128] In the sequel, Liang's two protagonists have eventually returned to China after completing their studies in Europe. Speaking in the voice of Liang, the anonymous author accentuates that Huang Keqiang and Li Qubing are those who know the "true" meaning of the revolution. But instead of elucidating what the "true" revolution is about, in the chapter the author goes on to expose and condemn the "fake" revolutionaries the protagonists encounter in Shanghai, as well as the hypocrisy of these "fake" revolutionary talks.

The word "revolution," as Liang notes, is violent and immoral. But at the same time, what he considers to be the "true," "authentic" revolution remains an intuitive imagining that cannot be materialized in the political reality. The kind of true political modernity Liang calls for remains an unnamable truth suspended in one's aesthetic conviction.

The enthusiasm for exposing the deceptiveness of the word "revolution" and other modern political concepts continued in the late 1910s.[129] In *Strange Things Witnessed in Twenty Years* 二十年目睹之怪現狀, the late Qing novelist Wu Jianren 吳趼人 (1866–1910) meticulously describes how modern terms such as "liberty," "women's rights," "national citizen," and "constitutional monarchy" had been abused to serve various insidious purposes.[130] A question one may go on exploring is how the late Qing public tried to make sense of "fake" or "deceptive" modern political languages. By examining how a reader's fear, laugher, anger, and frustration had been circulated *as* "meanings" through the rapidly developing print media in Shanghai, perhaps we could proceed to question whether the rise of the national community in late Qing China was in reality an emotional community hinged upon collective affective responses toward these modern concepts as unfulfilled promises.

Postscript

Let Us Be Taken by Affect, and to Be *Taken* Away and Afar

In 1905, Zhang Taiyan 章太炎 (1869–1936) asserted that the Chinese public shared the spirit of liberty (*ziyou* 自由), equality (*pingdeng* 平等), and fraternity (*boai* 博愛).[1] Knowing that these were attributes upon which republican constitutionalism is based, in *People's Journal* (*Minbao* 民報) Zhang called for an "ethnic political revolution" (*zhongzu geming* 種族革命) to expel the Manchurian and establish a republican government. Liang Qichao adamantly opposed this call. To renounce Zhang's exhortation, Liang argued that the parliamentary congress was a legislative body that held hearings to administer a country's law-making processes. Both the state and the two chambers enjoyed the right to propose motions to be discussed and voted on. Most motions could be highly controversial. Tax increase, for instance, might seem to violate the interests of the public and benefit the state.[2] But to be able to deduce the judicious reasoning that informed the state's motion and appraise its viability and cogency, a congressman must be closely informed of recent developments in global economy and international affairs, as well as of the operating principles of government and public administration. Once a congressman detects the negligence of the state or its abuse of power, he must step out, rectify the fault, and be ready to impeach the responsible agents.[3] Beyond the display of personal integrity, courage, and sensible judgment, all interrogations conducted in the congress must be courteous and civil.

At the time Liang protested against Zhang's call, as he was sad to report, prospective legislators in China did not possess the knowledge, the moral character, or the integrity to fulfil their civil obligations. Such a verdict applied correspondingly to the general public. "Politics in all democratic countries," Liang continued, "are founded on the basis of the citizens' civil consciousness, which evinces all citizens to decide and determine whether a legislative proposition is *truly* bad or *truly* good."[4] In a democratic assembly that requires participants' exercise of collective free will, each individual must respect law and order, possess *true* republican spirit, be competent in self-governance, be fully committed to the defense of public interests, and not be easily persuaded by external influences.[5] In China, however, people did not have any prior experience of self-governance.[6] For those who were accustomed to autocratic rule, the range of civil attributes mentioned above were not traits that could be acquired or cultivated in an instant.[7]

The people, Liang argued, were not the only ones who were not ready. Were the Qing monarchy to be replaced by republican constitutionalism, the country was not institutionally prepared to enact the election law to administer the democratic election.[8] Parliamentary democracy, to begin with, required the participation of all national citizens. So far, China had yet to draft its "nationality law" (*guoji fa* 國籍法) to define and determine its residents' legal citizenship. Prior to the advent of universal suffrage, most countries were inclined to impose restrictions on voters' age, gender, education level, and income. Since China did not enforce compulsory education among schoolchildren, at that time there was no feasible means to determine voters' education level. The Qing dynasty's existing taxation system also had many loopholes. These loopholes posed difficulties in estimating taxpayers' exact incomes and were likely to exclude a sizable population from exercising their civil rights. China's rural population, in addition, was sparsely strewn across sequestered geographical regions. Over the years neither the Qing monarchy nor any private political organizations had conducted systematic demographic surveys to quantify the rural populations or document their age, education, gender, and income. Without these statistics, the state could not draw the boundaries of electoral districts. Beyond that, since "rural committees" (*xiangshi hui* 鄉事會) had yet been formed in local regions, people had never been given the opportunity to elect representatives who were held accountable to the voters. If an election became embroiled in disputes, there was no legal institute to adjudicate and resolve these disagreements. In the vast majority of the provincial districts there was also no official police force to maintain law and order during the election.

Liangzhi Being as Affective as Affect

Coming to the late 1900s, Liang became firmly against the prospect of staging a political revolution. Perceiving this as a time in which "adventurists" (*yexinjia* 野心家) incited people with false promises of freedom and equality, Liang wished his contemporaries could stay calm and listen to his reasoning.[9] In his protests against what he considered to be Zhang Taiyan's instigation of violence, Liang returned to the abiding piece of faith the Ming philosopher Wang Yangming placed in man's possession of *liangzhi* (良知), the good moral knowing. In recent days, Liang said, man's display of affect (*ganqing* 感情) resembled fire (*huo* 火), raging torrents (*kuangquan* 狂泉), and deranged madness (*bingkuang* 病狂).[10] When affect is in motion, it acts as if the madman has been conferred with divine power. The force is so capricious that it breaks out in unpredictable trajectories.[11] But daunting as affect might be, people also share *liangzhi*, the illuminating censor innate to their heartmind.[12] Being the introspective cognitive compass that guides man's moral judgement, *liangzhi* is there to rectify and to guide, so that a person will not be enslaved, baffled, or ultimately consumed by affect.[13]

In his public denouncement of the political revolution, Liang presented his arguments with confidence and calm. But when Liang was alone by himself, he no longer felt certain. One day when Liang was at home drinking, all of a sudden the thought of expelling the Manchurian with a political insurrection resurged.[14] Incessantly this deep and dearest wish burst, blasted, and exploded within his chest, making his blood surge and gush.[15] Liang, as it turns out, had never been able to put behind the political revolution he had denounced in public. At a time when Liang the seemingly sensible reformer urged the people to return to their rational reasoning (*bianli xin* 辨理心) and exercise their free will (*ziyou yizhi* 自由意志), his own rationality collapsed in secret.[16] Not being able to control his own thoughts nor stop himself from steering toward the precarious end that he had warned people against, Liang was consumed by fear and horror. As Liang looked into himself, he began to accept that man has feelings. Like the burning flame, the affective intensity is so overpowering that it transcends logical reasoning.[17] As his heart throbs in abrupt, burning rage, it races and drifts along with the mad currents. Having "one's heart enslaved by external stimuli" (內心為外感之奴隸也), Liang noted, a person's *liangzhi* "cannot" (*buneng* 不能) and is "no longer capable of" (*bufu neng* 不復能) resisting the invasion of affect, nor can it "be aware of" (*bu zizhi* 不自知) its loss of self-control.[18] Oblivious to its own malfunctioning, *liangzhi* ceases to comprehend its own fault (不自知其非) nor be aware of the damages it causes (不自知其害).[19]

In his early defense of *liangzhi* as a cognitive faculty innately capable of defending itself against the intrusion of affect, Liang categorized *liangzhi* and affect as two incongruous properties emerging from the opposite ends of a psyche spectrum. *Liangzhi* the good moral knowing, on one hand, constituted the reasoning faculty; affect, on the other hand, was the wild beast, roaring with rage. While *liangzhi* is supposed to subdue affect with effective ease, in reality Liang's own reasoning failed, testifying in practice to the collapse of the entrenched philosophical binary in China's ongoing democratic movement. Liang did not question the configuration of *liangzhi* as a perfectly built piece of cognitive faculty. But this faculty did not seem to have absolute control over itself. Similar to a machine built without an on-and-off switch, *liangzhi* seems inherently incapable of activating its preconfigured functions. Being malfunctional and defective in operation, *liangzhi* becomes completely passive when it confronts affect. Absent of agency and self-control, this innate moral compass looks just *affective* as affect.[20]

"Why is *liangzhi* incapable of resisting what is apparently wrong? Is it because man's moral consciousness was flawed by nature? Or is it because such perfect moral consciousness has turned numb due to the lack of practice? But then isn't the numbness of moral consciousness the same as not having any (良心之麻木, 謂是無良心耶)? *What* is the result and *what is* the cause?"[21] Again and again Liang persisted in asking the same questions. Many times he strived to be certain that man's *liangzhi* was not defective by nature. Throughout the course of its history, as Liang said to himself, China had been fettered by autocratic rule. Knowing that people were forced to suppress their personal moral judgement, the part (of their cognitive endowment) that had been deserted and unutilized for long must have since declined and degenerated into a state of atrophy (其久廢不用之一部分, 恆致漸失其本).[22] Altogether the natural aptitude of *liangzhi* decayed and diminished (良心之本能, 既漸滅以盡).[23] Liang wished to be convinced by his reasoning, and yet he cannot. "The politics of a country," as he pondered on another occasion, "is the product of its people" (一國之政治者, 又一國國民之產物也).[24] "The expressions of a country's political phenomena epitomize the thought of its people and their character. . . . Were the Chinese's thought and character not defective in nature, they would not have induced and sustained autocratic rule" (凡一國之政象, 則皆其國民思想品格之放映而已. . . . 國民之品格思想非有缺點, 則不能造成專制政體).[25]

The Ironies of Oneness

In the world of neo-Confucianism, man's moral perfection epitomizes the cosmos. While the conception of such cosmic imagination had given Chinese intellectuals much-needed hope to hold on to during a time of historical turmoil, the anxiety and distrust they expressed for the oneness model, alongside their attempts to suppress or deny their deep suspicion of the model, seemed to have played an equally decisive role in shaping the development of Chinese philosophy.[26]

In his attempt to direct China's transition from imperial monarchy to democratic governance, Liang shared Wang Yangming's euphoric moral optimism and attempted to go even further. Perceiving his contemporaries as equal cosmic members of the metaphysical republic, Liang envisioned the prospect of people living as one organic cosmic, moral, and political body in a republican government.[27] Of the many things people can do to become one, there was *a way* that promised to remove all existing barriers that divide human from heaven, knowing from acting, and the people from the state. *The way* rested in people's collective participation in a political revolution. Liang strived to revive the euphoric cosmic oneness that neo-Confucian thinkers once endorsed amid China's transition to political modernity. His cosmic vision was most idealistic. While Liang's utopian attempt opened us to the finest possible ways our world can be, it prompts one to wonder whether a metaphysical hypothesis necessarily informs and corresponds to human reality.

In his contemporary reinterpretation of neo-Confucianism, Philip Ivanhoe embraces the comparable hope of sharing this "oneness" vision with readers of the Western world. In Ivanhoe's discussions on "oneness hypothesis," he notes that individuals of our times tend to be excessively concerned with their self-interest. To repudiate the "hyper-individualism" paradigm that dominates both contemporary Western consciousness and practice, Ivanhoe scrutinizes a wide spectrum of philosophical positions that neo-Confucian thinkers held in China, Japan, and Korea between the tenth and the nineteenth centuries. Thinkers he examines shared a firm conviction: being intricately and inextricably intertwined as an organic entity, human beings are caught in a shared destiny with all other creatures and the natural environment.[28] The proper scope of people's minds, for this reason, should no longer be limited by their selfish boundaries.

Ivanhoe's "oneness hypothesis" is blissfully gracious and altruistic. But at times when I look around at people in New York, the city where I live in, still I question: If human beings are indeed members of an undivided cosmic oneness, why do we proceed to live a life that is hopelessly estranged and divided? Why exactly do we fail to connect with each other? What makes it so difficult to put theory into practice? If these challenges are indeed valid and true, what do their presence imply? Being some of the most unconventional thinkers of their times, the early Song neo-Confucian thinkers Cheng Hao 程顥 (1032–1085) and Zhang Zai 張載 (1020–1077) were apparently more sensitive to and troubled by those questions than I am. If these neo-Confucian thinkers were aware of the persisting anxieties and uncertainties enshrouded in the purported cosmic oneness, why did they proceed, or even bother, to envision and defend the existence of a perfect cosmos? Why and how did their imagination of the perfect cosmos come into being? And how would anxieties and uncertainties suppressed in their cosmic conceptions recur to disrupt and defy the "modern moral-political oneness" Liang Qichao sought to restore in the early twentieth century?

Having reflected upon a comparable set of questions in alternate scholarly discussions, contemporary scholars including Michael Fuller, Thomas Metzger, and Qian Mu are careful to situate the evolution of neo-Confucian metaphysics in the Song dynasty's (960–1276) political turmoil. The three arrive at a comparable conclusion: instead of expressing the faith they share in human goodness, neo-Confucian thinkers' conception of cosmic oneness discloses precisely the painful realization of people's failure to be good. To retrieve the unprecedented moral and political rupture that warranted neo-Confucian thinkers' reimagination, or reparation of the cosmos, Michael Fuller presents the following account. Toward the end of the Northern Song dynasty (960–1127), Wang Anshi 王安石 (1021–1086), the state prime minister, instituted a range of reformist measures that enabled the state to intervene in the economy and expand the centralizing power of large-scale, statewide institutions.[29] To suppress those who disapproved of the reformist move, supporters of Wang Anshi's "New Policies" reforms drove their opponents from the court and prosecuted them with punitive measures. Wang Anshi's advocate, Emperor Shenzong 神宗, passed away in 1085 and China entered the reign of Yuanyou 元佑 (1086–1094). Instantly the new regime overturned Wang Anshi's establishments. And this time, Wang's followers became the ones driven into political exile. The factional strife caused by partisanship was corrosive of more than just the bureaucratic order. It tore apart what Fuller calls the a priori totality that learned individuals had once been able to identify between the coherence of heaven, the organization of text, and the moral sensibilities of men. As Wang Anshi's reforms left the Song court in a state of social, political, and moral chaos, it appeared to neo-Confucian thinkers as if the existing social political order was unmalleable, drained of any inherent power to renew and rejuvenate itself.[30] If one were to repair the outer realm, it seemed as if he could try to do so only by repairing the inner realm and refortifying the broken cosmic order.[31]

Both Cheng Hao and Zhang Zai made a preliminary attempt to defend man's moral perfection. Selfless and hopeful as it may seem, the very attempt reveals perhaps the most acute awareness of the *impossibility* of being moral in the *actual* social and political reality. "The world," as Thomas Metzger once said, "both in its history and in the present, was a moral wilderness."[32] What we would conceptualize today as "oneness" theory was in fact the greatest irony in the burning world of neo-Confucianism. (And more ironically, even the notion of "oneness," as Brook Ziporyn elaborates with great intellectual vigor, begins life as an irony in the Chinese philosophical tradition.[33]) Stuck in the chasm in which the realm of metaphysical transcendence had been severed from human existence, neo-Confucian thinkers were overshadowed by what Metzger calls the "sense of predicament."[34]

Liberal Autocracy

So what exactly had gone wrong? Could it be that China's sociopolitical circumstances had deformed the people's moral consciousness, or that the people had begun life as deformed creatures? While Liang could not bring a definitive conclusion to his metaphysical rumination, there was something he thought he knew for certain: in a modern nation, "only those who are capable of participating in congressal politics can be qualified as a republican citizen" (有能行議院政治之能力者，斯有可以為共和國民之資格).[35] These days, he lamented, his contemporaries tended to respond senselessly to the call of the revolutionary force. Absent of investigative spirit (研究的精神), incapable of conducting systematic analysis (歸納的研究), and being easily persuaded by rhetorical manipulation, the Chinese "has yet to be qualified as the Republican citizen" (未有共和國民之資格).[36] At a time when "the people's capricious impulse scorches as fire and the entire country acts in absolute madness" (夫民氣猶火也; 而舉國若狂),[37] what lay ahead in the approaching political revolution was not democratic governance but mayhem and chaos. "In today's China," Liang solemnly announced, "republican constitutionalism *cannot* be implemented under any possible circumstances" (今日中國萬不能行共和立憲制).[38] If "people with native command of political knowledge" (政治程度幼稚之國民) were prematurely given the right to vote, he foresaw the following consequence: to manipulate the results of state and regional elections, local interest groups would pressure congressional candidates to advance their selfish interests.[39] As voters were bribed, coaxed, or threatened to vote in favor of the local powers and abuse their civil rights, corruption would soon lead to election disputes. Since China had yet to establish an office of jurisdiction to adjudicate these disagreements, disputes would evolve into riots.

Liang's distrust of people forced him to draw an inevitable conclusion: in today's China, "the people had lost their ability to determine what was truly right and what was truly wrong" (國民無復判斷真是真非利害之能力).[40] To prevent needless damage and destruction, the country should consider implementing a conversative model of governance as a transition to prepare people for direct democratic elections.[41] In an elaborate constitutional blueprint he drafted, Liang contended: Sooner or later China should implement the form of parliamentary congress adopted by the United States.[42] Similar to the United States, China's national congress would consist of the Lower and Upper Houses. The Lower House of the Congress, which Liang called the "Left Chamber" (*Zuo yiyuan* 左議院), would be elected directly by voters to represent them in the Congress. The Upper House, or "Right Chamber" (*You yiyuan* 右議院), consists of senators representing all of the state provinces and possibly Tibet. To equitably represent diverse and often conflicting interests, all congressmen and senators would ideally be affiliated with contending political parties. Knowing that competitions between divided political forces were prone to create unsolicited deadlock, party members should aim to limit contending political parties to two major ones. Democracy, Liang argued, was consolidated through the repeated process of trial and error. For people who were accustomed to autocratic rule, it might take them years or perhaps decades to comprehend the contending political positions held by oppositional parties, rationales that informed these antagonistic positions, and to respect an election outcome that contradicts their personal preference. Before people were fully prepared to make an informed decision in a "direct election" (*zhijie xuanju* 直接選舉), they should first be granted restricted rights to participate in an "indirect election" (*jianjie xuanju* 間接選舉) and to choose the learned "representatives" to vote on their behalf in the final election.[43] By implementing what he called "liberal autocracy" (*kaiming zhuanzhi* 開明專制) as a form of transitional governance, people would be given ample opportunity to practice exercising their civil rights. Once the general public obtained a considerable level of political maturity, China would be officially ready for direct congressional election and parliamentary democracy.

Parting (Momentarily) from Wang Yangming

Being a faithful follower of Wang Yangming's moral teachings, Liang once believed that man was instinctively capable of moral deliberation. But having reflected upon the practical feasibility of implementing parliamentary democracy immediately after a political revolution, he hesitated. Liang's familiarity with modern American history further intensified these uncertainties. In the United States, he said, many early settlers were the Puritans, a community of religious partitioners who displayed exceptional self-restraint and discipline. Subsequently the Puritans incorporated worthy personal attributes into parliamentary governance and continued to work to strengthen these civil characters through years of democratic practices.[44] Compared with the Americans, the Chinese "were culturally naïve and feeble in self-discipline" (文化幼稚自治力薄之國民).[45] While their education level and ability to exercise rational judgement was inferior, the population significantly exceeded that of the United States.[46] Accompanying such a demoralized vision were Liang's growing despair and pessimism: "In my view, our race was inferior to others in so many aspects" (吾以爲吾國人之種性, 其不如人之處甚多):[47] "cruel, cunning, brutal, barbaric,"[48] "so despicable that they should not be able to survive in the course of natural selection" (以此卑鄙冗之人, 決不能競存於物競劇烈之世).[49] "Wicked as our people are, they have no intent to repent" (雖然國民惡德, 而不自湔祓).[50]

Whether as a national community or as cosmic existences, the Chinese people appeared to Liang as a cluster of defective residues. The reformer became so disappointed that he was ready to abandon Wang Yangming's teachings. Toward the end of the 1900s, Liang slowly took on the didactic voice of his teacher Kang Youwei, or even Zhu Xi, the neo-Confucian thinker of whom he once disapproved. And Liang seemed more reproachful than Zhu Xi. Being an optimist at heart, Zhu Xi had at least asserted that if a person could persist with his study of Confucian classics, there was a possibility that he could *learn* to become a sage. But Liang seemed to have given up hope of learning; rather than trying to become the better person one can never be, it appeared to him that perhaps the best a Chinese man could do was to live an ordinary life, look to conventional wisdom, and behave in accordance with the received canonical doctrines. In 1911, Liang said, "People of our nation are by nature deplorable" (吾國民根性劣敗).[51] "For those who feel personally responsible of being moral, I wish they do not indulge oneself in empty metaphysical discussion, nor try to display one's knowledge of new, quirky ideas" (吾願世之以德較為己任者, 毋騖玄遠之談, 毋衒新奇之說).[52] "Over the long course of Chinese history," he continued, some "mediocre virtues had effectively kept our society in good order. Let us cherish mediocre virtues our ancestor exemplified and magnify them to the fullest" (寶吾先民所率由之庸德, 而發揮光大之).[53]

Expressions of Liang's pessimistic cynicism did not end here. In the next ten years that followed, he continued to deny others and engulf himself in a prolonged period of self-denial. Coming to a point when Liang had finally relinquished his hope and his search for perfection, a moment of epiphany, at long last, arrived. His unexpected enlightenment reminds me of the comparison that the Ming political theorist Huang Zongxi 黃宗羲 (1601–1695) once drew between Qian Dehong 錢德洪 (1497–1574), the diligent student of Wang Yangming, and Wang Ji 王畿 (1498–1583), the deviated outcast:

> Eventually Longxi [Wang Ji] drifted into Chan Buddhism, and Qian never deviated from the norms of Confucian teaching. Why is this so? Longxi let go at the brink of the cliffs. While Longxi was not a person who could be contained by his master's teachings, Qian held on to the ropes as he sailed. And so, if his catch was not vast, neither did he have much to lose. 乃龍溪竟入於禪, 而先生不失儒者之矩矱, 何也? 龍溪懸崖撒手, 非師門宗旨所可系縛, 先生則把纜放船, 雖無大得亦無大失耳。[54]

Unlike Wang Ji, Liang did not intentionally hover around the brink of the cliffs. At one point, however, he slipped. Off the cliff Liang finally displayed what I consider to be the true spirit of Wang Yangming's teaching, and was liberated, however momentarily, from the self-limiting search for human perfection that neo-Confucian teaching had imposed upon him. In this sudden awakening Liang abruptly wondered: imperfect as I am, who has given me the right to determine the life of others, particularly in a "democratic" movement that belonged *to the people?*[55] History personifies the collective unfolding of the universe. Being part of a sprightly universe that incessantly evolves, what are deficiencies and dysfunctionalities to speak of when there has never been "perfection" to begin with? When there is no perfection, how can burgeoning possibilities be considered deficiencies and flaws?

In a medley of essays published in the early 1920s, Liang began to return to his metaphysical musing: in what neo-Confucians perceived to be a perfect universe, humans might indeed be defective cosmic beings. Confucius, however, "had never accepted the universe had a primordial body" (他是不承認宇宙有本體的).[56] If the universe exists, it can only be the unfolding of life activities taking place in the intersection of time (*shijian* 時間) and space (*kongjian* 空間). In the infinitude of space, man is a minute piece of dust, and a fleeting shard of fragment in the unceasingly evolving moment of time.[57] Living one's life as a piece of shattered fragment, a person stumbles and staggers to proceed forward in an ever-expanding universe that is thousands of years away from achieving perfection. Unlike what certain neo-Confucian thinkers claimed, the universe has never been elsewhere; it is here, and it is what we are. Being the living presence of the universe (rather than a creation *of* it), the impairment of man and his *liangzhi* discloses the impairment of the universe. In a universe and a life that can never be perfect (宇宙和人生是永遠不會圓滿的), the need to complete and perfect oneself is precisely that impetus that impels us to advance forward.[58] Without people's inadequacies and imperfections, the universe would stand stagnantly still and lose its strengthen and momentum to evolve. The imperfection of the universe is precisely what perfects it.

Being the primitive impulse that disrupts our rational comprehension, affect (*qinggan* 情感; *ganqing* 感情), as Liang knew perhaps better than anyone, is frantic, vicious, and impulsive. It is a blind destructive force that bounces recklessly to crush and destroy.[59] But aside from its frantic compulsion, "this piece of imperfection might also be the primitive force that promises to transport a person to a realm that transcends the human aptitude" (情感的性質是本能的, 但他的力量, 能引人到超本能的境界). Of the mysterious powers affect induces, one, as it appears to Liang, is "love" (*ai* 愛) and the other "beauty" (*mei* 美), the two impetuses that give life and form to the creation of human civilization.[60] If a person is "to expand and to be as boundlessly and endlessly expansive *as* the evolving universe," Liang said, "there is no other entrance beyond exposing oneself to the experience of affect" (把我的生命和宇宙和眾生進合為一, 除卻通過情感這一個關門, 別無他路).[61] Not holding anything back, nor letting anything to be taken aback, thereafter a person submits himself to this unknown affective force. By letting go of the narrowly defined sense of human perfection, a person goes beyond his limited human self and participates in the collective unfolding of the universe. "Affect," as Liang wanted us to believe, "is indeed a kind of great mystery in this universe" (所以情感是宇宙間一種大秘密).[62]

Democracy as Humans' Becoming

People's participation in China's democratic movement, Liang believed, marks precisely the process of humans' becoming in this imperfect universe. The politician had facilitated China's democratic movements since 1895. Looking back over his political career, Liang arrived at a disheartening self-realization: "Those who took part in China's political activities, regardless to which parties they belong, have completely failed to comprehend the true meaning of democratic politics. All the paths that they have taken were gravely mistaken" (中國做政治活動的人一無論何黨何派一都完全沒有了解民主政治的真意義, 所走的路都走錯了).[63] Over the years, "not a single individual had made a sustained effort to mobilize the people for collective political participation" (始終並沒有人從運動國民上痛下工夫).[64] Warlords, bureaucrats, and imposters caused malicious damage to the country. But in China's "democratic" movement, those who deserved the most blame were perhaps he himself and a handful of high-minded idealists who were sincerely committed to the well-being of the people.[65] Whether these individuals were in support of constitutional reform or political revolution, they seemed to be deluded by a false piece of conviction: in Confucian teaching, it is assumed that an able man must think and work on behalf of the people. As the benevolent gentlemen struggled to implement what they willfully believed to be an ideal form of democratic governance that thrived on the self-governance of the people, they had never quite included the participation *of* the people in this trying process.

In 1921, spirit and spark gradually returned to Liang's writing. In his later essays Liang proposed: from hereafter, let us mobilize the people.[66] To encourage their participation in politics, one might begin by organizing public gatherings. In these gatherings, one might give speeches, circulate flyers and pamphlets, communicate abstruse political theories in easily comprehensible languages, and, more importantly, encourage people to express their political views and form their own personal judgment.[67] When it comes to schooling and education, focus on developing students' character.[68] Divide students into camps when they compete in sports and let the spirit of fair play be fostered both on and off the field: respect one's opponents, make sure everyone participates, maintain self-control in all circumstances, and, more importantly, respect written rules as well as unspoken virtues such as integrity, solidarity, team spirit, friendship, equality, tolerance, and care.[69] The root of democracy, he said, was ingrained in deep, cryptic sites of people's daily habits.[70] Once the foundation is consolidated, "the kind of true, open democracy that awaits us in the future will naturally be established" (將來真正公開的民主政治,自然會漸漸確立起來).[71]

Liang expected China's democratic movement to evolve with this perpetually evolving universe. In this trying process, he wanted people to remember: what we want and create often turns out to be different from what we have anticipated.[72] The massive destruction the First World War created in Europe was a good example: so frightening that people end up being consumed and potentially destroyed by their own creations. But instead of shunning affect and becoming solely invested in logic, rationality, and science, mistakes and failures should be tolerated. To unfold responsibly with this imperfect universe, perhaps the best one can do is to *try* to transform affect into a positive constructive force: "Once the human creator identifies with his free will a place he wishes to arrive at, he must venture into the place with 'the power of his heart'" (創造者人類以自己的自由意志選定一個自己所想要到達的地位,便用自己的"心能"闖進那地位去).[73] Regardless how hard a person tries, there are destined to be tasks that he is incapable of completing. If this is the case, let these unfinished tasks be left to those who come after. Whether the universe can reach perfection, or whether its evolution will end on one day, are questions that do not have definite answers.[74] As long as each individual can contribute a small effort, the accumulation of everyone's collective attempts, as Liang wishfully believed, should bring humanity progressively to a new place.[75]

As I studied Liang's later writings, I do not know to what extent he was *truly* convinced by his self-persuasion. But in this trying process, the reformer had at least tried to put himself together again after nearly a decade of schizophrenic grief. Liang began his career as a radical revolutionary. In the years that followed, he introduced his contemporaries to modern school curricula, strove to help provinces declare independence from the Qing monarchy, assisted his teacher in implementing constitutional reform, founded modern newspapers to educate the new citizens, assisted in drafting China's first constitution, formed the Republican Party (*Gonghe dang* 共和黨) in the burgeoning national congress, fought in an armed combat to remove Yuan Shikai 袁世凱 (1859–1916) from the throne,[76] and lost some of his dearest friends in these uprisings and military combats. Many times Liang lost faith and hope. But just as he was about to abandon the hope of reaching an end that he had so steadfastly aspired to, he tried to make his universe expansive again. In the 1920s, Liang slowly retired from politics and began to devote himself to teaching and to scholarly research. The future of China continued to occupy his consciousness. To bring a finishing remark to this book, and perhaps to China's unfinished journey to democracy, allow me to conclude with a wish Liang Qichao, my protagonist, expressed toward the final years of his life: "For questions that require rational contemplation, we must resolve them with scientific methods. But for matters that concern feelings and emotions, they transcend and surpass science" (人生關涉理智方面的事項，絕對要用科學方法來解決。關涉情感方面的事項，絕對的超科學).[77] "These days," he said, "I feel blessed to live the life of a scholar. But often I think: if I keep away from politics, I am essentially neglecting my responsibilities. There, I believe, is something 'I' must do. I must pluck up my courage again, the courage that I had once had during of the years of my twenties" (容我專作學者生涯，但又常常感覺，我若不管政治，便是我逃避責任。我覺得"我"應該做的事，是恢復我二十幾歲時候的勇氣).[78]

Notes

Introduction

1. For the development of Chinese imperial history from the Yuan to the Qing Dynasties (1315–194), see Benjamin Elman, *A Cultural History of Civil Examinations in Late Imperial China* (Los Angeles: University of California Press, 2000).

2. Liang Qichao, "Xinmin shuo" 新民說 (On renewing the people), *Xinmin congbao* 新民叢報 (New Citizen Journal) 1 (hereafter XMCB) (1902): 5.

3. Rebecca Kingston, "The Political Relevance of Emotions from Descartes to Smith," in *Bringing the Passions Back In: The Emotions in Political Philosophy* (Vancouver: University of British Columbia Press, 2008), 108–25.

4. Paul Rekret, "Affect and Politics: A Critical Assessment," accessed April 17, 2024, https://pressbooks.pub/pauljreilly/chapter/affect-and-politics-a-critical-assessment/; also see Clare Hemmings, "INVOKING AFFECT: Cultural Theory and the Ontological Turn," *Cultural Studies* 19, no. 5 (Sept. 2005): 548–67.

5. Michael Walzer, *Politics and Passion: Toward a More Egalitarian Liberalism* (New Haven, CT: Yale University Press, 2005); Also see Rebecca Kingston and Leonard Ferry, eds., *Bringing the Passions Back In*.

6. Some of Massumi's key arguments first appeared in his essay "The Autonomy of Affect," *Cultural Critique* 31, The Politics of Systems and Environments, Part 2 (Autumn, 1995): 83–109. These arguments have been elaborated and unpacked in *Parables for the Virtual: Movement, Affect, Sensation* (Durham, NC: Duke University Press, 2002).

7. Gilles Deleuze draws a clear contrast between affect and emotion. While affect exhibits bodily states of being that confound social logic, emotion refers to the manifestation, containment, or interpretation of these asocial forces. As an autonomous intensity that passes from one state to another, affect and its movement are categorized by an increase or decrease in power. See Gilles Deleuze,

Essays Critical and Clinical, trans. D. W. Smith and M. A. Greco (Minneapolis: University of Minnesota Press, 1997), 181.

8. Historians pursuing "the emotional turn" are chiefly interested in exploring how "emotions do things to the world," and the ways these emotive accounts can open us to different versions of "histories." The transformative impacts of emotions can be manifested explicitly and inexplicitly. Barbara Rosenwein, for instance, believes that the attempt to resist and struggle against particular social norms in an "emotional community" is what constitutes historical actions. William Reddy's "emotives" theory more subtly suggests that in every human being there exists an unnamable zone that refuses to submit itself to linguistic representation. To elucidate the existence of this "unnamable zone" and the subversive potential it posts, in recent years Reddy has turned to the speculative regions of neuroscience. While neuroscience and cognitive science play an irreplaceable role in the development of the "history of emotions," historians pursuing this particular research trend are indebted to the British philosopher J. L. Austin's (1911–1960) "speech acts theory" as well as philosophical premises developed by hermeneutic thinkers that range from Friedrich Schleiermacher to Hans-Georg Gadamer. For an introduction to the general development of the field, see Jan Plamper's "The History of Emotions: An Interview with William Reddy, Barbara Rosenwein, and Peter Stearns," *History and Theory* 49 (May 2010): 237–65. For William Reddy's definition of "emotives," see his "Against Constructionism: The Historical Ethnography of Emotions," *Current Anthropology* 38, no. 2 (1997): 327–51.

9. See Kim Youngmin, "Moral Agency and the Unity of the World: The Neo-Confucian Critique of 'Vulgar Learning,'" *Journal of Chinese Philosophy* 33, no. 4 (2006): 479–89.

10. For a learned critique of Qing intellectuals' obsession with the textual investigation, Qian Mu's discussion on Gu Yanwu's 顧炎武 (1613–1682) intellectual position projects the critical voices coming from a Qing native and a modern commentator. See Qian Mu, *Zhongguo jin sanbai nian xueshu shi* (中國近三百年學術史) (A history of intellectual development in the last three hundred years) (Taipei: Taiwan shangwu yinshuguan, 1964), 121–57.

11. For larger moral and intellectual conditions that anticipated and justified the rise of evidential scholarship in the Qing dynasty, see Ori Sela's *China's Philological Turn: Scholars, Textualism, and The Dao in the Eighteen Century* (New York: Columbia University Press, 2018). For the roles the Ming-Qing dynastic transformation, literati's regional network, and academics' professionalization played, see Benjamin Elman's canonical survey *From Philosophy to Philology: Intellectual and Social Aspects of Change in Late Imperial China* (Council on East Asian Studies, Harvard University, 1984).

12. Liang Qichao believes that the rise of "evidential scholarship" was inspired by some reflective intellectuals' collective "quest for the truth" (*qiu zhen*

求真) and compares the movement and its speculative spirit to the Renaissance. For Liang's endorsement of evidential scholarship, see his *Qingdai xueshu gailun* 清代學術概論 (Intellectual trends of the Qing period) (Shanghai: Shanghai guji chubanshe, 1998), 4–51. For Immanuel C. Y. Hsü's English translation, see *Intellectual Trends in the Chi'ing Period* (Cambridge, MA: Harvard University Press, 1959).

13. Kai-wing Chow delineates the intellectual inertia that debilitated Qing intellectuals' critical reflexivity in "Writing for Success: Printing, Examinations, and Intellectual Change in Late Ming China," *Late Imperial China* 17 (June 1996): 12–57.

14. For the rise of New Text Confucianism in the Qing dynasty, and the roles Zhuang Cunyu 莊存與, Liu Fenglu 劉逢祿, and Gong Zizhen 龔自珍 played in this intellectual movement, see Benjamin Elman, *Classicism, Politics, and Kinship: The Ch'ang-Chou School of New Text Confucianism in Late Imperial China* (Berkeley: University of California Press, 1990); On-Cho Ng, "Text in Context: Chin-wen Learning in Ch'ing Thought" (PhD diss., University of Hawaii, 1986); On-Cho Ng and Q. Edward Wang, *Mirroring the Past: The Writing and Use of History in Imperial China* (Honolulu: University of Hawaii Press, 2005); Wang Hui, *Xiandai Zhongguo sixiang de xingqi* 現代中國思想的興起 (The rise of modern Chinese thought) (Beijing: Sanlian shudian, 2004), 489–519 and 737–829; Wang Hui, "Idea of China in New Text Confucianism, 1780–1911," in *Critical Zone 2: A Forum of Chinese and Western Knowledge*, ed. Q. S. Tong, Shouren Wang, and Douglas Kerr (Hong Kong: Hong Kong University Press, 2006), 167–80; Qian Mu, *Qian Binsi xiansheng quanji*; Pi Xirui 皮錫瑞, *Jingxue lishi* 經學歷史 (Confucian history) ([China]: Sixiang shuju, 1906; Philip Huang, "From New Text Confucianism to 'Democratic' Reform, 1890–1898," in in Philip Huang, *Liang Ch'i-ch'ao and Modern Chinese Liberalism* (Seattle: University of Washington Press, 1972), 11–35.

15. Qian Mu, *Lianghan jingxue jinguwen pingyi* 兩漢經學今古文評議 (Assessment of the Han Dynasty's Old Text and New Text controversy) (Taibei: Dongda tushu gongsi yinhang, 1983). For recent English discussions on the relationship between the academic and the political competition in the Han dynasty, see Yuri Pines, Paul Goldin, and Martin Kern, eds., *Ideology of Power and Power of Ideology in Early China* (Leiden: Brill Academic, 2015).

16. For Liang Qichao's personal account on the intellectual and political positions he developed for New Text studies, see his *Qingdai xueshu gailun*.

17. In her study of early Chinese cinema, Bao Weihong defines the term as "a distinct notion of the medium as mediating environment with the power to stir passions, frame perception, and mold experience." These early Chinese cinematic productions, to borrow her words, "operates as a rhetoric, or a politics that illuminates the changing operation of a medium through the triad process of unframing, deframing, and reframing, mobilizing the dynamic between the

old and the new in a sense of liberating from, annihilating, and redrawing medium boundaries." For Bao's stimulating discussions on "affective medium" and key theoretical assumptions that inform the coinage, see *Fiery Cinema: The Emergence of an Affective Medium in China, 1915–1945* (Minneapolis: University of Minnesota Press, 2015), 2. In addition to her monograph, Bao Weihong also presents an illuminating discussion on the concept of "intermediality" in "The Politics of Remediation: Mise-en-scène and the Subjunctive Body in Chinese Opera Film," *The Opera Quarterly*, 26, no. 2–3 (2010): 256–90.

18. On-cho Ng has studied most crucial but less examined Qing intellectual developments in his forthcoming monograph "Qing Thought as a Period Concept: Intellectual Trends in Late Imperial China." A summary of the book titled "Qing Philosophy" appears in the *Stanford Encyclopedia of Philosophy* (Summer 2019): 1–55. Yu Wen shares persisting interests in the correlation between late Qing intellectual history and its political reformist movement. Currently she is turning her dissertation, "The Search for the Chinese Way in a Modern World: From the Rise of Evidential Scholarship to the Birth of Chinese Identity" (PhD diss., Harvard University, 2018) into a book. Theodore Huters studies the relationship between the development of late Qing intellectual history and literary theory in "From Writing to Literature: The Development of Late Qing Theories of Prose," *Harvard Journal of Asiatic Studies* 47, no. 1 (June 1987): 51–96.

19. The "crisis of meaning" caused by Chinese intellectuals' obsession with textual knowledge remains an understudied research topic. But for those who look for more personal accounts, there are primary sources available. Concern and anxieties that came with Qing dynasty's excessive "intellectualism" are perhaps most vocally and elaborately expressed in *Rulin waishi* 儒林外史 (Unofficial history of the scholars), a novel, if not a first-hand account, completed by Wu Jingzi 吳敬梓 (1701–1754) in 1750. Shang Wei has carefully analyzed the intellectual implications of Wu Jingzi's work and the epistemic crisis the Qing novelist endeavored to grapple in *Rulin Waishi and Cultural Transformation in Late Imperial China* (Cambridge, MA: Harvard University Asian Center, 2003).

20. See *Mirror for Moral Cultivation* (*Deyu jian* 德育鑑), a 160-page collection Liang compiled and distributed in 1903. The anthology, issued complimentarily with one issue of the *New Citizen Journal*, is divided into six chapters, in which Liang systematically delineates how the Chinese public can become "*authentic nationalists*" (*zhen aiguo zhe* 真愛國者) in successive steps. Of these six steps, the first begins with "activating one's perceptual intuition" (*bianshu* 辨術). Following that, a person makes the effort of "becoming resolute" (*lizhi* 立志). Upon "recognizing the primal importance" (*zhiben* 知本), one should persist in "preserving it through nurturing cultivation" (*cunyang* 存養) as well as "self-reflection and restraint" (*xingke* 省克). As long as one can observe these five principles, he is capable of "realizing his conviction through application/action" (*yingyong* 應用). Liang Qichao (*Yinbing shi zhuren* 飲冰室主人), *Deyu jian* (Mirror for moral cultivation), in 新民叢報第二次臨時增刊 *Xinmin congbao dierci linshi zengkan* (The

second interim supplement to the New Citizen Journal) (Yokohama, Japan: Xinmin congbao she, 1903).

21. Thomas Metzger, *Escape from Predicament* (New York: Columbia University Press, 1986), 111–13.

22. For an elaborate explication on Wang Yangming's Buddhist-inspired moral metaphysics and Liang Qichao's incorporation of his metaphysics in China's transition to political modernity, see the third chapter of this book, "To Know Is to Act: The Realization of Cosmo-Moral-Political Oneness in Action." For the moral and intellectual lineage Philip Ivanhoe established between Mencius and Wang Yangming, see *Ethics in the Confucian Tradition: The Thought of Mencius and Wang Yang-Ming* (Indianapolis, IN: Hackett, 2002).

23. "Metaphysical Republic" is a term coined by Kim Youngmin. For his discussion and elaboration of this concept, see "The Metaphysical Republic," in *A History of Chinese Political Thought* (Beijing: Polity Press, 2017), 114–36.

24. Philip Ivanhoe devotes a book monograph to elaborate this concept. See his *Oneness: East Asian Conceptions of Virtue, Happiness, and How We Are All Connected* (Oxford University Press, 2017). For Wang Yangming, most people are unaware of their cosmic moral nature. They would rather *learn* to be moral by studying prescriptive moral doctrines as if it were textual knowledge that was external to them. The hierarchical socio-moral-emotive paradigm people subscribe to can be best captured in a debate between Thomas Metzger and Benjamin Schwartz. See Benjamin Schwartz, "Hierarchy, Status, and Authority in Chinese Culture," in *China and Other Matters*, 130–41; and Thomas Metzger, "The Definition of Self, the Group, the Cosmos, and Knowledge in Chou Thought: Some Comments on Professor Schwartz's Study," *American Asian Review* 4, no. 2 (Summer 1986): 68–116.

25. For the subversive potential Wang Yangming unpacked in Qing philosophy, see Araki Kengo 荒木見悟 *Bukkyō to Jukyō: Chūgoku Shisō wo keiseisuru mono* 仏教と儒教 中国思想を形成するもの (Confucianism and Buddhism: The formation of Chinese thought) (Kyōto, Heirakuji Shoten, Showa 38 [1963]); Yu Ying-shih 余英時, *Songminglixue yu zhengzhi wenhua* 宋明理學與政治文化 (Neo-Confucianism and political culture) (Taipei: Yongchen congkan, 2004)

26. Besides the work of Wang Yangming, Liang's thinking was heavily influenced by political theories developed by Wang Fuzi 王夫之 (1619–1692) and Huang Zongxi 黃宗羲 (1610–1695). For more details, see Yu Wen's unpublished dissertation, "The Search for the Chinese Way in a Modern World: From the Rise of Evidential Scholarship to the Birth of Chinese Identity."

27. This is an expression I borrow from Thomas Metzger's discussion on the relationship between the metaphysical and the experiential in neo-Confucianism. See Metzger's *Escape from Predicament*, 85.

28. To understand how Liang Qichao's historical thinking had evolved from a "global imaginary of identity" to a "global imaginary of difference" from 1902 to roughly 1922, how his early foresight had subtly subverted the

238 | Notes to Introduction

enlightenment concept of universal and progressive time, and how such foresight projects "a postnationalist cultural politics that questions the world system of nation-states" (234), see Tang Xiaobing, *Global Space and the Nationalist Discourse of Modernity: The Historical Thinking of Liang Qichao* (Standard, CA: Standard University Press, 1996).

29. See Michael Fuller, *Drifting among Rivers and Lakes: Southern Song Dynasty Poetry and the Problem of Literary History* (Cambridge, MA: Harvard University Asia Center, 2013).

30. Michael Fuller, "Shilun wenxueshi zhong Tangsong zhuanxing de yige lilun kuangjia" 試論文學史中唐宋轉型的一個理論框架, lecture presentation at Fudan University in August 2018.

31. For Fuller's full translation of the poem, see his *Introduction to Chinese Poetry: From the Canon of Poetry to the Lyrics of the Song Dynasty* (Cambridge, MA: Harvard University Asia Center, 2017), 234.

32. Michael Fuller (Fu Junmai 傅君勱), "The Aesthetic as Immanent Assent to Pattern within Heterogeneity, or 文," in *Zhongguo wenxue yanjiu de xin quxiang: ziran, shenmei yu bijiao yanjiu* 中國文學研究的新趨向：自然、審美與比較研究 (New Trends in Chinese literary studies: natural aesthetics and comparative studies), ed. Yu-yu Cheng 鄭毓瑜 (Taipei: Taida chuban zhongxin, 2005), 47–80.

33. Fuller, "Aesthetic as Immanent Assent," 17.

34. Fuller, "Aesthetic as Immanent Assent," 24.

35. Perhaps both Xun Kuang's and Kant's assumption are not overexaggerations. In recent scientific experiments conducted by neuroscientists, it appears that men's neural networks are built to extract patterns, and their brains are programed to identify, process, and react to patterns that matter to them. For a general summary, see Fuller, *Drifting among Rivers and Lakes*, 14–16.

36. The topic receives perhaps the most intelligent and elaborate treatment in Rodolphe Gasché's *The Idea of Form: Rethinking Kant's Aesthetics* (Stanford, CA: Stanford University Press, 1995).

37. "Judgment," according to Kant, "in general is the ability to think the particular as contained under the universal. If the universal (the rule, principle, law) is given, then judgment, which subsumes the particular under it, is determinative (even though [in its role] as transcendental judgment it states a priori conditions that must be met for subsumption under that universal to be possible). But if only the particular is given and judgment has to find the universal for it, then this power is merely reflective." See Immanuel Kant, *Critique of Judgment* (Indianapolis, IN: Hackett, 1987), 18–19.

38. See Theodor Adorno, "Music, Language, and Composition," trans. Susan Gillespie, *Musical Quarterly* 77 no. 3 (Autumn 1993): 401–14; and "Parataxis: On Hölderlin's Late Poetry," in *Notes to Literature*, vol. 2, ed. Rolf Tiedemann and trans. Shierry Weber Nicholsen (New York: Columbia University Press, 1991).

39. Liang's original words say: 陽明之良知，即康德之真我。其學說之基礎全同。See Liang Qichao, "Jinshi diyi dazhe kangde zhi xueshuo" 近世第一大哲康德

之學說 (Immanuel Kant the greatest philosopher in the early modern period), in XMCB 46 (1904): 57.

40. Liang Qichao, "Zhongguo yunwen litou suo biaoxian de qinggan" 中國韻文裡頭所表現的情感 (Feelings expressed in China's rhapsodic verses) in *Liang Qichao lun zhongguo wenxue* 梁啟超論中國文學 (Liang Qichao on Chinese Literature) (Beijing: Shangwu yinshuguan, 2012), 222.

41. See Wilhelm Dilthey, "Awareness, Reality: Time," and "The Understanding of Other Persons and Their Life-Expressions," in *The Hermeneutics Reader: Texts of the German Tradition from the Enlightenment to the Present*, ed. Kurt Mueller-Vollmer (New York: Continuum, 1985), 148–64.

42. Ruth Leys, *The Ascent of Affect: Genealogy and Critique* (Chicago, IL: University of Chicago Press, 2017).

43. Rei Terada, *Feeling in Theory: Emotion after the "Death of the Subject"* (Cambridge, MA: Harvard University Press, 2001).

44. Lydia Liu, for instance, raises the following questions: "The central questions I ask myself in this regard are How do people imagine and talk about the Chinese xiandai condition? and its corollary: What happens when certain types of discourses are preferred and legitimized over and above others? I am less concerned, though, with the question of the nature of the local character of the Chinese modern." See Lydia Liu, *Translingual Practice: Literature, National Culture, and Translated Modernity—China, 1900–1937* (Stanford, CA: Stanford University Press, 1995), xvii.

45. See Liu, *Translingual Practice*, 1–43.

46. Liu, *Translingual Practice*, 26.

47. Such imagination, as Liu elaborates in Leo Ou-fan Lee's famous observation, refers specifically to the way the "May Fourth generation, and their predecessors, attempt to define their difference from the past and articulate a new range of sensibilities which they would consider 'modern.'" See Liu, *Translingual Practice*, 28. For Leo Ou-fan's elaborate discussion on the relationship between emotions, subjectivity, and Chinese modernity, see *The Romantic Generation of Modern Chinese Writers* (Cambridge, MA: Harvard University Press, 1973); and his essays "Qinggan de lichen" 情感的歷程 (The journey of sentimentality) and "Zhuiqiu xiandai xing: Yiba jiuwu-yijiuerqi" 追求現代性：一八九五——一九二七 (Searching for modernity: 1895–1927), in *Xiandai xing de zhuiqiu* 現代性的追求：李歐梵文化評論精選集 (In search of modernity: Essays in cultural criticism) (Taibei: Maitian chuban, 1996), 139–60, and 229–300.

48. Theodore Huters, *Bringing the World Home: Appropriating the West in Late Qing and Early Republican China* (Honolulu: University of Hawai'i Press, 2005).

49. David Der-wei Wang, *The Lyrical in the Epic Time: Modern Chinese Intellectuals and Artists through the 1949 Crisis* (New York: Columbia University Press, 2015).

50. Wang, *Lyrical in the Epic Time*, xii.

51. For Mark Bevir's apt summary on Roland Barthes, see his "Meaning and Intention: A Defense of Procedural Individualism," *New Literary History* 31, no. 1 (July 2000): 385–403.

52. Prasenjit Duara, *Rescuing History from the Nation* (Chicago, IL: University of Chicago Press, 1997).

53. Lydia Liu, *The Clash of Empires: The Invention of China in Modern World Making* (Cambridge, MA: Harvard University Asia Center, 2004).

54. See Duara, *Rescuing History from the Nation*, 7. In addition to Duara, also see Rebecca Karl's *Staging the World and Failure, Nationalism, and Literature* (Durham, NC: Duke University Press, 2015). Karl believes that political and literary historians of late Qing and early modern China are helplessly trapped in a dogmatic dichotomy that divides the world into two binary oppositions: the colonizer and the colonized, and the dominator and the dominated. Informed by concepts such as domination versus resistance, identity, and agency, postcolonial scholars have been occupied by the task of reempowering the third world others and reversing the position of the colonizer and the colonized. And for postmodernists under the influence of Foucault, they focus on showing that the Western enlightenment discourse (or teleological, evolutionary Hegelian history) is a matter of knowledge construction. Certain (political) power forces, however, eventually come to endorse and legitimize the "constructiveness" by suppressing and appropriating other competing indigenous, alternative discourses. For Karl both of these two theoretical approaches have fallen prey to the imperial, hegemonic discourses they have aspired to subvert in the first place. While many postmodern and postcolonial scholars have tried hard to reempower the dominated/colonized and to place them in the dominating position, they make little if any attempt to escape from the dogmatic dichotomy of the dominator and the dominated. Sometimes someone might appear successful in reversing the position of the binary pair, but their framework of analysis and the languages associated with this framework remain imperialist in nature. It is true that different countries had been given a chance to exchange roles in these postmodern/postcolonial historical reinterpretations, but the world remains a system of hierarchical difference instead of a system of mutual differentiation. To demolish this dominator/dominated binary opposition, Karl's book seeks to represent positioned readings Hegelian histories from those third world perspectives. This way, the world history in the past two hundred years would cease to be a story of sovereignty expansion and domination and become instead a story of "struggle" or third world countries joining hands (i.e., China, India, Turkey, and the Philippines) to strive for survival. By reading history from a different "discursive positioning," the once "negative spaces of 'lack' and 'incompletion' will be replaced by 'positive spaces for an ongoing project of dynamic social-political and cultural transformation"; Rebecca Karl, *Staging the World: Chinese Nationalism at the Turn of the Twentieth Century* (Durham, NC: Duke University Press, 2002), 17.

55. Aristotle, "On the Soul," in *Aristotle: On the Soul. Parva Naturalia. On Breath* (Cambridge, MA: Harvard University Press, 1957).

56. Edmund Husserl, "Essential Distinction" and "Towards a Characterization of the Acts which Confer Meaning," in Kurt Mueller-Vollmer, *The Hermeneutics Reader: Texts of the German Tradition from the Enlightenment to the Present* (New York: Continuum, 1985), 165–86.

57. Maurice Merleau-Ponty, *Phenomenology of Perception* (Abingdon, UK: Routledge 2012). The book was originally published in 1945.

58. Michael Fuller, "Weary Night": A Reflection on Embodied Poetics in the Classical Chinese Tradition," paper presented at the Conference on Art and Ritual in Asian Cultures organized by the Center for Body, Mind and Culture at Florida Atlantic University on March 20, 2009. For Fuller's nuanced introduction to core elements of contemporary neuroscience and his explication for the relevance of neuroscientific models for a broader understanding of the nature of human experience, see his *Being Biological: Human Meaning in the Age of Neuroscience* (Self-published, December 20, 2022).

59. For the connection between Wang Yangming and Mencius, see Mou Zongsan 牟宗三, "Wangxue shi mengzi xue" 王學是孟子學 (The learning of Wang Yangming as the learning of Mencius), in *Cong Lu Xianshan dao Liu Jishan*, 從陸象山到劉蕺山 (From Lu Xianshan to Liu Jishan) (Taipei: Xuesheng shuju, 2011), 177–217; also see Philip Ivanhoe's book-length study titled *Ethics in the Confucian Tradition: The Thought of Mencius and Wang Yang-Ming* (Indianapolis, IN: Hackett, 2002).

60. Liang, *Qingdai xueshu gailun*, 84.

61. David Wang shares a comparable observation in his discussion of the *The Future of New China*. See his chapter "Confused Horizons: Science Fantasy," in *Fin-de-Siècle Splendor: Repressed Modernities of Late Qing Fiction, 1849–1911* (Stanford, CA: Stanford University Press, 1997), 252–311.

62. In the classical age, as James Kloppenberg notes, "democracy" was seen as the failure rather than the ideal of good governance. For how democracy has evolved from stories of chaotic, bloody battles to the ideal of good governance, see his *Toward Democracy: The Struggle for Self-Rule in European and American Thought* (New York: Oxford University Press, 2016). For skepticism early American statesmen expressed for human nature, see Arthur O. Lovejoy, "The Theory of Human Nature in the American Constitution and the Method of Counterpoise," in *Reflections on Human Nature* (Baltimore, MD: Johns Hopkins University Press, 1961), 37–66; for an excellent comparison on assumptions the Confucian and the Christian traditions' take on human nature, and the development of varying governmental construction in these cultural traditions, see Chang Hao's "Youan yishi yu minzhu chuantong" 幽暗意識與民主傳統 (Consciousness of darkness and the democratic tradition), in *Youan yishi yu minzhu chuantong* 幽暗意識與民主傳統 (Taipei: Lianjing, 2000), 3–32.

63. See Liang Qichao, "Xin zhongguo weilaiji" 新中國未來記 (The future of new China), *Xin xiaoshuo* 新小說 (New Fiction) 2 (1903): 29–79; and *Xin xiaoshuo* 3 (1903): 79–106.

64. Liang Qichao, "Lun zhongguo xueshu sixiang bianqian zhi da shi" 論中國學術思想變遷之大勢 (On the general transformational trend of Chinese academic thoughts), in XMCB 3 (1902): 41–56; XMCB 5 (1902): 57–80; XMCB 12 (1902): 39–56.

65. See Liang Qichao's *Qingdai xueshi gailun* 清代學術概論 (Intellectual trends of the Qing period) (Shanghai: Shanghai guji chubanshe, 1998).

66. Liang Qichao, *Liang Qichao Quanji* 梁啟超全集 (The complete works of Liang Qichao), vols. 1–21 (Beijing: Beijing chubanshe, 1999).

Chapter 1

1. For a recent study on the development of Qian Daxin's career as philologist, see Ori Sela's *China's Philological Turn: Textualism and the Dao in the Eighteenth Century* (New York: Columbia University Press, 2018).

2. Qian Daxin, "You maoshan ji" 遊茅山記 (Journey to Mountain Mao), in *Qian yan tang wenji* 潛研堂文集, *juan* 20 (China: n.p., 1806), 13–21.

3. Qian, "You maoshan ji," 13.

4. In contemporary scholarship the English translation of *li* 理 constitutes a constant topic of debate. The term has been conventionally translated as "principles" or "patterns." Willard Peterson, Peter Bol, and Brook Ziporyn rendered it as "coherence." Ziporyn justifies the translation with the following reason: "The word principle only says 'because of some reasons' without telling us what the reason is. Coherence, on the contrary, can be used to explain why something is what it is (because of the way it joins and interacts with other things, or as what emerges as newly intelligible if and only if some set of other things comes together in a certain way. It can give value to something being as it is." Philip Ivanhoe strongly opposes this usage, for "coherence" fails to indicate "what it is that coheres," and why this coherence takes place. For Ziporyn's reasons for translating *li* as "coherence," see his elaborate footnote in *Ironies of Oneness and Differences: Coherence in Early Chinese Thought; Prolegomena to the Study of Li* 理 (Albany, NY: State University of New York Press, 2013), 269–70. For Ivanhoe's protest against the usage of "coherence," see his "Book Review on Peter Bol's *Neo-Confucianism in History*," *Dao: A Journal of Comparative Philosophy* 9 (2010): 471–75.

5. Immanuel Kant, *Groundwork of the Metaphysic of Morals* (1785) (4:439).

6. To see how Liang reformulated the Kantian autonomous moral subject to make it conform with neo-Confucian ideals of virtuous self-cultivation, see Camila YaDeau's recent article, "Translingual Encounters: Freedom, Civic Virtue,

and the Social Organism in Liang Qichao's Reading of Kant," *TRANSIT* 13, no. 1 (2021): 115–229.

    7. In contrast to "deontological ethics," the rightness of action driven by man's natural moral obligation and determined by its intrinsic value rather than the consequences of the action, the performance of "virtue ethics" serves as a means to attain an end. It is goal-oriented. For a general definition on virtue ethics and its relevance with Confucian philosophy, see Bryan Van Norden, *Virtue Ethics and Consequentialism in Early Chinese Philosophy* (Cambridge: Cambridge University Press, 2007). For critiques and protests of Van Norden's and other contemporary Western philosophers' decision to approach Confucian morality as virtue ethics, see Lee Ming-huei, "Confucianism, Kant, and Virtue Ethics," in *Virtue Ethics and Confucianism*, ed. Stephen Angle and Michael Slote (New York: Routledge, 2013), 47–56.

    8. To see the various attempts neo-Confucian thinkers made to "say Yes to life," see Carsun Chang, *Development of Neo-Confucian Thought* (New York: Bookman Associates, 1957), 130.

    9. Jeeloo Liu, *Neo-Confucianism: Metaphysics, Mind, and Morality* (Hoboken, NJ: Wiley-Blackwell, 2017), 14.

    10. In ancient China, it was believed that the heart is the spring of all thoughts and emotions (萬事皆發於心). The doctrine that heart is in charge of cognition and wisdom was gravely challenged by missionaries arriving from Europe in the Ming dynasty. The most comprehensive description on the function of the brain in the mid-nineteenth century came with Benjamin Hobson's *Quanti xinlun*. In the chapter titled "Nao wei quanti zhi zhu" 腦為全體之主 (The brain governs the entire body), Hobson asserts that the seat of all mental activities rests in the brain (靈之在腦). It is the organ generating thoughts that may be translated into actions (以顯其思慮行為者). See Benjamin Hobson, *Quanti xinlun* 全體新論 (Treatise on physiology) (Beijing: Zhonghua shuju, 1991), 75. (The book was first published in 1851, by Huiai yiguan 惠愛醫館. The current edition is reprinted from the Haishan xianguan congshu ben 海山仙館叢書 edition.)

    11. Stephen Angel and Justin Tiwald, *Neo-Confucianism: A Philosophical Introduction* (Cambridge: Polity Press, 2017), 71.

    12. For Philip Ivanhoe's discussion on how "we understand the Way when we experience the feeling that all things are connected to and reflections of the principle within us," see *Three Streams: Confucian Reflections on Learning and the Moral Heart-Mind in China, Korea, and Japan* (New York: Oxford University Press, 2016), 29.

    13. In *The Analects* (論語), Confucius says that a benevolent person (*renzhe* 仁者) "is loving of others" (*airen* 愛人). When his loving care is universally transmitted, people (having presumably experienced the warmth of his loving kindness) will grow to appreciate and become benevolent (*fanai zhong, er qin ren* 泛愛眾, 而親仁).

14. To see how neo-Confucian thinkers turned the four incipiencies into moral propensities universally shared by mankind, see Carsun Chang's chapter, "Fundamental Principles of the Philosophy of Reason," in *Development of Neo-Confucian Thought*, 43–55.

15. Both Cheng Hao and Zhu Xi had made this same remark. Zhu Xi was apparently under the influence of Zhang Zai, who claimed that "性者理也, 性是體, 情是用, 性情皆出於心, 故心能統之。" See Zhang Zai, 後錄下 (Part Two in *Words of Zhang Zhai*) in Zhangzi yulu 張子語錄 (Words of Zhang Zhai).

16. See Peter Bol, "When Antiquity Matters: Thinking about and with Antiquity in the Tang-Song Transition," in *Perceptions of Antiquity in Chinese Civilization*, ed. Dieter Kuhn and Helga Stahl (Heidelburg, Germany: Edition Forum, 2008), 323. Peter Bol also made comparable remarks in his discussions on Wang Yangming; see Ivanhoe, *Neo-Confucianism in History*, 187–93.

17. See Thomas Metzger, *Escape from Predicament* (New York: Columbia University Press, 1986), 111–13. For a more detailed explication of Zhu Xi's moral metaphysics, see Qian Mu 錢穆, *Zhuzi xin xuean* 朱子新學案 (A new biography of Zhu Xi's academic life), vol. 1 (Beijing: Jiuzhou chuban she, 2011), 1–15, 300.

18. The irreconcilable discrepancy between the heartmind and the cosmic pattern has been most critically elaborated by Zhu Xi's follower Chen Baisha 陳白沙 (1428–1500). For an insightful summary of Chen Baisha's metaphysical position, see Araki Kengo, "Chen Baisha yu Zhan Ganquan 陳白沙與湛甘泉," *Journal of Renmin University of China* (中國人民大學學報) 6 (1991): 34–44.

19. Zhu Xi, "Da He Shujing" 答何叔景 (Response to He Shujing) in *Zhuzi yulei*, juan 4. Zhu Xi's words read "盖必有是理然后有是心, 有是心而后有是事。"

20. For a systematic description on the metaphysical organization of Zhu Xi's moral theory, see Metzger, *Escape from Predicament*, 70–93.

21. Metzger, *Escape from Predicament*, 87–89.

22. See Zhu Xi's *Dushu fa* 讀書法 (Methods of reading). See *Zhu zi yulei*, juan 44, 15, and 4. Besides emphasizing the importance of learning, Zhu Xi also placed considerable emphasis on meditative practices.

23. Philip Ivanhoe believes that "Neo-Confucianism developed into different schools primarily over disagreements about how to study or learn (*xue* 學)." These disagreements later informed the distinctive approaches they developed for learning. I disagree with this position and hope to trace their disagreements to more fundamental causes. For Ivanhoe's remark, see *Three Streams*, 22–23.

24. See Willard Peterson, "Confucian Learning in Late Ming Thought," in *The Cambridge History of China*, volume 8, ed. Denis Twitchett and Frederic E. Mote (Cambridge: Cambridge University Press, 1998), 709–88.

25. See Dai Zhen 戴震, "Da Peng Yunchu shu shu" 答彭允初書 (A letter reply to Peng Yunchu). Besides making this remark in his personal letter, Dai Zhen repeated this statement as many as three times in his magnum opus, *Mengzi ziyi shuzheng* 孟子字義疏證 (An evidential study of the meaning of terms of the Mengzi).

26. For Liang Qichao's summary on Dai Zhen's philological or linguistic investigation of the classics, see his "Dai Dongyuan zhexue" 戴東原哲學 (Philosophy of Dai Dongyuan), in *Liang Qichao lun yuejia zhexue* 梁啟超論儒家哲學 (Liang Qichao on the philosophy of Confucianism) (Beijing: Shangwu yinshu guan, 2012), 249–51.

27. In *Qingdai xueshu gailun* 清代學術概論 (Intellectual trends of the Qing period), Liang Qichao describes Dai Zhen's research practice with the words of his fellow evidential researcher Yu Tingcan 余廷燦 (1729–1798): "When there was a single character which was not based on the Six Scripts, or the interpretation of a single word which could not be uniformly applied to various classics, he would not believe it without evidence. When he doubted, he had no peace with himself until he had repeatedly checked the references and evidence." Translated by Immanuel Hsü, in *Intellectual Trends in the Chi'ing Period* (Cambridge, MA: Harvard University Press, 1959), 57.

28. In an evolutionary process that is universally applicable, a tribal group evolves to form a kinship society. It moves from a kinship society to a monarchy, and eventually develops into a nation-state administered by democratic governance. For Tang Xiaobing's discussion on Liang's reformist vision, see *Global Space and the Nationalist Discourse of Modernity* (Stanford, CA: Standard University Press, 1996), 36.

29. Liang Qichao, *Deyu jian* 德育鑑 (Mirror for moral cultivation) (Yokohama, Japan: Xinmin congbao she, 1903) (hereafter *DYJ*), 4, 6, 7.

30. Liang, *DYJ*, 52. Also see Liang Qichao, "Lun side," 論私德 (On private morality), XMCB 46/7/8 (1904), 8.

31. Liang, *DYJ*, 5 and 7.

32. Liang Qichao, "Lun gongde," 論公德 (On public morality), in XMCB 3 (1902), 2.

33. Liang, "Lun gongde," 6.

34. Liang, "Lun gongde," 3.

35. Liang, "Lun gongde," 1.

36. Liang Qichao, "Lun side," in XMCB 39 (1903): 1.

37. See Ori Sela's chapter "Philology and the Message of the Sages," in Sela, *China's Philological Turn*, 101–17.

38. Sela, *China's Philological Turn*, 103.

39. Among the few books I consider particularly solid and insightful are Chang Hao's *Liang Ch'i-ch'ao and Intellectual Transition in China, 1890–1907* (Cambridge, MA: Harvard University Press 1971); Peter Zarrow's *After Empire: The Conceptual Transformation of the Chinese State, 1885–1924* (Stanford, CA: Stanford University Press, 2012); and Wang Hui's *Xiandai zhongguo sixiang de xingqi* 現代中國思想的興起 (The rise of modern Chinese thought) (Beijing: Sanlian shudian, 2015). Stephen Angel is also careful to acknowledge the role neo-Confucianism plays in shaping Liang Qichao's conception of human rights.

See his chapter "Dynamism in the Early Twentieth Century," in *Human Rights and Chinese Thought: A Cross-Cultural Inquiry* (Cambridge: Cambridge University Press 2002), 140–77.

40. Liang, "Lun jiaoyu dangding zongzhi" 論教育當論宗旨 (On education and the importance of its purposes), XMCB 1 (1902): 65.

41. Liang, *DYJ*, 59.

42. Liang, *DYJ*, 52.

43. Liang, *DYJ*, 5. The two accusations Liang made against the people are originated from Mencius. "Being unfaithful to oneself" (自得於己) appears in 3A4 and 5B42, while "abandoning oneself with indulgence" (自暴自棄) can be found in 4A10.

44. Liang, "Lun guojia sixiang" 論國家思想 (On national thinking), XMCB 4 (1902): 1.

45. Nakae Chōmin's 中江兆民 rendition of Kant was based on *Histoire de la philosophie* (1875), a general introduction to the Western philosophy completed by Alfred Fouillée (1838–1912). Later Liang had creatively and rather liberally adapted Chōmin's translation into Chinese. For Liang Qichao's description of his translation background, see "Jinshi diyi dazhe Kangde zhi xueshuo" 近世第一大哲康德之學說 (The theories of Kant the greatest philosopher in the early modern period), in XMCB 25 (1903): 15. The first installment of Liang's translation of Kant was serialized in volume 25 of *New Citizen Journals*; the rest of the installments were published in XCMB volumes 26, 28, and the combined 46/7/8 volume. For Nakae Chōmin's translation of Fouillée's introduction to Kant, see his *Rigaku enkakushi* 理学沿革史 (Tokyo: Monbusho Henshukyoku, [1886]), 609–96.

46. Liang Qichao, "Jinshi diyi dazhe Kangde," in XMCB 25 (1903): 19–20.

47. In addition to *Qingdai xueshu gailun* and the final chapter of *Lun zhongguo xueshu sixiang bianqian zhi dashi* 論中國學術思想變遷之大勢 (On the general trend in changes of Chinese academic thought), Liang Qichao's familiarity with the methodological approaches adopted by Qing evidential research and the school's research output is demonstrated most evidently in *Zhongguo jin sanbainian xueshu shi* 中國近三百年學術史 (Chinese academic history of the recent three hundred years) (Shanghai: Shanghai guji chuban she, 2013).

48. Liang Qichao, "Jinshi diyi dazhe Kangde zhu xueshuo," in XMCB 25 (1903): 15.

49. Liang, "Jinshi diyi dazhe Kangde," XMCB 25 (1903): 21.

50. Liang, "Jinshi diyi dazhe Kangde," 16–21.

51. Unlike Yogācāra Buddhists, though, Kant does not deny the existence of the things of the world, only that we cannot have unmediated access to or knowledge of them.

52. To give just a summary of Yogācāra Buddhism: under the influence of Nāgārjuna, Vasubandhu (Chin: 世親) (fl. 4th to 5th century CE), and his half-

brother Asaṅga (Chin: 無著) (300–370 AD) converted the *Abhidharma* tradition to another branch of Buddhism, the school of Yogācāra or Cittamātra. To be empty, in the two's understanding, is not so much to be empty of *svabhāva* as to be "free from the distinction between object cognized and the consciousness cognizing." In Yogācāra Buddhism, it is believed that people possess eight kinds of consciousness. The first six are those to do with embodied sensations, including sight, hearing, touch, taste, smell, and introspection. The seventh consciousness is the home of our concepts, opinions, and inner discursiveness. It is a source of suffering and a place where people exhaust most of our mental energy. The eighth consciousness is *ālaya-vijñāna* (Chin: 阿賴耶識), the storehouse consciousness, or what Freud might call the unconscious. Being the place where variegated feelings and memories are kept, *ālaya-vijñāna* would bubble up and disturb other levels of consciousness. When a person looks around, they naturally form a subject-object duality between themself and other phenomenal objects. For Vasubandhu, however, the apparent self-other duality is a "perception" generated by *ālaya-vijñāna*. The moment one recognizes the illusory nature of imagined objects and overcomes all dualities as perceived, the person obtains spiritual transcendence. I borrow the apt summary from Graham Priest; see *The Fifth Corner of Four: An Essay on Buddhist Metaphysics and the Catuṣkoṭi* (New York: Oxford University Press, 2019), 5, and 108–10. Jiang Tao presents a critical examination on the existing interpretative frameworks in *Contexts and Dialogue: Yogacara Buddhism and Modern Psychology on the Subliminal Mind* (Hawaii: University of Hawaii Press, 2006).

53. Liang Qichao, "Jinshi diyi dazhe Kangde," in *XMCB* 25 (1093): 20.

54. Liang, "Jinshi diyi dazhe Kangde zhu xueshuo," 20.

55. For Liang's summary and personal discussion of "practice reason," see his "Jinshi diyi dazhe Kangde," in *XMCB* 25 (1093): 17–24.

56. Liang, "Jinshi diyi dazhe Kangde," *XMCB* 25 (1093): 21.

57. Liang, "Jinshi diyi dazhe Kangde," *XMCB* 25 (1093): 20.

58. Liang, "Jinshi diyi dazhe Kangde," *XMCB* 25 (1093): 21.

59. Max K. W. Huang (黃克武), "Liang Qichao yu Kangde" 梁啟超與康德 (Liang Qichao and Immanuel Kant), in *Bulletin of the Institute of Modern History Academia Sinica* 近代史研究所集刊 30 (December 1998): 101–48. For a clear and substantial critique on some contemporary Chinese historians' general misinterpretations of Kant, see Lee Ming-huei 李明輝, *Kangde zhexue zai dongya* 康德哲學在東亞 (Taipei: Taiwan National University Press, 2016), 11–80.

60. Immanuel Kant, *Critique of Pure Reason* (1781) (A 239).

61. Liang Qichao, "Jinshi diyi dazhe Kangde," in *XMCB* 28 (1903): 10.

62. Liang Qichao, "Jinshi diyi dazhe Kangde," in *XMCB* 46/47/48 (1904): 10.

63. Liang Qichao, "Jinshi diyi dazhe Kangde," in *XMCB* 46/47/48 (1904): 10.

64. For a concise comparison between Kantian-style deontology and the moral theory conceived by early neo-Confucian thinkers such as Cheng Yi 程頤 (1033–1107), see Ivanhoe, *Three Streams*, 62–63.

65. While most contemporary philosophers call *liangzhi* "the good moral knowing," JeeLoo Liu is careful to translate the term as a priori moral goodness. Her interpretation of Wang Yangming is under the clear influence of Mou Zongsan 牟宗三 (1909–1995), who shares a particular interest in juxtaposing the Ming philosopher's moral metaphysics with Kantian ethics in a comparative framework. For more details, see JeeLoo Liu's chapter "Wang Yangming's Intuitionist Model of Innate Moral Sense and Moral Reflexivism," in Liu, *Neo-Confucianism*, 245–64.

66. The group of modern philosophers Lederman refers to includes David Nivison, Philip Ivanhoe, Antonio Cua, and Stephen Angle. For Lederman's systematic summaries of, and disagreement with, this body of scholarship, see "Perception and Genuine Knowledge in Wang Yangming," in *Oxford Studies in Epistemology* 7 (2022): 134–75.

67. Lederman, "Perception and Genuine Knowledge," 135.

68. Harvey Lederman is certainly not the only one who holds such view. For a systematic endorsement on the mind's introspective function, see Lin Yueh-hui 林月惠, "Gengning dui Yangming houxue de quanshi yu pingjia" 耿寧對陽明後學的詮釋與評價 (Iso Kern's interpretation and evaluation on the moral teachings as explicated by students of Wang Yangming), in *Gengning xinxing xianxiangxue yanjiu wenji* 耿寧心性現象學研究文集 (Collected writings on Iso Kern's moral phenomenology), ed. Ni Liangkang 倪梁康 and Zhang Renzhi 張任之 (Beijing: Shangwu yanshuguan, 2020), 271–313.

69. Lederman, "Perception and Genuine Knowledge," 137.

70. Lederman, "Perception and Genuine Knowledge," 135–36.

71. See Liang Qichao, "Jinshi diyi dazhe Kangde," in *XMCB* 46 (1904): 57.

72. Liang, *DYJ*, 39.

73. For Liang Qichao's summary on the general social, historical background that anticipated the rise of Qing evidential research, see *Qingdai xueshu gailun*, 30–31; also see Benjamin Elman, *From Philosophy to Philology: Intellectual and Social Aspects of Change in Late Imperial China* (Cambridge, MA: Harvard University Asia Center, 1985).

74. Between 1902 and 1924, Liang Qichao was careful to retrieve, document, and acknowledge the protest early Qing intellectuals posted against neo-Confucianism in *Lun zhongguo xueshu sixiang bianqian zhi dashi* (1902–3), *Qingdai xueshi gailun* (1920), and *Zhongguo jin sanbainian xueshu shi* (1924).

75. Dai Zhen was one of the most gifted and prolific scholars of his times. Being impressed by his mastery command of mathematics, astrology, historical geography, etymology, and linguistics, Qian Daxin cordially invited him to work

as a collaborator for one state-sponsored and one privately funded research project as Dai visited the capital in the nineteenth year of the realm of Emperor Qianlong (1754). Having accepted Qian Daxin's invitation, Dai Zhen first worked as an official compiler of *Siku quanshu* 四庫全書 (The complete library in four sections) sponsored by the state. In addition, he worked as a collaborator on *A Comprehensive Study of the Five Rites* (五禮通考), a private research project supervised by the Hanlin scholar Qin Huitian 秦蕙田 (1702–1764). For more details, see Yu Ying-Shih, "Tai Chen's Choice between Philosophy and Philology," *Asia major* 2, no. 1 (1989): 79–108.

76. Sela, *China's Philological Turn*, 105.

77. Liang Qichao, "Lun zhongguo xueshu sixiang bianqian zhi dashi," in *XMCB* 41 (1904): 35.

78. For Liang Qichao, these renowned Qing scholars include Qian Daxin, Wang Mingsheng 王鳴盛 (西莊) (1722–1797), Ji Yun 紀昀 (曉嵐) (1724–1805), and Lu Wenchao 盧文弨 (抱經) (1717–96). See Liang Qichao, *Dai Dongyuan zhexue*, 255.

79. Liang, "Dai Dongyuan zhexue," 255.

80. Liang, *DYJ*, 37.

81. Liang, *DYJ*, 37.

82. Zhu Xi's missive to Lü Zujian is titled "Da Lü Ziyue shu" 答呂子約書 (A letter response to Lü Ziyue). For Liang Qichao's reference to the letter, see *DYJ*, 37.

83. In addition to Lü Zujian, Zhu Xi used the word "fragmented" to describe his study to two other friends. To comment on the confession Zhu Xi made in "Yu He Shujing shu" 與何叔京書 (Correspondences with He Shujing), Liang Qichao said: "Some days later Zhu Xi said in self-reproach: I am aware that those former remarks I've made and actions that I've taken were responses to issues that most gentlemen feel anxious about. But as I looked back to places I consider shaky and wobbling, I have come to realize that what I had learned previously was hopelessly fragmented." 朱子他日自悔曰: 多識前言往行, 固君子所急, 近因返求未得箇安穩處, 卻始知別此未免支離. Then in his "Letter to Zhou Shijin" 與周叔謹書, Zhu Xi made a comparable remark: "In recent days I have become aware that my words were in many ways fragmented. Even sitting in meditation and making my own personal effort do not feel as deep and earnest as I have wished." 某近日亦覺向來說話有太支離處, 反身以求, 正坐自己用功亦未切耳. See Liang Qichao, *DYJ*, 39.

84. Liang Qichao, "Lun side," *XMCB* 39 (1903):13.

85. Liang, "Lun side," 14.

86. Liang, "Lun side," 14.

87. Liang, "Lun side," 14.

88. Liang, *DYJ*, 45.

89. Liang, "*Lun side*," XMCB 39 (1903): 13.
90. Liang, *DYJ*, 45.
91. Liang, *DYJ*, 10.
92. Liang, "Lun side," in XMCB 41 (1903): 9.
93. Liang, *DYJ*, 45.
94. Liang, *DYJ*, 10.
95. For Araki Kengo's 荒木見悟 insightful discussion on Zhu Xi's rejection of Buddhism and his refusal to tolerate the Buddhist claim on "the absence of goodness and evil" (無善無惡), see "Yijing yu lengranjing" 易經與楞嚴經 (Yijing and the Śūraṅgama Sūtra), trans. Yang Baiyi 楊白衣, in *Yijiuqiba nian foxue yanjiu lunwen ji* 一九七八年佛學研究論文集 (Taiwan: Foguang wenhua, 1978), 206–17.
96. For recent English scholarship on Zhu Xi's appropriation and misinterpretation of Buddhism, see *The Buddhist Roots of Zhu Xi's Philosophical Thought*, ed. John Makehem (New York: Oxford University Press, 2018).
97. Liang Qichao, "Jinshi diyi dazhe Kangde," in XMCB 26 (1903): 16–17.
98. Liang, "Jinshi diyi dazhe Kangde," in XMCB 26 (1093): 16–17.
99. Liang, "Jinshi diyi dazhe Kangde," in XMCB 26 (1903): 14–15.
100. Liang, "Jinshi diyi dazhe Kangde," in XMCB 26 (1903): 15.
101. Liang, "Jinshi diyi dazhe Kangde," in XMCB 26 (1903): 15. His original words read: 眾生之身，既落於俗諦，為物理定例所束縛，則其所循一定之軌道，固無不可測知者。
102. Liang, "Jinshi diyi dazhe Kangde," in XMCB 26 (1903): 14.
103. *Treatise on Awakening Mahāyāna Faith*, translated by John Jorgensen, Dan Lusthaus, and John Makeham (New York: Oxford University Press, 2019), 69.
104. *Treatise on Awakening Mahāyāna Faith*, 578a.
105. In *Treatise on Awakening Mahāyāna Faith*, Paramārtha says the following: 以一切心識之相皆是無明，無明之相不離覺性，非可壞非不可壞 (576c). Because all the characteristics of the mind and consciousnesses are ignorance and, since the characteristic of ignorance is not separate from the nature of awakening, the mind and consciousnesses are indestructible and destructible. This English comes from Jorgensen's, Lusthaus's, and Makeham's rendition of *Treatise on Awakening Mahāyāna Faith*, 62–63.
106. Liang Qichao, "Jinshi diyi dazhe Kangde," in XMCB 28 (1903): 12.
107. Besides incorporating Kantian ethics and moral epistemology endorsed by the Wang Yangming school of neo-Confucianism, Liang's definition of right was informed by the German political theorist Rudolf von Jhering (1818–1892). For more details, see Angel, *Human Rights in Chinese Thought: A Cross-Cultural Inquiry*, 140–61.
108. Liang Qichao, "Jinshi diyi dazhe Kangde," in XMCB 46/47/48 (1904): 55.

109. Liang, "Jinshi diyi dazhe Kangde," in XMCB 46/47/48 (1904): 56.
110. Liang Qichao, "Jinshi diyi dazhe Kangde," in XMCB 26 (1904): 17.
111. Liang Qichao, "Jinshi diyi dazhe Kangde," in XMCB 28 (1903): 12.
112. Liang, "Jinshi diyi dazhe Kangde," in SMCB 28 (1903): 10.
113. Liang Qichao, "Lun guojia sixiang" 論國家思想 (On national thinking), in XMCB 4 (1902): 1.
114. Liang Qichao, "Lun side," in XMCB 39 (1903): 3.
115. Liang, "Lun side," 3.

Chapter 2

1. Liang Qichao, "Jinshi wenming chuzhu er dajia zhi xue" 近世文明初祖二大家之學 (The theories of two great precursors of modern civilization), in XMCB 2 (1902): 19.
2. Liang Qichao, *DYJ*, 41–42 and 52.
3. Liang Qichao, "Lun zhongguo xueshu sixiang bianqian zhi da shi," in XMCB 3 (1902): 41–56; XMCB 5 (1902): 57–80; XMCB 12 (1902): 39–56.
4. Liang, "Lun zhongguo xueshu sixiang," in XMCB 3 (1902): 44.
5. Liang, "Lun zhongguo xueshu sixiang," in XMCB 3 (1902): 44; also see Liang Qichao, "Lun gongde" 論公德 (On public morality), in XMCB 3 (1902): 7.
6. Liang, "Lun zhongguo xueshu sixiang," 44.
7. Liang, "Lun jiaoyu dangding zongzhi," 65.
8. Liang, "Lun jiaoyu dangding zongzhi," in XMCB 1 (1902): 65.
9. Liang, "Dili yu wenming zhi guanxi" 地理與文明之關係 (The relationship between geography and civilization), in XMCB 3 (1902): 49.
10. The term "empty word" (*kongyan*) appears frequently in the work of Luo Nianan 羅念菴 (1504–1564), a devoted student of Wang Yangming. Luo was strongly dissatisfied with the overintellectualism that dominates the intellectual practice during the Ming dynasty. In *Mirror for Moral Cultivation*, Liang asserted that his hope to combat the "empty words" was intended to continue Luo's unfinished intellectual endeavor. For a discussion on Luo's protest against the text-based approach to learning, see Chi Keung Chan 陳志強, "Acquiring Mere Knowledge and Empty Moralizing: Luo Nianan on the Faults of Confucian Practitioners" (知見空言──羅念菴論「學者」之過), *Chinese Studies* 漢學研究 34, no. 4 (2016): 99–130.
11. Liang Qichao, "Xinmin shuo yi: Diyijie: Sulun" 新民說一: 第一節·敘論, in XMCB 1 (1902): 3.
12. Liang Qichao, "Lun gongde," 1–7.
13. Liang, "Lun gongde," 6; emphasis added.
14. Liang Qichao, "Xinmin shuo yi: Xulun," 3.

15. In addition to Liang's "Lun gongde" also see his "Lun jiaoyu dangding zongzhi," in XMCB 1 (1902): 61–78, and XMCB 2 (1902): 21–28.

16. Liang Qichao, "Lun gongde,"1.

17. Liang Qichao, "Jinshi wenming chuzhu," in XMCB 2 (1902): 14.

18. In *Yige bei fangqi de xuanze: Liang Qichao tiaoshi sixiang zhi yanjiu* 一個被放棄的選擇: 梁啓超調適思想之研究 (The rejected path: A study of Liang Ch'i-ch'ao's accommodative thinking), Huang Ko-wu perceives Liang's *Discourse on the New Citizen* as a critique of the Chinese's public's intellectual slavishness, as well as their lack of public and private morality. For Huang's discussion, see *Yige bei fangqi de xuanze* (Taibei: Zhongyang yanjiuyuan jindaishi yanjiusuo, 1994), 44–60, 66–80, 93–106, and 114–15; Peter Zarrow also believes that Liang strongly emphasized the importance of cultivating the Chinese public's moral autonomy, for such quality is crucial in transforming the "people" into the "new citizen." See Peter Zarrow, "Citizenship in China and the West," in *Imagining the People: Chinese Intellectuals and the Concept of Citizenship, 1890–1920*, ed. Joshua Fogel and Peter Gue Zarrow (Armonk, NY: M. E. Sharpe, 1997), 17, and *After Empire: The Conceptual Transformation of the Chinese State, 1885–1924* (Stanford, CA: Stanford University Press, 2012), 80–81. In Philip Huang's view, Liang's *Discourse on the New Citizen* was "to advance new set of morals for the "new citizen" of a modern China" (65). See Philip Huang's *Liang Ch'i-Ch'ao and Modern Chinese Liberalism* (Seattle: University of Washington Press, 1972), 64–67. For Chang Hao, Liang's promotion of new morality was based on the keen awareness that "in the realm of social ethics and state ethics, traditional morality proved to be woefully inadequate" (154). See Chang's chapter "The New Citizen," in *Liang Ch'i-Ch'ao and Intellectual Transition in China, 1890–1907* (Cambridge, MA: Harvard University Press, 1971), 149–219.

19. Recently a considerable number of philosophers have tried to explicate the heartmind's epistemic configuration in Wang Yangming's moral philosophy. Their responses, according to Harvey Lederman's classification, can be divided into the "affective-perceptual model" and the "introspective model." Perceiving perfect moral knowing as an omniscient cosmic perspective, David Nivison, Philip Ivanhoe, Antonio Cua, and Stephen Angle follow the "affective-perceptual model" and regard what Wang Yangming calls *liangzhi* 良知 as a form of premeditated moral intuition that *latently informs* and *directs* people's embodied actions. Lederman rejects this acclaimed interpretation. *Liangzhi*, he argues, is neither a "form of 'seeing as,'" nor perceptual propensity, complemented by affect." Instead of the "mastermind" orchestrating, instructing, and overseeing virtuous actions, *liangzhi* is *introspective* "cognitive achievement" that occurs *simultaneously with* virtuous actions. For Harvey Lederman's discussion on Wang Yangming and his summary on relevant recent English scholarship, see "Perception and Genuine

Knowledge in Wang Yangming." The kind of view Lederman advocates has been systematically discussed by Mou Zongsan 牟宗三 (1909–1995), who shares particular interest in juxtaposing Wang Yangming's moral metaphysics with Kantian ethics in a comparative framework. For a brief and systematic summary on the mind's introspective function, see Lin Yueh-hui "Gengning dui Yangming houxue de quanshi yu pingjia," 271–313.

20. Philip Ivanhoe, *Ethics in the Confucian Tradition: The Thought of Mengzi and Wang Yangming* (Indianapolis, IN: Hackett, 2002), 22.

21. Qing philology and neo-Confucianism, according to Yu Ying-shih, are two intellectual/philosophical movements that appear "diametrically antithetical to each other." But having situated the rise of Qing philology in "the inner logic" that informed the development of neo-Confucianism, Yu contended that the rise of Qing philology was predicated on the pressing necessity of disentangling a philosophical conundrum failed to be resolved by contending schools of neo-Confucian thinkers. In "a new periodization of the whole neo-Confucian intellectual development," Yu sees the maturing of Qing philology as a response to the metaphysical controversies that occurred during the Ming dynasty. His argument can be summarized as follows: Before the eleventh century, early neo-Confucian thinkers believed that the moral way or substance (*ti* 體) should be put to practical political uses (*yong* 用). But soon Wang Anshi's sweeping political reform failed. Knowing that China had missed the opportunity to put conviction into practice, neo-Confucian thinkers turned inward to embark on a metaphysical search for moral meanings. Those who retreated to philosophical contemplation faced an immediate challenge: "What role would the Confucian literary tradition, especially the scriptural domain, play in this inner search for the substance of Dao?" (See Yu Ying-shih, "Some Preliminary Observations on the Rise of Qing Confucian Intellectualism," in *Chinese History and Culture: Seventeenth Century through Twentieth Century*, vol. 2 [New York: Columbia University Press, 2016], 20). Thinkers shared polarized views. Students of Zhu Xi, for instance, saw the scriptural tradition as a necessary intellectual prerequisite for the right kind of moral cultivation. Those associated with Wang Yangming, on the contrary, asserted that man's moral awakening consisted in an original discovery of his own mind. As contending thinkers failed to reach a general consensus, intellectuals of the Qing dynasty could break the philosophical deadlock only by seeking guidance from the early Confucian classics. For a more extensive treatment of this topic, see Yu Ying-shih's *Lun Dai Zhen yu Zhang Xuecheng* 論戴震與章學誠 (On Dai Zhen and Zhang Xuecheng) (Taipei: Sanmin shuju, 2016).

22. To my knowledge, no other scholars has been so bold to call early Qing philology a "perfection" of the Wang Yangming school of neo-Confucianism. But in the series of articles Professor Yu Ying-shih devoted to this topic, he discussed

a substantial number of Qing intellectuals (which included Fang Dongshu 方東樹, Chen Li 陳澧, Huang Yizhou 黃以周, Zhang Xuecheng 章學誠, Liu Zongzhou 劉宗周, Gong Zizhen 龔自珍, and Huang Zongxi 黃宗羲) who believed that "man's moral consciousness not only is inseparable from his intellectual nature but also depends on it for operation." For Yu Ying-shih's summaries of these underexamined intellectual positions, see his "Toward an Interpretation of the Intellectual Transition in Seventeenth Century China," in *Chinese History and Culture*, 1:355–74.

23. Liang Qichao, *Qingdai xueshu gailun*, 37.
24. Willard Peterson, "Confucian Learning in Late Ming Thought," 709–88.
25. Ori Sela, *China's Philological Turn*, 3. The original statement was made by the Qing philologist Ruan Yuan 阮元 (1764–1849) in *Rulin zhuan gao* 儒林傳稿 (Draft traditions of the forest of Ru).
26. Sela, *China's Philological Turn*, 5 and 16.
27. Liang Qichao, "Lun zhongguo xueshu sixiang," in XMCB 53 (1904): 53.
28. Liang, *Qingdai xueshu gailun*, 11.
29. Liang, *Qingdai xueshu gailun*, 11.
30. Liang Qichao, *Zhongguo jin sanbainian xueshu shi*, 64.
31. Liang, *Qingdai xueshu gailun*, 4.
32. Liang Qichao, "Jinshi diyi dazhe Kangde zhu xueshuo," in XMCB 25 (1903): 16–24.
33. Liang, *Qingdai xueshu gailun*, 3–50.
34. Liang, *Qingdai xueshu gailun*, 9–11.
35. Liang, *Qingdai xueshu gailun*, 10.
36. Liang, *DYJ*, 7.
37. Liang, *Qingdai xueshu gailun*, 12.
38. Liang, *Qingdai xueshu gailun*, 13.
39. Liang, *Qingdai xueshu gailun*, 14.
40. Liang, *Qingdai xueshu gailun*, 14.
41. Liang, *Qingdai xueshu gailun*, 13. For a select English translation of Gu Yanwu's book, see Ian Johnston's *Record of Daily Knowledge and Collected Poems and Essays* (New York: Columbia University Press, 2016).
42. In Gu Yanwu's preface to *Record of Daily Knowledge and Collected Poems and Essays*, he once declared, "Since I pursued my study in a young age, once I obtained certain understanding, I would jot down my note" (愚自少讀書, 有所得輒記之). Later Gu's student Pan Lei 潘耒 (1646–1708) made comparable observation in his editor's preface: once enlightened by his archeological study, immediately Gu recorded his words. Later these notes were assembled into a book.
43. Liang, *Qingdai xueshu gailun*, 13.
44. Liang, *Zhongguo jin sanbainian*, 67.
45. Liang, *Qingdai xueshu gailun*, 14.
46. Liang, *Qingdai xueshu gailun*, 14.

47. In my summary of Liang's introduction to Bacon and Descartes, I take the liberty of translating *zhihui* 智慧 and *yishi* 意識 as "reason" and "introspection." My rendition of these terms is not a personal invention; it is informed by a subsequent analogy Liang drew between Yogācāra Buddhism and the epistemology of Kant. When a person encounters a physical object with his five consciousnesses, the person, as Liang explicated in his long essay on Kant, needs to rely on his sixth consciousness, which is "introspection" (Chinese: 意識; Sanskrit: *manovijñāna*), to draw a meaningful connection between one's a priori intuition and the object he experiences. Operating under the a priori framework of time and space, the sixth consciousness is instinctively capable of "connecting" (聯結) and "synthesizing all perceptual elements in rational sequence" (綜合一切序次), "so that the logical order does not suffer from disarray" (使有先後而不相離). What practitioners of Yogācāra Buddhism call "introspection," as Liang believed, is what Kant means by "reason" (智慧), a cognitive faculty that is programmed to unify the disparate sensual information a person collects through the five consciousness into a coherent, unified, and systematic entity. For more details, see Liang Qichao, "Jinshi diyi dazhe Kangde," in XMCB 25 (1903): 16–21.

48. Liang, *Qingdai xueshu*, 18.
49. Liang Qichao, "Jinshi wenming chuzhu," XMCB 2 (1902): 10.
50. Liang, "Jinshi wenming chuzhu," XMCB 2 (1902): 10.
51. Liang, "Jinshi wenming chuzhu," XMCB 2 (1902): 11.
52. Liang Qichao, "Jinshi wenming chuzhu," in XMCB 1 (1902): 13–15.
53. Liang, "Jinshi wenming chuzhu," XMCB 2 (1902): 10 and 11.
54. Liang, "Jinshi wenming chuzhu," XMCB 2 (1902): 11.
55. Liang, "Jinshi wenming chuzhu," XMCB 2 (1902): 11.
56. For Liang's summary and personal discussion of "practice reason," see his "Jinshi diyi dazhe Kangde," in XMCB 25 (1093): 17–24.
57. Liang Qichao, *Zhongguo jin sanbainian xueshu shi*, 14. (His original words read: 用來做新政治建設的準備.)
58. Liang, *Qingdai xueshu gailun*, 16.
59. Liang, *Qingdai xueshu gailun*, 16. (His original words read: 心目中恆視為神聖不可侵犯.)
60. Liang, *Qingdai xueshu gailun*, 16.
61. Liang Qichao, "Jinshi diyi dazhe kangde zhi xueshuo," in XMCB 46/47/48 (1904): 57.
62. Liang Qichao, "Lun zhongguo xueshu sixiang," in XMCB 53 (1904): 46.
63. Liang, "Lun zhongguo xueshu sixiang," 46–48.
64. Liang, "Lun zhongguo xueshu sixiang," 57.
65. Liang, *Zhongguo sanbainian zhi xueshu sixiang shi*, 14.
66. Liang Qichao, "Lun zhongguo xueshu sixiang," in XMCB 53 (1904): 47.
67. Liang, *Zhongguo sanbainian zhi xueshu sixiang shi*, 13.

68. See Dai Zhen 戴震, *Dai Dongyuan ji* 戴東原集 (Collected work of Dai Dongyuan), vol. 1, *juan* 8 (Shanghai: Shangyu yinshuguan, 1929), 17–25. Besides making this remark in his personal letter, Dai Zhen repeated this statement as many as three times in *Mengzi ziyi shuzheng* 孟子字義疏證 (An evidential study of the meaning of terms of the Mengzi).

69. Philip Ivanhoe, *Confucian Moral Self Cultivation*, 2nd ed. (Indianapolis, IN: Hackett, 2000), 89.

70. Yu Ying-Shih, "Tai Chen's Choice between Philosophy and Philology," *Asia Major* 2, no. 1 (1989): 79–108.

71. Sela, *China's Philological Turn*, 105.

72. Sela, *China's Philological Turn*, 37.

73. Liang, *Qingdai xueshu gailun*, 5.

74. Liang, *Qingdai xueshu gailun*, 48.

75. Sela, *China's Philological Turn*, 6.

76. Sela, *China's Philological Turn*, 97.

77. Sela, *China's Philological Turn*, 3, 6.

78. Peter Bol argues that for individuals who pursued Daoxue, *yili* the moral principle is innate so that the real test (and the function of the classics) rests in one's ability to understand the mind of the sages and their rationale for conveying particular messages in the classics. For Bol's discussion on the role of learning between the seventh to the twelfth centuries, see *"This Culture of Ours": Intellectual Transitions in T'ang and Sung China* (Stanford, CA: Stanford University Press, 1994).

79. Sela, *China's Philological Turn*, 7.

80. Liang Qichao, "Jinshi diyi dazhe Kangde," in XMCB 25 (1903): 21. In his preface to the second edition of *The Critique of Pure Reason* (1787), Kant compares himself to Nicolaus Copernicus (1473–1543), the Renaissance polymath, and announces a Copernican revolution in philosophy.

81. Liang, *Qingdai xueshu gailun*, 38.

82. Liang, *Qingdai xueshu gailun*, 37.

83. Liang, *Qingdai xueshu gailun*, 40.

84. Liang, *Qingdai xueshu gailun*, 39.

85. Liang, *Qingdai xueshu gailun*, 38.

86. Of the men of extensive learning and powerful memory, Dai Zhen was referring specifically to Zheng Qiao 鄭樵 (1108–1166), the Song historian, and Yang Shen 楊慎 (1488–1529), the celebrated Ming scholar, poet, and literary historian. See Liang Qichao, *Qingdai xueshu gailun*, 41.

87. Liang, *Qingdai xueshu gailun*, 37.

88. Liang, *Qingdai xueshu gailin*, 50. Also see Liang's "Dai Dongyuan zhexue," 249–51.

89. Liang, *Qingdai xueshu gailun*, 41.

90. Liang, *Qingdai xueshu gailun*, 56.

91. Liang, *Qingdai xueshu gailun*, 16.

92. Linag, *Qingdai xueshu gailun*, 17.
93. Liang, *Qingdai xueshu gailun*, 17.
94. Liang Qichao, "Jinsi wenming chuzu," XMCB 2 (1902): 19.
95. Besides arguing that understanding is existential, Heidegger emphasizes the role time plays in people's understanding. For Heidegger, a person's being is essentially temporal: their lived horizon includes past, present, and future, but they projects themself primarily toward the future. Understanding is the mode through which the "possibilities" and "potentialities" of one's life are disclosed to a person. "Understanding," for this reason, "bears an inner relationship to his temporality." For a brief summary of Heidegger's philosophical assumption, see Kurt Mueller-Vollmer's *Hermeneutics Reader: Texts of the German Tradition from the Enlightenment to the Present* (New York: Continuum, 1985), 34–35.
96. Liang Qichao, "Jinshi diyi dazhe Kangde," in XMCB 46/47/48 (1904): 56. For Bodin's classical definition of sovereignty, see chapter 8 and 10 of book 1 of *On Sovereignty: The Six Books of the Commonwealth* (New York: Cambridge University Press, 1992).
97. Liang, "Jinshi diyi dazhe Kangde," in XMCB 46/47/48 (1904): 56.
98. Liang Qichao, "Jinshi diyi dazhe Kangde," in XMCB 46/47/48 (1904): 60.
99. Liang, "Jinshi diyi dazhe Kangde," in XMCB 28 (1903): 10.
100. Liang, "Jinshi diyi dazhe Kangde," in XMCB 46/47/48 (1904): 56–57.
101. Liang, "Jinshi diyi dazhe Kangde," in XMCB 46/47/48 (1904): 60.
102. Liang, "Jinshi diyi dazhe Kangde," in XMCB 46/47/48 (1904): 60.
103. Liang Qichao, "Jinshi diyi dazhe Kangde," in XMCB 28 (1903): 12.
104. Immanuel Kant, *Groundwork of the Metaphysics of Morals* (Cambridge: Cambridge University Press, 2012), 4:439.
105. Liang Qichao, "Jinshi diyi dazhe Kangde," in XMCB 46/47/48 (1904): 59.
106. Liang, "Jinshi diyi dazhe Kangde," in XMCB 46/47/48 (1904): 59.
107. Liang, *DYJ*, 4, 7, 8, 13, 15, 18, and 43.
108. Liang Qichao, "Jinshi diyi dazhe Kangde," in XMCB 46/47/48 (1904): 59.
109. Liang, "Jinshi diyi dazhe Kangde," in XMCB 46/47/48 (1904): 59.
110. Kant, *Groundwork*, 4:394.
111. Liang Qichao, "Jinshi diyi dazhe Kangde zhi xueshuo," in XMCB 46/47/48 (1904): 56–58.

Chapter 3

1. Liang Qichao, "Zhongguo lishi shang geming zhi yanjiu" 中國歷史上革命之研究 (A study on the political revolutions in Chinese history), in XMCB 46/47/48 (1904): 115.

2. Liang, "Zhongguo lishi shang geming," 117.

3. For a comprehensive introduction to recent studies on Tan Sitong, see Luke Kwong's *T'an Ssu-T'ung, 1865–1898: Life and Thought of a Reformer* (Leiden: E. J. Brill, 1996), 1–12.

4. For a summary on Liang Qichao's support for the revolution before 1897, see Zhang Pengyuan's *Liang Qichao yu qingji geming* 梁啟超與清季革命 (Liang Qichao and the Qing revolution) (Shanghai: Sanlian shudian, 2013), 31–78. (The book was originally published by Zhongyang yanjiuyuan jindaishi yanjiusuo in 1982, in Taipei.)

5. For a detailed description of this piece of history, see Wong Young-Tsu's "Revisionism Reconsidered: Kang Youwei and the Reform Movement of 1898," *Journal of Asian Studies* 51, no. 3 (Aug. 1992), 513–44.

6. Liang Qichao, "Lun Eluosi xuwudang" 論俄羅斯虛無黨 (On the Russian nihilist movement), in XMCB, 41 (1903): 67.

7. Liang Qichao, "Zhongguo lishi shang geming," in XMCB 46/47/48 (1904): 115.

8. Liang Qichao, "Renxue xu" (仁學序) (Preface to Renxue), in *Renxue*, 仁學 (An exposition of benevolence), annotated by Tang Zhijun 湯志鈞 and Tang Renze 湯仁澤 (Taibei: Taiwan xuesheng shuju, 1998), 102.

9. While Confucius emphasized the importance of sacrificing one's life for higher moral principles, Mencius celebrates comparable virtues with another proverb known as "relinquishing one's body for righteousness" (捨身取義). For a study of the depiction of political suicide in the Chinese philosophical and historical tradition, see Ping-cheung Lo (羅秉祥), "Confucian Ethic of Death with Dignity and Its Contemporary Relevance," *Annual of the Society of Christian Ethics* 19 (1999): 313–33.

10. Tan Sitong's *Renxue* was first serialized in Shanghai's *Yadong shibao* 亞東時報 (East Asia Times) in 1899 in issues 5 (January 31, 1899) through 19 (February 28, 1899). Later Liang Qichao decided to republish the manuscript sporadically in *China Discussion* in the same year. Hazama Naoki believes that Liang's peculiar arrangement is informed by his immediate political and strategic calculation. For his sensitive and insightful discussion, see Hazama Naoki 狹間直樹, "Liang Qichao bixia de Tan Sitong: Guanyu renxue de kanxing yu liang zhuan 'Tan Sitong zhuan'" 梁啟超筆下的譚嗣同——關於《仁學》的刊行與梁撰《譚嗣同傳》 (Tan Sitong in Liang Qichao's account: On the publication of *On Benevolence* and Liang's composition of the "Biography of Tan Sitong"), in *Liang Qichao yu jin dai Zhongguo she hui wen hua* 梁啟超與近代中國社會文化 (Liang Qichao and Contemporary Chinese Society and Culture), ed. Li Xisuo 李喜所 (Tianjin: Tianjin guji chubanshe, 2005), 618–32. The article was translated by Jiang Haibo 蔣海波 and was first published in *Wen shi zhe* 文史哲 (Journal of Literature, History, and Philosophy) 280, no. 1 (2004): 30–35. For more info on *Renxue*'s publication background and discrepancies between different editions,

also see Tang Zhijun, "Renxue banben tanyuan" 仁學版本探源 (An exploration of *Renxue*'s editions), in Tan Siting, *Renxue*, 104–41.

11. Liang, "Renxue xu," 101–3.
12. Tan, *Renxue*, 6.
13. Tan Sitong, *Renxue*, 6.
14. *Mūlamadhyamakakārikā* is written originally in Sanskrit. The translation is based on my modification of Jay L. Garfield's rendition of the foundational Buddhist classic from Tibetan to English. See Jay Garfield's *The Fundamental Wisdom of the Middle Way* (New York: Oxford University Press, 1995), 2 and 100.
15. Kumārajīva's Chinese rendition of *Mūlamadhyamakakārikā* has been collected in *Taishō Tripiṭaka* (大正新脩大藏经), trans. Kumārajīva, vol. 30 (Tokyo: Taishō Shinshū Daizōkyō Kankōkai, 1988).
16. This example derives from China's homegrown Huayan Buddhism, which emphasizes the "interpenetrative" relationship that goes beyond the kind of "interdependence" emphasized by Mahāyāna Buddhism.
17. Liang Qichao, *Hunan shiwu xuetang yibian* 湖南時務學堂遺編 (Rediscovered pieces from the Hunan Academy of Current Affairs) (Changsha: Hunan daxue chubanshe, 2017), 285.
18. Kang identified the following instances to exemplify these early philosophers' endorsement for parliamentary governance: "Whether one is qualified as a ruler is predicated on the will and predilection of the people, not his procurement of royal ornaments symbolizing his supreme authority" (王不王，專視民之聚散向背名之，非謂其黃屋左纛，權威無上). "What is agreeable to the people constitutes the basic fundamentals" (孟子大義，云民為貴。但以民義為主). Since "those who prosper and instruct the people are the thrones, whereas those impair, mutilate the people the assailants" (其能養民、教民者，則為王。其殘民、賊民者，則為民賊), men should be the ones to decide on the ruler. The *Canon of Yao* (*Yaodian*) 堯典, according to Kang Youwei, is a book that celebrates democracy in an explicit fashion. The *Canon of Yao* said, "Having observed the rotation of night and day," Emperor Yao 堯 (c. 2356—2255 BC) "decided to dismiss his royal successor and resign from his reign" (惟堯典特發民主義). "Later he received the reverberating assent of four luminaries and the commendation of the people. In the ancestor hall devoted to the worship of King Wen, Yao shut four doors and had the Congress convened" (自欽若昊天後，即舍嗣而異位。或四岳共和，或師錫在下。格文祖而集明堂，闔四門以開議院). To inherit and substantiate the historical precedent Emperor Yao established, "Confucius," according to Kang Youwei, "invented election to institutionalize the practice" (選舉者，孔子之制也). "In the *Spring and Autumn Annals*, Confucius stipulated the reform and established the constitution. Thrones of later generation upheld his stipulations until the present" (春秋改制，即立憲法，後王奉之，以至於今). These statements derive chiefly from *Kangzi gaizhi gai*, *juan* 8, 9, and 12. Comparable remarks also appear in Kang Youwei, "Qing ding kai

yihui zhe" 請定開議會折 (A Memorial pleading for the commencement of the congress), in *Kang Youwei quanji* 康有爲全集 (Completed work of Kang Youwei), vol. 4, ed. Jian Yihua 姜義華 and Zhang Ronghua 張榮華 (Beijing: Zhongguo renmin daxue chubanshe, 2007), 424.

19. Huang Zhangjian interprets Kang Youwei's "reformist" career as a "revolutionary" scheme in disguise. He tends to view Kang in a negative light, and "impenetrable" is a description that appears often in his discussion. For more details, see Huang Zhangjian 黃彰健, *Wuxu bianfa shi yanjiu* 戊戌變法研究 (A study of the 1898 reform) (Taipei: Institute of Linguistics and History, Academia Sinica, 1970).

20. For a critical analysis of Kang Youwei's political and philosophical thinking, see Yu Wen, "The Search for the Chinese Way in a Modern World: From the Rise of Evidential Scholarship to the Birth of Chinese Identity." For uncertainties Kang shared for man's moral nature, see the section "Modifying the Inferior Man," in the current chapter.

21. For more details, see Feng Youlan, 馮友蘭, "Qingdai daoxue zhi jixu" 清代道學之繼續 (The continuation of neo-Confucian philosophy in the Qing Dynasty), in *Zhongguo zhexue shi* 中國哲學史 (History of Chinese Philosophy) (Taipei: Taiwan shangwu yinshuguan, 2015), 830–58. In his forthcoming monograph, On-Cho Ng also describes the reversal between *li* and *qi* as the rise of vitalism. This new metaphysical imagination was believed to be the source that anticipated the rise of key intellectual movements such as historicism, utilitarianism, and intellectualism during the Qing dynasty. For a preliminary overview of Ng's key arguments, see his "Qing Philosophy," in the *Stanford Encyclopedia of Philosophy*, April 16, 2019, https://plato.stanford.edu/entries/qing-philosophy/.

22. See Kang Youwei, *Kangzi neiwai pian* (Beijing: Zhonghua shuju, 1988), 29. For systematic discussions on philosophical synthesis that Kang drew upon and incorporated into his political reformism, see Kung-Chuan Hsiao, *A Modern China and a New World: K'Ang Yu-Wei, Reformer and Utopian, 1858–1927* (Seattle: University of Washington Press, 1975), 137–89.

23. Kang Youwei, *Kangzi neiwai pian*, 11. Kang's original words read: 智, 無形也, 見之於愛惡.

24. For Kang Youwei's reflection on the French Revolution, see his "Jincheng faguo geming ji xu" 進呈《法國革命記》序 (Presenting Preface to *The French Revolution*) in *Kang Youwei quanji*, 4:371–72.

25. Kang Youwei, "Shang Qingdi disi shu" 上清帝第四書 (The fourth memorials submitted to the Qing emperor), in *Kang Youwei quanji*, 2:82–88.

26. Kang Youwei, "Qing ding lixian kaihui zhe" 請定立憲開會折 (A memorial requesting to draft the constitution and inaugurate the Congress), in *Kang Youwei quanji*, 4:424 and 426.

27. Kang, "Qing ding lixian kaihui zhe," 424 and 426. Also see Kang Youwei, "Shang Qingdi diliu shu" 上清帝第六書 (The sixth memorials submitted to the Qing emperor), in *Kang Youwei quanji*, 4:18.

28. Kang Youwei, "Wei liding guanzhi qing fenbie guanchai yi xing xinzheng" 為厘定官制請分別官差以行新政, in *Kang Youwei quanji*, 4:391.

29. Hsiao, *Modern China and a New World*, 267.

30. Kang Youwei, "Bianfa xianhou you xu qi su fen qian duan yi jiu jianwei zhe" 變法先後有序乞速奮乾斷以救艱危折, in *Kang Youwei quanji*, 4:86.

31. Kang, "Bianfa xianhou you xu," 86; also see his "Qing junmin he zhi manhan bufen zhe" 請君民合治滿漢不分折, in *Kang Youwei quanji*, 4:426.

32. Kang Youwei, "Xian xuan cai yizheng xu min shangshu yanzheng zhe" 先選才議政許民上書言政折, in *Kang Youwei quanji*, 4:389.

33. Liang, *Wuxu zhengbian ji*, 20. Liang's words read: 南學會實隱寓眾議院之規模, 課吏堂實隱寓貴族院之規模, 新政局實隱寓中央政府之規模.

34. Kang Youwei, "Waixin weipo fenge rong zhi yi jishi fafen da shi chen gong kai zhidu xin zhengju zhe" 外釁危迫分割溶至宜及時發憤大誓臣工開制度新政局折, in *Kang Youwei quanji*, 4:15.

35. To inherit the modern parliamentary model created by the New Planning Board, all provinces, prefectures, and counties should be prepared to establish their local legislative councils to discuss and stipulate public policies. These local regional councils would be formed by members appointed by the state government as well as spokespersons representing the local gentry. For a general description of Kang's regional reformist plan, see his "Waixin weipo fenge," 15.

36. Tan, *Renxue*, 23. For the influence of Western science on the philosophy of Tan Sitong, see David Wright, "Tan Sitong and the Ether Reconsidered," in *Bulletin of the School of Oriental and African Studies* 57 (1994): 551–57.

37. Tan, *Renxue*, 23.

38. Tan, *Renxue*, 30.

39. As Cheng Hao says, "As for the constancy of heaven and earth, their mind covers myriad things so that they have no mind; as for the constancy of the sages, their emotions follow myriad affairs so that they have no emotion. . . . That's why the sages' joy and anger are not tied to their hearts but to things" 天地之常, 心普物而無心, 此是天地之定. 二者, 聖人之常, 情順物而無情, 此是聖人之定 (程頤 <定性書>). Also see Ling Hon Lam, *The Spatiality of Emotion in Early Modern China* (New York: Columbia University Press, 2019), 62.

40. For Graham Priest's question to Ivanhoe, see "On Ivanhoe on Oneness," *Philosophy and Phenomenological Research* 99, no. 2 (Sept. 2019): 496; for Ivanhoe's reply to Priest, see "Replies," *Philosophy and Phenomenological Research* 99, no. 2 (Sept. 2019): 514–17.

41. Philip Ivanhoe devotes a book monograph to elaborate on this concept. See *Oneness: East Asian Conceptions of Virtue, Happiness, and How We Are All Connected*, 22. For more discussions on this topic, also see the collected volume Philip Ivanhoe, Victoria S. Harrison, Hagop Sarkissian, and Eric Schwitzgebel, *The Oneness Hypothesis: Beyond the Boundary of Self* (New York: Columbia University Press, 2018).

42. In modern Chinese vocabularies, there are terms such as *tihui* 體會 (to understand experientially), *titie* 體貼 (to be considerate), *tiyan* 體驗 (to experience) and *tiliang* 體諒 (to forgive, in the sense of understanding the offender's predicament). The usage of the word *ti* (體 body), as Brook Ziporyn aptly observes, refers precisely to the capacity for *a reversal of position*. See Ziporyn, *Ironies of Oneness and Differences: Coherence in Early Chinese Thought; Prolegomena to the Study of Li* 理 (New York: State University of New York Press, 2013), 151 and 361.

43. Tan, *Renxue*, 17.

44. Tan, *Renxue*, 17.

45. Toward the end of the nineteenth century, the expansion of Western imperialism was about to reach its apex. To consolidate white supremacy and justify the legitimacy of colonial expansion, colonizers from the West readily began to rate and classify discrete human races based on convoluted arguments and self-serving measurements of the size of their skulls and other shared physiological features. Drawing evidence from anthropology, anthropometry, and craniometry, these accounts asserted that the white people were designed and destined to subjugate the yellow, the brown, and the black.

Having appointed himself Kangzi 康子, the modern Confucian Sage, Kang was determined to guide humanity in realizing the Great Unity or state of global universalism in the contemporary context. In the hope of reviving New Text Confucianism and implementing the utopian oneness Confucius projected in the *Spring and Autumn Annals*, he was led to call for genetic modification and a series of radical sociopolitical reform. In his modern adaptation of *The Great Unity* (*Datong shu* 大同書), Kang proposes a systematic set of measures to eradicate racial, political, class, and gender hierarchy that had persisted to divide this world. Considering the brown and the black the most inferior races, Kang first wanted them to go extinct. Then, to remove physical differences between the yellow and white races, Kang expected the yellow to intermarry with the white and change their diet (eating beef, for instance, should give one a healthy, rosy complexion, while moving away from tropical zones can lighten their skin color). Once people become biologically and genetically identical, the barrier that divided the nations would naturally be dismantled. In the world of "political and racial oneness," people should proceed to dismantle the remaining class and gender hierarchies. By abandoning private property, abolishing the practice of marriage, and entrusting one's children to public nurseries, people ultimately would become one race, one family, and one country.

In *The Great Unity*, Kang Youwei classifies the world population into four races: white, yellow, brown, and black. The white are the most superior, and the black the least. While the Chinese are just as fine as the white, their yellowish skin complexion puts them in an embarrassing ranking. To make the Chinese as unambiguously superior as the white, Kang envisioned a number of racial modification proposals. While his proposals sound unabashedly racist to modern readers, Kang presented them for a reason. The racial classification system arrived in China in as early as the mid-1850s through the translation of works on medical science, anatomy, geography, and ethnography. Fearing that the physiologically based racial classification system would offend the Chinese public, missionaries such as Benjamin Hobson (1816–1873) deliberately tried to make the yellow race's biological features ambiguously similar to those of the white race. Leading Chinese intellectuals of the times were well informed of the racial hierarchy foreign researchers established among the white, yellow, brown, and black. And yet, they did not try to engage in the conversation nor make attempts to challenge these pseudoscientific premises. Being convinced that China was located in the center of the universe and that the Chinese people were the offspring of the Yellow Emperor, they dismissed the Western racial discourse as "non-sense" and "irrelevant." Kang Youwei was arguably one of the first late Qing intellectuals who sought to respond to the challenge to the West and to engage in a cross-cultural dialogues.

To ensure the yellow race's superiority, Kang was careful to take advantage of the gray areas that appeared in anatomy textbooks Benjamin Hobson compiled in the 1860s. He, for instance, tried to "fill in the blank" by placing the yellow race on an equal footing with the white and enthusiastically declared that the two would eventually "assimilate, dominate, or eliminate the Indian and the black."

Although Kang succeeded in exploiting those graphic and illustrative ambiguities to his advantage, his creative attempt ran the immediate risk of generating the opposite outcomes. His genetic modification project, most obviously, confirms the assumption that racial hierarchy should be determined by biological attributes (especially skin color) instead of one's familiarity with the Chinese culture, civilization, or other factors that appeared favorable to the Chinese. Based on the Western classification criterion, a younger generation of Chinese intellectuals soon expanded the racial hierarchy to include China's cultural and ideological shortcomings. For more details, see Kang Youwei, *Datong shu* 大同書 (The Great Unity), and Liang Zhan's 梁展 "Kang Youwei de weilai zhongguo" 康有為的未來中國 (Kang Youwei's futuristic China), *Zhonghua dushubao* 中华读书报, 15th ed. (China Reading Weekly) (May 20, 2015).

46. Tan Sitong, "Shang Ouyang Zhonggu shu," in *Tan Sitong quanji* 譚嗣同全集 (The complete collection of Tan Sitong), edited by Cai Shangsi and Fang Xing (Beijing: Sanlian shudian, 1954), 374.

47. Tan, "Shang Ouyang Zhonggu shu," 374.

48. Tan, "Shang Ouyang Zhonggu shu," 372.

49. The political transition between Wang and Liang does not happen right away. It is mediated through the work of Wang Fuzhi 王夫之 and Huang Zongxi 黄宗羲. For the subversive political potential concealed in Wang Yangming's moral philosophy, see Araki Kengo 荒木見悟, *Bukkyō to Jukyō: Chūgoku Shisō wo keiseisuru mono* 仏教と儒教中国思想を形成するもの (Confucianism and Buddhism: The formation of Chinese thought) (Kyōto, Heirakuji Shoten Shōwa 38 [1963]); and Philip Ivanhoe, *Ethics in the Confucian Tradition*. For the lingering political influence of Wang Yangming's moral philosophy, see Yu Ying-shih, 余英時, *Songminglixue yu zhengzhi wenhua* 宋明理學與政治文化 (Neo-Confucianism and political culture) (Taipei: Yongchen congkan, 2004).

50. See Ivanhoe et al., *Oneness Hypothesis*.

51. "Metaphysical Republic" is a term coined by Kim Youngmin. For his discussion and elaboration of this concept, see the "The Metaphysical Republic," in *A History of Chinese Political Thought* (Beijing: Polity Press, 2017), 114–36.

52. The passage is translated by Chan Sin Wai in his English rendition of *An Exposition of Benevolence* (Hong Kong: The Chinese University Press, 1984), 218 (emphasis added). To call attention to Tan's reference to Wang Yangming's formulation of the concept 真知 (*zhenzhi*), I have replaced Chan's translation of "truly knowing" with "genuine knowing."

53. In the existing English scholarship, Harvey Lederman is the only one who tries to analyze the concept "genuine knowing" in careful and systematic detail. For Lederman's articles on "genuine knowing," see "Perception and Genuine Knowledge in Wang Yangming," in *Oxford Studies in Epistemology* 7 (2022): 134–75, and "The Introspective Model of the Unity of Knowledge and Action," *Philosophical Review* 131 no. 2 (2022): 169–213. For Tan's own words, see Tan, *Renxue*, 96–97.

54. While Harvey Lederman explicates "genuine knowing" from the perspective of analytical philosophy, I try to reconstruct Wang Yangming's invention of the concept by retrieving underexamined hints that appear in his personal letters and philosophical writing. For a technical clarification, see a chapter section titled "Evil as Hesitation to Be True to Oneself" in chapter 5 of this volume.

55. For an elaborate, and often enlightening, interpretation of this concept, see Peter Hershock, *Liberating Intimacy: Enlightenment and Social Virtuosity in Ch'an Buddhism* (New York: State University of New York Press, 1996).

56. Peter Hershock, *Chan Buddhism* (Honolulu: University of Hawaii Press, 2004) 138.

57. The irreconcilable discrepancy between the heartmind and the cosmic pattern has been most critically elaborated by Zhu Xi's follower Chen Baisha 陳白沙 (1428–1500). For an insightful summary of Chen Baisha's metaphysical position, see Araki Kengo 荒木見悟, "Chen Baisha yu Zhan Ganquan."

58. Translated by Steven Miles, in Xinzhong Yao edited, *Routledge Encyclopedia of Confucianism*, vol. 2 (New York: Routledge, 2003), 486.
59. See Willard Peterson, "Confucian Learning in Late Ming Thought," 709–88.
60. Stephen Miles translated *siju jiao* as the "Four Dicta," while Justin Tiwald and Stephen Angel rendered it as "Doctrine in Four Axioms":

> In the inherent reality of heartmind, there is no distinction between good and bad;
> When intentions are activated, there is distinction between good and bad;
> Good knowing is that which knows good and bad;
> Getting a handle on things does good and removes bad.

Tiwald and Angle perceive the emphasis Wang placed on *"wu"* (absent of) a remark to deny "that there are rules of right and wrong action that apply across all contexts." For their interpretation and translation, see *Neo-Confucianism: A Philosophical Introduction* (Cambridge: Polity, 2017), 60–61.

61. See Zhong Lun 中論, *Mulamadhyamakakarika*, in *Taisho shinshu Daizokyo* 大正新脩大藏經, edited by Takakusu Junjiro (Tokyo: Taishō Shinshū Daizōkyō Kankōkai, 1988), 30:24. For a clear, precise, and illumination explication of *catuṣkoṭi*, see Graham Priest, *The Fifth Corner of Four: An Essay on Buddhist Metaphysics and the Catuskoti* (New York: Oxford University Press, 2019).

62. For the ways *catuṣkoṭi* can be employed as a "pedagogical device," see Richard H. Robinson, *Early Madhyamika in India and China* (Madison: University of Wisconsin Press, 1967), 56; and for the dialectical of function of the four-cornered doctrine, see R. D. Gunaratne, "Understanding Nāgārjuna's Catuṣkoṭi," *Philosophy East and West* 36, no. 3 (1986): 213–34.

63. See Gunaratne, "Understanding Nāgārjuna's Catuṣkoṭi," 213–34.

64. My general summary is based on Vasubandu's commentary on the *Abhidharmas*. His own words appear in *Commentary on the Treasury of Abhidharma* (*Abhidharmakośa-Bhāṣya*). See Vasubandhu, *Abhidharmakośa-Bhāṣya of Vasubandhu: The Treasury of the Abhidharma and Its (Auto) Commentary*, vol. 3, trans. De La Vallée Poussin and Lodrö Sangpo (Delhi: Motilal Banarsidass, 2012), 1891–92.

65. Frits Staal and Richard Robinson believe that Nāgārjuna had rejected all four positions. But having situated Nāgārjuna's argument in his debate with Theravada Buddhism, R. D. Gunaratne focuses on explicating Nagarjuna's refutation of the third position. For Frits Staal's study on *catuṣkoṭi*, see *Exploring Mysticism: A Methodological Essay* (Berkeley: University of California Press, 1975), 41.

66. Jay Garfield, "The Heart of Wisdom Sūtra Bhagavatī-Prajñāpāramitā-Hṛdaya-Sūtra," accessed December 24, 2023, https://jaygarfield.files.wordpress.com/2016/08/the-heart-of-wisdom-succ84tra-with-commentary.pdf.

67. For a brief introduction on the historical spread of Buddhism into China, differences between Indian and Chinese Buddhism, and the early developments in Chinese Buddhism, see Peter Hershock's *Chan Buddhism*, 29–65.

68. For Chan Wing Tsit's exclusion of Buddhist influences in Wang Yangming's moral philosophy, see his "How Buddhistic Is Wang Yang-ming?" in *Philosophy East and West*, 12, no. 3 (Oct. 1962): 203–15. For the subtle yet radical and substantial disagreements Professor Liu Ts'un-Yan 柳存仁 expresses for Chan's position, see his "Wang Yangming yu fodao erjiao" 王陽明與佛道二教 (Wang Yangming's association with Buddhism and Daoism), in *Tsing Hua Journal of Chinese Studies* 清華學報 13, no. 1 (Dec. 1981): 27–52.

69. In the history of neo-Confucianism, Wang Yangming was certainly not the first to emphasize the connection between the heartmind and the cosmic pattern. Both Cheng Hao and Cheng Yi (程頤), as A. C. Graham has noted, made comparable remarks. Besides that, even Zhu Xi himself mentioned in *Yulei* 18 that "the heartmind is cosmic pattern; the cosmic pattern is the heartmind" (心即理; 理即心). Instead of reiterating the superficial and familiar equivalence Wang Yangming establishes between the heartmind and the cosmic pattern, my goal is to explicate how the Ming philosopher had attempted to infuse the Buddhist notion of "emptiness" into the existing neo-Confucian debates on the nature and the function of the heartmind.

70. Zhu Xi, *Zhu zi yulei* 18.

71. Wang Yangming, 傳習錄 (Instructions for practical living), in *Wang Yangming quanji*, volume 2, 6.3–4.

72. Of the various English explications on the meaning on *xing* 行 (spontaneous actions or responses), I find the entry in Youngming Kim's encyclopedic entry illuminating and clear. See "Wang Yangming (1472—1529)," in *Internet Encyclopedia of Philosophy*, accessed December 23, 2023, https://iep.utm.edu/wangyang/.

73. This is an expression I borrow from Thomas Metzger's discussion on the relationship between the metaphysical and the experiential in neo-Confucianism. See Metzger's *Escape from Predicament*, 85.

74. For the role Chen Baozhen play in the 1898 reform, see Stephen R. Platt, *Provincial Patriots: The Hunanese and Modern China* (Cambridge, MA: Harvard University Press, 2007), 63–93.

75. Platt, *Provincial Patriots*, 63–93.

76. For concerns Kang Youwei expressed, see his "Shang qingdi diwu shu" 上清帝第五書 (The fifth memorial to the Qing Emperor), in *Kang Youwei Quanji*, 2; also see Kang's "Baoguo hui xu" 保國會序 (Introduction to the National Preservation Society), in *Kang Youwei quanji*, 4:52. For difficulties Kang encountered

in the process of delivering of his memorial, see Kang Youwei, *Kang Nanhai zibian nianpu* 康南海自編年譜 (Kang Youwei's self-compiled autobiography) (Beijing: Zhonghua shuju, 1992), 28.

77. Liang Qichao, "Shang Chen Baozhen shu lun Hunan yangban zhi shi" 上陳寶箴書論湖南應辦之事 (A letter to Chen Baozhen discussing policies that need to be implemented in Hunan), in *Wuxu bianfa ziliao* 戊戌變法資料 (Materials on the 1898 Reform), vol. 2, comp. Zhongguo shi xuehui 中國史學會 (Shanghai: Shanghai shudian chuban she, 1953), 550–58.

78. *Wuxu bianfa ziliao* 1:431; also see *Wuxu bianfa ziliao* 2:473 and 627.
79. Liang, "Shang Chen Baozhen shu," 533–34.
80. Liang, "Shang Chen Baozhen shu," 533–34.
81. Liang, "Shang Chen Baozhen shu," 534.
82. Liang, "Shang Chen Baozhen shu," 553, 554.
83. Liang, "Shang Chen Baozhen shu," 555.
84. Liang, "Shang Chen Baozhen shu," 554.
85. Liang, "Shang Chen Baozhen shu," 555.
86. Liang Qichao, *Wuxu zhenbian ji* 戊戌政變記 (Remembering the 1898 Reform) (Shanghai: Shanghai guji chubanshe, 2014), 20.
87. Liang, "Shang Chen Baozhen shu," 555.
88. Quoted from Huang Zhangjian, *Wuxu bianfa shi yanjiu*, 9–10.
89. Huang, *Wuxu bianfa shi yanjiu*, 360.
90. Huang, *Wuxu bianfa shi yanjiu*, 360.
91. Pi Xirui 皮錫瑞, *Jing xue lishi* 經學歷史 (Confucian history) (Shanghai: Shanghai shudian, 1996), and *Pi Xirui riji* 皮錫瑞日記 (The diary of Pi Xirui) (Beijing: Zhonghua shu ju, 2015).
92. Quoted from Huang, *Wuxu bianfa shi yanjiu*, 19.
93. In an article published in the *Chinese Progress*, Huang Zunxian wrote, "Among civilians who are clever and bright, they can nominate each other as legislative representatives and participate in the congress in Beijing. For state ministers bearing office titles above the third rank, they are automatically enlisted in the Senate. Positions of councilmen should also be created in state provinces, prefectures, and counties. . . . The new composition revamps the administrative structure of the central government" (使士民之明秀者，互相舉為議員，使至京入議院，而使中外大員自三品以上，俱入上議院；省府州縣，各設議員。... 改革中央政府組織). See Huang Zunxian, "Yiyuan minquan" 議院民權, in *Shiwu bao* 時務報 (Chinese Progress), August 1, 1897.
94. Wu xu bian fa dang an shi liao 戊戌變法檔案史料 (Archival documents for the 1898 reform), comp. Guojia danganju mingqing dangan guan 國家檔案局明清檔案館 (Beijing: Zhonghua shuju, 1958), 253.
95. Huang Zhangjian, *Wuxu bianfa shi yanjiu*, 347.
96. Huang Zhangjian, *Wuxu bianfa shi yanjiu*, 348.
97. Huang Zhangjian, *Wuxu bianfa shi yanjiu*, 18.

98. See *Hunan lishi ziliao* 湖南歷史資料, vol. 4 (Hunan historical documents), comp. Hunan lishi ziliao bianji weiyuanhui 湖南歷史資料編輯委員會 (Changsha, China: Hunan ren min chu ban she, 1959), 133. In this letter Tan wrote, "We seek your approval to found the Southern Learning Society in Hunan. With your endorsement and support, the foundation of the national congress is laid and the shape of Parliament is figuratively formed. . . . However drastic the changes and transformation would be, the sovereignty of the people would not perish and expire if we can zealously preserve the Congress" (湘省請立南學會。既蒙公優許矣，國會即是植基，而議院亦且隱寓焉。. . . 無論如何田天翻地覆。惟力保國會，則民權終無能盡失).

99. *Hunan lishi ziliao*, 59. Tan Sitong said, "我不速出而自任而誰任矣? 夫當速出而自任，寧止保衛一局，而保衛局乃一切政治之起點，而治地方之大權也。自州縣不事事，於是有保甲局之設，其治地方之權，反重於州縣官。今之所謂保衛，即昔之所謂保甲，特官權紳權之異焉耳。"

100. Pi Xirui, *Pi Xirui riji* (March 4, 1898): 昨見右帥，談至四鼓，右帥痛哭。其所上奏，皆為人所阻。

101. Pi Xirui, *Pi Xirui riji* (February 6, 1898): 夏觀察來拜 . . . 力請右帥練兵，厘金局每年可供十二萬金，為練二千人之用；開武備學堂。

102. Pi Xirui, *Pi Xirui riji*, 555 (February 6, 1898): 書籍圖器，定有講期，定有功課，長官時時臨X以鼓勵之 . . . 發明中國危亡之故，考政治之本原，講辦事之條理。

103. Liang Qichao, "Gu yiyuan kao" 古議院考 (A study of early parliaments), in *Yinbingshi heji* 飲冰室合集 (Collected volumes from Ice-Drinking Studio), 1:96.

104. Liang, "Shang Chen Baozhen shu," 553.

105. Liang, "Shang Chen Baozhen shu," 551.

106. Liang, "Shang Chen Baozhen shu," 551.

107. Liang Qichao, *Qingdai xueshu gailun*, 95.

108. For the modern syllabi and instructional structure Liang proposed for the new schools, see Liang Qichao, "Xuexiao zonglun" 學校總論 (Synopsis on school), "Lun shifan" 論師範 (On teacher's eduction), "Lun nüxue" 論女學 (On women's education), "Lun youxue" 論幼學 (On children's education), and "Xuexiao yulun" 學校餘論 (More discussions on schools), in YBSWJ 1:14–20, 34–36, 37–43, 44–59, 60–63.

109. *Wuxu bianfa ziliao*, 1:431; also see *Wuxu bianfa ziliao*, 2:473 and 627.

110. *Wuxu bianfa ziliao*, 1:431.

111. Liang, "Shang Chen Baozhen Shu," 534.

112. In fact, the plan to elect Tan Siting as China's president was Kang Youwei's suggestion. For Kang's letter to Liang, see Ye Dehui 葉德輝, ed., *Juemi yaolu* 覺迷要錄 (Record of an awaken scholar) (Beijing: Beijing chubanshe, 2000), 4:18b.

113. While it is "philosophically" feasible to assert that Tan had demonstrated what it meant to have obtained genuine knowing is his voluntary execution, the exact reasons for his death are complex and personal. The

young martyr experienced serious psychological distress after the sudden loss of his mother and three siblings in an epidemic. Having suffered the abuse of his stepmother for years, there were signs that Tan had lost the will to live a worldly existence long before his obtainment of "genuine knowing." For Chang Hao's sensitive and often compassionate interpretation of Tan's death, see *Liang Qichao yu zhongguo sixiang de guodu, 1890–1907* 梁啟超與中國思想的過渡 1890–1907 (Liang Ch'i-ch'ao and intellectual transition in China, 1890–1907); *Lieshi jingshen yu pipan yishi: Tan Sitong sixiang de fenxi* 烈士精神與批評意識: 譚嗣同思想分析 (The spirit of the martyr and critical consciousness: An analysis of Tan Sitong), translated by Cui Zhihai 崔志海 and Ge Fuping 葛夫平 (Beijing: Xinxing chubanshe, 2006), 215–314.

114. For the guilt and psychological torment Liang experienced after Tan's death, see Hu Ying's "Naming the First 'New Woman,'" in *Rethinking the 1898 Reform Period: Political and Cultural Change in Late Qing China*, ed. Rebecca E. Karl and Peter Zarrow (Cambridge, MA: Harvard University Press, 2002), 181–211.

115. Liang Qichao, "Preface to *Renxue*," in Tan, *Renxue*, 101–2.

116. Liang Qichao, "Wang Yangming zhixing heyi zhi jiao" 王陽明知行合一之教 (Wang Yangming's Teaching on the Unity of Knowing and Being), in *Chuangxi lu jiping* 傳習錄集評 (Collected commentaries on Instructions for Practical Living) (Beijing: Jiuzhou chuban she, 2015), 6.

117. Liang, "Wang Yangming zhixing heyi," 18.

118. Liang, "Wang Yangming zhixing heyi," 16.

119. Liang, "Wang Yangming zhixing heyi," 27. Liang Qichao's words read: 良知並不是一成不變的, 實是跟着經驗來天天長進 (Perfect moral knowing is not stagnant and unchanged. Each day it progresses and grows along with one's experiences.)

120. Liang Qichao, *DYJ* 4. For Liang's additional protests of his contemporaries' intellectual inertia, also see *Deju jian*, 41–42 and 52.

121. For the significance of mirror in traditional Chinese thought, see Erin M. Cline, "Mirrors, Minds, and Metaphors, *Philosophy East and West* 58, no. 3 (2008): 337–57.

122. Liang Qichao, *Zhongguo zhi wushidao* 中國之武士道 (*China's Bushido Spirit*) (Shanghai: Guangzhi shuju, 1904), 9.

123. Liang, *Zhongguo zhi wushidao*, 9.

124. Liang, "Wang Yangming zhixing heyi zhi jiao," 111.

125. See Liang Qichao, "Yidali Jianguo sanjie zhuan" 意大利建國三傑傳 (The Biography of the Three Heroes Who Founded Italy), XMCB 10 (1902): 43–53.

126. Liang, "Yidali Jianguo sanjie zhuan" XMCB 10 (1902): 51.

127. Liang, "Yidali Jianguo sanjie zhuan" XMCB 14 (1902): 39.

128. Liang, "Yidali Jianguo sanjie zhuan" XMCB 14 (1902): 41.

129. Liang, "Yidali Jianguo sanjie zhuan" XMCB 22 (1902): 15.

130. See Thomas Metzger, "The Neo-Confucian Sense of Predicament," in *Escape from Predicament*, 49–165.

131. The "perfect" moral vision that Wang Yangming circulated can well be rhetorical. In fact the Ming philosopher was sharply awareness of the human darkness. For a recent and excellent study of the hidden pessimism of his moral philosophy, see Chi-keung Chan 陳志強's *Wangming Wangxue yuane lun* 晚明王學原惡論 (On the original sin in Wang Yangming's teaching in the late Ming period) (Taipei: Guoli Taiwan daxue chuban zhongxin, 2018). For a comparatively brief but insightful discussion on Wang Yangming's and his proceeding neo-Confucian thinkers' collective recognition of human evil, see Chang Hao's 張灝 "Youan yishi yu minzhu chuantong" 幽暗意識與民主傳統 (Consciousness of darkness and the democratic tradition) and "chaoyue yishi yu youan yishi" 超越意識與幽暗意識 (Consciousness of transcendence and consciousness of darkness) in *Youan yishi yu minzhu chuantong* 幽暗意識與民主傳統 (Consciousness of darkness and the democratic tradition) (Taipei: Lianjing chuban she, 1989), 3–78.

132. For the subversive political potential concealed in Wang Yangming's moral philosophy, see Araki Kengo, *Bukkyō to Jukyō*; and Yu Ying-shih, *Songminglixue yu zhengzhi wenhua*.

Chapter 4

1. Liang Qichao, "Xin zhongguo weilaiji" 新中國未來記, *Xin xiaoshuo* 新小說 (New fiction) (hereafter XXS) 1 (1902): 53.

2. Liang, "Xin zhongguo weilaiji," 2: 54.

3. Liang, "Xin zhongguo weilaiji," 2: 56.

4. Liang, "Xin zhongguo weilaiji," 2: 58. For very brief summaries on narrative features that vernacular Chinese fiction retains from the oral storytelling tradition, see John Bishop, "Some Limitations of Chinese Fiction," *Far Eastern Quarterly*, 15, no. 2 (Feb. 1956): 239–47; Vibeke Børdahl, "The Storyteller's Manner in Chinese Storytelling," *Asian Folklore Studies* 62 (2003): 1–48. For a recent study on the incorporation of features of "oral telling" into vernacular fiction, see Paize Keulemans, "Acts of Ventriloquism: Literati Appropriations of the Storyteller's voice," chap. 1 of *Sound Rising from the Paper: Nineteenth-Century Martial Arts Fiction and the Chinese Acoustic Imagination* (Cambridge, MA: Harvard University Asia Center, 2014), 33–64.

5. Liang, "Xin zhongguo weilaiji," 2: 58.

6. Liang, "Xin zhongguo weilaiji," 2: 58.

7. Liang Qichao, "Lun xiaoshuo yu qunzhi zhi guanxi" 論小說與群治之關係 (On the relationship between fiction and public governance), XXS 1(1902): 1–8. For Gek Nai Cheng's translation of the article, see Liang Qichao, "On the Relationship between Fiction and the Government of the People," in *Modern*

Chinese Literary Thought: Writings on Literature, 1893–1945, ed. Kirk Denton (Stanford, CA: Stanford University Press, 1996), 74–81. For Liang's remark, see "Lun xiaoshuo," 2.

8. Liang, "Lun xiaoshuo," 3.

9. In modern literary studies, many believe that Liang has helped to construct a "discourse" of utopic imagination in his creation of *The Future of New China*. Later this new discourse had proved instrumental in generating a new consciousness of the global space, exemplifying the modern nation-state building process, and assisting the general public in forming a new national identity. For more details, see Xiaobing Tang, *Global Space and the Nationalist Discourse of Modernity*; Chen Jianhua 陳建華, "Minzu 'xiangxiang' de moli: Chong du Liang Qichao 'Lun xiaoshuo yu qunzhi zhi guanxi'" 民族"想像"的魔力: 重讀梁啟超《論小說與群治之關係》 (The magical power of national "imagination": Rereading Liang Qichao's "On the Relationship between Fiction and People's Governance), in *Cong geming dao gonghe: Qingmo zhi Minguo shiqi wenxue, dianying yu wenhua de zhuanxing* 從革命到共和: 清末至民初時期文學、電影與文化的轉型 (From revolution to the republic: Literary, cinematic, and cultural transformations) (Guilin, China: Guangxi shifan daxue chubanshe, 2009), 65–84; Ban Wang, "Geopolitics, Moral Reform, and Poetic Internationalism: Liang Qichao's *The Future of New China*," *Frontiers of Literary Studies in China* 6, no. 1 (2012): 2–18; Guan Kean-Fung 顏健富, *Cong "shen ti" dao "shi jie": Wanqing xiaoshuo de xin gainian ditu* 從「身體」到「世界」——晚清小說的新概念地圖 (From the "body" to the "world": New conceptual maps in late Qing fiction) (Taibei: National Taiwan University Press, 2014), 15–58; Mei Chia-ling 梅家玲, "Faxiang shaonian, xiangxiang zhongguo: Liang Qichao 'Shaonian zhongguo shuo' de xiandai xing, qimeng lunshu yu guozu xiangxiang" 發現少年, 想像中國—梁啟超〈少年中國說〉的現代性、啟蒙論述與國族想像 ("Discovering youth" and "imagining China": Modernity, enlightenment discourse, and national imagination in Liang Qichao's "The Youth of China"), *Hanxue yanjiu* 漢學研究 (Chinese Studies) 19, no. 1 (June 2001): 249–75; Leung Shuk Man, "The Discursive Formation of the Utopian Imagination in New Fiction, 1902–1911" (PhD diss., SOAS, University of London, 2013). Many of the above titles' discussions on "discourse," "space," and "national communities" are informed by Michel Foucault's theory on discursive formation, Anderson Benedict's *Imagined Communities: Reflections on the Origin and Spread of Nationalism* (London: Verso, 1983), and Jürgen Habermas's *The Structural Transformation of the Public Sphere* (Cambridge, MA: MIT Press, 1989).

10. See Plato, "Book X," *The Republic* (London: Penguin Books, 2003), 335–353; emphasis added.

11. See Murray Krieger, *Ekphrasis: The Illusion of the Natural Sign* (Baltimore, MD: Johns Hopkins University Press, 1992), 6. Also see Roland Barthes' "The Reality Effect," in *French Literary Theory Today: A Reader*, ed. Tzvetan Todorov (Cambridge: Cambridge University Press, 1982), 11–17.

12. Derrida refers the logocentric desire to "the naive desire that leads us to prefer the immediacy of the picture to the mediation of the code in our search for a tangible, 'real' referent that would render the sign transparent." For more details on Derrida's discussion on "logocentrism," see the chapter "Linguistics and Grammatology" in *Of Grammatology* (Baltimore, MD: Johns Hopkins University Press, 1976), 29–73.

13. Liang, "Lun xiaoshuo," 8. The passage is translated by Gek Nai Cheng. See her translation "On the Relationship between Fiction and the Government of the People," in *Modern Chinese Literary Thought*, 81.

14. Anne Friedberg, "Introduction" to *The Virtual Window: From Alberti to Microsoft* (Cambridge, MA: MIT Press, 2006), 1–25.

15. Jill Bennett, "Aesthetics of Intermediality," *Art History*, 30, no. 3 (June 2007): 436.

16. Bennett, "Aesthetics of Intermediality," 6.

17. See Jay David Bolter, "Ekphrasis, Virtual Reality, and the Future of Writing," in *The Future of The Book*, ed. Geoffrey Nunberg (Berkeley: University of California Press, 1996), 253–72.

18. Bolter, "Ekphrasis," 269.

19. Bolter, "Ekphrasis," 265.

20. See Jay David Bolter and Richard Grusin, *Remediation: Understanding New Media* (Cambridge, MA: MIT Press, 1999).

21. Rather than focusing on these terms' Buddhist origins, C. T. Hsia provides a highly imaginative and vivid interpretation of their connotative meanings. Hsia says that "by 1902 he (Liang) has somewhat refined his understanding of fiction so that he is able to illustrate its power with four metaphors: fiction spreads a cloud of smoke or incense (*hsün*) around the reader so that his senses and power of judgment are conditioned by his reading; it immerses (*chin*) him in the situations and problems depicted in its pages so that even for days or weeks after the reading he is still seized by sorrow or anger or other appropriate emotion; it pricks (*tz'u*) him into an unusual state of excitement over scenes depicted with great power; lastly, it lifts (*t'i*) him to the level of the hero and motivates him to imitate him." See *C. T. Hsia on Chinese Literature*, 233–34. Unlike scholars who try to explain how these Buddhist terms characterize the ways the novel affects the individual mind, David Wang believes that their importance rests in emphasizing man's capacity in experiencing and generating intense emotions. Wang's words read, 這是在討論梁啟超的小說學時，最常提到的四字真言：薰、浸、刺、提。它的重要意義，在於強調情感本身所產生的強烈的、動人心魄的力量. See Wang Dewei 王德威, *Xian dangdai wenxue xinlun: Yili, lunli, dili* 現當代文學新論：義理・倫理・地理 (New perspectives on modern and contemporary literature: Morality, ethics, and geography) (Beijing: Shenghuo dushu, xinzhi sanlian shudian, 2014), 61. In the entry Wang contributed earlier to *The Cambridge History of Chinese Literature*, he interprets these four terms as

"methods that can disturb one's emotional equilibrium and thus lead one to a changed apprehension of the world." See David Der-wei Wang's "Reforming and Re-forming Literature: 1895–1919," in *The Cambridge History of Chinese Literature*, ed. Kang-i Sun Chang and Stephen Owen (Cambridge: Cambridge University Press, 2010), 443.

22. For brief discussions on the relationship between the Buddhist theory of cognition and the faith Liang invested in fiction's emotive power and "motivational function," see Theodore Huters, *Bringing the World Home: Appropriating the West in Late Qing and Early Republican China* (Honolulu: University of Hawai'i Press, 2005), 113–16; Chang Hao, *Liang Ch'i-Ch'ao*, 232–37; Milena Doleželová-Velingerová's introduction to *The Chinese Novel at the Turn of the Century* (Toronto: University of Toronto Press, 1980), 3–17; Marian Galikm, "On the Influence of Foreign Ideas on Chinese Literary Criticism (1898–1904)," *Asian and African Studies* (Bratislava) 2 (1966): 38–48; Mori Noriko, "Liang Qichao, Late Qing Buddhism, and Modern Japan," in *The Role of Japan in Liang Qichao's Introduction of Modern Western Civilization to China*, ed. Joshua A. Fogel (Berkeley, CA: Center for Chinese Studies, 2004), 223–46. For the general influence of Buddhism on Liang's reformism, see Chan Sin-wai, *Buddhism in Late Ch'ing Political Thought* (Hong Kong: Chinese University Press, 1985), 40–43.

23. See Theodore Huters's discussion on "The New Novel," in *Bringing the World Home*, 112–20. Also see Chang Hao's *Liang Ch'i-ich'ao*, 232–37.

24. Liang Qichao, "Zongjiao yu zhexue zhi changduan deshi" 宗教與哲學家之長短得失" (The strengths and shortcomings of religious thinkers and philosophers), in *XMCB* 19 (1902): 59–68.

25. Marianne Bastid-Bruguière conducts a meticulous study on Liang's use of the word "zongjiao" 宗教 (religion). She believes that before Liang went into political exile in Japan, he used to use *zongjiao* loosely to refer to a number of general concepts such as "teaching," "thinking," or "idea." But under the influence of the Japanese intellectual world, from 1901 onward Liang began to define the word straightly as the Western concept "religion," the faith one invests in the divine power or the transcendental. At the same time, Liang's familiarity with "religion" also helps to clarify his definition of *zhexue* 哲學 (philosophy). See Marianne Bastid-Bruguière, "Liang Qichao yu zongjiao wenji" 梁啓超與宗教問題 (Liang Qichao and the question of Religion), *Toho Gakuho* 東方學報 (Journal of Oriental Studies, Kyoto) 70 (1998): 329–73.

26. Liang, "Zongjiao yu zhexue," 61.

27. For the key words Liang uses to describe philosophy in "Zongjiao yu zhexue," scholarly knowledge (*xuewen*) appears on page 61, academic study (*xueshu*) on page 66, and theoretical thinking (*xueshuo*) and the theory of science (*gezhi xueshi*) on page 64.

28. Liang, "Zongjiao yu zhexue," 65.

29. Liang, "Zongjiao yu zhexue," 64.

30. Liang, "Zongjiao yu zhexue," 64.
31. Liang, "Zongjiao yu zhexue," 64.
32. For Benjamin Schwartz's landmark studies on Yan Fu's translation of Adam Smith, see *In Search of Wealth and Power: Yen Fu and the West Benjamin Schwartz* (Cambridge, MA: Belknap Press of Harvard University Press, 1964).
33. Liang, "Zongjiao yu zhexue," 64.
34. Liang, "Zongjiao yu zhexue," 64.
35. Liang, "Zongjiao yu zhexue," 64.
36. For studies on the importation of foreign social, scientific, and medical knowledge to late Qing China, some important references include Benjamin A. Elman, *On Their Own Terms: Science in China, 1550–1900* (Cambridge, MA: Harvard University Press, 2005); David Wright, *Translating Science: The Transmission of Western Chemistry into Late Imperial China, 1840–1900* (Leiden: Brill, 2000); Michael Lackner and Natasha Vittinghoff, *Mapping Meanings: The Field of New Learning in Late Qing China* (Leiden: Brill, 2004); Michael Lackner, Iwo Amelung, and Joachim Kurtz, eds., *New Terms for New Ideas: Western Knowledge and Lexical Change in Late Imperial China* (Leiden: Brill, 2001); Xiong Yuezhi 熊月之, *Xixue dongjian yu wanqing shehui* 西學東漸與晚清社會 (The dissemination of Western learning and the Late Qing Society) (Shanghai: Shanghai renmin chubanshe, 1994); Chan Man Sing 陳萬成, *Zhongwai wenhua jiaoliu tanyi: Xingxue, yixue, qita* 中外文化交流探繹：星學・醫學・其他 (Exploration of East-West cultural exchanges: Astrology, medicine, and others) (Beijing Shi: Zhonghua shuju, 2010).
37. Liang, "Zongjiao yu zhexue," 64.
38. Liang, "Zongjiao yu zhexue," 59–68. Also see Liang Qichao, "Jiateng boshi tianze baihua" 加藤博士天則百話 (Dr. Kato Hiroyuki's *Hundred Essays on the Law of Evolution*) in XMCB 21 (1902): 52. Liang's original words are: 羣治之開化, 卻非徒恃有形之物質也。而更賴無形之精神。無形有形, 相需為用, 而始得完全圓滿之真文明。
39. Liang, "Zongjiao yu zhexue," 65.
40. Liang, "Zongjiao yu zhexue," 61.
41. Liang, "Zongjiao yu zhexue," 60.
42. See Liang Qichao, "Xin zhongguo weilaiji," XXS 2 (1902): 29.
43. Liang, "Zongjiao yu zhexue," 61.
44. For an introduction to the "mind school" of neo-Confucianism, see Tang Chun-i's "The Development of the Concept of Moral Mind from Wang Yang-ming to Wang Chi" and Theodore de Bary's "Individualism and Humanitarianism in Late Ming Thought" in *Self and Society in Ming Thought*, ed. Theodore de Bary (New York: Columbia University Press, 1970), 93–118 and 145–247.
45. See Liang Qichao, "Yalishiduode zhi zhengzhi xueshuo" 亞里士多德之政治學說 (The political theory of Aristotle), in XMCB 20 (1902): 9.

46. Liang Qichao, "Lun xiaoshuo," in *XXS* 1 (1902): 5. The translation derives from Gek Nai's translation of "On the Relationship between Fiction and the Government," 77.

47. Liang Qichao, "Lun zhongguo xueshu sixiang zhi dashi" 論中國學術思想變遷之大勢 (On general transformational trends of Chinese academic thoughts), in *XMCB* 21 (1902): 48. The statement "不立文字, 直指本心, 見性成佛" derives from the *Flower Ornament Scripture* (*Avataṃsaka Sūtra*). In the late Qing period, Liang's contemporaries often recited the statement to summarize Chan Buddhism. One example derives from Yang Wenhui's 楊文會 *Fojiao zongpai xiangzhu* 佛教宗派詳諸 (Detailed annotation on Buddhist sects), annotated by Wan Jun (Yangzhou: Guanling shushe, 2008), 66. (The book was first published by in 1921, in Shanghai, by Yixue shuju.)

48. Liang, "Lun zhongguo xueshu sixiang zhi dashi," *XMCB* 21 (1902): 48.

49. Liang, "Lun xiaoshuo," 3.

50. Liang, "Lun xiaoshuo," 3.

51. Liang Qichao, "Lun fojiao yu qunzhi zhi guanxi" 論佛教與群治之關係 (On the relationship between Buddhism and public governance), in *XMCB* 23 (1902): 49.

52. Liang Qichao, "Shijie mori ji" 世界末日記 (Last days of the world), *XXS* 1 (1902): 101–18.

53. Tokutomi Roka's translation was serialized in *Kokumin no tomo* 國民之友 (The nation's friend) and published by Minyūsha 民友社 in Tokyo between 1887 and 1892. For the reprint of Tokutomi's translation, see *Kokumin no tomo* 国民之友 (Tokyo: Meiji Bunken, 1966–1968), 119:766–68, and 120:814–16. Tokutomi's *Sekai no matsujitsu* is a retranslation of Camille Flammarion's (1842–1925) *Omega: The Last Days of the World* (New York: Cosmopolitan, 1894).

54. Liang, "Shijie mori ji," 117. Besides attaching a translator's afterword to "Last Days of the World," Liang made a number of revisions and introduced a good number of Buddhist elements in his (re)translation of Tokutomi's *Sekai no matsujitsu*. For a brief comparison between Flammarion's novel, Tokutomi's free Japanese adaptation, and Liang's retranslation of Tokutomi's adaptation, see Li Yanli 李艷麗, "Qingmo kexue xiaoshuo yu shiji mo sichao: Yi lianbian 'shijie mori ji' wei li" 清末科學小說與世紀末思潮——以兩篇《世界末日記》为例 (Late Qing science fiction and the *fin-de-siècle* intellectual trend), *Shehui kexue* 社會科學 (Journal of Social Science) 2 (2009): 157–67.

55. Liang, "Shijie mori ji," 117.

56. Liang, "Shijie mori ji," 117.

57. Liang, "Shijie mori ji," 117–18.

58. In "Zongjiao yu zhexue," Liang Qichao unambiguously indicates that the imperishable being means the soul (*linghun* 靈魂). Liang says, "There rests in me an imperishable being. Its name is the soul. Since it is persistently here,

death isn't something that I am fearful of." 吾自有不死者存, 曰靈魂。既常有不死者存, 則死吾奚畏. See Liang, "Zongjiao yu zhexue," 65.

59. Liang, "Zongjiao yu zhexue," 65.

60. Guan Kean-Fung, for instance, interprets the story from the perspective of Edward Said's "travel theory" and Max Nordau's discussion on the phenomenon of *fin de siècle*. See Guan Kean-Fung, *Cong "shenti" dao "shijie,"* 47–49.

61. Guan Kean-Fung, *Cong "shenti" dao "shijie,"* 116–17.

62. Liang, "Shijie mori ji," 116. Having compared Liang's translation with the Japanese original, it seems evident that the statement is Liang's personal addition rather than words found in the Japanese text.

63. Liang, "Shijie mori ji," 115.
64. Liang, "Shijie mori ji," 115.
65. Liang, "Shijie mori ji," 116.
66. Liang, "Shijie mori ji," 117.
67. Liang, "Shijie mori ji," 117–18.
68. Liang, "Shijie mori ji," 60.
69. Liang, "Xin zhongguo weilaiji," XXS 1 (1902): 60.
70. Liang, "Xin zhongguo weilaiji," XXS 1 (1902): 60.
71. Liang, "Shijie mori ji," 52.
72. Liang Qichao, "Xin zhongguo weilaiji," XXS 1 (1902): 56.
73. Liang, "Xin zhongguo weilaiji," 2: 57.

74. See Lawrence Wang-chi Wong, "'The Sole Purpose Is to Express My Political Views': Liang Qichao and the Translation and Writing of Political Novels in the Late Qing," in *Translation and Creation Readings of Western Literature in Early Modern China, 1840–1918*, ed. David Pollard (Amsterdam: J. Benjamins, 1998), 105–26; Chen Pingyuan 陳平原, *Zhongguo xian dai xiao shuo de qi dian: Qingmo minchu xiaoshuo yanjiu* 中國現代小說的起點: 清末民初小說研究 (Origins of modern Chinese fiction: A study of late Qing and early republican fiction) (Beijing: Beijing daxue chubanshe, 2005), 6–12, and 104–13.

75. For the rise of evidential studies in the early Qing dynasty, representative scholars of this intellectual trend, and its distinct academic practices, see Elman Benjamin, *From Philosophy to Philology*.

76. See Benjamin Elman, "The Relevance of Sung Learning in the Late Qing: Wei Yuan and the Huang-ch'ao Ching-shih Wen-pien," *Late Imperial China* 9, no. 2 (Dec. 1988): 56–85.

77. For a general introduction on the composition, circulation, and interpretation of the *Annals*, see Michael Nylan, "The Spring and Autumn Annals (*Chunqiu*), as Read through Its Three Traditions," in *The Five "Confucian" Classics* (New Haven, CT: Yale University Press, 2001), 253–306.

78. Dong's and He's assumption is informed by a classical historical tradition: following the establishment of a new dynasty, the new ruler in China governed with the fully developed institutional practices it inherited from the two preceding dynasties as well as with the law and order they invented for

the new state. Such a convention, however, can no longer be observed in Confucius's time. The Sage lived in the Warring States period (475–221 BC). At that time, China was divided by the rule of local warlords. The country did not have standardized institutional measures and there was not a sound legal system. To make things worse, the Western Zhou dynasty 西周 (1045–771 BC) that preceded the Warring States period was so corrupt that it failed to provide any valuable reference to pacify the social unrest. In the hope of averting further chaos, Confucius soon decided to assign himself the personal responsibility of prescribing proper institutional measures for future rulers. For a detailed study of Dong's interpretation of the *Gongyang Commentary* and the rise of New Text studies in the Han dynasty as the first state-sponsored Confucian orthodoxy, see Sarah Queen's *From Chronicle to Canon: The Hermeneutics of the Spring and Autumn according to Tung Chung-shu* (Cambridge: Cambridge University Press, 1996); also see Michael Loewe's *Dong Zhongshu, a Confucian Heritage and the Chunqiu Fanlu* (Leiden: Brill, 2011).

79. See Qian Mu, *Lianghan jingxue jinguwen pingyi* 兩漢經學今古文評議 (Assessment of the Han old and New Text controversy) (Taibei: Dongda tushu gongsi yinhang, 1983). For recent English discussions on the relationship between the academic and the political competition in the Han dynasty, see Yuri Pines, Paul Goldin, and Martin Kern, eds., *Ideology of Power and Power of Ideology in Early China* (Leiden: Brill Academic, 2015).

80. Liang Qichao, *Qingdai xueshu gailun*, 79–80. Kang's *On Confucius as a Reformer* was completed in 1892 and published in 1897.

81. Hsiao Kung-ch'uan, *A Modern China and a New World*, 47; also see Wei Leong Tay, "Kang Youwei, The Martin Luther of Confucianism and his Vision of Confucian Modernity and Nation," in *Secularization, Religion, and State*, ed. Haneda Masashi (Tokyo: University of Tokyo Center for Philosophy), 101–2.

82. Liang, *Qingdai xueshu gailun*, 83. In the hope of popularizing Kang's teachings to the general public, Liang wrote, "For any scholar-officials with a proper understanding of their study, whenever shortcomings they notice in the institutional construct, they conceive solutions to make up for these shortcomings. This is such a common practice. Confucius composed the *Spring and Autumn Annals* for the same reasons. If one believes that Wang Fuzhi and Huang Zongxi can formulate their reformist proposals, why wouldn't one allow Confucius to have done the same? This is senseless." 凡士大夫之讀書有心得者，每覺當時之制度，有未善處，而思有以變通之。此最尋常事。孔子之作春秋,亦猶是耳。夫以梨洲船山林一之所能為者，而必不許我孔子為之, 此何理也. See Liang Qichao, "Du Chunqiu jieshuo" 讀春秋界說 (Definitions for reading Spring and Autumn Annals), in *Hunan shiwu xuetang yibian* 湖南時務學堂遺編 (Unpublished writing from the Hunan School of Current Affairs) (Hunan: Hunan daxue chubanshe, 2017) 1:4.

83. Liang Qichao, "Lun zhongguo xueshu sixiang," in XMCB 2 (1902): 39–55.

84. Liang, "Lun Zhongguo xueshu sixiang," 45–55.
85. Liang Qichao, "Du Mengzi jieshuo," 讀孟子界說 (Definitions for reading Mencius). *Qingyi bao* 21 (1898): 1–3. Also see Liang Qichao, "Lun Zhongguo xueshu sixinag," in XMCB 4 (1902): 46, and XMCB 12 (1902): 45–55.
86. Liang, *Qingdai xueshu gailun*, 84. See Immanuel C. Y. Hsü's translation in *Intellectual Trends in the Ch'ing Period* (Cambridge, MA: Harvard University Press, 1959), 100.
87. Liang, *Qingdai xueshu gailun*, 84. For divided views on Xunzi shared by late Qing intellectuals, see Zhu Weizheng, "Wanqing hanxue: 'Pai Xun' yu Zhun xun'" 晚清漢學: 排荀與尊荀 (Han learning in late Qing China: Protest Against Xunzi and support for Xunzi), in *Wanqing xueshu shilun: Qiusuo zhen wenming* 晚清學術史論: 求索真文明 (Discussions on the late Qing academic history: The search of the true civilization) (Shanghai: Shanghai guji chubanshe, 1996), 333–50.
88. Liang, "Du Mengzi jieshuo," 2.
89. Liang, "Du Mengzi jieshuo," 2.
90. Liang, *Qingdai xueshu gailun*, 88.
91. Liang Qichao, "Baojiao fei souyi zun kong lun" 保教非所以尊孔論 (The preservation of teaching is not the reason to venerate Confucius), XMCB 2 (1902): 72.
92. Liang Qichao, "Baojiao fei souyi zun kong lun," 72.
93. Liang, "Du Mengzi jieshuo," 67.
94. Liang, "Du Mengzi jieshuo," 67.
95. Liang, "Xin zhongguo weilaiji," XXS 1 (1902): 51. Kou Zhengfeng points out that Liang's *The Future of New China* is structured on the basis of the interplay between the abstract fictionality (虛 *xu*) and the factual historicity (實 *shi*). In Kuo's article, he focuses on exploring influences Liang received from Japanese fiction published in the Meiji period. See Ko Zhenfeng 寇振鋒, "Xin zhongguo weilaiji zhong de Mingzhi zhengzhi xiaoshuo yinsu"《新中國未來記》中的日本明治政治小說因素 (Elements of Meiji Japan's political fiction in the future of new China), accessed May 11, 2015, http://www.jsc.fudan.edu.cn/picture/jl080210.pdf. While Liang calls his fictional creation an "allegory," Chen Jianhua insightfully suggests that Liang's promotion of fiction has achieved the paradoxical ends of subverting the prestige of more respected literary genres such as poetry, Confucian classics, and historical writing. See Chen Jianhua, "Minzu 'xiangxiang' de moli," 69.
96. Liang's promotion of "public morality" has received a good deal of scholarly attention. In Wang Hui's and Peter Zarrow's insightful study, they carefully trace Liang's close affiliation with New Text studies and the ways in which his reformism were informed by New Text principles. Similar to Wang and Zarrow, I agree that examining Liang's engagement with New Text studies is instrumental in revealing the intellectual complexity and logical order of his seemingly incongruous political thinking. But in addition, in the first two chapters

of the book I hope to discover and make clear how encouraging the Chinese public to internalize Western political knowledge as moral, ethical, and religious principles reconfigured the epistemological status of Western knowledge, and in turn revised the Chinese public's "perceptual distance" with translated political modernity at a precarious historical junction. For more details, see Peter Zarrow, *After Empire*, 56–89; Wang Hui, *Zhongguo xiandai sixiang de xingqi*, 924–1010.

97. Liang Qichao, "Xin zhongguo weilaiji," XXS 2 (1902): 60.
98. Liang, "Xin zhongguo weilaiji," 2: 60.
99. Liang, "Xin zhongguo weilaiji," 2: 37.
100. Liang, "Xin zhongguo weilaiji," 2: 37.
101. Liang, "Xin zhongguo weilaiji," 2: 37; emphasis added.
102. Liang, "Xin zhongguo weilaiji," 2: 75.
103. Liang, "Xin zhongguo weilaiji," 2: 37. In Liang's historical *Biography of the Three Heroes Who Founded Italy* (意大利建國三傑傳), he unmistakably classifies Mazzini as a revolutionary and Cavour as a reformer. Liang portrays Mazzini as a national hero who pursues "liberty, equality, independence, and self-governance" as lofty moral goals. While Mazzini sees the prospect of launching a revolution for Italy as the materialization of his moral pursuit, Cavour is interested only in implementing political reform on an institutional level. See Liang, "Yidali jianguo sanjie zhuan" 意大利建國三傑傳 (Biographies on the three Italian heroes who founded Italy). XMCB 9 (1902): 31–44; XMCB 10 (1902): 43–53; and XMCB 14 (1902): 31–42.
104. Liang Qichao, "Xin zhongguo weilaiji," XXS 2 (1902): 39.
105. Liang, "Xin zhongguo weilaiji," 2: 37 and 39–40.
106. Liang, "Xin zhongguo weilaiji," 2: 60.
107. Liang, "Xin zhongguo weilaiji," 2: 59.
108. Liang, "Xin zhongguo weilaiji," 2: 65. Liang's original reads, 直至廣東自治時代, 這憲政黨黨員已有了一千四百萬人, 廣東一省四百多萬, 其餘各省, 合共九百多萬, 所以同聲一呼, 天子動容, 權奸褫魄, 便把廣東自治的憲法得到手了, 隨後各省紛紛繼起, 到底做成了今天的局面。
109. Liang, "Xin zhongguo weilaiji," 2: 58.
110. Yamada Keizō is one of the very few scholars who are sensitive to note that the word "reform" (*weixin* 維新) that Liang uses in *New China* refers neither to republicanism nor to the kind of constitutional monarchy Japan established based on the Prusso-German model. Keizō believes that the reason Liang chooses to use "reform" instead of "revolution" (*geming* 革命) is that the word emphasizes the prospect of achieving the revolutionary ends through peaceful instead of violent means. In Keizō's discussion, he unambiguously suggests that the "reform" Liang envisions in his novella is directly opposite of the kind reform Kang Youwei endorses. In addition, Keizō believes that it would be extremely unlikely for Liang to propose a kind of reformism that completely excludes revolutionary elements. Keizō words read, 「維新」は、しかし共和制

ではない。それはあくまでも帝政のもとに憲法を制定し、国会を召集するものであって、日本の明治維新をモデルとした「立憲君主制」の確立こそが変法維新の理念であった。にもかかわらず、梁が十年後に共和制国家の実現を描いたのは、むろんそれが当時の彼の願望に合致する目標であったからにほかならない。だが、それが「革命」ではなく「維新」と表記されているのは、彼の理想が武力によってではなく、平和的な手段----ここでは光緒帝の自発的な退位と初代大統領への就任----によるものと想定されているからであろう...ただこの時点で、一〇年後の一九=一年に共和国家の成立を夢見ることは、変法維新運動のプログラムにはなく、師の康有為の見解にも違背する先走った提言であった。See Yamada Keizō 山田敬三, "Shin chūgoku miraiki o megutte: Ryō Keichō ni okeru kakumei to henkaku no ronri" 新中国未来記」をめぐって:梁啓超における革命と変革の論理 (On "The future of new China": Liang's logic on reform and revolution), in *Kyōdō kenkyū Ryō Keichō: Seiyō kindai shisō juyō to Meiji Nihon* 共同研究梁啓超: 西洋近代思想受容と明治日本 (Collaborative research on Liang Qichao: The reception of modern Western thought and Meiji Japan) (Tokyo: Misuzu shobo, 1999), 342. For a Chinese translation of Keizō's article, see "Weirao xin zhongguo weilai ji suo jian Liang Qichao geming yu biange sixiang" 圍繞新中國未來記所見梁啟超革命與變革思想, in *Liang Qichao, Mingzhi Riben, xifang Riben Jingdu daxue renwen kexue yanjiusuo gongyong yanjiu baogao*" 梁啟超・明治日本・西方: 日本京都大學人文科學研究所共同研究報告 (Liang Qichao, Meiji Japan, and the west: Collaborative research reports from Institute for Research in Humanities, Kyoto University) (Beijing: Shehui kexue wenxian chubanshe, 2001), 321–46. Zhu Lin has made a similar remark as Keizō, suggesting that the "reform" Liang refers to is *not* a binary opposition to "revolution" as it is generally assumed. See Zhu Lin 朱琳, "Liang Qichao de 'geming' lun" 梁启超的'革命'论 (Liang Qichao on "revolution"), *Higashi Ajia bunka kōshō kenkyū* 東アジア文化交涉研究 (Journal of East Asian cultural interaction studies) 5 ([n.d.]): 119. For Chen Jianhua, the utopic reformist construct Liang envisions in *New China* is neither an epitome of constitutional monarchy nor a representative democracy. It is a medley of the different modern political models that Liang was interested in implementing in China. See Chen Jianhua, "The magic power of national 'imagination,'" 67.

111. Liang Qichao, "Shi ge" 釋革 (Exegesis on Ge), in *XMCB* 22 (1902): 1–8.

112. Liang, "Shi ge" 1.

113. Liang, "Shi ge," 1.

114. Liang, "Shi ge," 4.

115. For Yamada Keizō's discussion on Liang's ambiguous uses of the words *weixin* 維新, *geming* 革命, and *biange* 變革, see Keizo, "Shin chūgoku miraiki kōsetsu," 353–56.

116. Ding Wenjiang 丁文江 and Zhao Fengtian, 趙豐田, eds., *Liang Qichao nianpu changbian* 梁啟超年譜長編 (An unabridged chronicle of Liang Qichao) (Shanghai: Shanghai renmin chubanshe, 2009), 147.

117. Ding and Zhao, *Liang Qichao nianpu changbian*, 132–34, and 144.

118. Ding and Zhao, *Liang Qichao nianpu changbian*, 133–34 (港澳同人速謀運械入口的地方；專販我急需之物).

119. Ding and Zhao, *Liang Qichao nianpu changbian*, 152–53 (集股十萬為之；擇一地開蠶桑公司，并招年少與曾入蠶桑學堂者教以中西文，以此為招，選其壯健樸誠者，日日練之，日日講之，可以暗成一有勇知方之軍。).

120. Ding and Zhao, *Liang Qichao nianpu changbian*, 156.

121. Ding and Zhao, *Liang Qichao nianpu changbian*, 152.

122. Ding and Zhao, *Liang Qichao nianpu changbian*, 132.

123. Ding and Zhao, *Liang Qichao nianpu changbian*, 141 and 144.

124. Ding and Zhao, *Liang Qichao nianpu changbian*, 117 and 119. Ding Wenjiang and Zhang Fengtian documented the friendship between Liang and Sun with the following words: 相與談論排滿方略，極為相得。春夏間，先生因為和孫中山來往日密，所以漸有贊成革命的趨向，當時也曾商兩黨合作問題，以南海之阻，又未成。

125. For the growing antagonism between Kang Youwei and Sun Yat-sen, see Feng Ziyou 馮自由, *Zhonghua minguo kaiguo qian geming shi* 中國民國開國前革命史 (Revolution history that precedes the establishment of the Republic of China) (Guilin, China: Guangxi shifan daxue chubanshe, 2011), 26–33.

126. For Liang's support for the political revolution, see Tang Xiaobing, *Global Space*, 1–79; and Chang Hao's chapters "Liang in Exile" and "The New Citizen" in *Liang Ch'i-ch'ao and Intellectual Transition in China, 1890–1907* (Cambridge, MA: Harvard University Press, 1971), 121–219. Zhang Pengyuan provides the most detailed, convincing, and sympathetic analysis on Liang's unfailing hope in launching a revolution and the emotional torment from which Liang suffered. See *Liang Qichao yu qingji geming* 梁啟超與清季革命 (Liang Qichao and the Qing revolution) (Shanghai: Sanlian shudian, 2007).

127. Ding and Zhao, *Liang Qichao nianpu changbian*, 189.

128. Ding and Zhao, *Liang Qichao nianpu changbian*, 197.

129. In personal letters he exchanged with his friends between 1902 and 1903, Liang candidly revealed his frustration for not being able to initiate a political revolution in China. For a detailed historical documentation of these exchanges, see Ding and Zhao, *Liang Qichao nianpu changbian*, 179–219.

130. For Liang's first meeting with Sun Yat-sen in Yokohama, Japan, see Ding and Zhao, *Liang Qichao nianpu changbian*, 117 and 119. For Liang's alliance with Sun, see Feng Ziyou, *Zhonghua minguo kaiguo qian geming shi*, 1:44. Feng describes their collaboration as 矢言合作到底，至死不渝.

131. See Chang Hao, *Liang Ch'i-ch'ao*, 121–48. For the growing antagonism between Kang Youwei and Sun Yat-sen, see Feng Ziyou 馮自由, *Zhonghua minguo kaiguo qian geming shi*, 26–33.

132. In contrast, Huang Keqiang's definition of "reform" is completely different from the "reform" Dr. Kong describes in his speech. In the debate,

Huang is firmly convinced that the Chinese public is not ready for political revolution. Instead of seeking to form a constitutional party and gather millions of members in Guangzhou and other provinces, Huang strongly emphasizes that the Chinese public "do not have any spirit of self-governance, and they haven't made any process in the past few thousand years" 自治毫無精神, 幾千年沒有一點進步. For Huang, the Chinese public is completely uninformed of their rights and obligations in a democratic society. This disorganized crowd of ignorant people, he says, is "directly opposite from the 'organic' body as defined in the modern political philosophy" (和那政治學上所謂"有機體"正相反). Revolution, theoretically speaking, can transform China from an imperial monarchy into a "self-governed community" (自治團體). But since the people are not ready for self-governance, Huang says, it would take only one or two powerful figures to ruin and destroy the self-governed community the Chinese forms (只要一兩個官吏紳士有權勢的人, 可以任意把他的自治團體糟蹋敗壞). After listing the Chinese public's shortcomings and the destructive consequences of a revolution, Huang says that it would be a better idea to set up legislative councils in different provincial regions. But as for the national congress, it would be better to wait for another twenty to thirty years (先把地方議會開了, 這就遲二三十年再開國會也是無妨的). Since different provinces could begin to have trial legislative councils, Huang completely denies the prospect of declaring different provinces independent from the Qing monarchy. He says that if this ever happens, internal conflicts will turn China into a state of chaos, and different imperial powers will make the country their colonial states. See Liang, "Xin zhongguo weilaiji," XXS 2 (1902): 69.

133. Liang Qichao, "Xin zhongguo weilaiji," XXS 2 (1902): 37.
134. Liang, "Xin zhongguo weilaiji," XXS 1 (1902): 37.
135. Liang Qichao, "Shi ge," 1–2; emphasis added.
136. See Chang Hao, *Liang Ch'i-ch'ao*, 121–48.
137. Jean Tsui, "Political Modernity and Its Musical Dissociation: A Study of Guomin and Geming in Liang Qichao's Historical Biographies," *Frontiers of Literary Studies in China* 8, no. 2 (2014): 302–30.
138. Liang Qichao, "Lun gongde" 論公德 (On public morality) *Xinmin congbao* 17 (1902): 7.
139. Liang, "Lun gongde," 7.

Chapter 5

1. Liang Qichao, "Jinggao wo tongye zhujun" 敬告我同業諸君 (A respectful announcement to my fellow reformists), in XMCB 17 (1902): 1–8.
2. Liang, "Jinggao wo tongye zhujun," 4.
3. Liang, "Jinggao wo tongye zhujun," 4.

4. Liang, "Jinggao wo tongye zhujun," 4.

5. Liang, "Jinggao wo tongye zhujun," 5.

6. Werner Jaegar, *Paideia: The Ideals of Greek Culture*, vol. 2 (New York: Oxford University Press), 144.

7. Liang, "Jinggao wo tongye zhujun," 4.

8. Xia Xiaohong 夏曉紅, *Jueshi yu chuanshi: Liang Qichao de wenxue daolu* 覺世與傳世: 梁啟超的文學道理 (Enlightenment and permanence: The literary road of Liang Qichao) (Shanghai: Shanghai renmin chubanshe, 1991), 28. *Qinggan* can be finely divided into "emotion," "affect," "feeling," and "pathos" in recent scholarly discussions. In this statement, it seems likely that by *qinggan* Liang was referring to the "appeal" to the audience's emotions, and "pathos" is thus the most appropriate translation.

9. For more details, see Xia's *Jueshi yu chuanshi*, 13–39.

10. See Xia's chapter 5, "Kai wenzhang zhi xinti, ji minqi zhi anchao" 開文學之新體, 啟民氣之暗潮 (Inventing a new style for literature, and inspiring the undercurrent of people's civil thinking), in Xia Xiaohong, *Jueshi yu chuanshi*, 109–48. Elisabeth Kaske has compiled a detailed list of references on the relationship between Liang's new prose style and the circulation of modern political knowledge. For the list, see *The Politics of Language in Chinese Education, 1895–1919* (Leiden: Brill, 2008), 114; for Kaske's discussions on this topic, see 114–23.

11. Quoted from Ding Wenjiang 丁文江 and Zhao Fengtian 趙豐田, eds., *Liang Qichao nianpu changbian* 梁啟超年譜長編 (An unabridged chronicle of Liang Qichao) (Shanghai: Shanghai renmin chubanshe, 2009), 181.

12. Ding and Zhao, *Liang Qichao nianpu changbian*, 196.

13. Liang Qichao, "Xiongyali aiguozhe Gesushi zhuan" 匈牙利愛國者噶蘇士 (Biography of the Hungarian patriot Kossuth), in XMCB 4 (1902): 32.

14. Liang Qichao, "Lun zizhi" (On self-governance) XMCB 9 (1902): 36. Both the terms "righteousness" (*yi*) and "knight-errant" (*xia*) are loaded with heavy cultural connotations. When Confucius mentions the term "the right," he refers to what is right in general and does not have any specific virtue in mind. While "the right" refers to the existence of the moral norm in *The Analects*, it is being interpreted as what ought to be done, particularly in terms of honoring the worthy, in *Means and Harmony* (*Zhong yong*). Coming to Mencius (Mengzi), righteousness and benevolence (*ren*) are being defined as a binomial pair, which is *renyi* (benevolence and a sense of righteousness). Although these virtues are two fundamental moral principles, benevolence, according to D. C. Lau's introduction to *Mencius*, is considered more basic, and it is the place where righteousness takes root. Only a man with benevolence can proceed to righteousness, which, in Lau's words, "can be applied to an act which is right, to the agent who does what is right and to a duty which an agent ought to do." See D. C. Lau. trans., *Mencius* (Harmondsworth, UK: Penguin Books, 1970), 12. Apart from benevolence, *ren* has been translated variously as "goodness" (Arthur

Waley), "human-heartedness" (E. R. Hughes), "love" (Derk Bodde), "humanity" (Peter Boodberg), "true manhood" (Lin Yutang), and so on. For the relative merits, or shortcomings, of each translation, see Wing-tsit Chan, A *Source Book in Chinese Philosophy* (Princeton, NJ: Princeton University Press, 1963), 788–89. While *yi* refers to the moral disposition to do good, "knight errant" is not such a philosophical concept. A knight-errant is someone who often appears in the marvel tales (*chuanqi*) that thrived in the Tang dynasty (618–907). According to Yau-woon Ma and Joseph Lau, a knight-errant is "usually seen as a man of extraordinary martial and spiritual discipline. Subscribing to what seems to us to be a very narrow and personal code of honor, a *xia* would often offer his services in the name of justice and benevolence to anyone who happens to cater to his fancy." See Yau-woon Ma and Joseph S. M. Lau, eds., *Traditional Chinese Stories: Themes and Variations* (New York: Columbia University Press, 1978), 39.

15. Liang, "Lun zizhi," 36.
16. Liang, "Lun zizhi," 5.
17. Liang Qichao, "Xiongyali aiguozhe Gesushi zhuan," in XMCB 4 (1902): 40.
18. Liang, "Xiongyali aiguozhe Gesushi zhuan," 42.
19. Liang, "Xiongyali aiguozhe Gesushi zhuan," 39.
20. Liang, "Xiongyali aiguozhe Gesushi zhuan," 42.
21. Liang, "Xiongyali aiguozhe Gesushi zhuan," 43.
22. Liang, "Xiongyali aiguozhe Gesushi zhuan," 43.
23. "Morality," as Liang says, "is an organic oneness. But once it is expressed outward, there rises the categorical differences between the public and the private. When one focuses on cultivating his personal moral well-being, it is private morality. And as he extends his moral goodness to his peers, it becomes public morality." 道德之一本體而已。但其發表於外，則公私之名立焉。人人獨善其身者，謂之私德，人人相善其群者，謂之公德。See Liang's "Lun gongde," 論公德 (On public morality) XMCB 17 (1902): 1.
24. Liang Qichao, "Lun guojia sixiang," 論國家思想 (On nationalistic thought) XMCB 4 (1902): 4.
25. Chung-ying Cheng, "Confucian Onto-Hermeneutics: Morality and Ontology," *Journal of Chinese Philosophy* 27 no. 1 (March 2000): 33–68. For Cheng's extensive elaboration on onto-hermeneutics, see *Yixue bengti lun* 易學本體論 (Body, mind, and spirit) (Taibei: Kangde chubanshe, 2008).
26. While "hermeneutics" refers to a general science of interpretation that applies to all texts, thinkers such Wilhelm Dilthey, Martin Heidegger, and Hans-Georg Gadamer are sharply aware that the reader's existential experience often subjectively reinvents the text they try to make sense of. Ng shows that while these theorists see the reader's psychology as the subjective component of comprehension, their understanding of hermeneutic is epistemological in nature. What Cheng is interested in doing is showing how "Confucian insights

and ideas can be fruitfully and meaningfully appropriated to construct a hermeneutics that is truly ontological." See On-cho Ng, "Toward a Hermeneutic Turn in Chinese Philosophy: Western Theory, Confucian Tradition, and Cheng Chung-ying's Onto-hermeneutics," *Dao: A Journal of Comparative Philosophy* 6, no. 4 (Dec. 2007): 383–95; On-cho Ng, "Chinese Philosophy, Hermeneutics, and Onto-Hermeneutics," *Journal of Chinese Philosophy* 30 no. 3/4 (Sept./Dec. 2003): 373–85; and On-cho Ng, "Religious Hermeneutics: Text and Truth in Neo-Confucian Readings of the Yijing," *Journal of Chinese Philosophy*, 34, no. 1(March 2007): 5–24.

27. Inspired by his study of *Yijing* 易經 (The book of changes), Chung-ying Cheng's "onto-hermeneutics" theory consists of four correlated principles. The first, the "principle of comprehensive observation," refers to the "careful and wide-ranging investigation of both the graphic and symbolic meaning of the universe represented by the hexagrams." The second, the "principle of congruence of reciprocal feelings," designates the "cultivation of the moral ability to feel the sentiments of others and thereby experiences reality as it really is." The third is the "principle of practice and self-cultivation." It refers to the realization of one's comprehension of knowledge in action. The fourth is the "principle of unity of virtues and reason." Derived from the Confucian dictum and injunction of "rectification of names" (*zhengming* 正名), this principle emphasizes that reality must be both recognized and rectified in order to ensure that its descriptions are true. For more details, see On-cho Ng, "Chinese Philosophy," 378–81.

28. Liang, "Xiongyali aiguozhe Gesushi zhuan," 6:36; emphasis added. Satoru Hashimoto has recently conducted a detailed analysis of Liang's translation of the biography from Japanese in his dissertation. See Satoru Hashimoto, "Afterlives of the Culture: Engaging with the Trans-East Asian Cultural Tradition in Modern Chinese, Japanese, Korean, and Taiwanese Literatures, 1880s–1940s" (PhD diss., Harvard University, 2014). To see differences between Liang's historical biography and that of Hisahi, see Hirata Hisashi, 平田久 *Itarī kenkoku sanketsu* 伊太利建国三傑 (Three heroes who founded Italy) (Tokyo: Min'yūsha, 1892), accessed April 18, 2015, at the online database *Kindai dejitaruraiburari* 近代デジタルライブラリー (Digital library from the Meiji era), http://kindai.ndl.go.jp/info:ndljp/pid/777020. For an English rendition of Kossuth's speech, see Phineas Camp Headley, *The Life of Louis Kossuth, Governor of Hungary* (Ann Arbor: University of Michigan, 1995), 103–4.

29. Liang Qichao, "Xiongyali aiguozhe Gesushi zhuan," 4: 32.

30. In the early 1900s, Liang warmly celebrated the effectiveness of circulating modern political knowledge through the orality of speech. For more details, see Chen Pingyuan 陳平原, "Yousheng de Zhongguo: Yanshuo yu jinxiandai Zhongguo wenzhang bianqe" 有聲的中國：演說'與近現代中國文章變革 (On the relationship between "public speaking" and the development of Chinese prose), *Wenxue pinglun* 文學評論 (Literary Criticism) 3 (2007): 5–21. For a book-length

study on the crucial role sound and orality played in forming the Chinese public's national identity and shaping one's imagination of the political modern in the twentieth century, see John Crespi, *Voices in Revolution: Poetry and the Auditory Imagination in Modern China*. (Honolulu: University of Hawai'i Press, 2009).

31. Barbara Mittler, *A Newspaper for China: Power, Identity, and Change in Shanghai's News Media, 1872–1912* (Cambridge, MA: Harvard University Press, 2004), 110.

32. Ronald Egan, "The Prose Style of Fan Yeh," *Harvard Journal of Asiatic Studies* 39, no. 2 (1979): 352.

33. Egan, "Prose Style of Fan Yeh," 353.

34. Egan, "Prose Style of Fan Yeh," 353.

35. George Steiner, "Silence and the Poet," in *Language and Silence: Essays on Language, Literature, and the Inhumane* (New York, NY: Atheneum, 1967), 43.

36. Steiner, "Silence and the Poet," 34; emphasis added. In the *Analects* (*Lunyu* 論語), *yi* means what is right in general and it is not associated with any particular virtues. While the word is broadly defined as the presence of the moral norm in the *Analects*, it refers to "what ought to be done," particularly in terms of honoring the worthy, in *Means and Harmony* (*Zhongyong*). In *Mencius* (*Mengzi*), *yi* and *ren* (benevolence) are understood as a binomial pair, which is *renyi* (benevolence and a sense of righteousness). For more details, see Zhang Dainian, *Key Concepts in Chinese Philosophy*, ed. and trans. Edmund Ryden (New Haven, CT: Yale University Press, 2002), 285–310; also see Chan, *Source Book in Chinese Philosophy*, 788–89.

37. Liang Qichao, "Xiongyali aiguozhe Gesushi zhuan," in XMCB 6 (1902): 42.

38. Liang, "Xiongyali aiguozhe Gesushi zhuan," 6: 43.

39. Liang, "Xiongyali aiguozhe Gesushi zhuan," 6: 49.

40. In the historical biography, Kossuth the Hungarian patriot skillfully connects the national citizen with the shared code of righteousness (*yi* 義) and appoints them the role of knight-errant (*xiayi* 俠義) in marvel tales (*chuanqi* 傳奇) that have thrived since the Tang dynasty (618–907). According to Yau-woon Ma and Joseph Lau, a knight-errant (*xia*) is "usually seen as a man of extraordinary martial and spiritual discipline. Subscribing to what seems to us to be a very narrow and personal code of honor, a *xia* would often offer his services in the name of justice and benevolence to anyone who happens to cater to his fancy." See Yau-woon and Joseph Lau, *Traditional Chinese Stories*, 39.

41. Liang Qichao, "Lun guojia sixiang," in XMCB 4 (1902): 1.

42. For more details on Gong Zichen's political thinking and his view on music, see Judith Whitbeck, "The Historical Vision of Kung Tzu-chen (1792–1841)" (PhD diss., UC Berkeley, 1980); for English scholarships that focus on eighteenth-century Chinese political thinking, see Susan Mann, *Hung Liang-Chi (1746–1809): The Perception and Articulation of Political Problems in Late*

Eighteenth-Century China (PhD diss., Stanford University, 1972); Kent Guy, *The Scholar and the State in Late Imperial China* (PhD thesis, Harvard University, 1980); James Polachek, *Literati Groups and Literati Politics in Early Nineteenth-Century China* (PhD thesis, University of California, Berkeley, 1976); On-Cho Ng, *Cheng-Zhu Confucianism in the Early Qing: Li Guangdi and Qing Learning* (New York: SUNY University Press, 2001); and Susan Mann and Philip Kuhn, "Dynastic Decline and the Roots of Rebellion," in *Cambridge History of China*, vol. 10, ed. John Fairbank (Cambridge: Cambridge University Press, 1978), 107–62.

43. Whitbeck, "Historical Vision," 127–28.

44. Liang Qichao, "Xiongyali aiguozhe Gesushi zhuan," in XMCB 6 (1902): 42.

45. Liang, "Xiongyali aiguozhe Gesushi zhuan," 6: 42.

46. Ken Berthel, "*Zhiyin* 知音 and *Zhiyan* 知言, Knowing Notes and Knowing Words: Aurality and Reality in Ancient China" (PhD diss., University of California, Irvine, 2010), 101.

47. Berthel, "*Zhiyin*," 102.

48. Berthel, "*Zhiyin*," 99.

49. "Great Preface to Mao's Odes" 毛氏大序. See *Hou hanshu* 後漢書 (The book of later Han) (Peking: Zhonghua shuju, 1965), 9:2575–76.

50. For a theoretical exegesis on the "mediating interaction" between an artist's interiority and the "structural frame," see Kao Yu-kung, "Chinese Lyric Aesthetics," in *Words and Images: Chinese Poetry, Calligraphy, and Painting*, ed. Alfveda Mumck and Wen Fong (New York: The Metropolitan Museum of Arts, 1991), 47–90.

51. Kao Yu-kung, "The Aesthetics of Regulated Verse," in *The Vitality of the Lyric Voice: Shih Poetry from the Late Han to T'ang*, ed. Shuen-fu Lin and Stephen Owen (Princeton, NJ: Princeton University Press, 1986), 339. For the book-length monograph Kao devoted to the study of the Chinese lyrical aesthetics, see his *Zhongguo meidian yu wenxue yanjiu lunji* 中國美典與文學研究論集 (Collected essays on researches on the Chinese aesthetic tradition and literature) (Taibei: Guoli Taiwan daxue chuban zhongxin, 2004).

52. Kao, "Aesthetics of Regulated Verse," 333.

53. Kao, "Aesthetics of Regulated Verse," 333.

54. Theodore Adorno, "Parataxis: On Hölderlin's Late Poetry," in *Notes to Literature*, vol. 2, ed. Rolf Tiedemann and translated by Shierry Weber Nicholsen (New York: Columbia University Press, 1991), 130.

55. Theodore Adorno, "Music, Language, and Composition," trans. Susan Gillespie *Musical Quarterly* 77, no. 3 (Autumn 1993): 404.

56. Adorno, "Music, Language, and Composition," 404. Something important to note is that Adorno does not exclude music's potential to articulate the conceptual. In "Music, Language, and Composition," Adorno draws a distinction between the good "music" and bad "musical language." What differentiates the

two is whether the composer tries to impose logic and an informed structure on his musical composition. Adorno believes that good music should be the spontaneous overflow of powerful feelings, and to compose music through rational organization and careful manipulation of its expressive potential is not so different from conceptualizing the unmediated experience into language. For more details, see Adorno, "Music, Language, and Composition," 401–14.

57. Adorno, "Parataxis," 130.
58. Adorno, "Parataxis," 112.
59. See Peter V. Zima, *Subjectivity and Identity: Between Modernity and Postmodernity* (New York: Bloomsbury Academic, 2015).
60. For the subversive political potential concealed in Wang Yangming's moral philosophy, see Araki Kengo 荒木見悟 *Bukkyō to Jukyō: Chūgoku Shisō wo keiseisuru mono* 仏教と儒教 中国思想を形成するも (Confucianism and Buddhism: The formation of Chinese Thought) (Kyōto: Heirakuji Shoten Shōwa 1963); Yu Ying-shih, *Songminglixue yu zhengzhi wenhua*; and Philip Ivanhoe, *Ethics in the Confucian Tradition*.
61. Kao, "Aesthetics of Regulated Verse," 340.
62. Kao, "Aesthetics of Regulated Verse," 333.
63. Kao, "Aesthetics of Regulated Verse," 333–34.
64. Liang Qichao, "Luoran furen zhuan" 羅蘭夫人傳 (A biography of Madame Roland), in XMCB 18 (1902): 48–49.
65. Liang, "Luoran furen zhuan" 45.
66. Wang Yangming's discussion of *yi* 意 (natural inclination) remains an underexamined topic in the study of neo-Confucianism. So far, Harvey Lederman is one of few individuals who has conducted a critical analysis of *yi* in English scholarship. Perceiving *yi* as a "cognitive" expression informed by one's "introspective reasoning, Lederman translates *yi* as "intention" in his unpublished article "Perception and Genuine Knowledge in Wang Yangming," in *Oxford Studies in Epistemology*, accessed December 27, 2023, http://www.harveylederman.com/Perception%20and%20Genuine%20Knowledge.pdf.
67. Wang, *Chuanxi lu, juan* 2 and 6.
68. Wang, *Chuanxi lu*, 91.
69. As the philosopher says, "Object is a matter of affairs" (物者，事也). See *Wang Yangming quanji*, 26: 972.
70. Wang Yangming, *Chuanxi lu*, in *Wang Yangming quanji, juan* 2 and 6.
71. Wang Yangming, Chuanxi lu, in *Wang Yangming quanji*, 3: 111.
72. Wang Yangming, *Daxue wen* 大學問 (Inquiry on the great learning), in *Wang Yangming quanji*, 26:971.
73. Wang Yangming, 別錄五—計處地方疏 (Appendix 5—Memorial from a remote land), in *Wang Yangming quanji*, 23.
74. Wang Yangming, 贛州書示四侄正思等 (Letter from Ganzhou: To my fourth nephew Zhensi and other family members), in *Wang Yangming quanji*, 23: 987.

75. Wang, "Letter from Ganzhou," in *Wang Yangming quanji*, 23:987. Wang's original words go: "習俗移人, 如油漬面, 雖賢者不免, 況爾曹初學小子能無溺乎?"

76. Wang, "Letter from Ganzhou," in *Wang Yangming quanji*, 23:1036. Wang's original words go: "與不善人居, 如入鮑魚之肆, 久而不覺其臭, 則與之俱化。"

77. Wang Yangming, 與克彰太叔 (Letter to Grand Uncle Kezhang), in *Wang Yangming quanji*, 23:1032.

78. Wang, "Letter to Grand Uncle Kezhang," in *Wang Yangming quanji*, 23:1032.

79. Peng Guoxiang 彭國翔, "Zhong wangming de xiancheng liangzhi zhi bian" 中晚明的現成良知之辨 (Debates on the presence of perfect moral knowing from the mid to the late Ming period), *Guoxue yanjiu* 國學研究 (Studies in Sinology) 11 (June 2003): 15–46.

80. For a very brief summary of Huayan Buddhism, see the section titled "The Emptiness of the Heart" in chapter 3 in this volume.

81. Fung Yiu-ming and I share a comparable conclusion. While I try to reinterpret Wang Yangming's emphasis on the "unity of knowing and being" from the perspective of Huayan Buddhism, Fung returns to the metaphysical roots of neo-Confucianism. His careful analysis yields the following conclusion: "*Liang-zhi* cannot simply be described as non-empirical, more importantly, I show that it cannot be identified as any kind of knowledge or knowing capacity, enlightenment or enlightening capacity, intellectual intuition or mystical feeling. *Liang-zhi* is not an *epistemic* concept in any sense. To treat *liangzhi* as some kind of knowing faculty or mental capacity is to stray from Wang Yangming's main philosophical train of thought." See Fung Yiu-ming 馮耀明, "Wang Yang-ming's Theory of *Liang-zhi*—A New Interpretation of Wang Yang-ming's Philosophy" (王陽明的良知理論: 王陽明哲學新詮), *Tsing Hua Journal of Chinese Studies* 42, no. 2 (June 2012): 261.

82. Wang's words go: 又如知痛, 必已自痛方知痛; 知寒, 必已自寒; 知飢, 必已自飢. See his "Dialogues with Xu Ai" 徐愛記 in *Chuanxi lu* 傳習錄.

83. Liang Qichao, "Wang Yangming zhixing heyi zhi jiao" 王陽明知行合一之教 (Wang Yangming's teaching on the unity of knowing and being), in *Chuangxi lu jiping* 傳習錄集評 (Collected commentaries on Instructions for Practical Living) (Beijing: Jiuzhou chuban she, 2015), 5.

84. Wang Yangming, 傳習錄 (Instructions for practical living), in *Wang Yangming quanji*, juan 2.

85. For Wai-yee Li's exemplary study on this topic, see "Shuo zhen: Mudan ting yu mingmo qingchu wenhua" 說真:《牡丹亭》與明末清初文化 (On being genuine: *Peony Pavilion* from Late Ming to Early Qing), in *Qunqu chun saner yue tian—miandui shijie de kunqu yu mudanting* 崑曲春三二月天—面對世界的崑曲與牡丹亭 (Kun Opera and the Peony Pavilion from comparative perspectives), ed. Hua Wei (Shanghai: Shanghai guji chubanshe, 2010), 448–65.

86. See Richard G. Wang, "The Cult of Qing: Romanticism in the Late Ming Period and in the Novel Jiao Hong Ji," *Ming Studies* 33 (1994): 12–55.

87. Ling Hon Lam, *The Spatiality of Emotion in Early Modern China: From Dreamscapes to Theatricality* (New York: Columbia University Press, 2018), 3.

88. Lam, *Spatiality of Emotions*, 25.

89. In the "Society" chapter of *Aesthetic Theory*, Adorno notes that modern artists often perceive art as an autonomous force: people make art to articulate an individual voice and to speak against established norms in an administered capitalist society. But for the theorist, neither does good art "try" to resist social norms, nor does it express or trigger personal, otherwise repressed emotions. The will to resist exposes the very failure of breaking away from the confinement of norms. Instead of bringing one closer to oneself, good art removes one from it. When a person experiences good art, he is *taken by* it and loses one's footing: "The possibility of truth, embodied in the aesthetic image, becomes tangible" (244). Adorno describes the moments of having "self-preservation fall away" and the "liquidation, or annihilation, of I." His description reveals precisely how emotion is being experienced in the first place and how, after all, the reflection of one's emotional experience implies living (from now on) in the representation of the emotional experience and being expelled from the experience itself. The self who experiences and the subjectivity that conceptualizes the self's experience become strangers at the moment of reflection. For more details, see Theodor Adorno, *Aesthetic Theory* (Minneapolis: University of Minnesota Press, 1997), 244–45.

90. See Ling Hon Lam's chapter 1, "Winds, Dreams, Theater: A Genealogy of Emotion-Realms," in *Spatiality of Emotions*, 19–52.

91. Marta Figlerowicz, "Affect Dossier," *Qui Parle* 20, no. 2 (2012): 6.

92. Figlerowicz, "Affect Dossier," 12.

93. See Xiaobing Tang's chapter "The Nation and Revolution: Narrating the Modern Event," in *Global Space and the Nationalist Discourse of Modernity: The Historical Thinking of Liang Qichao*, 80–116.

94. Chen believes that since Meiji intellectuals were dissatisfied with the Tokugawa bureaucracy and wished to restore the emperor, their use of *kakumei* suggests reform instead of dynastic overthrow.

95. See Chen Jianhua, "Chinese Revolution in the Syntax of World Revolution," in *Tokens of Exchange: The Problem of Translation in Global Circulation*, ed. Lydia Liu (Durham, NC: Duke University Press, 1999), 357.

96. For more details, see Chen, "Chinese Revolution in the Syntax of World Revolution," 355–74; also see Chen's *Geming de xiandaixing: Zhongguo geming huayu kaolun* 革命的現代性: 中國革命話語考論 (The modernity of Geming: A study of the discourse on revolution in China) (Shanghai: Shanghai guji chubanshe, 2000), 1–59.

97. Liang Qichao, "Luolan furen zhuang," in XMCB 18 (1902): 38.

98. For more details, see Michel Poizat, *The Angel's Cry: Beyond the Pleasure Principle in Opera*, trans. Arthur Denner (Ithaca, NY: Cornell University Press, 1992). For a study on the acoustic excitement generated by the sound

effects storytellers created in Chinese vernacular and martial arts fiction, see Paize Keulemans's chapter 3, "Sound That Sell: Vendor Calls and the Acoustic Aesthetics of the Market Place," and chapter 4, "Listening to the Martial Arts Scene: Onomatopoeia in *The Three Knights Series*," in *Sound Rising from the Paper: Nineteenth-Century Martial Arts Fiction and the Chinese Acoustic Imagination* (Cambridge, MA: Harvard University Asia Center, 2014), 96–144 and 145–78.

99. Poizat, *Angel's Cry*, 75.

100. Mladen Dolar, *A Voice and Nothing More* (Cambridge, MA: MIT Press, 2006), 4.

101. Dolar, *Voice*, 75.

102. Dolar, *Voice*, 30.

103. Dolar, *Voice*, 8.

104. My use of the word "unwork" is inspired by John Hamilton's monograph *Music, Madness, and the Unworking of Language* (New York: Columbia University Press, 2013). For Hamilton's discussion on the dissociative power of music, see his introduction, "The Subject of Music and Madness," 1–19.

105. Roland Barthes, *The Responsibility of Forms: Critical Essays on Music, Art, and Representation* (New York: Hill and Wang, 1985), 249.

106. Barthes, *Responsibility of Forms*, 255.

107. Derrida, Writing and Difference, 211.

108. Barthes, *Responsibility of Forms*, 207.

109. Paul de Man, *Allegories of Reading: Figural Language in Rousseau, Nietzsche, Rilke, and Proust* (New Haven, CT: Yale University Press, 1979), 12; emphasis added.

110. Liang Qichao, "Xiongyali aiguozhe Gesushi zhuan," in XMCB 6 (1902): 36.

111. For more details, see Liang Qichao, "Yidali jianguo sanjie zhuan," in XMCB 9 (1902): 31–44; XMCB 10 (1902): 40–53; XMCB 14 (1902): 31–42.

112. Liang Qichao, "Luolan furen zhuan," in XMCB 17 (1902): 36.

113. Liang Qichao, "Sibada xiaozhi," in XMCB 13 (1902): 22–24.

114. Liang Qichao, "Luanlan furen zhuan," in XMCB 17 (1902): 39–40.

115. Liang, "Luanlan furen zhuan," 40.

116. See Liang Qichao, "Luolan furen zhuan," in XMCB 18 (1902): 51. Matsuo Yoji's study of Liang's historical biography shows that the "Biography of Madame Roland" is based on Tokutomi Roka's 德富蘆花 biography "Futsukoku kakumei no hana" 佛國革命の花 (Flower of the French Revolution), which is collected in *Sekai kokon meifu kagami* 世界古今名婦鑑 (Mirror of renowned women from ancient and modern Times) (Tokyo: Min'yūsha, 1898), 1–48. The monologues that I discuss are again Liang's invention instead of his translation of Tokutomi's original work. Tokutomi's biography is available at "Digital Library from the Meiji Era," accessed December 27, 2023, http://kindai.ndl.go.jp/info:ndljp/pid/777148?itemId=info%3Andljp%2Fpid%2F777148&__lang=en.

For Xia Xiaohong's comparison of Liang's "Biography of Madame Roland" and Tokutomi's "Flower of the French Revolution," see "Shijie gujin mingfu jian yu wanqing waiguo nüjie zhuang"《世界古今名婦鑑》與晚清外國女傑傳 (Mirror of renowned women from ancient and modern times and Western heroines in late Qing China), *Beijing daxue xuebao (zhexue shehui bao)* 北京大學學報 (哲学社會科學版) (Journal of Peking University: Philosophy and Social Science Edition) 46, no. 2 (March 2009): 35–48. Also see Xia's "Wanqing nübao hong de xifang nüjie—mingzhi 'furen lizhi' duwu de zhongguo zhilu" 晚清女報中的西方女傑—明治'婦人立志 (Western heroines in late Qing's women's newspaper—The journal of Meiji Japan's women's magazines in China), in *Wen shi zhe* 文史哲 (Literature, History, and Philosophy) 4 (2012): 20–34.

117. Liang Qichao, "Luolan furen zhuan," in XMCB 17 (1902): 35.

118. Liang Qichao, "Luolan furen zhuan," in XMCB 18 (1902): 50. Emphasis added.

119. Chang Hao and Tang Xiaobing offer two alternative readings for this final episode. Chang Hao, for instance, believes that "Madame Roland's sacrifice at the altar of liberty conveyed clearly his (Liang's) disenchantment with Rousseau's ideals of liberty and natural rights." See C. Philip. Chang, *Liang Ch'i-ch'ao and Modern Chinese Liberalism*, 193. For Tang, Madame Roland's last words indicate that the "radical destruction" had prompted Liang to ponder consequences created by the revolution as well as the "individual and personal dimension of collective action." See Xiaobing Tang, *Global Space*, 112.

120. *Gudai hanyu xuci cidian* 古代漢語虛詞詞典 (A dictionary of empty words in classical Chinese) (Beijing: Shangwu yinshuguan, 1999), 606.

121. Liang, "Jinggao wo tongyue zhujun," 6.

122. Liang, "Jinggao wo tongyue zhujun," 6.

123. Liang, "Jinggao wo tongyue zhujun," 6.

124. Liang, "Jinggao wo tongyue zhujun," 6.

125. Liang Qichao, "Jinggao dangdaozhe" 敬告當道者 (A respectful note to those in power), in XMCB 18 (1902): 1–16.

126. Liang, "Jinggao dangdaozhe," 13–5.

127. Liang, "Jinggao dangdaozhe," 9.

128. See the fifth chapter of the "Xin Zhongguo weilaiji," in XXS 7 (1902): 107–40. The editor of the journal did not include the name of its author, but there are at least two pieces of evidence indicating that the fifth chapter was composed by someone other than Liang Qichao. First, in intertextual commentaries inserted in previous chapters of the "Xin Zhongguo weilaiji," Liang said that he had intended to write only three chapters; the fourth chapter is an unexpected addition. C. T. Hsia arrives at a similar observation. He points out that "He (Liang) says he had written two or three chapters, but since the second and third chapters are equally inventive in technique, while the fourth chapter departs in mood and method completely from the preceding narrative,

I believe Liang must have completed three chapters by the time he wrote the preface, and it was his realization that chapter 4 was a false start that led him to discontinue the novel." See C. T. Hsia, *C. T. Hsia on Chinese Literature* (New York: Columbia University Press, 2004), 242. Second, there are considerable stylistic differences between the first four chapters of the novella and the fifth one. For a study on these differences, see Yu Lixin 余立新, "Xin zhongguo weilaiji di wu hui bushi chuzi Liang Qichao zhi shou"《新中國未來記》第五回不是出自梁啟超之手 (The future of new China's fifth chapter did not derive from Liang Qichao), *Guji yanjiu* 古籍研究 (Journal of Ancient Books Studies) 2 (1997): 85–87. For an investigation of the fifth chapter's authorship, see Yamada Keizō's "Shin chūgoku miraiki o megutte," in *Kyōdō kenkyū Ryō Keichō: Seiyō kindai shisō juyō to Meiji Nihon* 共同研究梁啓超：西洋近代思想受容と明治日本 (Collaborative research on Liang Qichao: The reception of modern Western thought and Meiji Japan) (Tokyo: Misuzu shobo, 1999), 331–58. For Xia Xiaohong's responses to Yu and Yamada, see "Shui shi xin zhongguo weilai ji di wu hui de zuozhe" 誰是《新中國未來記第五回》的作者 (Who is the author of the future of the China's chapter five?), in *Zhonghua dushu bao* 中華讀書報 (China Reading Weekly), May 21, 2003.

129. Juan Wang has devoted a book-length study exploring why late Qing tabloid writers such as Wu Jianren and Li Baojia (李寶嘉) (courtesy name Li Boyuan 李伯元) (1867–1906) shared particular enthusiasm in making fun of Liang Qichao and his fellow reformists. See *Merry Laughter and Angry Curses: The Shanghai Tabloid Press, 1897–1911* (Vancouver: University of British Columbia Press, 2012). For discussions on sarcastic allusions to late Qing tabloid writers made on Liang Qichao, see A. Ying 阿英, "Lixian yundong liangmian guan" 立憲運動兩面觀 (Two faces of the constitutional movement), in *Wanqing xiaoshuo shi* 晚清小說史 (A history of late Qing fiction) (Jiangsu: Fenghuang chuban jituan, 2009), 76–89; Xia Xiaohong, "Wu Jianren yu Liang Qichao guanxi gouchen" 吳趼人與梁啟超關係鉤沉 (Complicated liaisons between Wu Jianren and Liang Qichao), in *Wan Qing bao kan, xing bie yu wen hua zhuan xing: Xia Xiaohong xuan ji* 晚清報刊、性別與文化轉型：夏曉虹選集 (Late Qing newspapers and journals, gender, and cultural transformation: Selected works by Xia Xiaohong), comp. and ed. LüWencui 呂文翠 (Taibei: Renjian chubanshe, 2013), 87–99 (originally published in *Anhui shifan daxue xuebao* 安徽師範大學學報 (Journal of Anhui Normal University) 30, no. 6 (Nov. 2002): 636–40). Leo Lee has also pointed out that the use of the word *xiao* 笑 (laugh) became increasingly frequent in journals and newspapers as late Qing China's political situation deteriorated. See Lee Ou-fan, "Dizhi mo de xuanwa—wanqing wenxue chongtan" 帝制末日的喧嘩—晚清文學重探 (Uproar at the end of imperial China: Re-exploration of the late Qing literature), *Zhongguo wenzhe yanjiu tongxun* 中國文哲研究通訊 (Newsletter from the Institute of Chinese Literature and Philosophy, Academia Sinica) 20, no. 2 (June 2010): 215.

130. Wu Jianren 吳研人, *Jin shi nian zhi guai xian zhuang* 二十年目睹之怪現狀 (Strange things of the past ten years) (Tianjin: Tianjin guji chubanshe, 1986). In addition to *Strange Things*, Wu expresses sarcastic mockery toward the reformer in titles such as *Xin shitou ji* 新石頭記 (New story of the stone) (Zhengzhou: Zhongzhou guji chubanshe, 1986), and *Shanghai youcan lu* 上海游驂錄 (Travels in Shanghai), collected in *Wu Jianren quanji: San* 吳趼人全集 (3) (Ha'erbin, China: Beifang wenyi chubanshe, 1998), 437–91.

Postscript

1. To indicate that he had built a convincing case against Zhang Taiyan, Liang Qichao took the liberty of publishing Zhang's manifesto alongside his refutation. For Liang's summary of Zhang's key arguments and the Zhang's original writing, see Liang Qichao, "Da moubao disihao duiyu xinmin congbao zhi bolun" 答某報第四號對於新民叢報之駁論 (Reply to the refutation certain newspaper posted against the fourth volume of New Citizen Journal) (1905), in *Yinbingshi heji* 飲冰室合集 (Collected volumes from ice-drinking studio) (From hereafter *YBSHJ*) 18:101; also see Zhang Taiyan, "Bo Xinmin Congbao zuijin zhi fei geming lun" 駁新民叢報最近之非革命論 (Refutations on New Citizen Journal's protest against the political revolution), in *YBSHJ* 18:102–31.

2. Liang Qichao, "Kaiming zhuanzhi lun" 開明專制論 (On literal autocracy) (1905), in *YBSHJ* 17:78.

3. Liang, "Kaiming zhuanzhi lun," 17:78.

4. Liang Qichao, "Shimin de qunzhong huodong zhi yiyi ji jiazhi" (市民的群衆運動之意義及價值) (The meaning and value of citizen's public movements) (1921), in *YBSHJ* 39:36.

5. Liang Qichao, "Da moubao disihao," 78/81.

6. Liang, "Da moubao disihao," 66, 62.

7. Liang, "Da moubao disihao," 78.

8. Liang Qichao listed a total of thirteen reasons that had prevented China from conceiving its election law. For more details, see his "Kaiming zhuanzhi lun," 81–82.

9. Liang, "Da moubao disihao," 78.

10. See Liang Qichao, "Shenlun zhongzu geming yu zhengzhi geming zhi deshi" 申論種族革命與政治革命之得失 (Further discussions on the pros and cons between ethnic revolution and political revolution) (1905), in *YBSHJ* 19:19 and 41.

11. Liang Qichao, "Baodong yu waiguo ganshe" 暴動與外國干涉 (Riots and foreign countries' interference) (1905), in *YBSHJ* 19:55.

12. Liang, "Da moubao disihao," 92.

13. Liang, "Shenlun zhongzu geming," 7.

14. Liang, "Shenlun zhongzu geming," 43.
15. Liang, "Shenlun zhongzu geming," 43.
16. Liang, "Da moubao disihao," 74.
17. Liang, "Shenlun zhongzu geming," 7.
18. Liang, "Shenlun zhongzu geming," 9.
19. Liang, "Shenlun zhongzu geming," 9.

20. My definition of *liangzhi* being "affective" is different from what Harvey Lederman perceived to be the mainstream "affective-perceptual model," which regards *liangzhi* as a form of premeditated moral intuition that subsconsciously informs and directs people's embodied actions. I agree with Harvey Lederman that *liangzhi* refers to cognitive introspection. By *liangzhi* being "affective," I am referring solely to *liangzhi*'s inability to activate, or "switch on," its cognitive functions when it is in operation.

21. Liang Qichao, "Liangxin mamu zhi guomin" 良心麻木之國民 (National citizens with their consciousness numb) (1915), *YBSHJ* 33:55.

22. Liang, "Liangxin mamu zhi guomin," 56.

23. Liang, "Liangxin mamu zhi guomin," 56.

24. Liang Qichao, "Zhongguo guohui zhidu siyi" 中國國會制度私議 (My personal proposals on China's congress design) (1912), in *YBSHJ* 24:2.

25. Liang Qichao, "Yinian lai zhi zhengxiang yu guomin chendu zhi toushe" 一年來之政象與國民程度之投射 (Between the political situation of the past one year and its projection of citizens' level of performance) (1912), in *YBSHJ* 30:16.

26. See Thomas Metzger, "The Neo-Confucian Sense of Predicament," in *Escape from Predicament*, 49–165.

27. For the subversive political potential concealed in Wang Yangming's moral philosophy, see Araki Kengo, *Bukkyō to Jukyō: Chūgoku Shisō wo keiseisuru mono* 佛教と儒教: 中国思想を形成するもの (Confucianism and Buddhism: The formation of Chinese thought) (Kyōto, Heirakuji Shoten [Shōwa 38; 1963]); Yu Ying-shih, *Songminglixue yu zhengzhi wenhua* 宋明理學與政治文化 (Neo-Confucianism and political culture) (Taipei: Yongchen congkan, 2004); Ivanhoe, *Ethics in the Confucian Tradition: The Thought of Mencius and Wang Yang-Ming*, 2nd ed. (Indianapolis, IN: Hackett, 2002).

28. Ivanhoe elaborates this argument in two books and one collected volume. See his *Three Streams: Confucian Reflections on Learning and the Moral Heart-Mind in China, Korea, and Japan*; *Oneness: East Asian Conceptions of Virtue, Happiness, and How We Are All Connected*; and the collected volume *The Oneness Hypothesis: Beyond the Boundary of Self*, ed. Philip J. Ivanhoe, Owen J. Flanagan, Victoria S. Harrison, Hagop Sarkissian, and Eric Schwitzgebel.

29. See Fuller, *Drifting among Rivers and Lakes: Southern Song Dynasty Poetry and the Problem of Literary History* (Cambridge, MA: Harvard University Asia Center, 2013). The second chapter, "The Source and Streams Flowing from It," is particularly relevant. For a discussion of the question of cosmic correspondence

in Tang Poetry, see Stephen Owen, *Traditional Chinese Poetry and Poetics: Omen of the World* (Madison: University of Wisconsin Press, 1985).

30. Metzger, *Escape from Predicament*, 75; Qian Mu 錢穆, *Zhuzi xin xuean* 朱子新學案 (A new biography of Zhu Xi's academic life), vol. 1 (Beijing: Jiuzhou chuban she, 2011), 1–15, 300.

31. For the relationship between the rise of Zhu Xi's *lixue* and Wang Anshi's political reform, see Yu Ying-shih, *Zhu Xi de lishi shijie* 朱熹的歷史世界 (The historical world of Zhu Xi) (Taipei: Yunchen congkan, 1996–97).

32. See Metzger, *Escape from Predicament*, 158. Metzger's book was published in 1977. To quote him in 2020 evokes strong and mixed feelings.

33. See Brook Ziporyn, *Ironies of Oneness and Differences* (New York: State University of New York Press, 2012).

34. See Metzger, "Neo-Confucian Sense of Predicament," 49–165.

35. Liang, "Da moubao disihao," 60.

36. Liang, "Da moubao disihao," 81.

37. Liang, "Da moubao disihao," 19.

38. Liang also said: 今日中國政治非可采用共和立憲者也 in "Da moubao disihao," 59.

39. Liang Qichao, "Shuo youzhi" 說幼稚 (On nativity) (1912), in *YBSHJ* 30:45–46; comparable remarks also appear in Liang Qichao, "Zhengzhi shang zhi duikang li" (Confrontational force in politics) 政治上之對抗力 (1912) in *YBSHJ* 30:32.

40. Liang, "Shenlun zhongzu geming," 15.

41. Liang, "Kaiming zhuanzhi lun," 49–83.

42. For the meticulous roadmap Liang envisioned for China's burgeoning national congress, see "Zhongguo guohui zhidu siyi," 1–147.

43. Liang, "Zhongguo guohui zhidu siyi," 73–76.

44. Liang Qichao, "Zhongguo daode zhi dayuan" 中國道德之大原 (The great origins of Chinese morality) (1911), in *YBSHJ* 28:13; for Liang's discussion of the development of parliamentary democracy in the United States, also see his "Ouzhou zhengzhi gejing zhi yuanyi" 歐洲政治革進之原因 (Reasons that contribute to Europe's political progress) (1912), in *YBSHJ* 30:39–44.

45. Liang, "Zhongguo daode zhi dayuan," 32.

46. Liang, "Da moubao disihao," 85.

47. Liang, "Zhongguo daode zhi dayuan," 12.

48. Liang Qichao, "Guoxing pian" 國性篇 (On national temperament) (1911), in *YBSHJ* 28:88. In this article, Liang describe people as 桀黠凶戾之民.

49. Liang, "Zhongguo daode zhi dayuan," 12.

50. Liang, "Yinian lai zhi zhenxiang yu guomin chendu zhi toushe," 18.

51. Liang, "Zhongguo daode zhi dayuan," 13.

52. Liang, "Zhongguo daode zhi dayuan," 20.

53. Liang, "Zhongguo daode zhi dayuan," 20.

54. Huang Zongxi 黃宗羲, "Zhezhong Wang meng xuean yi" 浙中王門學案一 (The first record on Scholars from Zhejiang), in *Mingru xuean* 明儒學案 (The records of Ming scholars). Huang Zongxi. *The Records of Ming Scholars*, edited and translated by Julia Ching (in collaboration with Chaoying Fang) (Honolulu: University of Hawaii Press, 1987), 113.

55. Liang, "Shimin de qunzhong huodong," 35–39.

56. Liang Qichao, "Pinglun Hu Shi zhi zhongguo zhexue shi dagang" 評論胡適之中國哲學史大綱 (Comments on Hu Shi's An Outline of the History of Chinese philosophy) (1921), in *YBSHJ* 38:61.

57. Liang Qichao, "Zhi buke erwei zhuyi yu wei er buyou zhuyi" "知不可而為"主義與 "為而不有"主義 (Between knowing what is impossible but working toward and working and not expecting an result) (1921), in *YBSHJ* 37:63.

58. Liang Qichao, "Weixue yu zuoren" 為學與做人 (Between learning and being a good person) (1921), in *YBSHJ* 39:107.

59. Liang Qichao, "Zhongguo yunwen litou suo biaoxiang de qinggan" 中國韻文裏頭所表現的情感 (Feelings expressed in China's rhapsodic verses) (1922), in *YBSHJ* 37:71.

60. Liang Qichao, "Renshengguan yu kexue" 人生觀與科學 (Outlook on life and science) (1922), in *YBSHJ* 40:26.

61. Liang, "Zhongguo yunwen," 71.

62. Liang, "Zhongguo yunwen," 71.

63. Liang, "Shimin de qunzhong huodong," 36.

64. Liang Qichao, "Waijiao yu neizheng yu" 外交歟內政歟 (Sighs to foreign affairs, and sighs to inner affairs) (1920), in *YBSHJ*, 37:59.

65. Liang, "Waijiao yu neizheng yu," 54.

66. Liang, "Shimin de qunzhong huodong," 37.

67. Liang, "Shimin de qunzhong huodong," 38.

68. Liang Qichao, "Jiaoyu yu zhengzhi" 教育與政治 (Education and politics) (1922), in *YBSHJ* 38:76 (把知識教育放在第二位, 把人格教育放在第一位。所謂人格, 其實只是團體生活所必要的人格。)

69. Liang, "Jiaoyu yu zhengzhi," 77.

70. Liang, "Jiaoyu yu zhengzhi," 75.

71. Liang, "Shimin de qunzhong huodong," 39.

72. Liang Qichao, "Shenme shi wenhua" 什麼是文化 (What is culture?) (1922), in *YBSHJ* 39:100; Liang also made a comparable remark in his "Ouyou xinying lu" 歐遊心影錄 (A record of the heart's reflection in the travel to Europe) (Beijing: Shangwu yinshuguan, 2017), 6–7.

73. Liang, "Shenme shi wenhua," 100.

74. Liang, "Zhi buke erwei zhuyi yu wei er buyou zhuyi," 62.

75. Liang, "Zhi buke erwei zhuyi yu wei er buyou zhuyi," 63.

76. Liang Qichao, "Huguo zhi yi huigu tan" 護國之役回顧談 (Looking back to the battle of protecting nation) (1922), in *YBSHJ* 39:86–96.
77. Liang, "Renshengguan yu kexue," 26.
78. Liang, "Waijiao yu neizheng yu," 59.

Bibliography

Abbreviations

DYJ *Deyu jian* 德育鑑 [Mirror for moral cultivation]
XMCB *Xinmin congbao* 新民叢報 [New Citizen Journal]
XXS *Xin xiaoshuo* 新小說 [New fiction]
YBSHJ *Yinbingshi heji* 飲冰室合集 [Collected volumes from ice-drinking studio]

Adorno, Theodor. *Aesthetic Theory*. Minneapolis: University of Minnesota Press, 1997.
———. "Music, Language, and Composition." Translated by Susan Gillespie. *Musical Quarterly* 77, no. 3 (Autumn 1993): 401–14.
———. "Parataxis: On Hölderlin's Late Poetry." In *Notes to Literature*, vol. 2, edited by Rolf Tiedemann, translated by Shierry Weber Nicholsen, 109–49. New York: Columbia University Press, 1991.
Anderson, Benedict. *Imagined Communities: Reflections on the Origin and Spread of Nationalism*. London: Verso, 1983.
Angel, Stephen. *Human Rights and Chinese Thought: A Cross-Cultural Inquiry*. Cambridge: Cambridge University Press, 2002.
Araki Kengo 荒木見悟. *Bukkyō to Jukyō: Chūgoku Shisō wo keiseisuru mono* 佛教と儒教: 中国思想を形成するもの [Confucianism and Buddhism: The formation of Chinese thought]. Kyōto, Heirakuji Shoten (Shōwa 38; 1963).
———. "Chen Baisha yu Zhan Ganquan" 陳白沙與湛甘泉 [Chen Baisha and Zhan Ganquan] *Journal of Renmin University of China* [中國人民大學學報] 6 (1991): 34–44.
———. "Yijing yu lengranjing" 易經與楞嚴經 [Yijing and the Śūraṅgama Sūtra]. Translated by Yang Baiyi 楊白衣. In *Yijiuqiba nian foxue yanjiu lunwen ji* 一九七八年佛學研究論文集. Taiwan: Foguang wenhua, 1978.
Aristotle. "On the Soul." In *Aristotle: On the Soul. Parva Naturalia. On Breath*, 2–203. Cambridge, MA: Harvard University Press, 1957.
A. Ying 阿英. *Wanqing xiaoshuo shi* 晚清小說史 [A history of late Qing fiction]. Jiangsu: Fenghuang chuban jituan, 2009.

Bao Weihong. *Fiery Cinema: The Emergence of an Affective Medium in China, 1915–1945*. Minneapolis: University of Minnesota Press, 2015.

———. "The Politics of Remediation: Mise-en-scène and the Subjunctive Body in Chinese Opera Film." *Opera Quarterly* 26, no. 2–3 (2010): 256–90.

Barthes, Roland. "The Reality Effect." In *French Literary Theory Today: A Reader*, edited by Tzvetan Todorov, 141–48. Cambridge: Cambridge University Press, 1982.

———. *The Responsibility of Forms: Critical Essays on Music, Art, and Representation*. Translated by Richard Howard. New York: Hill and Wang, 1985.

Bass, Alan. *Difference and Disavowal: The Trauma of Eros*. Stanford, CA: Stanford University Press, 2000.

Bastid-Bruguière, Marianne. "Liang Qichao yu zongjiao wenji" 梁啓超与宗教問題 [Inquiries on Liang Qichao and religion. *Toho Gakuho* 東方學報 [Journal of Oriental Studies, Kyoto] 70 (1998): 329–73.

Bennett, Jill. "Aesthetics of Intermediality." *Art History*, 30, no. 3 (June 2007): 436.

Bevir, Mark. "Meaning and Intention: A Defense of Procedural Individualism." *New Literary History* 31, no. 1 (July 2000): 385–403.

Bishop, John. "Some Limitations of Chinese Fiction." *Far Eastern Quarterly* 15, no. 2 (Feb. 1956): 239–47.

Bodin, Jean. *On Sovereignty: The Six Books of the Commonwealth*. New York: Cambridge University Press, 1992.

Bol, Peter. "When Antiquity Matters: Thinking about and with Antiquity in the Tang-Song Transition." In *Perceptions of Antiquity in Chinese Civilization*, edited by Dieter Kuhn and Helga Stahl, 209–36. Heidelburg, Germany: Edition Forum, 2008.

Bolter, Jay David. "Ekphrasis, Virtual Reality, and the Future of Writing." In *The Future of The Book*, edited by Geoffrey Nunberg, 253–72. Berkeley: University of California Press, 1996.

Bolter, Jay David, and Richard Grusin. *Remediation: Understanding New Media*. Cambridge, MA: MIT Press, 1999.

Børdahl, Vibeke. "The Storyteller's Manner in Chinese Storytelling." *Asian Folklore Studies* 62 (2003): 1–48.

Cai Lesu 蔡樂蘇, Zhang Yong 張勇, and Wang Xianming 王憲明. *Wuxu bianfa shishu lungao* 戊戌變法史述論稿 [Draft on the historical narrative and discussion on the 1898 reformist movement]. Beijing: Qinghua daxue chuban she, 2001.

Cai, Zongqi. "The Rethinking of Emotion: The Transformation of Traditional Literary Criticism in the Late Qing Era." *Monumenta Serica* 45 (1997): 63–100.

Chan Chi-keung 陳志強. "Acquiring Mere Knowledge and Empty Moralizing: Luo Nianan on the Faults of Confucian Practitioners" [知見空言——羅念菴論「學者」之過]. *Chinese Studies* 漢學研究 34, no. 4 (2016): 99–130.

———. *Wangming Wangxue yuane lun* 晚明王學原惡論 [On the original sin in Wang Yangming's teaching in the late Ming period]. Taipei: Guoli Taiwan daxue chuban zhongxin, 2018.

Chan Man Sing 陳萬成. *Zhongwai wenhua jiaoliu tanyi: Xingxue, yixue, qita* 中外文化交流探繹: 星學・醫學・其他 [Exploration of the East-West cultural exchange: Astrology, medicine, and others]. Beijing: Zhonghua shuju, 2010.

Chan, Sin-wai. *Buddhism in Late Ch'ing Political Thought*. Hong Kong: Chinese University Press, 1985.

———. *An Exposition of Benevolence: The "Jen-hsüeh" of T'an Ssu-t'ung*. Hong Kong: The Chinese University Press, 1984.

Chan, Wing-tsit, trans. *A Source Book in Chinese Philosophy*. Princeton, NJ: Princeton University Press, 1963.

———. "How Buddhistic Is Wang Yang-ming?" *Philosophy East and West*, 12, no. 3 (Oct. 1962): 203–15.

Chang, Carsun. *Development of Neo-Confucian Thought*. New York: Bookman Associates, 1957.

Chang, Hao. *Chinese Intellectuals in Crisis: Search for Order and Meaning, 1890–1911*. Berkeley: University of California Press, 1987.

———. *Liang Ch'i-Ch'ao and Intellectual Transition in China, 1890–1907*. Cambridge, MA: Harvard University Press, 1971.

———. *Liang Qichao yu zhongguo sixiang de guodu, 1890–1907* 梁啟超與中國思想的過渡 1890–1907 [Liang Ch'i-ch'ao and intellectual transition in China, 1890–1907]; *Lieshi jingshen yu pipan yishi: Tan Sitong sixiang de fenxi*.; 烈士精神與批評意識: 譚嗣同思想分析 [The spirit of the martyr and his critical consciousness: An analysis of Tan Sitong]. Translated by Cui Zhihai 崔志海 and Ge Fuping 葛夫平. Beijing: Xinxing chubanshe, 2006.

———. "Youan yishi yu minzhu chuantong" 幽暗意識與民主傳統 [Consciousness of darkness and the democratic tradition]. In *Youan yishi yu minzhu chuantong* 幽暗意識與民主傳統, 3–32. Taipei: Lianjing chubanshe, 2000.

———. "Zhuanxing shidai zai zhongguo jindai sixiangshi yu wenhuashi shang de zhongyao xing" 轉型時代在中國近代思想史與文化史上的重要性 [The significance of the transformational era in modern Chinese intellectual and cultural history]. In *Zhang Hao zixuan ji* 張灝自選集 [Selected works of Chang Hao]. Shanghai: Shanghai jiaoyu chubanshe, 2002.

Chang, Kang-i Sun, and Stephen Owen, eds. *The Cambridge History of Chinese Literature*. Cambridge: Cambridge University Press, 2010.

Chen, Jianhua 陳建華. "Chinese Revolution in the Syntax of World Revolution." In *Tokens of Exchange: The Problem of Translation in Global Circulation*, edited by Lydia Liu, 355–74. Durham, NC: Duke University Press, 1999.

———. *Cong geming dao gonghe: Qingmo zhi minguo shiqi wenxue, dian ying yu wenhua de zhuanxing* 從革命到共和: 清末至民初時期文學、電影與文化的轉型 [From revolution to the republic: Literary, cinematic, and cultural transformations]. Guilin, China: Guangxi shifan daxue chubanshe, 2009.

———. *Geming de xiandaixing: Zhongguo Geming huayu kaolun* 革命的現代性: 中國革命話語考論 [The modernity of *Geming*: A study of the discourse on revolution in China]. Shanghai: Shanghai guji chubanshe, 2000.

Chen Junqi 陳俊啟. "Conggu Liang Qichao xiaoshuo guan ji qi zai xiaoshuo shi shang de yiyi" 重估梁啟超小說觀及其在小說史上的意義 [A reassessment of Liang Qichao's theory of fiction and its significance in the history of Chinese fiction]. *Hanxue yanjiu* 漢學研究 (Chinese Studies) 20, no. 1 (2002): 309–38.

Chen Pingyuan 陳平原. *Zhongguo xiandai xiaoshuo de qidian: Qingmo minchu xiaoshuo yanjiu* 中國現代小說的起點: 清末民初小說研究 [Origins of modern Chinese fiction: A study of late Qing and early republican fiction]. Beijing: Beijing daxue chubanshe, 2005.

———. "Yousheng de Zhongguo: Yanshuo yu jinxiandai Zhongguo wenzhang biange" 有聲的中國: '演說' 與近現代中國文章變革 [On the relationship between "public speaking" and the development of Chinese prose]. *Wenxue pinglun* 文學評論 [Literary Criticism] 3 (2007): 5–21.

Chen, Pingyuan 陳平原, and Xia Xiaohong 夏曉紅, eds. *Ershi shiji Zhongguo xiaoshuo lilun ziliao: Diyi juan "yiba jiuqi yijiu yiliu"* 二十世紀中國小說理論資料: 第一卷 (一八九七——一九一六) [Materials on twentieth century fiction theory: Volume one (1897–1916)]. Beijing: Beijing daxue chubanshe, 1989.

Cheng, Chung-ying 成中英. "Confucian Onto-Hermeneutics: Morality and Ontology." *Journal of Chinese Philosophy* 27, no. 1 (March 2000): 33–68.

———. *Yixue bengti lun* 易學本體論 [Body, mind, and spirit]. Taipei: Kangde chubanshe, 2008.

Chow, Kai-wing. "Writing for Success: Printing, Examinations, and Intellectual Change in Late Ming China." *Late Imperial China* 17 (June 1996): 12–57.

Chu Hung-lam 朱鴻林. *Zhu Honglin du Huang Zongxi: "Mingru xuean" jianggao* 朱鴻林讀黃宗羲: 明儒學案講稿 [Chu Hung-lam reads Huang Zongxi: Lectures on The Records of Ming Scholars]. Hong Kong: Hong Kong Chinese University Press, 2013.

Cline, Erin. "Mirrors, Minds, and Metaphors." *Philosophy East and West* 58, no. 3 (2008): 337–57.

Crespi, John. *Voices in Revolution: Poetry and the Auditory Imagination in Modern China*. Honolulu: University of Hawai'i Press, 2009.

Dai Zhen 戴震. *Dai Dongyuan ji* 戴東原集 [Collected work of Dai Dongyuan], vol. 1, *juan* 8, 17–25. Shanghai: Shangyu yinshuguan, 1929.

———. *Mengzi ziyi shuzheng* 孟子字義疏證 [An evidential study of the meaning of terms of the Mengzi]. Shanghai: Shanghai shudian chuban she, 2012.

de Bary, William Theodore. *Self and Society in Ming Thought*. New York: Columbia University Press, 1970.

———. "Waiting for the Dawn: Huang Zongxi's Critique of the Chinese Dynastic System." In *Finding Wisdom in East Asian Classics*, 199–208. New York: Columbia University Press, 2011.
Deleuze, Gilles. *Essays Critical and Clinical*. Translated by D. W. Smith and M. A. Greco. Minneapolis: University of Minnesota Press, 1997.
De Man, Paul. *Allegories of Reading: Figural Language in Rousseau, Nietzsche, Rilke, and Proust*. New Haven, CT: Yale University Press, 1979.
Denton, Kirk, ed. *Modern Chinese Literary Thought: Writings on Literature, 1893–1945*. Stanford, CA: Stanford University Press, 1996.
Derrida, Jacques. *Writing and Difference*. Translated by Alan Bass. Chicago, IL: University of Chicago Press, 1978.
Des Forges, Alexander. "The Uses of Fiction: Liang Qichao and His Contemporaries." In *The Columbia Companion to Modern Chinese Literature*, edited by Kirk Denton, 97–103. New York: Columbia University Press, 2016.
Ding Wenjiang 丁文江 and Zhao Fengtian 趙豐田, eds. *Liang Qichao nianpu changbian* 梁啟超年譜長編 [An unabridged chronicle of Liang Qichao]. Shanghai: Shanghai renmin chubanshe, 2009.
Dolar, Mladen. *A Voice and Nothing More*. Cambridge, MA: MIT Press, 2006.
Doleželová-Velingerová, Milena. *The Chinese Novel at the Turn of the Century*. Toronto: University of Toronto Press, 1980.
Duara, Prasenjit. *Rescuing History from the Nation*. Chicago, IL: University of Chicago Press, 1997.
Egan, Ronald. "The Prose Style of Fan Yeh." *Harvard Journal of Asiatic Studies* 39 no. 2 (1979): 339–401.
Elman, Benjamin A. *A Cultural History of Civil Examinations in Late Imperial China*. Los Angeles: University of California Press, 2000.
———. *Classicism, Politics, and Kinship: The Ch'ang-Chou School of New Text Confucianism in Late Imperial China*. Berkeley: University of California Press, 1990.
———. *From Philosophy to Philology: Intellectual and Social Aspects of Change in Late Imperial China*. Council on East Asian Studies, Harvard University, 1984.
———. *On Their Own Terms: Science in China, 1550–1900*. Cambridge, MA: Harvard University Press, 2005.
———. "The Relevance of Sung Learning in the Late Qing: Wei Yuan and the Huang-ch'ao Ching-shih Wen-pien." *Late Imperial China* 9, no. 2 (Dec. 1988): 56–85.
Flatley, Jonathan. *Affective Mapping: Melancholia and the Politics of Modernism*. Cambridge, MA: Harvard University Press, 2008.
Feng Banggan 馮邦幹. "Falü pingtan 法律平談 [A general discussion on legal matters]. In *Xinmin congbao* 新民叢報 [New Citizen Journal] 4 (1902): 69–76.
Feng Youlan 馮友蘭. *Zhongguo zhexue shi* 中國哲學史 [History of Chinese philosophy]. Taipei: Taiwan shangwu yinshuguan, 2015.

Feng Ziyou 馮自由. *Zhonghua minguo kaiguo qian geming shi* 中國民國開國前革命史 [Revolution history that precedes the establishment of the Republic of China]. Guilin, China: Guangxi shifan daxue chubanshe, 2011.

Flammarion, Camille. *Omega: The Last Days of the World*. New York: Cosmopolitan, 1894.

Fogel, Joshua, ed. *The Role of Japan in Liang Qichao's Introduction of Modern Western Civilization to China*. Berkeley: Center for Chinese Studies, 2004.

Fogel, Joshua, and Peter Zarrow, eds. *Imagining the People: Chinese Intellectuals and the Concept of Citizenship, 1890–1920*. Armonk, NY: M. E. Sharpe, 1997.

Freud, Sigmund. *Beyond the Pleasure Principle*. Translated and edited by James Strachey. New York: Norton, 1961.

Friedberg, Anne. *The Virtual Window: From Alberti to Microsoft*. Cambridge, MS: MIT Press, 2006.

Fuller, Michael. "The Aesthetic as Immanent Assent to Pattern within Heterogeneity, or 文." In 中國文學研究的新趨向自然、審美與比較研究, 東亞文明研究叢書, vol. 53. Taipei: Taida chuban zhongxin, 2005.

———. *Being Biological: Human Meaning in the Age of Neuroscience*. Self-published: Michael Fuller, 2022.

———. *Drifting among Rivers and Lakes: Southern Song Dynasty Poetry and the Problem of Literary History*. Cambridge, MA: Harvard University Asia Center, 2013.

———. *Introduction to Chinese Poetry: From the Canon of Poetry to the Lyrics of the Song Dynasty*. Cambridge, MA: Harvard University Asia Center, 2017.

———. "Shilun wenxueshi zhong Tangsong zhuanxing de yige lilun kuangjia" 試論文學史中唐宋轉型的一個理論框架. Lecture presentation at Fudan University in August 2018.

Galikm, Marian. "On the Influence of Foreign Ideas on Chinese Literary Criticism (1898–1904)." *Asian and African Studies* (Bratislava) 2 (1966): 38–48.

Garfield, Jay L. *The Fundamental Wisdom of the Middle Way*. New York: Oxford University Press, 1995.

———. "The Heart of Wisdom Sūtra Bhagavatī-Prajñāpāramitā-Hṛdaya-Sūtra." Online access at https://jaygarfield.files.wordpress.com/2016/08/the-heart-of-wisdom-succ84tra-with-commentary.pdf.

Gasché, Rodolphe. *The Idea of Form: Rethinking Kant's Aesthetics*. Stanford, CA: Stanford University Press, 1995.

Gek Nai Cheng. "On the Relationship between Fiction and the Government of the People." In *Modern Chinese Literary Thought: Writings on Literature, 1893–1945*, edited by Kirk Denton, 74–81. Stanford, CA: Stanford University Press, 1996.

Gu, Yanwu. *Record of Daily Knowledge and Collected Poems and Essays*. Translated by Ian Johnston. New York: Columbia University Press, 2016.

Guan Kean-Fung 顏健富. *Cong "shenti" dao "shijie": Wanqing xiaoshuo de xin gainian ditu* 從「身體」到「世界」——晚清小說的新概念地圖 [From the "body" to the "world": New conceptual maps in late Qing fiction]. Taipei: National Taiwan University Press, 2014.

Gudai hanyu xuci cidian 古代漢語虛詞詞典 [A dictionary of empty words in classical Chinese]. Beijing: Shangwu yinshuguan, 1999.

Gunaratne, R. D. "Understanding Nāgārjuna's Catuṣkoṭi." *Philosophy East and West* 36, no. 3 (1986): 213–34.

Guy, Kent Guy. *The Scholar and the State in Late Imperial China*. PhD thesis, Harvard University, 1980.

Habermas, Jürgen. *The Structural Transformation of the Public Sphere*. Cambridge, MA: MIT Press, 1989.

Hamilton, John. *Music, Madness, and the Unworking of Language*. New York: Columbia University Press, 2008.

Hashimoto, Satoru. "Afterlives of the Culture: Engaging with the Trans-East Asian Cultural Tradition in Modern Chinese, Japanese, Korean, and Taiwanese Literatures, 1880s–1940s." PhD diss., Harvard University, 2014.

Hazama Naoki 狹間直樹. *Kyōdō kenkyū Ryō Keichō: Seiyō kindai shisō juyō to Meiji Nihon* 共同研究梁啓超: 西洋近代思想受容と明治日本 [Collaborative research on Liang Qichao: The reception of modern Western thought and Meiji Japan]. Tokyo: Misuzu shobo, 1999.

———. "Liang Qichao bixia de Tan Sitong: Guanyu renxue de kanxing yu liang zhuan 'Tan Sitong zhuan'" 梁啟超筆下的譚嗣同——關於《仁學》的刊行與梁撰《譚嗣同傳》" [Tan Sitong in Liang Qichao's account: On the publication of *On Benevolence* and Liang's composition of the "Biography of Tan Sitong"]. In *Liang Qichao yu jin dai Zhongguo she hui wen hua* 梁啟超與近代中國社會文化 [Liang Qichao and contemporary Chinese society and culture], edited by Li Xisuo 李喜所. Tianjin: Tianjin guji chubanshe, 2005.

———. *Liang Qichao, Mingzhi Riben, xifang Riben Jingdu daxue renwen kexue yanjiusuo gongyong yanjiu baogao* 梁啟超‧明治日本‧西方: 日本京都大學人文科學研究所共同研究報告 [Liang Qichao, Meiji Japan, and the west: collaborative research reports from Institute for Research in Humanities, Kyoto University]. Beijing: Shehui kexue wenxian chubanshe, 2001.

Headley, Phineas Camp. *The Life of Louis Kossuth, Governor of Hungary*. Ann Arbor: University of Michigan, 1995.

Hemmings, Clare. "INVOKING AFFECT: Cultural Theory and the Ontological Turn." *Cultural Studies* 19, no. 5 (2005): 548–67.

Hershock, Peter. *Chan Buddhism*. Honolulu: University of Hawaii Press, 2004.

———. *Liberating Intimacy: Enlightenment and Social Virtuosity in Ch'an Buddhism*. New York: State University of New York Press, 1996.

Hirata Hisashi 平田久. *Itarī kenkoku sanketsu* 伊太利建国三傑 [Three heroes who founded Italy]. Tokyo: Min'yūsha, 1892. Accessed April 18, 2015. http://kindai.ndl.go.jp/info:ndljp/pid/777020.

Hobson, Benjamin. *Quanti xinlun* 全體新論 [Treatise on physiology]. Beijing: Zhonghua shuju, 1991.

Hsia, Chih-tsing. *C. T. Hsia on Chinese Literature*. New York: Columbia University Press, 2004.

Hsiao, Kung-chuan. *A Modern China and a New World: K'ang Yu-Wei, Reformer and Utopian, 1858–1927*. Seattle: University of Washington Press, 1975.

Hsü, Immanuel, C. Y. *Intellectual Trends in the Chi'ing Period*. Cambridge, MA: Harvard University Press, 1959.

Hu Xiaozhen 胡曉眞. *Minzu guojia lunshu—cong wanqing, wusi dao riju shidai Taiwan xin wenxue* 民族國家論述: 從晚清, 五四到日據時代臺灣新文學 [Narratives on the nation-state: Taiwan's new literature from late Qing, may fourth, to the Japanese occupation]. Taipei: Zhongyang yanjiuyuan Zhongguo wenzhe yanjiusuo choubeichu, 1995.

Hu, Ying. "Late Qing Fiction." *The Columbia Companion to Modern Chinese Literature*, edited by Kirk Denton, 104–110. New York: Columbia University Press, 2016.

——. "Naming the First 'New Woman.'" In *Rethinking the 1898 Reform Period: Political and Cultural Change in Late Qing China*, edited by Rebecca E. Karl and Peter Zarrow, 180–211. Cambridge, MA: Harvard University Press, 2002.

Huang, C. Philip. *Liang Ch'i-Ch'ao and Modern Chinese Liberalism*. Seattle: University of Washington Press, 1972.

Huang Jinzhu 黃錦珠. *Wanqing shiqi xiaoshuo guannian zhi zhuanbian* 晚清時期小說觀念之演變 [Transformation in the concept of fiction during the late Qing period]. Taipei: Wenshizhe chubanshe, 1995.

Huang ko-wu 黃克武. "Liang Qichao yu Kangde" 梁啟超與康德 [Liang Qichao and Immanuel Kant]. *Bulletin of the Institute of Modern History Academia Sinica* 近代史研究所集刊 30 (Dec. 1998): 101–48.

——. *Yige bei fangqi de xuanze: Liang Qichao tiaoshi sixiang zhi yanjiu* 一個被放棄的選擇: 梁啟超調適思想之研究 [The rejected path: A study of Liang Ch'i-ch'ao's accommodative thinking]. Taipei: Zhongyang yanjiuyuan jindaishi yanjiusuo, 1994.

Huang Zhangjian 黃彰建. *Wuxu bianfa shi yanjiu* 戊戌變法研究 [A study of the 1898 reform]. Taipei: Institute of Linguistics and History, Academia Sinica, 1970.

Huang, Zongxi. *The Records of Ming Scholars*. Edited by Julia Ching with collaboration of Chaoying Fang. Honolulu: University of Hawaii Press, 1987.

Hughes, Theodore. *Literature and Film in Cold War South Korea Freedom's Frontier*. New York: Columbia University Press, 2012.

Hunan lishi ziliao 湖南歷史資料 [Hunan historical documents]. Vol. 4. Compiled by Hunan lishi ziliao bianji weiyuanhui 湖南歷史資料編輯委員會. Changsha, China: Hunan renmin chubanshe, 1959.

Hunan shiwu xuetang yigao 湖南時務學堂遺稿 [Unpublished writing from the Hunan School of Current Affairs]. Hunan: Hunan daxue chubanshe, 2017.

Huters, Theodore. *Bringing the World Home: Appropriating the West in Late Qing and Early Republican China*. Honolulu: University of Hawai'i Press, 2005.

———. "From Writing to Literature: The Development of Late Qing Theories of Prose." *Harvard Journal of Asiatic Studies* 47, no. 1 (June 1987): 51–96.

Jaeger, Werner. *Paideia: The Ideals of Greek Culture*. Translated by Gilbert Highet. New York: Columbia University Press, 1970.

Jiang, Tao. *Contexts and Dialogue: Yogacara Buddhism and Modern Psychology on the Subliminal Mind*. Hawaii: University of Hawaii Press, 2006.

Judge, Joan. "The Factional Function of Print: Liang Qichao, Shibao, and the Fissures in the Late Qing Reform Movement." *Late Imperial China* 16, no. 1 (1995): 120–40.

———. *Print and Politics: "Shibao" and the Culture of Reform in Late Qing China*. Stanford, CA: Stanford University Press, 1996.

Ivanhoe, Philip. "Book Review on Peter Bol's *Neo-Confucianism in History*." *Dao: A Journal of Comparative Philosophy* 9 (2010): 471–75.

———. *Ethics in the Confucian Tradition: The Thought of Mencius and Wang Yang-Ming*. 2nd ed. Indianapolis, IN: Hackett, 2002.

———. *Oneness: East Asian Conceptions of Virtue, Happiness, and How We Are All Connected*. Oxford: Oxford University Press, 2017.

———. *Three Streams: Confucian Reflections on Learning and the Moral Heart-Mind in China, Korea, and Japan*. New York: Oxford University Press, 2016.

Ivanhoe, Philip, Owen Flanagan, Victoria S. Harrison, Hagop Sarkissian, and Eric Schwitzgebel, eds. *The Oneness Hypothesis: Beyond the Boundary of Self*. New York: Columbia University Press, 2018.

Lackner, Michael, and Natasha Vittinghoff, eds. *Mapping Meanings: The Field of New Learning in Late Qing China*. Leiden: Brill, 2004.

Lackner, Michael, Iwo Amelung, and Joachim Kurtz, eds. *New Terms for New Ideas: Western Knowledge and Lexical Change in Late Imperial China*. Leiden: Brill, 2001.

Lam, Ling Hon. *The Spatiality of Emotion in Early Modern China*. New York: Columbia University Press, 2019.

Lau, D. C. trans. *Mencius*. Harmondsworth, UK: Penguin Books, 1970.

Lee, Leo Ou-fan. "Dizhi mo de xuanwa—wanqing wenxue chongtan" 帝制末日的喧嘩—晚清文學重探 [Uproar at the end of imperial China: Re-exploration of the late Qing literature]. *Zhongguo wenzhe yanjiu tongxun* 中國文哲研究

通訊 [Newsletter from the Institute of Chinese Literature and Philosophy, Academia Sinica] 20, no. 2 (June 2010): 211–21.

———. *The Romantic Generation of Modern Chinese Writers*. Cambridge, MA: Harvard University Press, 1973.

———. *Shanghai Modern: The Flowering of a New Urban Culture in China, 1930–1945*. Cambridge, MA: Harvard University Press, 1999.

———. *Xiandai xing de zhuiqiu: Li Oufan wenhua pinglun jingxuan ji* 現代性的追求：李歐梵文化評論精選集 [In search of modernity: Essays in cultural criticism]. Taipei: Maitian, 1996.

Lee, Leo Ou-fan, and Andrew Nathan. "The Beginnings of Mass Culture." In *Popular Culture in Late Imperial China*, edited by David Johnson, Andrew J. Nathan, and Evelyn S. Rawski, 360–97. Berkeley: University of California Press, 1985.

Lee Ming-huei 李明輝. "Confucianism, Kant, and Virtue Ethics." In *Virtue Ethics and Confucianism*, edited by Stephen Angle and Michael Slote, 47–55. New York: Routledge, 2013.

———. *Kangde zhexue zai dongya* 康德哲學在東亞. Taipei: Taiwan National University Press, 2016.

Lederman, Harvey. "The Introspective Model of the Unity of Knowledge and Action." *Philosophical Review* 131, no. 2 (2022): 169–213.

———. "Perception and Genuine Knowledge in Wang Yangming." In *Oxford Studies in Epistemology* 7 (2022): 134–75.

Leung, Shuk Man. "The Discursive Formation of the Utopian Imagination in New Fiction, 1902–1911." PhD diss., SOAS, University of London, 2013.

Leys, Ruth. *The Ascent of Affect: Genealogy and Critique*. Chicago, IL: University of Chicago Press, 2017.

Liang Qichao. "Baodong yu waiguo ganshe" 暴動與外國干涉 [Riots and foreign countries' interference] (1905), in *YBSHJ* 19:52–68.

———. "Baojiao fei souyi zun kong lun" 保教非所以尊孔論 [The preservation of teaching is not the reason to venerate Confucius]. *Xinmin congbao* 2 (1902): 59–72.

———. "Da moubao disihao duiyu xinmin congbao zhi bolun" 答某報第四號對於新民叢報之駁論 [Reply to the refutation certain newspaper posted against the fourth volume of New Citizen Journal] (1905), in *YBSHJ* 18:59–131.

———. "Dai Dongyuan zhexue." 戴東原哲學 [Philosophy of Dai Dongyuan]. In *Liang Qichao lun yuejia zhexue* 梁啟超論儒家哲學 [Liang Qichao on the philosophy of Confucianism]. Beijing: Shangwu yinshu guan, 2012.

———. *Deyu jian* 德育鑑 [Mirror for moral cultivation]. Yokohama, Japan: Xinmin congbao she, 1903.

———. "Dili yu wenmin zhi guanxi" 地理與文明之關係 [On the relationship between geography and civilization]. *Xinmin congbao* 2 (1902): 53–60.

———. "Du Chunqiu jieshuo" 讀春秋說 [Definitions for reading Spring and Autumn Annals], in *Hunan shiwu xuetang yibian* 湖南時務學堂遺編 [Unpublished writing from the Hunan School of Current Affairs]. Hunan: Hunan daxue chubanshe, 2017.

———. "Du Mengzi jieshuo." 讀孟子界說 [Definitions for reading Mencius]. *Qingyi bao* 21 (1898): 1–3.

———. "Fali xue dajia Mengdesijiu zhi xueshuo" 法理學大家孟德斯鳩之學說 [The legal studies master Montesquieu's theory]. *Xinmin congbao* 4 (1902): 13–22.

———. "Falansi diyi nüjie—Luolan furen zhuang" 羅蘭夫人傳 [Biography of Madame Roland, the most prominent French heroine]. *Xinmin congbao* 17 (1902): 35–43; *Xinmin congbao* 18 (1902): 35–43.

———. "Guoxing pian" 國性篇 [On national temperament] (1911), in *YBSHJ* 28:88.

———. "Gu yiyuan kao" 古議院考 [A Study of Early Parliaments], in *YBSHJ* 飲冰室合集 [Collected volumes from ice-drinking studio] 1:94–96.

———. "Huguo zhi yi huigu tan" 護國之役回顧談 [Looking back to the battle of protecting nation] (1922), in *YBSHJ* 39:86–96.

———. *Hunan shiwu xuetang yibian* 湖南時務學堂遺編 [Rediscovered pieces from the Hunan Academy of Current Affairs]. Changsha, China: Hunan daxue chubanshe, 2017.

———. *Intellectual Trends in the Chi'ing Period*. Translated by Immanuel C. Y. Hsü. Cambridge, MA: Harvard University Press, 1959.

———. "Jiaoyu yu zhengzhi" 教育與政治 [Education and politics] (1922), in *YBSHJ* 38:68–83.

———. "Jiateng boshi tianze baihua" 加藤博士天則百話 [Dr. Kato Hiroyuki's *Hundred Essays on the Law of Evolution*]. *Xinmin congbao* 21 (1902): 51–61.

———. "Jinggao dangdaozhe" 敬告當道者 [A respectful note to those in power]. *Xinmin congbao* 18 (1902): 1–16.

———. "Jinggao wo tongye zhujun" 敬告同業諸君 [A respectful announcement to my fellow reformists]. *Xinmin congbao* 17 (1902): 1–7.

———. "Jinshi diyi dazhe Kangde zhi xueshuo" 近世第一大哲康德之學說 [The theories of Kant the greatest philosopher in the early modern period]. *Xinmin congbao* 25 (1903): 16–24; *Xinmin congbao* 26 (1903): 9–18; *Xinmin congbao* 28 (1903): 9–12; *Xinmin congbao* 46/47/48 (1903): 68–76.

———. "Jinshi wenming chuzhu er dajia zhi xue" 近世文明初祖二大家之學 [The theories of two great precursors of modern civilization]. *Xinmin congbao* 1 (1902): 11–7; and *Xinmin congbao* 2 (1902): 9–19.

———. "Kaiming zhuanzhi lun" 開明專制論 [On Literal Autocracy] (1905), in *Yinbingshi heji* 飲冰室合集 [Collected volumes from Ice-Drinking Studio] 17:13–78.

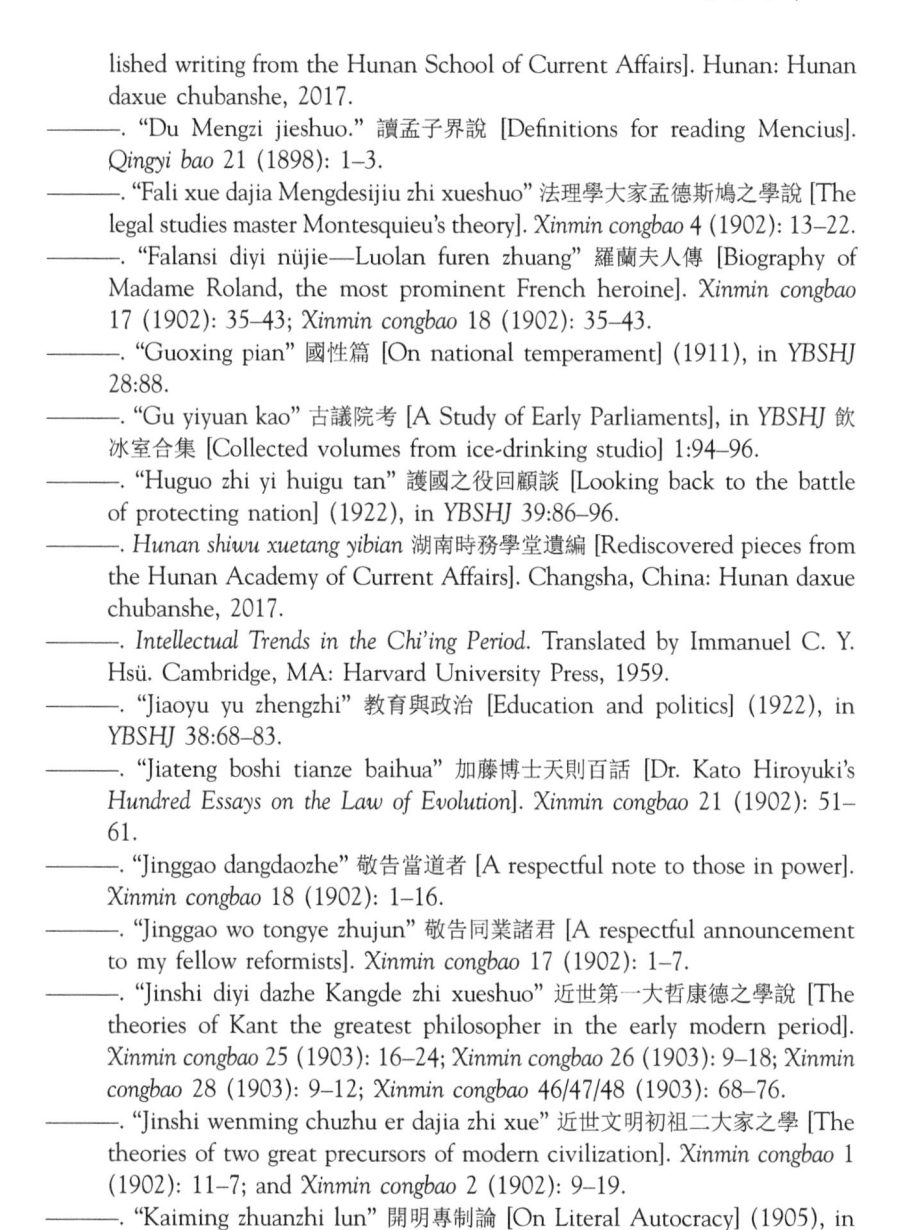

———. *Liang Qichao lun Zhongguo wenxue* 梁啟超論中國文學 [Liang Qichao on Chinese literature]. Beijing: Shangwu yinshuguan, 2012.

———. *Liang Qichao Quanji* 梁啟超全集 [The complete works of Liang Qichao. Vols. 1–21. Beijing: Beijing chubanshe, 1999.

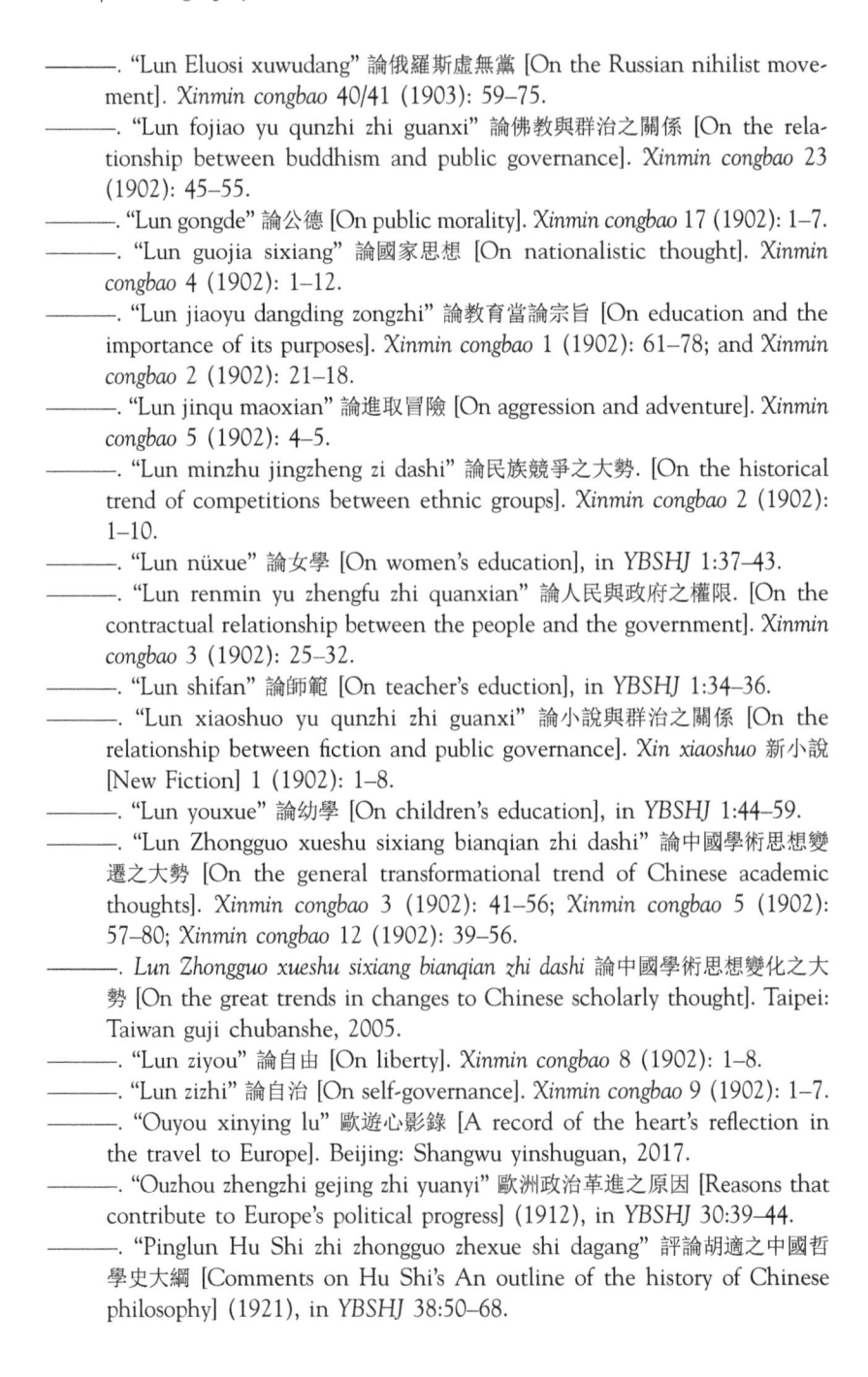

———. "Lun Eluosi xuwudang" 論俄羅斯虛無黨 [On the Russian nihilist movement]. *Xinmin congbao* 40/41 (1903): 59–75.

———. "Lun fojiao yu qunzhi zhi guanxi" 論佛教與群治之關係 [On the relationship between buddhism and public governance]. *Xinmin congbao* 23 (1902): 45–55.

———. "Lun gongde" 論公德 [On public morality]. *Xinmin congbao* 17 (1902): 1–7.

———. "Lun guojia sixiang" 論國家思想 [On nationalistic thought]. *Xinmin congbao* 4 (1902): 1–12.

———. "Lun jiaoyu dangding zongzhi" 論教育當論宗旨 [On education and the importance of its purposes]. *Xinmin congbao* 1 (1902): 61–78; and *Xinmin congbao* 2 (1902): 21–18.

———. "Lun jinqu maoxian" 論進取冒險 [On aggression and adventure]. *Xinmin congbao* 5 (1902): 4–5.

———. "Lun minzhu jingzheng zi dashi" 論民族競爭之大勢. [On the historical trend of competitions between ethnic groups]. *Xinmin congbao* 2 (1902): 1–10.

———. "Lun nüxue" 論女學 [On women's education], in *YBSHJ* 1:37–43.

———. "Lun renmin yu zhengfu zhi quanxian" 論人民與政府之權限. [On the contractual relationship between the people and the government]. *Xinmin congbao* 3 (1902): 25–32.

———. "Lun shifan" 論師範 [On teacher's eduction], in *YBSHJ* 1:34–36.

———. "Lun xiaoshuo yu qunzhi zhi guanxi" 論小說與群治之關係 [On the relationship between fiction and public governance]. *Xin xiaoshuo* 新小說 [New Fiction] 1 (1902): 1–8.

———. "Lun youxue" 論幼學 [On children's education], in *YBSHJ* 1:44–59.

———. "Lun Zhongguo xueshu sixiang bianqian zhi dashi" 論中國學術思想變遷之大勢 [On the general transformational trend of Chinese academic thoughts]. *Xinmin congbao* 3 (1902): 41–56; *Xinmin congbao* 5 (1902): 57–80; *Xinmin congbao* 12 (1902): 39–56.

———. *Lun Zhongguo xueshu sixiang bianqian zhi dashi* 論中國學術思想變化之大勢 [On the great trends in changes to Chinese scholarly thought]. Taipei: Taiwan guji chubanshe, 2005.

———. "Lun ziyou" 論自由 [On liberty]. *Xinmin congbao* 8 (1902): 1–8.

———. "Lun zizhi" 論自治 [On self-governance]. *Xinmin congbao* 9 (1902): 1–7.

———. "Ouyou xinying lu" 歐遊心影錄 [A record of the heart's reflection in the travel to Europe]. Beijing: Shangwu yinshuguan, 2017.

———. "Ouzhou zhengzhi gejing zhi yuanyi" 歐洲政治革進之原因 [Reasons that contribute to Europe's political progress] (1912), in *YBSHJ* 30:39–44.

———. "Pinglun Hu Shi zhi zhongguo zhexue shi dagang" 評論胡適之中國哲學史大綱 [Comments on Hu Shi's An outline of the history of Chinese philosophy] (1921), in *YBSHJ* 38:50–68.

———. *Qingdai xueshi gailun* 清代學術概論 [Intellectual trends of the Qing period]. Shanghai: Shanghai guji chubanshe, 1998.

———. "Renshengguan yu kexue" 人生觀與科學 [Outlook on life and science] (1922), in *YBSHJ* 40:21–27.

———. "Renxue 仁學" [Book review on an exposition of benevolence]. *Xinmin congbao* 1 (1902): 116–17.

———. "Renxue xu" (仁學序) [Preface to Renxue], in *Renxue* 仁學 [An exposition of benevolence], annotated by Tang Zhijun 湯志鈞 and Tang Renze 湯仁澤. Taipei: Taiwan xuesheng shuju, 1998.

———. "Shang Chen Baozhen shu lun Hunan yangban zhi shi" 上陳寶箴書論湖南應辦之事 [A letter to Chen Baozhen discussing policies that need to be implemented in Hunan]. In *Wuxu bianfa ziliao* 戊戌變法資料 [Materials on the 1898 Reform], vol. 2, comp. Zhongguo shi xuehui 中國史學會, 550–58. Shanghai: Shanghai shudian chuban she, 1953.

———. "Shenlun zhongzu geming yu zhengzhi geming zhi deshi" 申論種族革命與政治革命之得失 [Further discussions on the pros and cons between ethnic revolution and political revolution] (1905), in *YBSHJ* 19:1–45.

———. "Shenme shi wenhua" 什麼是文化 [What is culture?] (1922), in *YBSHJ* 39:97–104.

———. "Shi ge" 釋革 [Exegesis on ge]. *Xinmin congbao* 22 (1902): 1–8.

———. "Shijie mori ji" 世界末日記 [Last days of the world]. *Xin xiaoshuo* 1 (1902): 101–18.

———. "Shimin de qunzhong huodong zhi yiyi ji jiazhi" [市民的群衆運動之意義及價值] [The meaning and value of citizen's public movements] (1921), in *YBSHJ* 39:35–39.

———. "Shuo youzhi" 說幼稚 [On nativity] (1912), in *YBSHJ* 30:45–51.

———. "Sibada xiaozhi" 斯巴達小志 [A brief historical record on Sparta]. *Xinmin congbao* 13 (1902): 27–42.

———. "Waijiao yu neizheng yu" 外交歟內政歟 [Sighs to foreign affairs, and sighs to inner affairs] (1920), in *YBSHJ* 37:41–59.

———. "Wang Yangming zhixing heyi zhi jiao" 王陽明知行合一之教 [Wang Yangming's teaching on the unity of knowing and being]. In *Chuangxi lu jiping* 傳習錄集評 [Collected commentaries on Instructions for Practical Living]. Beijing: Jiuzhou chuban she, 2015.

———. "Weixue yu zuoren" 為學與做人 [Between learning and being a good person] (1921), in *YBSHJ* 39:104–10.

———. *Wuxu zhengbian ji* 戊戌政變記 [Remembering the 1898 Reform]. Shanghai: Shanghai guji chubanshe, 2014.

———. "Xinmin shuo yi: Diyijie-sulun" 新民說一：第一節-敘論 [Discourse on the new citizen 1: Chapter 1: General introduction]. *Xinmin congbao* 1 (1902): 1–10.

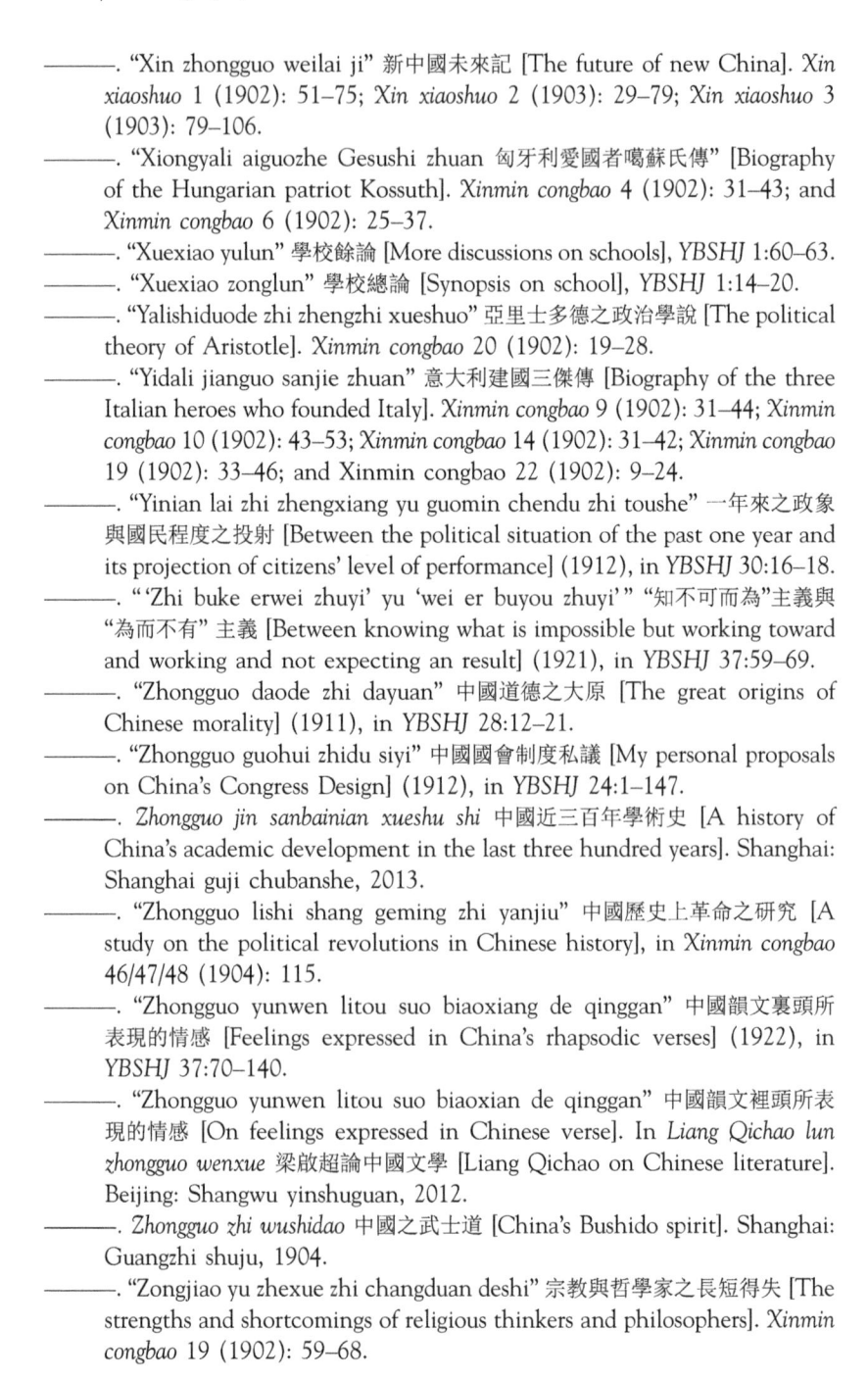

———. "Xin zhongguo weilai ji" 新中國未來記 [The future of new China]. *Xin xiaoshuo* 1 (1902): 51–75; *Xin xiaoshuo* 2 (1903): 29–79; *Xin xiaoshuo* 3 (1903): 79–106.

———. "Xiongyali aiguozhe Gesushi zhuan 匈牙利愛國者噶蘇氏傳" [Biography of the Hungarian patriot Kossuth]. *Xinmin congbao* 4 (1902): 31–43; and *Xinmin congbao* 6 (1902): 25–37.

———. "Xuexiao yulun" 學校餘論 [More discussions on schools], *YBSHJ* 1:60–63.

———. "Xuexiao zonglun" 學校總論 [Synopsis on school], *YBSHJ* 1:14–20.

———. "Yalishiduode zhi zhengzhi xueshuo" 亞里士多德之政治學說 [The political theory of Aristotle]. *Xinmin congbao* 20 (1902): 19–28.

———. "Yidali jianguo sanjie zhuan" 意大利建國三傑傳 [Biography of the three Italian heroes who founded Italy]. *Xinmin congbao* 9 (1902): 31–44; *Xinmin congbao* 10 (1902): 43–53; *Xinmin congbao* 14 (1902): 31–42; *Xinmin congbao* 19 (1902): 33–46; and Xinmin congbao 22 (1902): 9–24.

———. "Yinian lai zhi zhengxiang yu guomin chendu zhi toushe" 一年來之政象與國民程度之投射 [Between the political situation of the past one year and its projection of citizens' level of performance] (1912), in *YBSHJ* 30:16–18.

———. "'Zhi buke erwei zhuyi' yu 'wei er buyou zhuyi'" "知不可而為"主義與"為而不有" 主義 [Between knowing what is impossible but working toward and working and not expecting an result] (1921), in *YBSHJ* 37:59–69.

———. "Zhongguo daode zhi dayuan" 中國道德之大原 [The great origins of Chinese morality] (1911), in *YBSHJ* 28:12–21.

———. "Zhongguo guohui zhidu siyi" 中國國會制度私議 [My personal proposals on China's Congress Design] (1912), in *YBSHJ* 24:1–147.

———. *Zhongguo jin sanbainian xueshu shi* 中國近三百年學術史 [A history of China's academic development in the last three hundred years]. Shanghai: Shanghai guji chubanshe, 2013.

———. "Zhongguo lishi shang geming zhi yanjiu" 中國歷史上革命之研究 [A study on the political revolutions in Chinese history], in *Xinmin congbao* 46/47/48 (1904): 115.

———. "Zhongguo yunwen litou suo biaoxiang de qinggan" 中國韻文裏頭所表現的情感 [Feelings expressed in China's rhapsodic verses] (1922), in *YBSHJ* 37:70–140.

———. "Zhongguo yunwen litou suo biaoxian de qinggan" 中國韻文裡頭所表現的情感 [On feelings expressed in Chinese verse]. In *Liang Qichao lun zhongguo wenxue* 梁啟超論中國文學 [Liang Qichao on Chinese literature]. Beijing: Shangwu yinshuguan, 2012.

———. *Zhongguo zhi wushidao* 中國之武士道 [China's Bushido spirit]. Shanghai: Guangzhi shuju, 1904.

———. "Zongjiao yu zhexue zhi changduan deshi" 宗教與哲學家之長短得失 [The strengths and shortcomings of religious thinkers and philosophers]. *Xinmin congbao* 19 (1902): 59–68.

Liang Zhan. 梁展 "Kang Youwei de weilai zhongguo" 康有為的未來中國 [Kang Youwei's futuristic China]. *Zhonghua dushubao* 中华读书报 [China Reading Weekly] (May 20, 2015, edition, 15).

Li Yanli 李艷麗. "Qingmo kexue xiaoshuo yu shiji mo sichao: Yi lianbian 'shijie mori ji' wei li" 清末科學小說與世紀末思潮—以兩篇《世界末日記》为例 [Late Qing science fiction and the *fin-de-siècle* intellectual trend]. *Shehui kexue* 社會科學 [Journal of Social Science] 2 (2009): 157–67.

Lin Mingde 林明德. "Liang Qichao yu xin xiaoshuo" 梁啟超與新小說 [Liang Qichao and new fiction]. In *Minzu gu jia lunshu—cong Wanqing, wusi dao riju shidai Taiwan xin wenxue* 民族國家論述: 從晚清, 五四到日據時代臺灣新文學 [Narratives on nation-state: New Taiwan literature from late Qing, may fourth, to the Japanese occupation], edited by Hu Siao-chen 胡曉眞. Taipei: Zhongyang yanjiuyuan Zhongguo wenzhe yanjiusuo choubeichu, 1995.

Liu, Jeeloo. *Neo-Confucianism: Metaphysics, Mind, and Morality*. Hoboken, NJ: Wiley-Blackwell, 2017.

Liu, Lydia. *Translingual Practice: Literature, National Culture, and Translated Modernity—China, 1900–1937*. Stanford, CA: Stanford University Press, 1995.

Liu Ts'un-Yan 柳存仁. "Wang Yangming yu fodao erjiao" 王陽明與佛道二教 [Wang Yangming's association with Buddhism and Daoism]. *Tsing Hua Journal of Chinese Studies* 清華學報 13, no. 1 (Dec. 1981): 27–52.

Li Xisuo 李喜所. *Liang Qichao yu jindai Zhongguo shehui wenhua* 梁啟超與近代中國社會文化 [Liang Qichao and the modern Chinese society and culture]. Tianjin, China: Tianjin guji chubanshe, 2005.

Lo, Ping-cheung 羅秉祥. "Confucian Ethic of Death with Dignity and Its Contemporary Relevance." *Annual of the Society of Christian Ethics* 19 (1999): 313–33.

Loewe, Michael. *Dong Zhongshu, a Confucian Heritage and the Chunqiu Fanlu*. Leiden: Brill, 2011.

Lovejoy, Arthur O. "The Theory of Human Nature in the American Constitution and the Method of Counterpoise." In *Reflections on Human Nature*, 35–65. Baltimore, MD: Johns Hopkins University Press, 2020.

Karl, Rebecca. *Staging the World and Failure, Nationalism, and Literature*. Durham, NC: Duke University Press, 2002.

Kang Youwei 康有為. *Kang Nanhai zibian nianpu: Wai erzhong* 康南海自編年譜: 外二種 [Kang Youwei's self-compiled chronicle and two others], edited by LouYulie 樓宇烈. Beijing: Zhonghua shuju, 1992.

Kang Youwei Quanji 康有爲全集. [The complete works of Kang Youwei]. Edited by Jian Yihua 姜義華 and Zhang Ronghua 張榮華. Beijing: Zhongguo renmin daxue chubanshe, 2007.

———. *Kongzi gaizhi kao* 孔子改制考 [Study of the reforms of Confucius]. Shanghai: Shanghai shudian, 1991.

Kant, Immanuel. *Critique of Judgment*. Indianapolis, IN: Hackett, 1987.
———. *Critique of Pure Reason*. Indianapolis, IN: Hackett, 1996.
———. *Groundwork of the Metaphysics of Morals*. Cambridge: Cambridge University Press, 2012.
Kao, Yu-kung. "The Aesthetics of Regulated Verse." In *The Vitality of the Lyric Voice: Shih Poetry from the Late Han to T'ang*, edited by Shuen-fu Lin and Stephen Owen, 332–86. Princeton, NJ: Princeton University Press, 1986.
———. "Chinese Lyric Aesthetics." In *Words and Images: Chinese Poetry, Calligraphy, and Painting*, edited by Alfveda Mumck and Wen Fong, 47–90. New York: The Metropolitan Museum of Arts, 1991.
———. *Zhongguo meidian yu wenxue yanjiu lunji* 中國美典與文學研究論集 [Collected works on researches on the Chinese aesthetic tradition and literature]. Taipei: National Taiwan University Press, 2004.
Kaske, Elisabeth. *The Politics of Language in Chinese Education, 1895–1919*. Leiden: Brill, 2008.
Keulemans, Paize. *Sound Rising from the Paper: Nineteenth-Century Martial Arts Fiction and the Chinese Acoustic Imagination*. Cambridge, MA: Harvard University Asia Center, 2014.
Krieger, Murray. *Ekphrasis: The Illusion of the Natural Sign*. Baltimore, MD: Johns Hopkins University Press, 1992. New York: Columbia University Press, 1978.
Kim, Youngmin. *A History of Chinese Political Thought*. Beijing: Polity Press, 2017.
———. "Moral Agency and the Unity of the World: The Neo-Confucian Critique of 'Vulgar Learning.'" *Journal of Chinese Philosophy* 33, no. 4 (2006): 479–89.
Kingston, Rebecca. "The Political Relevance of Emotions from Descartes to Smith." In *Bringing the Passions Back in: The Emotions in Political Philosophy*, edited by Rebecca Kingston and Leonard Ferry, 108–25. Vancouver: University of British Columbia Press, 2008.
Kloppenberg, James. *Toward Democracy: The Struggle for Self-Rule in European and American Thought*. New York: Oxford University Press, 2016.
Kockum, Keiko. *Japanese Achievement, Chinese Aspiration: A Study of the Japanese Influence on the Modernisation of the Late Qing Novel*. Löberöd, Sweden: Plus Ultra, 1990.
Kokumin no tomo 國民之友 [The nation's friend]. 1887; repr., Tokyo: Meiji Bunken, 1968.
Ko Zhenfeng 寇振鋒. "Xin zhongguo weilai ji zhong de Mingzhi zhengzhi xiaoshuo yinsu"《新中国未来记》中的日本明治政治小说因素 [Elements of Meiji Japan's political fiction in the future of new China]. Accessed May 11, 2015. http://www.jsc.fudan.edu.cn/picture/jl080210.pdf.
Kwong, Luke S. K. "An Aspect of Modern China in Transition: The Life and Thought of T'an Ssu-t'ung (1865–1898)." PhD diss., University of Toronto, 1973.

———. *A Mosaic of the Hundred Days: Personalities, Politics, and Ideas of 1898*. Cambridge, MA: Council on East Asian Studies, Harvard University, 1984.

———. "Reflections on an Aspect of Modern China in Transition: T'an Ssu-t'ung (1865–1898) as a Reformer." In *Reform in Nineteenth-Century China*, edited by Paul Cohen and John E. Schrecker, 184–93. Cambridge, MA: Harvard University, East Asian Research Center, 1976.

Ma, Yau-woon, and Joseph S. M. Lau, eds. *Traditional Chinese Stories: Themes and Variations*. New York: Columbia University Press, 1978.

Mueller-Vollmer, Kurt. *The Hermeneutics Reader: Texts of the German Tradition from the Enlightenment to the Present*. New York: Continuum, 1985.

Makehem, John, ed. *The Buddhist Roots of Zhu Xi's Philosophical Thought*, edited by John Makehem. New York: Oxford University Press, 2018.

Mann, Susan. *Hung Liang-Chi (1746–1809): The Perception and Articulation of Political Problems in Late Eighteenth-Century China*. PhD diss., Stanford University, 1972.

Mann, Susan, and Philip Kuhn. "Dynastic Decline and the Roots of Rebellion." In *Cambridge History of China*. Vol. 10. Edited by John Fairbank. Cambridge: Cambridge University Press, 1978.

Marriott, J. A. R. *The Makers of Modern Italy: Mazzini, Cavour, Garibaldi: Three Lectures Delivered at Oxford*. London: Macmillan, 1889.

Martin, Helmut. "A Transitional Concept of Chinese Literature 1897–1917: Liang Ch'i-chao on Poetry Reform, Historical Drama and the Political Novel." *Oriens Extremus* 20 (1973): 175–217.

Massumi, Brian. "The Autonomy of Affect." *Cultural Critique* 31, The Politics of Systems and Environments, Part 2 (Autumn 1995): 83–109.

———. *Parables for the Virtual: Movement, Affect, Sensation*. Durham, NC: Duke University Press, 2002.

Matsuo Yoji 松尾洋二. "Liang Qichao yu shizhuan—dongya jindai jingshen shi de bengliu" 梁啟超與史傳—東亞近代精神史的奔流 [Liang Qichao and his historical biography: The torrent of modern Asian intellectual history]. In *Mingzhi Riben, xifang Riben Jingdu daxue renwen kexue yanjiusuo gongyong yanjiu baogao* 梁啟超・明治日本・西方: 日本京都大學人文科學研究所共同研究報告 [Liang Qichao, Meiji Japan, and the west: Collaborative research reports from Institute for Research in Humanities, Kyoto University]. Beijing: Shehui kexue wenxian chubanshe, 2001.

Mei Chia-ling 梅家玲. "Faxiang shaonian, xiangxiang zhongguo: Liang Qichao 'Shaonian zhongguo shuo' de xiandai xing, qimeng lunshu yu guozu xiangxiang" 發現少年, 想像中國—梁啟超〈少年中國說〉的現代性、啟蒙論述與國族想像 ["Discovering youth" and "imagining China": Modernity, enlightenment discourse and national imagination in Liang Qichao's "The Youth of China"]. *Hanxue yanjiu* 漢學研究 [Chinese Studies] 19, no. 1 (June 2001): 249–76.

Merleau-Ponty, Maurice. *Phenomenology of Perception*. Abingdon, UK: Routledge, 2012.
Metzger, Thomas. "The Definition of Self, the Group, the Cosmos, and Knowledge in Chou Thought: Some Comments on Professor Schwartz's Study." *American Asian Review* 4, no. 2 (Summer 1986): 68–116.
———. *Escape from Predicament*. New York: Columbia University Press, 1986.
Mittler, Barbara. *A Newspaper for China: Power, Identity, and Change in Shanghai's News Media, 1872–1912*. Cambridge, MA: Harvard University Press, 2004.
Mori, Noriko. "Liang Qichao, Late Qing Buddhism, and Modern Japan." In *The Role of Japan in Liang Qichao's Introduction of Modern Western Civilization to China*, edited by Joshua A. Fogel, 222–46. Berkeley, CA: Center for Chinese Studies, 2004.
Mou Zongsan 牟宗三. "Wangxue shi mengzi xue" 王學是孟子學 [The learning of Wang Yangming as the learning of Mencius]. In *Cong Lu Xianshan dao Liu Jishan* 從陸象山到劉蕺山 [From Lu Xianshan to Liu Jishan]. Taipei: Xuesheng shuju, 2011.
Mūlamadhyamakakārikā. *Taishō Tripiṭaka* 大正新脩大藏经. Vol. 30. Translated by Kumārajīva. Tokyo: Taishō Shinshū Daizōkyō Kankōkai, 1988.
Nakae, Chōmin 中江兆民. *Rigaku enkakushi* 理学沿革史. Tokyo: Monbusho Henshukyoku, [1886].
Ng, On-cho. *Cheng-Zhu Confucianism in the Early Qing: Li Guangdi and Qing Learning*. Albany, NY: State University of New York Press, 2001.
———. "Chinese Philosophy, Hermeneutics, and Onto-Hermeneutics." *Journal of Chinese Philosophy* 30, no. 3/4 (Sept./Dec. 2003): 373–85.
———. "Qing Philosophy." In *Stanford Encyclopedia of Philosophy*. April 16, 2019. https://plato.stanford.edu/entries/qing-philosophy/.
———. "Religious Hermeneutics: Text and Truth in Neo-Confucian Readings of the *Yijing*." *Journal of Chinese Philosophy* 34, no. 1 (March 2007): 5–24.
———. "Text in Context: Chin-wen Learning in Ch'ing Thought." PhD diss., University of Hawaii, 1986.
———. "Toward a Hermeneutic Turn in Chinese Philosophy: Western Theory, Confucian Tradition, and Cheng Chung-ying's Onto-hermeneutics." *Dao: A Journal of Comparative Philosophy* 6, no. 4 (Dec. 2007): 383–95.
Ng, On-Cho, and Q. Edward Wang. *Mirroring the Past: The Writing and Use of History in Imperial China*. Honolulu: University of Hawaii Press, 2005.
Nylan, Michael. "The Spring and Autumn Annals (*Chunqiu*), as Read through Its Three Traditions." In *The Five "Confucian" Classics*, 253–306. New Haven, CT: Yale University Press, 2001.
Peterson, Willard. "Confucian Learning in Late Ming Thought." In *The Cambridge History of China*, vol. 8, edited by Denis Twitchett and Frederic E. Mote, 709–88. Cambridge: Cambridge University Press, 1998.
Pi Xirui 皮錫瑞. *Jing xue li shi* 經學歷史 [Confucian history]. Shanghai: Shanghai shudian, 1906.

———. *Pi Xirui riji* 皮錫瑞日記 [The diary of Pi Xirui]. Beijing: Zhonghua shu ju, 2015.
Pines, Yuri, Paul Goldin, and Martin Kern, eds. *Ideology of Power and Power of Ideology in Early China*. Leiden: Brill Academic, 2015.
Plamper, Jan. "The History of Emotions: An Interview with William Reddy, Barbara Rosenwein, and Peter Stearns." *History and Theory* 49 (May 2010): 237–65.
Plato. *The Republic*. London: Penguin Books, 2003.
Platt, Stephen R. *Provincial Patriots: The Hunanese and Modern China*. Cambridge, MA: Harvard University Press, 2007.
Poizat, Michel. *The Angel's Cry: Beyond the Pleasure Principle in Opera*. Translated by Arthur Denner. Ithaca, NY: Cornell University Press, 1992.
Polachek, James. *Literati Groups and Literati Politics in Early Nineteenth-Century China*. PhD thesis, University of California, Berkeley, 1976.
Pollard, David E, ed. *Translation and Creation Readings of Western Literature in Early Modern China, 1840–1918*. Amsterdam: J. Benjamins, 1998.
Prasenjit, Duara. *Rescuing History from the Nation: Questioning Narratives of Modern China*. Chicago, IL: University of Chicago Press, 1995.
Priest, Graham. *The Fifth Corner of Four: An Essay on Buddhist Metaphysics and the Catuskoti*. New York: Oxford University Press, 2019.
———. "On Ivanhoe on Oneness." *Philosophy and Phenomenological Research* 99, no. 2 (Sept. 2019): 495–500.
Qian Mu 錢穆. *Lianghan jingxue jinguwen pingyi* 兩漢經學今古文評議 [Assessment of the Han old and new text controversy]. Taipei: Dongda tushu gongsi yinhang, 1983.
———. *Zhongguo jin sanbai nian xueshu shi* 中國近三百年學術史 [A history of intellectual development in the last three hundred years]. Taipei: Taiwan shangwu yinshuguan, 1964.
———. *Zhuzi xin xuean* 朱子新學案 [A new biography of Zhu Xi's academic life]. Vol. 1. Beiing: Jiuzhou chuban she, 2011.
Qin Shaode 秦紹德. *Shanghai jindai baokan shilun* 上海近代報刊實錄 [Empirical records on modern Shanghai newspapers and periodicals]. Shanghai: Fudan daxue, 1993.
Qiu Weixuan 邱煒萲. "Xiaoshuo yu minzhi guanxi" 小說與民智關係 [The relationship between fiction and people's intelligence]. In *Ershi shiji Zhongguo xiaoshuo lilun ziliao: Diyi juan "yiba jiuqi yijiu yiliu"* 二十世紀中國小說理論資料：第一卷 (一八九七——一九一六), edited by Chen Pingyuan 陳平原 and Xia Xiaohong 夏曉紅. Beijing: Beijing daxue chubanshe, 1989.
Queen, Sarah. *From Chronicle to Canon: The Hermeneutics of the Spring and Autumn according to Tung Chung-shu*. Cambridge: Cambridge University Press, 1996.
Reddy, William. "Against Constructionism: The Historical Ethnography of Emotions." *Current Anthropology* 38, no. 2 (1997): 327–51.

Rekret, Paul. "Affect and Politics: A Critical Assessment." Online access on April 17, 2024, https://pressbooks.pub/pauljreilly/chapter/affect-and-politics-a-critical-assessment/.
Rickett, Adele, and Chia-ying Yeh, eds. *Chinese Approaches to Literature from Confucius to Liang Ch'i-Chao*. Princeton, NJ: Princeton University Press, 1978.
Robinson, Richard H. *Early Madhyamika in India and China*. Madison: University of Wisconsin Press, 1967.
Routledge Encyclopedia of Confucianism. Vol. 2. Edited by Xinzhong Yao. New York: Routledge, 2003.
Saitō Mareshi 齋藤希史. "Jindai wenxue guannian xingcheng qi de Liang Qichao" 近代文學觀念形成期的梁啟超 [Liang Qichao in the formational years of modern literary thought]. In *Liang Qichao, Mingzhi Riben, xifang: Riben Jingdu daxue renwen kexue yanjiusuo gongtong yanjiu baogao* 梁啟超・明治日本・西方: 日本京都大學人文科學研究所共同研究報告 [Liang Qichao, Meiji Japan, and the west: Collaborative research reports from Institute for Research in Humanities, Kyoto University], edited by Hazama Naoki 狹間直樹. Beijing: Shehui kexue wenxian chubanshe, 2001.
Sang Bing 桑兵, and Xiaohong Guan 關曉紅. *Xian yin hou chuang yu bu po bu li: Jindai Zhongguo xueshu liupai yanjiu* 先因後創與不破不立: 近代中國學術流派研究. Beijing: Sanlian shudian, 2007.
Schwartz, Benjamin I. "Hierarchy, Status, and Authority in Chinese Culture." In *China and Other Matters*. Cambridge, MA: Harvard University Press, 1996.
———. *In Search of Wealth and Power: Yen Fu and the West*. Cambridge, MA: Belknap Press of Harvard University Press, 1964.
Sela, Ori. *China's Philological Turn: Scholars, Textualism and The Dao in the Eighteen Century*. New York: Columbia University Press, 2018.
Shang, Wei. *Rulin Waishi and Cultural Transformation in Late Imperial China*. Cambridge, MA: Harvard University Asian Center, 2003.
Shek, H. Richard. "Some Western Influences of T'an Ssu-t'ung's Thought." In *Reform in Nineteenth-Century China*, edited by Paul A. Cohen and John E. Schrecker, 194–303. Cambridge, MA: East Asian Research Center, Harvard University, 1976.
Shi Gexin 史革新. *Wanqing lixue yanjiu* 晚清理學研究 [A study of neo-Confucianism in late Qing China]. Beijing: Shangwu yinshu guan, 2007.
Staal, Frits. *Exploring Mysticism: A Methodological Essay*. Berkeley: University of California Press, 1975.
Steiner, George. *Language and Silence: Essays on Language, Literature, and the Inhumane*. New York: Atheneum, 1967.
Su Yu 蘇輿, ed. *Yijiao congbian* 翼教叢編 [A general collection to protect the faith]. Taipei: Wenhai chubanshe, 1971.
Tan Sitong. *Renxue* 仁學 [An exposition of benevolence]. Annotated by Tang Zhijun 湯志鈞 and Tang Renze 湯仁澤. Taipei: Taiwan xuesheng shuju, 1998.

———. *Tan Sitong quanji* 譚嗣同全集 [The complete collection of Tan Sitong]. Edited by Cai Shangsi and Fang Xing. Beijing: Sanlian shudian, 1954.

Tang, Chun-i. "The Development of the Concept of Moral Mind from Wang Yang-ming to Wang Chi." In *Self and Society in Ming Thought*, edited by Theodore De Bary, 93–119. New York: Columbia University Press, 1970.

Tang, Xiaobing. *Global Space and the Nationalist Discourse of Modernity: The Historical Thinking of Liang Qichao*. Stanford, CA: Stanford University Press, 1996.

Tang Zhijun 湯志鈞. *Kang Youwei yu wu xu bian fa* 康有為与戊戌變法 [Kang Youwei and the 1898 reform]. Beijing: Zhonghua shuju, 1984.

———. "Renxue banben tanyuan" 仁學版本探源 [An exploration of Renxue's editions]. In *Renxue*. Annotated by Tang Zhijun 湯志鈞 and Tang Renze 湯仁澤. Taipei: Taiwan xuesheng shuju, 1998.

Tay, Wei Leong. "Kang Youwei: The Martin Luther of Confucianism and His Vision of Confucian Modernity and Nation." In *Secularization, Religion, and State*, ed. Haneda Masashi, 97–109. Tokyo: University of Tokyo Center for Philosophy, 2010.

Terada, Rei. *Feeling in Theory: Emotion after the "Death of the Subject."* Cambridge, MA: Harvard University Press, 2001.

Tiwald, Justin, and Stephen C. Angle. *Neo-Confucianism: A Philosophical Introduction*. Cambridge: Polity, 2017.

Tokutomi Roka 德富蘆花. *Sekai kokon meifu kagami* 世界古今名婦鑑 [Mirror of renowned women from ancient and modern times]. Tokyo: Minyusha, 1898.

Tong, Q. S., Shouren Wang, and Douglas Kerr, eds. *Critical Zone 2: A Forum of Chinese and Western Knowledge*. Hong Kong: Hong Kong University Press, 2006.

Treatise on Awakening Mahāyāna Faith. Translated by John Jorgensen, Dan Lusthaus, and John Makeham. New York: Oxford University Press, 2019.

Van Norden, Bryan. *Virtue Ethics and Consequentialism in Early Chinese Philosophy*. Cambridge: Cambridge University Press, 2007.

Vasubandhu. *Abhidharmakośa-Bhāṣya of Vasubandhu: The Treasury of the Abhidharma and Its (Auto) Commentary*. Vol. 3. Translated by De La Vallée Poussin and Lodrö Sangpo. Delhi: Motilal Banarsidass, 2012.

Vittinghoff, Natascha. "Unity v. Uniformity: Liang Qichao and the Invention of a 'New Journalism' for China." *Late Imperial China* 23, no. 1 (2002): 91–143.

Walzer, Michael. *Politics and Passion: Toward a More Egalitarian Liberalism*. New Haven, CT: Yale University Press, 2005.

Wang, Ban. "Geopolitics, Moral Reform, and Poetic Internationalism: Liang Qichao's *The Future of New China*." *Frontiers of Literary Studies in China* 6, no. 1 (2012) 2–18.

Wang, David Der-wei. "Reforming and Re-forming Literature: 1895–1919." In *The Cambridge History of Chinese Literature*, edited by Kang-i Sun Chang and Stephen Owen, 440–66. Cambridge: Cambridge University Press, 2010.

———. *Fin-de-Siècle Splendor: Repressed Modernities of Late Qing Fiction, 1849–1911*. Stanford, CA: Stanford University Press, 1997.

———. *The Lyrical in the Epic Time: Modern Chinese Intellectuals and Artists through the 1949 Crisis*. New York: Columbia University Press, 2015.

Wang, Dewei 王德威. *Xiandai shuqing chuantong si lun* 現代抒情傳統四論 [Four readings of the modern lyrical tradition]. Taipei: National Taiwan University Press, 2011.

———. *Xian dangdai wenxue xinlun: Yili, lunli, dili* 現當代文學新論：義理・倫理・地理 [New perspectives on modern and contemporary literature: Morality, ethics, and geography]. Beijing: Shenghuo dushu, xinzhi sanlian shudian, 2014.

Wang, Fansen. "Cong xinmin dao xinren—jindai sixiang zhong de ziwo yu zhengzhi" 從新民到新人—近代思想中的自我與政治 [From the new citizen to the new man: Self and politics in the modern though]). In *Zhongguo jindai sixiangshi de zhuanxing shidai* 中國近代思想史的轉型時代 [Transitional periods in modern Chinese intellectual history]. Taipei: Lianjing, 2007.

———. *Zhiniu de diyin: Yixie lishi sikao fangshi de fansi* 執拗的低音：一些歷史思考方式的反思 [The stubborn bass: Reflections on some historical thinking methods]. Taipei: Yunchen wenhua shiye gufen youxian gongsi, 2014.

———. *Zhongguo jindai sixiang yu xueshu xipu* 中國近代思想與學術的系譜 [Genealogy of modern Chinese thought and academic trends]. Shijiazhuang: Hebei jiaoyu chubanshe, 2001.

Wang, Hui 汪暉. "Idea of China in New Text Confucianism, 1780–1911." In *Critical Zone 2: A Forum of Chinese and Western Knowledge*, edited by Q. S. Tong, Shouren Wang, and Douglas Kerr, 167–80. Hong Kong: Hong Kong University Press, 2006.

———. *Xiandai Zhongguo sixiang de xingqi* 現代中國思想的興起 [The rise of modern Chinese thought]. Beijing: Shenghuo, dushu, xinzhi sanlian shudian, 2004.

Wang, Juan. *Merry Laughter and Angry Curses: The Shanghai Tabloid Press, 1897–1911*. Vancouver: University of British Columbia Press, 2012.

Wei Chaoyong 魏朝勇. *Minguo shiqi wenxue de zhengzhi xiangxiang* 民國時期文學的政治想像 [Political imaginations in republican Chinese literature]. Beijing: Huaxia chubanshe, 2006.

Whitbeck, Judith. "The Historical Vision of Kung Tzu-chen (1792–1841)." PhD diss., UC Berkeley, 1980.

Willcock, Hiroko. "Japanese Modernization and the Emergence of New Fiction in Early Twentieth Century China: A Study of Liang Qichao." *Modern Asian Studies* 27, no. 4 (1995): 817–40.

Wong, Lawrence Wang-chi. "'The Sole Purpose Is to Express My Political Views': Liang Qichao and the Translation and Writing of Political Novels in the Late Qing." In *Translation and Creation Readings of Western Litera-*

ture in *Early Modern China, 1840–1918*, edited by David Pollard, 105–26. Amsterdam: J. Benjamins, 1998.
Wong Young-Tsu. "Revisionism Reconsidered: Kang Youwei and the Reform Movement of 1898." *Journal of Asian Studies* 51 no. 3 (Aug. 1992): 532.
Wright, David. *Translating Science: The Transmission of Western Chemistry into Late Imperial China, 1840–1900*. Leiden: Brill, 2000.
Wu, Hung. "A Ghost Rebellion: Notes on Xu Bing's 'Nonsense Writing' and Other Works." *Public Culture* 6 (1994): 411–18.
Wu, Jianren. *Ershi nian zhi guai xian zhuang* 二十年目睹之怪現狀 [Strange things witnessed in the past twenty years]. Tianjin, China: Tianjin guji chubanshe, 1986.
———. *Shanghai youcan lu* 上海游驂錄 [Travels in Shanghai]. In *Wu Jianren quanji: San* 吳趼人全集 (3) [Collected works of Wu Jianren (3)]. Ha'erbin, China: Beifang wenyi chubanshe, 1998.
———. *Xin shitou ji* 新石頭記 [New story of the stone]. Zhengzhou, China: Zhongzhou guji chubanshe, 1986.
Wuxu bian fa dang an shi liao 戊戌變法檔案史料 [Archival documents for the 1898 reform]. Compiled by Guojia danganju mingqing dangan guan 國家檔案局明清檔案館. Beijing: Zhonghua shuju, 1958.
Wuxu bianfa ziliao 戊戌變法資料 [Materials on the 1898 Reform]. Vol. 2. Compiled by Zhongguo shi xuehui 中國史學會. Shanghai: Shanghai shudian chuban she, 1953.
Xia, Xiaohong 夏曉虹. *Jueshi yu chuanshi: Liang Qichao de wenxue daolu* 覺世與傳世: 梁啟超的文學道路 [Enlightenment and permanence: The literary path of Liang Qichao]. Shanghai: Shanghai renmin chubanshe, 1991.
———. "Shui shi xin zhongguo weilai ji diwuhui de zuozhe" 誰是新中國未來記第五回的作者 [Who is the author of the fifth chapter of the future of the China's chapter five] *Zhonghua dushu bao* 中華讀書報 [China Reading Weekly], May 21, 2003.
———. "'Sijie gujin minfu jian' yu wanqing waiguo nüjie zhuan"《世界古今名婦鑑》與晚清外國女傑傳 ["Mirror of renowned women from ancient and modern Times" and Western heroines in late Qing China]. *Beijing daxue xuebao (zhexue shehui bao)* 北京大學學報 (哲学社會科學版) [Journal of Peking University: Philosophy and Social Science Edition] 46, no. 2 (March 2009): 35–48.
———. *Wanqing baokan, xingbie yu wenhua zhuanxing: Xia Xiaohong xuanji* 晚清報刊、性別與文化轉型: 夏曉虹選集 [Late Qing newspapers and journals, gender, and cultural transformation: Selected works by Xia Xiaohong], edited by LüWencui 呂文翠. Taipei: Renjian chubanshe, 2013.
———. "Wanqing nübao zhong de xifang nüjie—Mingzhi 'furen lizhi' duwu de zhongguo zhi lü" 晚清女報中的西方女傑—明治'婦人立志'讀物的中國之

旅 [Western heroines in late Qing's women's newspaper—The journal of Meiji Japan's women's magazines in China]. *Wen shi zhe* 文史哲 [Literature, history, and Philosophy] 4 (2012): 20–34.

Xiao Chi 蕭馳. "Lun Ruan Ji yonghuai dui shuqing chuantong zhi zaizao" 論阮籍詠懷對抒情傳統之再造 [On Ruan Ji's reinvention of the Chinese lyrical tradition in his poem "Yonghuai"]. In *Zhongguo shuqing chuantong de zai faxian: Yige xiandai xueshu sichao de lunwen xuanji* 中國抒情傳統的再發現：一個現代學術思潮的論文選集 [Rediscovering the Chinese lyrical tradition: Selected essays on a recent academic trend], edited by Xiao Chi and Ke Qingming 柯慶明, 437–85. Taipei: Taida chuban zhongxin, 2009.

Xiong Yuezhi 熊月之. *Xixue dongjian yu wanqing shehui* 西學東漸與晚清社會 [The dissemination of Western learning and the late Qing society]. Shanghai: Shanghai renmin chubanshe, 1994.

YaDeau, Camila. "Translingual Encounters: Freedom, Civic Virtue, and the Social Organism in Liang Qichao's Reading of Kant." *TRANSIT* 13, no. 1 (2021): 115–229.

Yamada Keizō 山田敬三. "Shin chūgoku miraiki o megutte: Ryō Keichō ni okeru kakumei to henkaku no ronri"「新中国未来記」をめぐって：梁啓超における革命と変革の論理 [On "The future of New China": Liang's logic on reform and revolution]. In *Kyōdō kenkyū Ryō Keichō: Seiyō kindai shisō juyō to Meiji Nihon* 共同研究梁啓超：西洋近代思想受容と明治日本 [Collaborative research on Liang Qichao: The reception of modern Western thought and Meiji Japan]. Tokyo: Misuzu shobo, 1999.

Yang Shiqun 楊師群. *Zhongguo xinwen chuanboshi* 中國新聞傳播史 [A history of China news and media]. Beijing: Beijing daxue chubanshe, 2007.

Yang Wenhui 楊文會. *Fojiao zongpai xiangzhu* 佛教宗派詳諸 [Detailed annotation on buddhist sects]. Yangzhou: Guanling shushe, 2008.

Yang Zhende 楊貞德. *Zhuan xiang ziwo: Jindai Zhongguo zhengzhi sixiang shang de geren* 轉向自我：近代中國政治思想上的個人 [An inward turn: The individual in modern Chinese political thought]. Taipei: Zhongyang yanjiuyuan Zhongguo wenzhe yanjiusuo, 2009.

Ye Dehui 葉德輝, ed. *Juemi yaolu* 覺迷要錄 [Record of an awoken schola]. Vol. 4. Beijing: Beijing chubanshe, 2000.

Yijiao congbian 翼教叢編 [A general collection to protect the faith. Edited by Su Yu 蘇輿. Taipei: Wenhai chubanshe, 1971.

Yu, Wen. "The Search for the Chinese Way in a Modern World: From the Rise of Evidential Scholarship to the Birth of Chinese Identity." PhD diss., Harvard University, 2017.

Yuan Jin 袁進. *Zhongguo wenxue guannian de jindai biange* 中國文學觀念的近代變革 [Chinese literary concepts' modern transformations]. Shanghai: Shanghai shehui kexueyuan chubanshe, 1996.

Yu Lixin 余立新. "Xin zhongguo weilai jidiwu hui bushi chuzi Liang Qichao zhi shou"《新中國未來記》第五回不是出自梁啟超之手 [The fifth chapter of the future of new China did not derive from Liang Qichao]. *Guji yanjiu* 古籍研究 [Journal of Ancient Books Studies] 2 (1997): 85–87.

Yu, Ying-shih 余英時. *Chinese History and Culture: Seventeenth Century through Twentieth Century*, vol. 2. New York: Columbia University Press, 2016.

———. *Lun Dai Zhen yu Zhang Xuecheng* 論戴震與章學誠 [On Dai Zhen and Zhang Xuecheng]. Taipei: Sanmin shuju, 2016.

———. *Neizai chaoyue zhi lu: Yu Yingshi xin ruxue lunzhu jiyao* 內在超越之路: 余英時新儒學論著輯要 [The path to internal transcedence: Collected essays on Yu Ying-shih's discussions on new confucianism]. Beijing: Zhongguo guangbo dianshi chubanshe, 1992.

———. *Songminglixue yu zhengzhi wenhua* 宋明理學與政治文化 [Neo-Confucianism and political culture]. Taipei: Yongchen congkan, 2004.

———. "Tai Chen's Choice between Philosophy and Philology." *Asia Major* 2, no. 1 (1989): 79–108.

———. *Zhishi ren yu zhongguo wenhua* Taipei *jiazhi* 知識人與中國文化的價值 [Intellectuals and the value of Chinese culture]. Taipei: Shibao chubanshe, 2007.

———. *Zhu Xi de lishi shijie* 朱熹的歷史世界 [The historical world of Zhu Xi]. Taipei: Yunchen congkan, 1996–97.

Zarrow Peter. *After Empire: The Conceptual Transformation of the Chinese State, 1885–1924*. Stanford, CA: Stanford University Press, 2012.

———. "Citizenship in China and the West." In *Imagining the People: Chinese Intellectuals and the Concept of Citizenship, 1890–1920*, edited by Joshua Fogel, and Peter Gue Zarrow, 113–41. Armonk, NY: M. E. Sharpe, 1997.

Zhao Jiheng 趙毅衡. "Ershi Shiji Zhongguo Weilai Xiaoshuo" 二十世紀中國未來小說. [Twentieth-century Chinese futuristic fiction]. *Ershiyi shiji shuang zhoukang* 二十一世紀雙周刊 [Twenty-First Century Bimonthly] 56 (Dec. 1999): 103–12.

Zhang, Dainian. *Key Concepts in Chinese Philosophy*. Edited and translated by Edmund Ryden. New Haven, CT: Yale University Press, 2002.

Zhang Pengyuan 張朋園. *Liang Qichao yu qingji geming* 梁啟超與清季革命 [Liang Qichao and the Qing revolution]. Shanghai: Sanlian shudian, 2007.

Zhang Taiyan. "Bo Xinmin Congbao zuijin zhi fei geming lun" 駁新民叢報最近之非革命論 [Refutations on New Citizen Journal's protest against the political revolution], in *YBSHJ* 18:102–31.

Zhou Yutong 周予同. *Jingjin guwen xue* 經今古文學 [Old text and new text studies]. Taipei: Taiwan shangwu yinshuguan, 1965.

Zhu Lin 朱琳. "Liang Qichao de 'geming' lun" 梁啟超的'革命'論 [Liang Qichao's thoughts on "revolution"]. *Higashi Ajia bunka kōshō kenkyū* 東アジア文化交渉研究 [Studies on East Asian Cultural Exchange] 5 ([n.d.]): 115–29.

Zhu Weizheng 朱維錚. *Wanqing xueshu shilun: Qiusuo zhen wenming* 晚清學術史論: 求索真文明 [Discussions on the late Qing academic history: The search of the true civilization]. Shanghai: Shanghai guji chubanshe, 1996.

Ziporyn, Brook. *Ironies of Oneness and Differences: Coherence in Early Chinese Thought; Prolegomena to the Study of Li* 理. New York: State University of New York Press, 2013.

Index

Action. *See* oneness of knowledge and action
Adorno, Theodor, 15, 193, 202, 238n38, 287n54, n55, n56, 288n56, n57, n58, 290n89
Affect, 7, 17–19, 126, 181–182, 192, 202–203; affect and democratic politics, 4–6, 9–10; and its destructive potentials, 26–27; and *liangzhi*, 58, 221–223, 229–230
Araki Kengo, 237n25, 244n18, 264n5, 264n57, 270n132, 288n60, 295n27
Aristotle, 4, 20, 155
Authenticity, 106–107, 142, 144, 171, 176–177, 182–183, 185–187, 193–194, 201, 213, 236n20; authentic freedom, 31, 37, 106; authentic political revolution, 213–214, 217

Bacon, Francis (comparison with René Descartes), 88–89, 102–103, 255n47, 240n51
Barthes, Roland, 19, 209, 211
benevolence (*ren*), 40–41, 57, 122, 110, 141, 183, 205
Bergson, Henri, 5
Bol, Peter, 41, 96

Buddhism, 266; affective knowledge transmission, 151, 155; basic doctrines, 10, 114–115; Chan, 228; comparisons between Theravada and Mahayana, 11, 113–114, 130–132, 134–135; heretical Chan Buddhism (*xie chan*), 128, 177, 155–156, 228; Huayan, 132–134, 200, 289n81; on intuitive understanding, 155, 158; and Kant, 53–54, 65–75; Madhyamaka, 16, 113–115, 129–130; and new fiction, 153, 155–157; and oneness, 120–121; relationship with neo-Confucianism, 45; Theravada Buddhism, 130; and Wang Yangming, 126–135; Yogācāra, 53–54, 247n52, 255n47; Zhu Xi's rejection of, 250n95

Camillo Cavour, 169–170, 279n103
Cartesian Dualism, 4, 10, 15–18; challenges against, 58–59, 125
Catuṣkoṭi, 33, 58, 127–128, 130–131, 197
China's Bushido, 143
Chen Baozhen, 136–139
Cheng Chung-ying, 185–186, 285n27
Chen Jianhua, 204, 278n95, 280n110

Cheng Hao, 39, 92, 119, 121, 134, 224–225, 261n39, 266n69
Chunqiu. See *Spring and Autumn Annals*
Confucianism, 24, 26; anxieties of, 34; fake Confucian scholars, 36, 64; Mencian school of, 7, 23, 28; true Confucianism (*zhen kongxue*), 22, 24, 165; Xunzi school of, 28
Confucius, 23–26, 29, 34, 40, 98, 142–143, 283n14; on benevolence, 110, 243n13, 258n9; compilation of *Chunqiu*, 115, 118, 121, 122–124, 163–167, 259n18, 262n45, 277n78, 277n82; on time and space, 229

Dacheng qixin lin (Treatise on Awakening Mahayana Faith), 70–71
Dai Zhen, 45; disagreement with Qian Daxin, 93–94, 248–249n75; Liang Qichao's reinterpretation on, 96–101; protest against neo-Confucianism, 45–46, 92–93
De Man, Paul, 211
Deleuze, Gilles, 5, 126, 233n7
Democratic governance, 47, 79, 110, 157, 245n28; and Confucianism, 22–24, 164; as human's becoming, 229–232; Kang Youwei on, 164–165; Kant on, 37–48, 103–108; Liang Qichao's endeavor to implement, 7, 137–140, 166–167, 191; man's failure to participate in, 26–27, 34, 220–223, 226–227, 282n132; and Neo-Confucianism, 12, 32–33, 49–51, 60, 82, 115–124, 136; as public expression of natural moral deposition, 3–4, 9–10, 22, 25, 27–28, 31–32, 36–37, 75–76, 103, 109, 162, 182–185, 194 (*also see* Kant on democratic governance); Rousseau on, 47, 123
Derrida, Jacques, 17, 202–203, 210, 272n12
Descartes, René, 203 (*also see* Bacon)
Deyu jian (Mirror for Moral Cultivation), 10, 142–143, 236n31
Di Baoxiang (Chuqing), 140
Discourse construction, critique of, 1–2, 9, 29–30
Discourse on the New Citizen (*Xinmin shuo*), 80, 176
Dilthey, Wilhelm, 17
Dolar, Mladen, 209
Dong Zhongshu, 163
Duara, Prasenjit, 19

Egan, Ronald, 118
Elder Brothers Society (*Gelaohui*), 172
ekphrasis, 148, 151
emotions, 7, 17–18, 181–182, 192, 201–203, 233n7, 290n89; and heartmind, 40, 70
evidential research, 7–8, 32, 35, 45–46, 50, 60, 82–84, 162, 234–23, 246n475n12; divide between Song learning and Han learning, 49, 83; divide between the enlightenment and the orthodox school, 61, 94; and Kant, 32, 52–53, 85–86, 89, 90–91, 97; Liang Qichao's critique of, 47, 52–53, 60–61, 64–65, 79, 83; Ori Sela on, 95–96; and scientific research methods, 32, 83, 100–102; and Wang Yangming, 82–83, 91–92, 101–102; and Zhu Xi, 61–63, 65; *also see* Dai Zhen

feeling (as a middle man between affect and emotion), 18, 203
Feng, Menglong, 202

Ferry, Leonard, 5
freedom, 1, 76, 88–89, 103–106, 153, 193, 216, 219; authentic freedom, 31, 37, 106–107, 182; false promises of, 213–214, 221
French Revolution, 146, 291–292n116; as embodied actions, 195–197, 200; Kang Youwei on, 117, 260n24; Liang Qichao's ambivalence toward, 26, 28, 34, 203–213
Fuller, Michael, on *wen* and *yan*, 13–14; on Song Dynasty's frictional divide, 224–225
Future of New China, The (*Xin Zhongguo weilai ji*), 25–26, 33–34, 147–150, 153, 157, 216, 271n9, 278n95; as modern rendition of *Chunqiu*, 160, 162, 166–168; on reform and revolution, 171–176, 279–280n110

Gadamer, Hans-Georg, 102–103, 186, 234n8, 284n26
Garfield, Jay, 132
Gelaohui. See Elder Brothers Society
Gong, Zizhen, 191
Gu Yanwu, 254n42; critique of Song learning, 84–85; on *li* and *qi*, 116; Liang Qichao's reinterpretation of, 85–92, 94, 96–97, 100, 101–102
Guangxu, Emperor, 110, 117, 136
Gongyang Commentary (*Gongyang zhuan*), 24–25, 163–164, 166
Great Unity, the (*datong*), 23, 115, 118, 121–123, 141, 164, 262–263n45

He Xiu, 163
Heartmind (*xin*), 25, 31–32, 39–44, 84–86, 90, 119–120, 195, 200, 221, 265n60, 266n69; Dai Zhen on, 92–94, 98; fragmentation of the heartmind, 43, 63; Wang Ji on, 199–200; Wang Yangming on, 100, 126–128, 133–134, 135–136, 194, 196–199, 201, 203; Zhu Xi's split of the 42, 127, 133, 201
Heidegger, Martin, 21, 102–103, 186, 257n95, 284n26
Hermeneutics, 17, 102–103, 234n8; hermeneutic phenomenology, 20–21; onto-hermeneutics, 185–186, 284–285n26
History of emotions, 7
Hölderlin, Fredrich, 193
Huayan Buddhism. See Buddhism
Huang Zunxian, 138, 267n93
Hunan Academy of Current Affairs (*Hunan shiwu xuetang*), 110, 115, 140
Hundred Days' Reform, 109, 172, 179
Husserl, Edmund, 20
Huters, Theodore, 18, 273n22

intellectual inertia, 8, 269n120, 191, 235n13
Ivanhoe, Philip, 120, 223–224, 237n22, 237n24, 242n4, 244n23, 248n66, 252n19, 262n41

Kang Youwei, 22, 44, 46, 52, 179, 228; on China's incipient constitutional construct, 117–118, 136, 259n18, 260n19, 262–263n45, 268n112, 281n125; on Confucius as a prophet, 163–164; on human nature, 115–116; Liang Qichao's disagreement with, 165–168, 173–174, 279n110; on rescuing Emperor Guangxu, 172–173; Tan Sitong's protest against, 118–123, 141

Kant, Immanuel, 15, 152–153; aesthetic judgement, 14–15; between Buddhism and Zhu Xi, 39, 67–75; and Buddhist metaphysics, 39; comparison with Wang Yangming, 31, 58–60; Copernican revolution of philosophy, 97–98; *Groundwork of the Metaphysic of Morals*, 37–38, 106; Kingdom of Ends, 37, 106–107; political ethics, 37–38, 104–108; transcendental idealism, 31, 37, 52–55, 85–86
Kao Yukung, 192, 194
Kingston, Rebecca, 5
Knowledge. See learning
Kossuth Lajos, 24, 26, 181, 183–186, 189–192, 195, 211, 286n40

Lam Ling Hon, 201–202
Last Days of the World, 157, 158–160 275n54
learning, 190, 228; alternative approaches to learning, 4–5, 9, 13, 17, 75, 92–93, 142–144; of the classics, 84–85; fake learning, 64; heart-based approach to knowledge, 4, 9–10, 32, 41, 45–46, 154–158, 201; Liang Qichao's critique of, 2, 5–6, 29, 47–50, 52–55, 57, 62–65, 79–81, 94, 151–153, 157, 168, 177; Qing learning, 100–102; text-based approach to, 1–4, 7–8, 9, 31, 43–44, 61–62, 201; Western learning, 153, 215
Lederman, Harvey, 58, 248n66, 248n68, 252–253n19, 264n53, 264n54, 288n66, 295n20
Lee Ming-huei, 243n7
Leys, Ruth, 17
Kumārajīva, 113
Li (cosmic pattern or principle), 10–11, 16, 32, 36, 39–41, 62, 76, 84–90, 120–121, 133, 242n4; Dai Zhen on, 61, 92–93, 98; and heartmind, 32, 44–45, 49, 57–60, 72, 82, 133–135; and Kant, 55–57; Liang Qichao on, 142; and *qi*, 41–43, 71, 74–75, 116, 118–119, 260n21; Tang Sitong on, 118–119
liangzhi (good moral knowing), 10, 58–59, 82–84, 90, 127, 135, 248n65, 252n19; malfunctioning of, 221–222, 229, 295n20; Wang Ji on, 199–200; *zhenzhi* (genuine knowing), 59–60
liberal autocracy, 225–227
Liu, Lydia, 18–19
Lu Xiangshan, 154

Massumi, Brian, 5–6, 15–17, 126, 202
Mazzini, Giuseppe, 24, 26, 169, 195, 211, 216, 279n103
Mencius (Mengzi) 21, 24, 28, 143, 164–165, 199, 246n43; Dai Zhen on 93–94, 98; on human nature 40, 63, 199; on *yi* (righteousness) 258n9, 283n14, 286n36
Metzger, Thomas, 224–225, 237n24, 237n27
Middle Way, The (*Mūlamadhyamakakārikā*), 11, 113–114
Montesquieu, Charles de, 117
Morality; contrast with learning, 62, 80–81; as modern political governance, 20–23, 28, 29, 34, 50–51, 57, 146, 164, 184, 278–279n96; public and private, 48–50, 76–77, 184–185, 252n18
Music, 13, 19, 163, 191–193, 209–212, 287–288n56; Liang Qichao's musical representation, 3–5, 13–15, 17, 23, 28, 33–34, 180, 186–192, 194, 204–209

Nāgārjuna, 11, 16, 39, 113–115, 131–134
Nakae Chomin, 52, 246n45
neo-Confucianism, 11, 31, 34, 36–38, 55, 59, 116, 201, 223–225, 266n69; and Buddhism, 39–40, 128–135, 153–157; Buddhism and Learning of Mind school of, 153–155; Learning of the Heart/Mind school of, 7, 10, 16, 38, 44–45, 51–52, 82–83; Learning of Principle school of, 7, 38, 40–43, 51–52, 61–62; modern political relevance of, 49–52, 62, 101–102, 126, 143–146; and Qing philology, 92–96, 253n21, 253n22
Neuroscience, 5, 17, 21
New Citizen Journal (*Xinmin congbao*), 2–3, 47, 51, 80–81, 151, 160, 177, 179–183, 214–215
New Fiction (*Xin xiaoshuo*), 3, 22, 25–26, 81–82, 148–149, 151, 155–162, 166, 171
new prose style, 3, 13, 23, 28, 34, 81–82, 180, 189, 205, 210
New Text studies/Confucianism, 7, 24–26, 262n45, 277n78, 278n96; and democracy, 118, 123–124, 141–142; and new fiction, 162–168; and Old Text Studies, 7–8, 162
Ng On-cho, 185–186, 236n18, 260n21, 284n26

Old Text studies. *See* New Text Studies
Oneness, cosmic moral-political, 11–12, 32–34, 109–112, 120–126, 136, 141; ironies of, 223–225
Oneness of knowledge and action (*zhixing heyi*; also unity of knowledge and action), 28, 58–59, 125–136, 145, 200; explained from a Buddhist perspective, 126–135; Wang Yangming on, 126, 129

Paramārtha, 70
Plato, 4, 148
Ponty-Merleau, Maurice, 20
Pozait, Michel, 209
Pratītyasamutpāda (dependently arisen upon temporal and situational conditions), 33, 59, 66, 114
Priest, Graham, 119, 247n52

qi (physical substance). *See li*
Qian Daxin, 35–35, 38, 49, 52, 61–62, 64; disagreement with Dai Zhen, 92–95, 99, 248n75
Qian Dehong, 228
Qian Mu, 224, 234n10
qing (human feelings), 42–44, 63, 127, 135, 191, 197, 201, 261n39, 283n8

Records of the Grand Historian (*Shiji*), 24, 143
restoration (*weixin*). *See* revolution
revolution (*geming*), 24, 110; in Confucianism, 24, 143; as cosmic instinctive impulse, 17, 33, 145; French Revolution, the, 26, 28, 34, 117, 146, 195–197, 200; and Great Unity, 23; Liang Qichao and, 26, 29, 30, 33–34, 109–110, 138–140, 149–150, 180–183, 203–209, 212–217, 219, 221, 223, 226, 230, 281n129; and restoration (*weixin*), 33, 168–176, 279–280n110, 281–282n132
Roland, Madame, 24, 26, 34, 182, 195–196, 203–207, 209, 211–216, 292n116
Rousseau, Jean-Jacques, 47, 103

scientific research methods. *See* evidential research
Sela, Ori, 95–97
Sima Qian, 23–24, 143, 179
Shiwu bao (Chinese Progress), 138
Southern Learning Society (*Nanxue hui*), 118, 137–139, 268n98
Spinoza, de Baruch, 6
Spring and Autumn Annals (*Chunqiu*) 24–25, 33, 163–164; modern interpretations on, 115, 118, 121–122, 163–164, 166–167, 259n18, 262n45, 277n82
Sun Yat-sen, 110, 173–174, 176, 204, 281n130

Tan Sitong, on benevolence, 110–113; on democratic governance, 123–124, 136, 136, 138; on genuine knowing, 124–125; on interdependence, 111–113, 119, 125; on protest against Kang Youwei, 118–123; political suicide, 109, 140–141, 144
Tang, Xiaobing, 204, 292n119
Terada, Rei, 17–18, 202–203
Tibet, 226

virtue ethics, 38

Walzer, Michael, 5
Wang Anshi, 139, 224–225
Wang, David, 18–19
Wang Fuzhi, 91
Wang Ji, 199, 228
Wang Kangnian, 138
Wang, Yangming, 7, 21, 27, 64; and democratic governance, 12, 22–23, 25–28, 31–32, 72–73, 76, 136, 143; and evidential research, 82–86; on evil, 197–199; on human nature, 21, 36–38, 44–45, 145, 154, 182, 194; and Kant, 38, 58–60; on *liangzhi*, 10, 58, 62; on oneness of knowledge and action, 11, 16–18, 32–33, 125–127, 128–135, 142; pitfalls in his teaching, 28–29, 34, 199–200, 221–224; protest against Zhu Xi, 10, 44, 91–92, 101–102, 127–128, 133–135
Wang Wu, 172
weiyan dayi, 25, 33, 163, 166, 168
wen (aesthetic patterns), in contrast to yan (words), 18–19
Whitbeck, Judith, 191
Wu Jianren, 217

Xun Kuang (Xunzi), 13–14, 28

Yan Fu, 152
Yang Wenhui, 114
Yoshida Shoin, 216
Yuan Shikai, 232

Zhang Taiyan, 219, 221
Zhang Zai, 41, 116, 224–225
Zhixing heyi. See Oneness of Knowing and Being
Zhu Xi, 7, 10, 45, 92, 98, 134, 228; on human nature, 10, 31, 38, 41, 145, 198–199; on learning, 61–64, 135; misinterpretation of Buddhism, 65–71; on *qing*, 127, 135; separation of the heartmind, 42–43, 44, 72–75, 133
Zhuangzi, 64
Zhuang Cunyu, 162–163, 235n14
Zili hui (Independence Society), 140

Milton Keynes UK
Ingram Content Group UK Ltd.
UKHW020458270824
447373UK00004B/38